P9-DUE-797

RETHINKING SEXISM, GENDER, AND SEXUALITY

Edited by:

Annika Butler-Wall, Kim Cosier, Rachel L. S. Harper, Jeff Sapp,
Jody Sokolower, Melissa Bollow Tempel

A RETHINKING SCHOOLS PUBLICATION

Rethinking Sexism, Gender, and Sexuality
Edited by Annika Butler-Wall, Kim Cosier, Rachel L. S. Harper, Jeff Sapp, Jody Sokolower, and Melissa Bollow Tempel

A Rethinking Schools Publication

Rethinking Schools is a nonprofit publisher and advocacy organization dedicated to sustaining and strengthening public education through social justice teaching and education activism. Our magazine, books, and other resources promote equity and racial justice in the classroom. We encourage grassroots efforts in our schools and communities to enhance the learning and well-being of our children, and to build broad democratic movements for social and environmental justice.

To request additional copies of this book or a catalog of other publications, or to subscribe to *Rethinking Schools* magazine, contact:
Rethinking Schools
6737 W. Washington St.
Suite 3249
Milwaukee, Wisconsin 53214
800-669-4192
rethinkingschools.org

© 2016 Rethinking Schools, Ltd.
First edition

Cover and Book Design: Design Action Collective
Cover Illustration: Favianna Rodriguez
Managing Editor: Jody Sokolower
Copyeditors: Elizabeth Barbian, Annika Butler-Wall
Production: Mike Trokan
Proofreading/Corrections: Hayley German Fisher, Lawrence Sanfilippo
Indexer: Carol Roberts

All rights reserved. Except as permitted below, no part of this book may be reproduced in any form or by any means, including electronic, without the express prior written permission of the publisher, except for brief quotation in an acknowledged review. Individuals may photocopy excerpts from this book for use in educational settings (physical settings only; internet use is not permitted), as long as such material is furnished free to students or workshop participants. For sale of any portion of this book as part of course packets, contact the Copyright Clearance Center for permissions and appropriate fees. If you have any questions, contact Rethinking Schools at the address above.

ISBN: 978-0-942961-59-1

Library of Congress Control Number: 2015959057

ACKNOWLEDGMENTS

Rethinking Sexism, Gender, and Sexuality has been a labor of love for the past three years. We have learned so much from the many teachers, parents, and youth who have shared their work and their writing with us. We want to thank everyone who sent us articles, and especially the authors who wrote, revised, and revised again. Thanks to the editorial board of Rethinking Schools for their thoughtful comments on many of these articles: Wayne Au, Bill Bigelow, Linda Christensen, Grace Cornell Gonzales, Jesse Hagopian, Stan Karp, David Levine, Larry Miller, Bob Peterson, Adam Sanchez, Stephanie Walters, Dyan Watson, and Moé Yonamine. The beautiful cover was created by activist/artist Favianna Rodriguez. Special thanks to Sabiha Basrai, of Design Action Collective, who designed the cover and the layout, waited patiently when we were behind schedule, and made us a priority when we were in a rush. Elizabeth Barbian put countless hours into skillful copyediting, proofreading, and everything else. Thanks also to proofreader Lawrence Sanfilippo and to Hayley German Fisher, who leapt in at the last minute to make corrections in layout. Although Mike Trokan retired from Rethinking Schools last year, he helped with permissions and much-appreciated support in the production process. Thanks also to Ericka Sokolower-Shain for producing our crowdsourcing video, and to our actors. The strengths of this book rest on all of your generous and wise shoulders.

And, of course, as editors we thank our families and friends, who have heard way too much about this book over the years, and tolerated the disruption of our early Sunday morning phone calls.

This book wouldn't have been possible without the support of the New Visions Foundation and other Rethinking Schools donors, and especially the many folks who contributed to our crowdfunding campaign. Huge thanks to:

Sara Berg
Teresa Chegwidden
William and Barbara Chinitz
Educators' Network for Social Justice
The Felton-Koestler Family
Karen Giuffre
John R. Harris
Nekicia D. Luckett
Beth Ludeman
McConnell Family Partnership
Barbara and Gary Mackman
Linda Munn
In memory of Elissa Nelson
Diana Porter and Len Webb
Jeff Sapp, Sino Donato, and their daughter, Helena Lourdes Donato-Sapp
Dennis Sayers
Rita Tenorio and Mike Trokan
and everyone else who contributed!

To all who have the courage to keep learning and to those who teach us how to imagine better worlds.

— Annika Butler-Wall

For Melissa, whose fierce dedication to fighting the good fight warms my heart and fans the flames of my own activism. And for Maya and Masami—apples that didn't fall too far from their mama's tree.

— Kim Cosier

For Kerry Downey, and all teachers, with love.

— Rachel L. S. Harper

To the thousands of teachers I've had the pleasure of bringing into the profession throughout my career in teacher credential and graduate courses. May you continue to interrogate the common everyday injustices you see in education, work for change, and keep pushing yourselves in rigorous ways to become more and more nuanced about identity issues in the classrooms where you teach. As always, I remain inspired by you all. And for my daughter, Helena Lourdes Donato-Sapp. May you continue to be strong and bold.

— Jeff Sapp

To Ericka, whose core integrity and courage lit my path to this book, and to Karen, the love of my life. To all the students who have opened my eyes and my heart. And to those dykes smoking pipes, sitting in the window ledges high above the Black Panthers' Washington, D.C., convention in 1970.

— Jody Sokolower

For my dear friend Susie, who long ago patiently answered all my questions about the birds and the birds and the bees and the bees. For Tony, a fabulous gay teacher and friend who has taught me so much. Lastly, I would never have worked on this book if it weren't for one amazing 1st grader who inspired me to learn and grow in ways I never imagined.

— Melissa Bollow Tempel

TABLE OF CONTENTS

Chapter 4: When Teachers Come Out 263

Chapter 5: Beyond the Classroom 301

Chapter 6: Teacher Education, Continuing Education

CHAPTER 1

Meredith Stern

Rethinking Sexism, Gender, and Sexuality: Introduction

By Jody Sokolower

Jody Sokolower is a political activist, teacher, writer, and editor. She is the managing editor at Rethinking Schools.

What if schools were places where children could explore their identities and passions without worrying about gender roles—without worrying about gender at all?

What if all groups marginalized by our history books—including women and LGBTQ people—were central to the content we teach and learn?

What if age-appropriate, supportive discussions of sexuality were welcome across grade levels and subject areas?

What if LGBTQ teachers and family members were embraced by schools as essential to the diversity that makes a community strong?

Questions like these inspired this book. We began work in the midst of increasing discussion about LGBTQ issues, fueled by campaigns to legalize gay marriage; recognition by school districts—in the face of a series of murders and suicides—that they had to do something about harassment of LGBTQ students; and the end of the military's "don't ask, don't tell" policy.

We are encouraged by the momentum, but concerned that "gay rights" is too narrow a focus and separated from an overall understanding of social justice. For example, we're sure the "It Gets Better" project, with half a million videos by everyone from Ellen DeGeneres to President Obama telling LGBTQ students to hang on, has helped many youth who felt isolated and alone. But it relies on a very individualized way of looking at the problem—everyone should be nice to each other, and your life will be better once you're out of school. That's a pretty low bar, and it doesn't say much about the ways that schools need to change.

We're also concerned about the ironic reality of marriage equality surging forward as patriarchy—the systemic control of women by men—reasserts its grip: Abortion and even birth control are less and less available to the women who need them most; the growing economic disparities have plunged single mothers into crisis (one-third of households headed by women are below the poverty line); violence against women continues unabated.

Finally, as I write this introduction, the Black Lives Matter movement is erupting in city after city. Protests against the police murders of African Americans have brought to center stage the systemic racism that continues to plague our country—and our schools. The urgency of that movement reinforces our conviction that LGBTQ struggles cannot be separated from the fabric of all struggles for social justice. Making schools safe for LGBTQ students, staff, and families is inextricably interwoven with the fight against racism.

> We're concerned about the ironic reality of marriage equality surging forward as patriarchy reasserts it grip.

Feminism—A Broad View

We needed a frame for this book that encompassed all those concerns. And one more, too: We wanted to be sex positive. Age appropriate, but sex positive. We wanted to model an approach to gender, sexuality, and sex that is fluid and respectful of feelings and questions at all levels of development. One that presumes that knowledge, respect, and communication are the basis of healthy and fulfilling relationships—to oneself and to others.

As we reviewed the many articles that were submitted, we had far-ranging discussions about how to frame the vision for this book. The five of us on the editorial committee for *Rethinking Sexism, Gender, and Sexuality* are spread across the country and the generations. We all brought something different to the table. In Rethinking Schools style, we wanted to avoid abstract and academic language. But we needed a way to talk about what we were fighting for, where we hope all this work is going.

The term *feminism* has had a conflicted history; in the 1970s, in particular, it was identified with a movement centered on the perspective and needs of white, middle-class, Western women. In the years since, radical scholar bell hooks and others have reclaimed the word and recast it in a broader, more progressive worldview.

In *Feminist Theory, From Margin to Center*, hooks defines feminism this way:

> Feminism is not simply a struggle to end male chauvinism or a movement to ensure that women will have equal rights with men; it is a commitment to eradicating the ideology of domination that permeates Western culture on various levels—sex, race, and class, to name a few—and a commitment to reorganizing society . . . so that the self-development of people can take precedence over imperialism, expansion, and material desires.

Margaret Randall, who spent many years participating in, documenting, and analyzing revolutionary movements in Latin America, adds this:

> Feminism is about . . . confronting and making useful the painful memories that surface in our lives. It is about the conception and uses of power, about relationships in the human, animal, and nature worlds—who holds power and over whom. It requires rethinking and reorganizing both our notions of society and society itself, so that we all may make our unique contributions and participate to our fullest potential.

Hooks and Randall are pointing to a better world for all of us. Our job, in part, is to figure out what that means for education and schools. Children need to be learning about sexism, gender, and sexuality within a framework that includes an understanding of racism and other forms of oppression, and looks honestly at history and current events. For example, we can't talk about gay rights in the military—or violence against women in the military—without asking what the U.S. military is doing in the Middle East these days.

We want students to feel supported and empowered at school; we also want them to see themselves as part of a world that needs fixing and that they can help fix. We want boys to feel comfortable wearing necklaces and girls to believe they can become physicists. But we are also trying to move the conversation toward something bigger—toward the vision that hooks and Randall articulate.

Teaching the Unspeakable

Most of the articles in this book concern topics often seen as taboo at school—including gay people, transgender people, and sex. Responding to questions from students or planning a unit can raise a lot of anxiety; all of us have been there. It's easy to worry that once the conversation starts, all hell will break loose. But it's a mistake to think that silence is neutral. Or that kids, even preschool kids, aren't already exposed to and thinking about these topics.

The key, as with so much of good teaching, lies in building community in the classroom from the beginning. In constantly teaching and modeling thoughtful, honest, and empathic conversation. So much of teaching young children, for example, is translating content into what is developmentally appropriate. This book is filled with master teachers describing concretely how they do that at every grade level and what rich discussions emerge as a result.

For the sake of all our children, it's critical to break the silences, but please do it in a way that works for you, given your own history, experience, and school situation. There is an enormous variation in school climates. A unit that will be welcomed and supported at one school could get you fired at another. We hope you will collaborate whenever possible, and think about and prepare yourself ahead of time for possible problems. You know your own situation best. This is not a test; we hope it feels like an invitation.

The articles are as explicit about content and teaching as we could make them. We wanted it to be easy to see what the author-teacher said and did, so it would be easy to see how to apply or adapt their work. Many of these articles pushed us to be more self-reflective. When an article made us nervous, we tried to ask ourselves why: How did it relate to our own history or the school where we teach? What would it take to move beyond our fear? We were lucky to have each other as sounding boards. It's hard to do this work alone; we hope you find others in your school community for discussion, collaboration, and support.

In Praise of Fluidity

In general, the articles in this collection reject binary thinking. "Are you pregnant?" is a fairly yes/no question, but almost everything else is more complicated. We lean toward fluidity, and use the terminology current in queer and gender studies.

Take, for example, our perspective on sex, gender, and sexuality. *Sex* refers to the biological differences between male and female, which scientists now see as more of a continuum than a binary. Far more people have complex combinations of sex characteristics than society recognizes.

> "Just Say No" is as ineffective and reactionary in relationship to sex as it is to drugs.

Gender is socially constructed, in the same way that race is. In other words, society has created definitions for "masculinity" and "femininity." Although they are made up, they have an enormous impact on all our lives. Some people feel comfortable with the gender they were assigned at birth; some people feel deeply that they are the other gender than the one assigned to them based on external sex characteristics. Some people have a fluid approach to gender—they feel differently at different stages of their lives. Others reject being gendered entirely.

Sexuality refers both to sexual feelings in general and with whom you feel drawn toward intimacy. Sex, gender, and sexuality are different for everyone— some people feel very strongly at one end of a continuum or another, others experience themselves as in the middle or not on a line at all. When working with children and young people, we need to allow them to be who they are and to support their safe exploration. What's harmful is being critical, silencing, or making assumptions. Some children who explore identifying as the other sex grow up to be trans men or women, while others do not. Being comfortable with ambiguity is key.

The teachers writing about sex education in *RSGS* are focused on being age appropriate and sex positive. It's important for students to learn about the risks associated with unequal, un-negotiated, and unprotected sex, but we oppose sex education that is based in fear and blanket prohibition. "Just Say No" is as ineffective and reactionary in relationship to sex as it is to drugs. And, although comprehensive sex education is far better than abstinence-only models, we are also critical of approaches based on the harm-reduction models of drug education—"It's best not to have sex until you're married, but if you must. . . ."

Positive sexual intimacy requires self-respect, equality, maturity, communication, affection, and protection from communicable diseases, but it is one of the great joys of life. We should not be teaching children that it is only fraught with peril. In Chapter 3, Lena Solow, Ericka Hart, Valdine Ciwko, and Jody Sokolower offer ways to provide students with age-appropriate, accurate information and lots of opportunity to discuss it.

Before We Get Started . . .

If you glance at the table of contents, you'll see how we decided (after a few false starts) to organize *Rethinking Sexism, Gender, and Sexuality*. There is a short introductory chapter that sets the tone. Chapter 2 focuses on what it takes at different grade levels to create a nurturing classroom for all children in terms of these issues. Chapter 3 centers on curriculum.

Then we have Chapter 4, "When Teachers Come Out." *RSGS* is essentially a book of curriculum, but we couldn't ignore the dozens of coming out at school stories we received as submissions. That topic deserves a book of its own; we've narrowed it to a short chapter here. But we don't mean to minimize the significance of out teachers. At too many schools, there's a Gay-Straight Alliance and some effort to support LGBTQ students, but it's not safe for teachers to come out. If a school is not safe for LGBTQ teachers, staff, and parents, it's not safe for students, either.

In Chapter 5, parents, teachers, activists, and administrators share their stories about advocating and organizing beyond classroom walls. Finally, Chapter 6 focuses on integrating LGBTQ content into teacher education programs and ongoing teacher education.

This book is just a beginning. There are many critical teaching pieces and perspectives that are missing. We hope you will discover new ideas and approaches, and that they will inspire you to develop and teach new curriculum, to organize and collaborate in creative new ways. Then, please, write about your work and contribute to this exciting, ongoing effort.

A final note: Student names have been changed throughout.

The New Misogyny
What it means for teachers and classrooms

By THE EDITORS OF RETHINKING SCHOOLS

As we go marching, marching, we're standing proud and tall
The rising of the women means the rising of us all.
Our lives shall not be sweated from birth until life closes,
Hearts starve as well as bodies: bread and roses, bread and roses.

T he song "Bread and Roses" and the 1912 strike in Lawrence, Massachusetts, where the phrase originated, remind us how important women's struggles have been in U.S. history, and that the liberation of women is central to progress toward social justice. There hasn't been much talk about women's liberation lately. Women have the vote; more than half the students at universities are women; rape is classified as a crime; there are women doctors, lawyers, soccer players, and secretaries of state. A lot of young professionals—and a lot of our students— would say the whole idea of women's liberation is passé, a non-issue.

A few years ago, the 2012 political campaigns revealed a deep and ugly wound: misogyny that ranged from Rush Limbaugh's crass attack on Georgetown Law School student Sandra Fluke to the repeal of Wisconsin's pay equity law, from the Republican attacks on Title X (which subsidizes cervical and breast cancer screening, testing for HIV and other sexually transmitted diseases, and birth control for 5 million low-income women) to Virginia's mandated vaginal ultrasounds for women who want abortions.

What was exposed is that the notion that we are "post-sexist" is a lie. There is a disturbing similarity to how the election of an African American president has masked the worsening realities for large numbers of African Americans— in the words of prison rights activist and scholar Ruth Wilson Gilmore, "One African American in the White House and a million in prison." Professional opportunities for a narrow stratum of women have masked the worsening realities of life for millions of women caught up in the welfare system, the prison system, low-paying service jobs, domestic violence, and the ideological misogyny of growing fundamentalist religious and political perspectives.

The Stereotype of the "Lazy Teacher"

The vilification of K–12 teachers is part and parcel of this misogyny. In 2011, when teachers led the occupation of the Wisconsin state capitol, many pointed out the obvious: Attacks on teachers—and other public sector workers like nurses and social workers—are overwhelmingly attacks on women. When "reformers," from former D.C. superintendent Michelle Rhee to New Jersey Gov. Chris Christie, portray teachers as incompetent, incapable of leadership, and selfish, they don't need to specify *women* teachers for that to be the image in people's minds—76 percent of U.S. teachers are women; at the elementary school level, it's nearly 90 percent. As education blogger Sabrina Stevens Shupe wrote recently, "The predominantly female teaching profession [is] among the latest [targets] in a long tradition of projecting community/social anxieties onto 'bad' women—from 'witches' to bad mothers to feminists and beyond."

> As education activists, we need to expose and confront the misogynist underpinnings of the current attacks on teachers.

The decimation of teachers unions and tenure structures seems aimed at forcing K–12 teaching back to the era before teaching became a profession, when young women—barely trained and constrained by regulations enforcing their clothing, living situations, and drinking—taught for a few years before they got married. Here are some requirements from a typical teacher's contract in 1923: The teacher is "not to ride in a carriage or automobile with any man except her brother or father" and "not to dress in bright colors." She is "to wear at least two petticoats" and "to sweep the classroom floor at least once daily."

More Than "Add a Woman and Stir"

These attacks on women—as teachers, as those with the right to control their own childbearing, as human beings who deserve respect from politicians and the media—are being taken on by unions, political organizations, and activists across the country. But one aspect rarely discussed is what this new misogyny means for us in the classroom. As we have seen in other social justice struggles, claiming and passing on the history is integral to fighting for the future. It's impossible to confront racism, militarism, or environmental degradation without understanding the history. The same is true for the oppression of

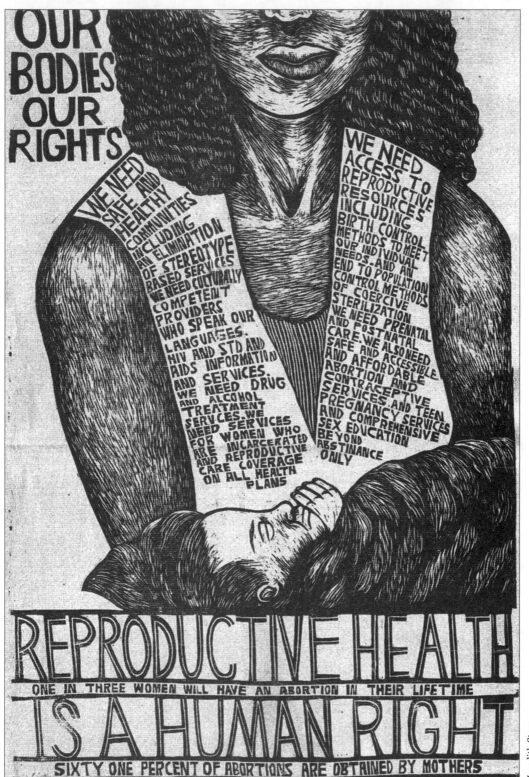

Meredith Stern

women. Our students need a critical understanding of women's lives and struggles in the past to understand and respond to the present.

If you go by most U.S. history texts, the only piece of women's history worth space in the curriculum is the fight for suffrage. But women defining and fighting for freedom for themselves and their communities has been at the center of American history from the beginning. The everyday lives of women are half the story in every historical moment—as Native Americans forced out of their lands, Black mothers enslaved and resisting, white settlers crossing the plains in covered wagons, immigrants at Angel Island and in New York's Lower East Side.

And, if we move past what Geraldine Clifford named the "add a woman and stir" approach to incorporating women into historical study, we can see that a feminist perspective calls into question how history is usually organized: centered on heroes, villains, and wars. For example, the Civil Rights Movement is often narrated as the story of Martin Luther King Jr.'s charismatic leadership of a mass movement. No doubt, any treatment of the Civil Rights Movement that did not discuss King's work would be incomplete. But a more accurate and more helpful-for-the-future narration might start with the many years of house-by-house organizing by the Women's Political Council in Montgomery, long before King arrived in that city; and the grassroots, democratic leadership modeled by Ella Baker that was responsible for so much of the success of the movement. As Student Nonviolent Coordinating Committee (SNCC) volunteer and historian Joanne Grant explains, Baker "taught the SNCC students the importance of nurturing local leaders, the value of organizing local groups who would make their own decisions, and the vital concept of a group-centered leadership as opposed to a leadership-centered group."

When we relegate these stories to a captioned photo, a colorful "historical highlight" box, or a paragraph at the end of the chapter, we miss an opportunity to tell a richer history, and we disarm our students from understandings they need to navigate a world of militarized masculinity and misogynist femininity.

The History of Birth Control

Take, for example, a controversial piece of history that relates directly to the current political debates: women's control over reproduction. Birth control, if taught at all in our schools, is usually segregated in health classes. But women's control over childbearing has actually been a key issue in U.S. history. As the women's rights movement grew before the Civil War, white middle-class women became interested in controlling how many children they had; they wanted time to extend their experiences beyond the home. For Black and Native American women, control of their bodies meant primarily the ability to make choices about fertility that weren't dominated by rape and the inability to keep their children safe and free. In the early 20th century, when Margaret Sanger first started handing out birth control—a crime for which she was repeatedly arrested—she saw it as part of a larger fight for the emancipation of the poor.

But, only a few years later, influenced by the eugenics movement that fueled Jim Crow at home and imperial designs abroad, she was defining the "chief issue of birth control" as "more children from the fit, less from the unfit." A generation later, many activists fighting for the legalization of abortion ignored the sterilization of Black women in the South, Native American women on reservations, and colonized women in Puerto Rico.

What a rich, complex historical vein—all the contradictions around gender, class, and race that lie at the heart of supporting students to think critically about history and social justice strategies. When we open up history in this way, we encompass gender issues, homophobia, and LGBTQ history. Many aspects of current society that don't show up in the standard curriculum—mass incarceration, poverty and the welfare system, the impact of militarization at home and abroad—are arenas where an exploration from a more feminist perspective can connect to students' lives and expose them to a more expansive view of what history is and why it matters.

The "new misogyny" is a wake-up call. As education activists, we need to expose and confront the misogynist underpinnings of the current attacks on teachers. And, as teachers and teacher educators, we need to center women's lives and history in our curricula; there is no way to build for the future without it.

Olive Earley

Queering Our Schools

By THE EDITORS OF RETHINKING SCHOOLS

O n Nov. 5, 2013, Illinois became the 16th state to legalize same-sex marriage. And Sasha Fleischman's skirt was set on fire on an Oakland, California, bus by a 16-year-old student from another school (Sasha is an agender youth). What a contradiction. And what a clear example of the complex state of LGBTQ issues at this moment in history. What does this contradiction mean for students, teachers, and schools?

One reason the tragedy in Oakland is significant is because of what happened after Sasha was seriously burned and the Oakland High junior who set the fire was charged as an adult with two felony hate crimes. Students and teachers at Oakland High responded by mobilizing support for Sasha. They collected money for medical expenses and sponsored a "Stroll for Sasha" along the bus route, which was spontaneously marked by rainbow ribbons. The varsity basketball team wore "No H8" T-shirts with Sasha's name on the back.

Meanwhile, Sasha and Sasha's family stressed education rather than law and order, urging that the accused student be tried as a child, not an adult. Sasha's dad, Karl, who is a teacher at Sequoia Elementary School, focused on how to talk with students. In a letter to the Sequoia community, he said:

> None of us can know the mind of the kid who lit a flame to Sasha's skirt. But I have a feeling that if he had seen Sasha's skirt as an expression of another kid's unique, beautiful self, and had smiled and thought "I hella love Oakland," I wouldn't be writing this now.

And that's the question, isn't it? How do we create classrooms and schools where each child, parent, and staff member's unique, beautiful self is appreciated and nurtured? The terrain, in terms of legal rights and public conversation, is shifting rapidly, creating space for enormous advances in curriculum and school climate. At the same time, homophobia, misogyny, and other forms of hatred are alive and well, and even progressive schools and classrooms have a long way to go in creating nurturing spaces for students, parents, and staff who don't conform to gender and/or sexuality "norms." So how do we move forward?

> How do we create classrooms and schools where each child, parent, and staff member's unique, beautiful self is appreciated and nurtured?

Build Community

Despite the recent advances in LGBTQ rights, most schools aren't safe for queer students. In a recent survey, six out of 10 LGBTQ teens said they felt unsafe at school and 82 percent had been verbally harassed because of their sexual orientation. In response to a series of high-publicity tragedies, 49 states have passed "anti-bullying" legislation. That's a good first step. But there are serious problems with focusing on bullying rather than social justice.

Talking about "bullies" makes it seem like an individual problem and glosses over homophobia, sexism, racism, Islamophobia—all the critical issues that underlie conflicts among children and adults. As Lyn Mikel Brown explains ("10 Ways to Move Beyond Bully Prevention and Why We Should"):

> To lump disparate behaviors under the generic "bullying" is to efface real differences that affect young people's lives. Bullying is a broad term that de-genders, de-races, de-everythings school safety.

There are reasons why teachers and administrators are reluctant to adopt schoolwide approaches that open up discussions of LGBTQ rights and homophobia. We worry about backlash from parents. As the movement has developed past its early "gay liberation" beginnings, it has become more complex; teachers who felt comfortable talking about lesbians and gay men need to wrap their hearts and minds around transgender issues and challenges to the socially constructed gender binary. And when you invite kids to talk openly and ask questions about gender and sexuality, you have to be ready for whatever happens. It's trickier than geometry.

But it's also a critical key to building community where no one is silenced, where everyone's reality is recognized and valued. And it's definitely possible. As Karl Fleischman explained in his letter:

Being agender simply means that the person doesn't feel they are "either a boy or a girl." I realize this is a concept that even adults have difficulty wrapping their heads around . . . so I can't pretend that it's an issue that all young children will grasp. But what they certainly can and should understand is that different people like different things. Different people dress or behave or look differently. And that's a GOOD thing.

The cornerstone of nurturing classrooms and schools is community, where everyone talks out problems, gets to know each other, and feels that they are part of something larger than themselves. Part of this is emphasizing empathy, which is at the heart of both solidarity and social justice teaching, and thus at the heart of creating safe spaces for everyone. This means a school filled with adults who are prepared to talk and listen to children talk about gender and sexuality, as well as other controversial and sensitive topics—adults who are willing to learn from youth as well as lead them. Community is built by working through differences, not sweeping them under the rug.

One beginning step is making sure that school structures support all families. A few examples: forms that ask for information for Parent/Family Members instead of Mother and Father; easily accessible gender-neutral bathrooms for everyone; no lining kids up in girls' lines and boys' lines; gym classes and locker rooms that accommodate a range of gender identities; honorary positions (for prom, homecoming, etc.) that are neutral for gender and sexual identity; diverse representation in posters, curriculum, library and classroom books, speakers, the arts, and school leadership. Equally important is empowering students to participate—at school and in the community—in organizations fighting for all kinds of social justice, including gay/straight alliances.

Safe Adults, Safe Students

A couple of years ago, several of us from around the country participated in a workshop sponsored by Educators' Network for Social Justice in Milwaukee. The topic was teachers coming out at school. It was a good discussion, but the talk kept drifting back to making schools safe for kids. It was hard to stay focused on making schools safe for LGBTQ teachers and staff. Even talking about it felt risky.

But no number of classroom discussions about gender stereotypes and homophobia will create a nurturing environment if teachers and parents are afraid to come out. A school that's a protective community for LGBTQ adults is a school that's going to be safe for kids.

What might that look like? When Jody Sokolower, Rethinking Schools' managing editor, came out to her 7th-grade students her first year of teaching, the principal and vice principal accused her of "talking about her sex life" and put a disciplinary letter in her file. When she called the union, her district rep immediately promised that the union would fight for her, and sent letters to that effect to the principal and to Jody's file. That backing was enormously important, both emotionally and practically. Union support is critical.

> Community is built by working
> through differences, not sweeping
> them under the rug.

So is educating and uniting teachers and staff. And mobilizing parents. At many elementary schools, parents have joined together to form LGBTQ parent committees that go into classes to lead workshops and advise teachers. If some parents in the school are worried about LGBTQ content, PTA discussions can be invaluable. *It's Elementary*, a documentary with age-appropriate teaching about LGBTQ issues from kindergarten through middle school, is a great resource.

Queering the Curriculum

Educators and scholars of color have argued for many years that multicultural education means moving beyond "heroes and holidays" to integrating the history and lives of people of color into curriculum at every point. The same is true for LGBTQ issues and people. Participating in the Day of Silence can be a good start, but a social justice frame demands an approach to curriculum that integrates queer people—their problems, history, struggles, and contributions—into day-to-day curriculum, K–12, across the subject areas.

In elementary school, for example, does the literature read in the classroom reflect children with gay and lesbian parents, as well as a broad range of other family structures? What is the approach to activities like Father's Day, Mother's Day, and "family tree" assignments? (It's worth noting that the "traditional" mom-dad-and-kids family is a minority—not a majority—experience, so many children and their families are affected by what are often oppressive school customs.)

Adam Grant Kelley's article on teaching the school-to-prison pipeline to high school students is just one example of the process of queering a piece of curriculum (see p. 235). *Rethinking Sexism, Gender, and Sexuality* has dozens of other examples that we hope will set your imagination aflame. What about enlarging a study of the Harlem Renaissance to explore the lives and impact of such LGBTQ poets, authors, and musicians as Langston Hughes, Countee Cullen, Angelina Weld Grimké, Ethel Waters, Gertrude "Ma" Rainey, Bessie Smith, and Josephine Baker? What about including the Lavender Scare in the study of the McCarthy era? Or the Stonewall Riots as part of the political foment of the late '60s? Or considering implications of the campaign for LGBTQ acceptance in the military in the context of questioning current U.S. military strategy?

None of this is easy. But every step leads to the next one. A friend of ours was recently mentoring a preservice teacher whose students were changing singular verbs to plural. One student looked at the example in the book: "My mom is swimming." After hesitating for a minute, the student pulled out a solution: "My parents are swimming." The teacher moved on to the next child. Later, the mentor suggested gently, "You know, that was an opportunity to mention the fact that some kids have two moms, and that it would be fine to say, "My moms are swimming."

> When you invite kids to talk openly and ask questions about gender and sexuality, you have to be ready for whatever happens. It's trickier than geometry.

Looking Forward

Meanwhile, Sasha was home for Thanksgiving and back at school shortly thereafter, using media interest in the case as an opportunity to explain different aspects of nonbinary gender identity. Sasha told reporters they probably won't ride the bus alone for a while, but concluded the interview: "I'm going to keep wearing a skirt. It's a big part of who I am."

Sharing current stories of history-making activists like Sasha—or Jeydon Loredo, a transgender student who successfully sued his school district to have his senior picture included in his high school yearbook; Destin Holmes, a lesbian student who stood up to abusive treatment by teachers and her principal; or the student body of Waukegan High School, which elected a gay and lesbian duo as their king and queen—can inspire dialogue and understanding as we work to help schools catch up in the march toward justice.

Seneca Falls, Selma, Stonewall
Moving beyond equality

By Therese Quinn and Erica R. Meiners

Our name order reflects a publishing rotation and not an authorship hierarchy; this is a co-written article.

Erica R. Meiners teaches and organizes in Chicago. She has written about her ongoing labor and learning in anti-militarization campaigns, educational justice struggles, prison abolition and reform movements, and queer and immigrant rights organizing in *Flaunt It! Queers Organizing for Public Education and Justice* (2009, Peter Lang), *Right to Be Hostile: Schools, Prisons, and the Making of Public Enemies* (2007), and articles in *Radical Teacher, Meridians, AREA Chicago, and Social Justice.*

Therese Quinn is an associate professor of art history and director of the Museum and Exhibition Studies Program at the University of Illinois at Chicago. She is a founding member of Chicagoland Researchers and Advocates for Transformative Education (CReATE at createchicago.org). Her most recent books are *Art and Social Justice Education: Culture as Commons* (2012), *Sexualities in Education: A Reader* (2012), *and Teaching Toward Democracy* (2010).

With same-sex marriage legal, trans woman Laverne Cox from the television series *Orange Is the New Black* on the cover of *Time* magazine, lots of queer sex on *Game of Thrones*, and President Obama's invocation of the Stonewall rebellion in his 2013 Inaugural Address,[1] gay people have, in full fabulous fashion, clearly arrived. With marriage certificates in our tuxedo pockets, our military uniforms pressed and ready, and anti-bullying initiatives in our schools, we—the LGBTQ justice movement—have left behind our worst problems and soared past the finish line to equality and rights. Right?

This view of social progress strikes a familiar chord for many of us working in schools, where the difficulties of the past are often explained as vastly distant, just folktales from an incomprehensible time, place, and people. Slavery? Women couldn't vote or own property? Gay people arrested, fired, castrated? Who would *do* that? Not us, that's for sure. Who *were* those people?

The ideas that *we* are different from *they*, and that *now* is better than *then*, form a kind of comfortable common sense; the feeling that things are getting better can be a relief when we are confronted with history's horrors. For that reason, it's not surprising that progress narratives, often paired with a focus on changing individual behavior by promoting respect for difference, fairness, and tolerance, are dominant in so many diversity and multicultural curriculum frameworks. Ongoing examples of systemic violations of human dignity and safety are often ignored and even banned from discussion in public education settings. It's easier and, let's face it, more profitable, to tout the right to gay marriage than the epidemic plight of homeless gay and trans youth. After the 2014 killing of Michael Brown, an unarmed Black youth in Ferguson, Missouri, by a white police officer, the superintendent of a school district in Illinois banned discussion of the shooting and related protests. "Teachers have been told not to discuss [the shooting] and if students bring it up, they should change the subject."[2] The implied message: What's terrible is past; everything is better now. What isn't better can be attributed to a few bad people, not bad social structures and oppressive policies. And, finally, what isn't better it's OK to ignore; in fact, silence might be mandatory.

Progress narratives support dangerously ahistoric understandings of social change, narrowing our attention. For example, why does everyone study the Civil Rights Movement but not the criminal justice system?

Progress narratives almost always focus on individuals in ways that isolate them from their historical context and erase the importance of collective efforts. Every individualizing hero story—Rosa Parks wouldn't move to the back of the bus, and just like that, everything changed—obscures the labor of the many others who dreamed up and tried out similar tactics earlier and those who turned a precipitating event into a movement. Trained as an organizer at the Highlander Folk School, Rosa Parks was an active member of racial justice organizations long before and long after the Montgomery bus boycott. Keeping organizations and other people in the story doesn't diminish Parks; rather, it puts her action into a context—the actual planning and hard work that it takes to achieve justice.

Not surprisingly, just as curriculum on racial justice often centers on individual struggle in the past and the need to be individually "nice" now, most schools' approaches to LGBTQ issues (when not silenced completely) also admonish us to plant a flag for dauntless progress. But what's the reality?

Standing on Their Shoulders

When Obama's inaugural speech linked Seneca Falls, Selma, and Stonewall—important milestones in the struggle for gender, racial, and sexual equality—he reminded us how much things have, in fact, changed. The 1848 Women's Rights Convention at Seneca Falls, New York, was critical in the movement for (white) women's enfranchisement, and the "Declaration of Sentiments" presented and endorsed at the gathering is still a powerful articulation of what the writers' described as men's "absolute tyranny" over women.[3] Patriarchy lingers on, but we are at some distance from absolute tyranny today.

In 1965, at the conclusion of the Selma to Montgomery March, Martin Luther King Jr. described the impact of racial apartheid (he used the term "segregated society"), repeatedly reminding his audience: "We've come a long way. . . . We are not about to turn around. . . . We are on the move."[4] The next year, Stokely Carmichael called for Black Power and the Black Panthers were formed in Oakland, California.

Also in 1966, transgendered women and gay "hustlers" at the Compton Cafeteria in San Francisco resisted when police attempted to arrest them for congregating in the restaurant—one of the first examples of queer resistance to being criminalized. Then, in 1969, during a brutal raid of the Stonewall Inn, a gay bar in New York's Greenwich Village, LGBTQ people fought back:

> Led by people described by many as drag queens and butch lesbians, bar patrons, joined by street people, began yelling "Gay Power!" and throwing shoes, coins, and bricks at the officers. Over the next several nights, police and queers clashed repeatedly in the streets of the West Village.[5]

Stonewall is now often referred to as the beginning of the present-day LGBTQ rights movement in the United States. In our view, it was a moment that was inspired by and built on many others, including the movement against the war in Vietnam; Compton; the birth of the Black Power Movement and the Black Panthers; the Young Lords, a Puerto Rican liberation organization; Chicana/o and women's liberation organizing; and marches and protests everywhere. Each of these eruptions, assertions, and coalescings sent similar messages about the importance of mobilization to demand transformations of the status quo. Stonewall was immediately, locally, an uprising against police brutality and, broadly, one wave among many against oppression and for social change. The whole world was erupting with demands for justice, and LGBTQ people were organizing, too. And we still are.

But now, given the broad social vision that inspired those movements, we have to question our current strategies and goals. Sure, some of us have come some distance, but where do we want to end up? In particular, the visible surge of support for selected lesbian and gay lives—often those who are white and well-resourced, want to marry, have children, or join the military, are "people of faith," and so on—places pressure on those of us working for queer justice in school and other contexts to critically reevaluate our organizing. To that end, we raise three interrelated questions:

- What are the aims of our work—liberation or assimilation?
- With whom are we in coalition, community, and conversation?
- In our labors for just schools and communities, how can we ensure that we leave no one behind?

And, for those new to this area, we use *queer* in multiple ways in this article—as an adjective and as a noun that refers to all sexualities and gender identities that are outside and challenging of normative, binary categories. To this end, we include Q for queer with LGBT, and use the term *queer* as a replacement for the letters. We also invoke *queer* as a verb, a stance that assumes and honors human complexities, and demands action toward ending oppressive social systems that limit our gendered, sexual, and creative lives (as, for example, in "queering the curriculum").

Of course, not all queers are white or able-bodied or wealthy, so LGBTQ liberation necessarily includes struggles against racism, ableism, and capitalism. These forms of domination are inseparable. The Q, therefore, signifies a political stance that our struggles for freedom and self-determination are one. As poet and activist Audre Lorde noted in 1982: "There is no such thing as a single-issue struggle, because we do not live single-issue lives."[6]

From Equality to Liberation

As we said earlier, the increased legitimacy and limited success of LGBT rights-based movements in the United States motivate us to step back and critically assess LGBTQ and other social justice organizing. What are our goals? Equality—full participation in the status quo—or liberation and collective transformation? Over the last 20 years, the focus of mainstream lesbian and gay organizations in the United States, while never monolithic, has been assimilation, characterized by a prioritization of issues such as full and equal participation in the military and marriage.

> It's easier and, let's face it, more profitable, to tout the right to gay marriage than the epidemic plight of homeless gay and trans youth.

This wasn't always the case. Many earlier LGBTQ organizers drew on international perspectives and movements. Henry Gerber, who founded the nation's first LGBTQ group, the Society for Human Rights, in 1924, was inspired by the efforts of German activists. Gay and feminist liberationists in the 1960s and '70s were often internationalist in their politics, linking their own freedom to the liberation of nations and peoples globally, and identifying with anti-colonial and anti-imperialist movements everywhere.[7] And, as policing and punishment were central to queer lives, early LGBTQ liberation movements analyzed the prison system, offered legal services, and created pen-pal programs with people inside. They saw anti-prison organizing as central because LGBTQ lives and communities were criminalized. Being gay or lesbian was against the law and, therefore, supporting LGBTQ lives required not only prisoner support work but also fighting against police harassment. Many of the gay publications of that period, including *Lesbian Tide, off our backs,* and *Gay Community News*, included letters and articles by people in prison and supported anti-prison organizing. The cover of the 1972 issue of *Gay Sunshine: A Newspaper of Gay Liberation* featured a collage titled "We Are All Fugitives" that visually connected queer struggles with anti-prison, anti-colonial, feminist, Black

Power, and other liberation movements.[8] Lesbian and gay organizers were at the forefront of the anti-war, civil rights, and feminist movements of the 1960s and '70s.

Now, together with grassroots justice organizations across the United States, including the Audre Lorde Project in New York and Communities United Against Violence in San Francisco, we question the current focus of most mainstream LGBTQ organizations. For example, although marriage brings with it a host of benefits, this access is offered at a moment when fewer individuals receive *any* state support or protection. Readers, we are sure, can name the markers of our crumbling public sphere: ongoing struggles to access quality and affordable healthcare; the decimation of unions and concurrent explosion of contingent and "just in time" workers without any benefits; the eradication of public housing and decimation of rent control; and the dearth of childcare and parental leave benefits.

> "There is no such thing as a single-issue struggle, because we do not live single-issue lives." —Audre Lorde

We're also concerned about the political and practical implications of the successful campaign to give LGBTQ people equality in the U.S. military. Of course we're not for inequality, but promoting lesbian and gay participation in the permanent war economy is problematic. Drone strikes by driverless aerial vehicles, initiated by the Obama administration and endorsed by then-Secretary of State Hillary Clinton, have killed thousands, including children, in Pakistan, Yemen, and other parts of the world, in attacks described as a "mass torture" of residents of these countries. Queer justice movements, we argue, must reject militarism and all forms of violent domination.

The narrow aim of equality pursued by mainstream lesbian and gay organizations—including access to marriage and the military—signifies acceptance of an unequal and unjust world. Assimilation into this status quo should not be our goal.

Building Coalition, Community, and Conversation

The trade-off of goodies for some and crumbs for many is nowhere more apparent than in schools today. We can't begin the meaningful conversations that lead to effective coalitions and strong communities without understanding the context: the abandonment of any form of wealth redistribution for K–12 public education, frontal assaults on teacher unions, bipartisan support for the privatization of schools through charters and vouchers, and the school-to-prison pipeline, with its high suspension and expulsion rates for Black and Latina/o students.

Our Chicago context offers an on-the-ground example of the effects of the national trends toward expanding school privatization: The number of charter schools doubled in the city between 2005 and 2012. The overwhelming majority of teachers at charter schools locally and nationally are not unionized; in Chicago these teachers are prevented by law from joining the Chicago Teachers Union.

A nonunion workforce is flexible—without the right to due process that contracts and tenure guarantee—and cheaper. In Chicago, the teachers laid off, predominantly older and African American, were replaced by newer, and whiter, teachers, often with little connection to the schools and surrounding community. A nonunion workforce also has less ability to push back against regressive policies and to support students.

As schools are increasingly sites of temporary and precarious, unprotected labor, this reshapes how teachers and other adults are likely to advocate for queer youth and take potentially unpopular positions. Our own research and

Molly Fair

experience indicate that where school personnel work at will, students often find themselves without "out" LGBTQ teachers and staff, and without vocal allies. This reduces the number of advocates for queer youth and facilitators for Gay-Straight Alliances and similar student organizations.[9] More broadly, the national trend toward "right to work" laws, such as in Michigan, Indiana, and Mississippi, makes it difficult for workers to organize and to call out unjust school conditions—from racist discipline practices to violence against LGBTQ students. Students benefit when school employees have workplace protections that foster speech, independent thinking, and advocacy. Pushing back on school privatization and making alliances with teacher unions has not been on the agenda of safe-school movements, and it must be.

An agenda for queer liberation and transformation translates into building democratic and well-resourced public schools in flourishing communities that are invested in challenging all injustices. For those of us trying to make schools safer spaces for LGBTQ youth, our work is absolutely inseparable from other struggles. More broadly, the goal of making schools strong is a community concern. The work for fair and just schools is not just an LGBTQ struggle: It is the push for just and quality funding, it is the movement to end white supremacy, it is the work for meaningful immigration reform that does not leave anyone behind, it is the campaign to end sexual harassment and assault. All of these intertwined movements shape LGBTQ lives, are central to education justice, and are core to building schools as open and affirming spaces for LGBTQ—and *all*—students, staff, and communities.

Students, teachers, unions, grassroots community organizers: We all need to work together to ensure that schools are worksites with good and fair working conditions. Educators, like students and communities, need secure and supportive environments to most effectively help create spaces for radical and queer curricular possibilities, and to be visible and out LGBTQ role models.

Leave No One Behind

LGBTQ education justice movements are being officially invited to participate in, and de facto legitimate, the "new normal" in education. There is a serious problem when "gay equality" means a network of strong and punitive anti-bullying laws that feed into zero-tolerance discipline policies and the school-to-prison pipeline. In this context, LGBTQ school safety organizing runs the risk of both being isolated from and not in dialogue with interrelated justice struggles, and of too narrowly defining who counts as a member of the LGBTQ community.

In fact, anti-bullying programs that rely on criminalization and closer ties to law enforcement and punishment increase racialized and homophobic forms of school push-out.[10] In efforts to make learning safer for LGBTQ students, punishing policies and closer partnerships with the juvenile justice system create profoundly unsafe schools for many young people. As just one example, disabled youth, especially those who are Black and Brown, experience more and harsher discipline than others in school.[11]

Transgender and gender nonconforming individuals face some of the most vitriolic backlash and punishment on our streets and in our classrooms, and this is particularly so for those who are nonwhite and/or poor. Standing up for transgender rights, dignity, and safety is often more threatening than advocating for lesbian and gay youth. For example, in October 2012, the East Aurora School Board in Illinois backtracked on a policy they had just five days earlier unanimously supported, to create a range of school protections and support for transgender and gender nonconforming students. Buckling under pressure, the school district rescinded the policy. In November 2012, a judge in Maine ruled that the Orono school district was not in violation of Maine's Human Rights Act when it blocked a 5th-grade transgender student from choosing which school bathroom to use.

On the positive side, in December 2012, after a packed six-hour meeting, the Orange County School Board in Florida added protections for gay, lesbian, and transgender students and staff to the district's nondiscrimination policy. However, these battles are hard fought. Fear of moving "too far, too fast" can result in movements, policymakers, and communities dropping the T or Q when the work gets tough. At the forefront of the Stonewall uprising were transgender and gender nonconforming people of color, angry and tired of systemic state and police repression. As we work to support LGBTQ youth in schools, let's not forget the T and Q.

Leaving no one behind demands that we analyze and critique what the state and the schools identify as LGBTQ educational justice issues—Why not school policing and school privatization? It also demands that we ensure that the strategies engaged build community and don't harm or isolate others.

Rising Up!

Seneca Falls, Selma, Stonewall—these were movements that pushed back, arguing that the "same old" politics of patriarchy, white supremacy, trans- and homophobia that structure our everyday lives and institutions, from schools to courtrooms, must be dismantled. As the transgender sex workers and queer bar patrons at Stonewall who fought back against police brutality and marched against forms of state repression demonstrated, queer movements have grounded histories demanding structural and systemic change for all. To continue their work is to not settle for the status quo or the crumbs offered. We need to put "our queer shoulders to the wheel," to quote Allen Ginsberg, exercise our radical imaginations, and work together to build the world we need.

What can this look like in schools? The possibilities are endless! Schools should all be beautiful and resource-rich spaces, filled with art, light, and well-rested and supported teachers. Their students and staffs should be encouraged to speak and act.

An important piece of transforming schools lies in the curriculum—remembering, surfacing, and teaching radical queer history. And always, as we mentioned at the beginning, situating individuals in the broader context of the movements in which they worked. Bayard Rustin, for example, was a queer, communist-to-socialist pacifist strategist who was critical to the Civil Rights Movement—he was a central organizer of the 1963 March on Washington for Jobs and Freedom—yet his contributions were purposely obscured because of his political views and homosexuality, and he was marginalized by many civil rights leaders. Harry Hay used skills he learned through labor organizing and in the Communist Party USA to co-found the Mattachine Society, the first sustained gay organization in the United States; the Gay Liberation Front; and the Radical Faeries, which continues today. Sylvia Rivera, a transgender Latina sex worker, was a member of the Young Lords and played a central role in the Stonewall uprising; she spoke powerfully and organized against police repression.

Poet and activist Adrienne Rich's life of resistance was exemplified by her refusal to accept the 1974 National Book Award as an individual, instead claiming the award on behalf of all women and sharing it with her other fierce, queer artist and activist nominees: Alice Walker and Audre Lorde. Lorde's powerful ideas are infused throughout this essay, and Walker's organizing and activism has continued across decades, from the civil rights and women's movements of the 1960s to her current support for the Boycott, Divestment, and Sanctions Campaign against the occupation of Palestine by Israel. All of these people remind us of the importance of persistence, of the power of community, and that there are no single-issue struggles. They were all in it for the long haul, and not interested in assimilation.

As these histories, *hir*stories,[12] and herstories ground us, our work extends to include unfolding and yet-to-be-imagined tactics and strategies. We are particularly energized by networks of youth, parents, and teachers, from Los Angeles to Atlanta, who are organizing, speaking out, and pushing back against punishing and undemocratic schools and communities. These folks are not settling for business as usual in our public schools, nor are they

Mary Tremonte

pitting teachers and labor struggles against the needs of Black and Brown parents. The conditions that necessitate these labors and the work itself seem daunting, but many of these groups—including New York's Audre Lorde Project, which works to make communities safer and stronger for LGBTQ youth of color—offer friendship and support along with radical visions that challenge the "new normal" and foster social justice everywhere.

These powerful examples of the many who are struggling for transformation, not assimilation—liberation, not equality—inspire and remind us that we are not alone. Raising radical (from the root) questions creates more opportunities for solidarity, more sites for building community, and more people to joyfully work alongside. We *can* build the communities we know we need, and leave no one behind along the way. During the 2012 strike, the Chicago Teachers Union rejected attempts to divide working and poor parents, often people of color, from public school teachers, and countered claims that educators cared more about benefits and salaries than the well-being of Chicago's children. Good teaching conditions are good learning conditions, they insisted. We insist on this, too, and on an expanded version of the idea: The conditions for flourishing lives are exactly the same as the conditions for justice. It will take all of us to do the work to build this world. We will be there! *Presente*!

Endnotes

1   Inaugural Address by President Barack Obama, Jan. 21, 2013. whitehouse. gov/the-press-office/2013/01/21/inaugural-address-president-barack-obama

2   Strauss, Valerie. 2014. "School District Bans Discussion on Michael Brown, Ferguson." *Washington Post*, Aug. 26. washingtonpost.com/blogs/answer-sheet/wp/2014/08/26/school-district-bans-classroom-discussion-on-michael-brown-ferguson/

3   "Declaration of Sentiments and Resolutions." 1848. Women's Rights Convention at Seneca Falls. ecssba.rutgers.edu/docs/seneca.html

4   "Address at the Conclusion of the Selma to Montgomery March, March 25, 1965." mlk-kpp01.stanford.edu/index.php/encyclopedia/documentsentry/doc_address_at_the_conclusion_of_selma_march/

5   Mogul, Joey, Andrea Ritchie, and Kay Whitlock. 2011. *Queer (In)justice: The Criminalization of LGBT People in the United States.* pp. 45–46. Beacon.

6   Lorde, Audre. 1982. "Learning from the 60s." blackpast.org/1982-audre-lorde-learning-60s

7   Many representations of these movements and ideas are available in:

Blasius, Mark, and Shane Phelan. 1997. *We Are Everywhere: A Historical Sourcebook of Gay and Lesbian Politics*. Routledge.

8   Kunzel. Regina. 2008. "Lessons in Being Gay: Queer Encounters in Gay and Lesbian Prison Activism." *Radical History Review* 100: 11–37.

9   Quinn, Therese. 2007. "'You Make Me Erect': Queer Girls of Color Negotiating Heteronormative Leadership at an Urban All-Girls' Public School." *Journal of Gay and Lesbian Issues in Education* 4.3: 31–47.

10 Meiners, Erica. 2007. *Right to Be Hostile: Schools, Prisons, and the Making of Public Enemies*. Routledge.

11 Lewin, Tamar. 2012. "Black Students Face More Discipline, Data Suggests." *New York Times,* March 6. nytimes.com/2012/03/06/education/black-students-face-more-harsh-discipline-data-shows.html?_r=0

12 *Hir*, a trans-sensitive gender pronoun. See more at "A gender neutral pronoun." genderneutralpronoun.wordpress.com/tag/transgender/

CHAPTER 2

Boys can wear dress-up clothes and play with dolls. Boys can jump rope. Girls can play with trucks and wrestle. Girls can play football. It's OK for girls and boys to do what they enjoy doing.

By: Vanessa and Xia
Room 27

No matter how long your hair is, or no matter how you look or what language you speak, or where you come from ... WE ARE ALL THE SAME ON THE INSIDE!

By: David and Adelais
Room 27

Artwork by students in Dale Weiss' class

If you are not sure if someone is a boy or a girl, Just ask them. And then believe what they tell you the first time. Let people be who they are!

Boys and girls can wear whatever clothes they feel comfortable in. Girls and boys can be whoever they want to be.

Our Classrooms: Introduction

By Melissa Bollow Tempel

Melissa Bollow Tempel has worked as a bilingual elementary school teacher, teacher educator, and culturally responsive teacher leader. She has been a Rethinking Schools editor and is currently an organizer with the Milwaukee Educators' Network for Social Justice. Melissa and her partner live in Milwaukee with their two daughters and their menagerie of pets.

The summer before 5th grade, my daughter Maya decided to get a short haircut. It was an adorable pixie cut that framed her face and fit her style perfectly. She got compliments almost every day—not just from friends and neighbors, but also from random people like the cashier at the grocery store. Maya walked around with more confidence and blushed each time she received a positive remark about her hair.

By the end of fall, the haircut had grown shaggy and her bangs fell across her face, hiding her eyes. I told Maya we should go get it cleaned up.

"I don't want short hair anymore," Maya said.

"But why? It's such a cute haircut, everyone thinks so!"

"I don't want short hair anymore, and I don't care what anyone else thinks!" she insisted and stomped off.

For a moment I contemplated forcing her to get a haircut but then came to my senses. After some cool-down time, I started probing to see why Maya didn't want short hair anymore. After the careful dance of questioning and letting it drop that parents of tweens know all too well, the truth finally came out. At school, one boy told another boy that Maya must be gay since she had short hair. Of course the comment got back to Maya.

Even though Maya knows many of our gay friends, even though Maya has friends with gay parents, even though we support marriage equality and openly resist gender stereotypes in our home, that one comment was enough to squash more than a month's worth of compliments. How could that be? Why didn't Maya feel liberated, tell that kid to buzz off, carry herself with confidence, and move on, knowing that her haircut was awesome?

Unfortunately, despite all the information Maya had about equality, she also knew that the societal message is still that calling someone "gay" is a horrible insult. She didn't feel empowered, she didn't feel supported by her friends and teachers, and she wasn't able to speak up. She didn't feel she could take the risk that kids at school would say she was one of "them."

It's not easy for kids to brush off homophobia. And it can be difficult for adults to confront the issue, too. For two years, I held the position of culturally responsive teacher leader in Milwaukee. The first year I focused on cultural identity issues like race, religion, and language. I felt like a coward for ignoring LGBTQ issues. During the summer before year two, I mentioned to a teacher friend that I needed to integrate gender and sexuality into my work, but I was nervous about it. She said: "This is your job. If not you, who?"

Then a colleague in my district told me a story. She saw a transgender student introduced to their teacher on the first day at school by another teacher, who knocked on the classroom door and said, "You have got to see *this*." I knew it was time to address the issues with explicit curriculum, not just for students but for staff as well.

Freedom from sexism and gender roles is liberating for all children.

I started slowly, going into classrooms to model lessons using books about gender nonconforming children, including *William's Doll* and *Oliver Button Is a Sissy*, and the lessons I wrote about in "It's OK to Be Neither."

Then, to address sexuality and sexism, I developed a series of lessons based on two picture books. The first one, *The Great Big Book of Families*, by Mary Hoffman, is simple and nonthreatening. It begins:

> Once upon a time, most families in books looked like this: One daddy, one mommy, one little boy, one little girl, one dog, and one cat.
> But in real life, families come in all sorts of shapes and sizes.

The next page nonchalantly states:

> Some children have two mommies or two daddies.

I asked students to "turn and talk" every few pages. "Talk about who you live with," I suggested. "Share whether you have a pet." As a class, we discussed different ways a family can have two mommies or two daddies. "I have two mommies—my mommy and my godmother," one child said. "I have a stepdad and a real dad," another said. As I added that some families have two moms or two dads who love each other and are a couple, I realized how important class discussion is; without time to talk about that page, the impact on the students would have been minimal.

The first time I read *The Great Big Book of Families* aloud, I felt that it was written for a middle-class audience. Although it does have pictures that contradict sexist stereotypes, like one of a stay-at-home father, I had to accommodate for the lack of cultural relevance by adding some of my own commentary. For example: "Some moms don't work because they're going to school," "Some children live with grandparents, aunties, and uncles," "Sometimes two families live together in one house," and "Some parents work at night."

Families, by Susan Kuklin, is based on interviews with children from a broad range of families. Issues include interracial relationships, divorce, disabilities, and gay parents. The first-person narratives and compelling photographs draw children in. Once again, it was important to look at what kinds of families were missing from this book, including blended families with stepbrothers and stepsisters, grandparents or relatives living in the home, and families with an incarcerated parent.

> # Teaching LGBTQ issues isn't something to save for the year when a child has lesbian parents or is visibly struggling with gender identity.

Most teachers welcomed my lessons, but I did encounter a teacher who was uncomfortable with what I was presenting. She had welcomed me into her room for many lessons on race and culture, but told me that *And Tango Makes Three* was out of her comfort zone; she wasn't ready to deal with potential parental or administrative pushback.

In part to respond to her concerns, I created a two-part workshop for teachers about sexism, gender, and sexuality. After doing research and talking with school social workers and LGBTQ education experts, including our state's Gay-Straight Alliance, I developed a presentation to explain the gender binary and the differences among the terms sex, sexuality, and gender. I cited research that demonstrates that separating children by gender—"Time to line up, boys and girls" or "Girls on team A, boys on team B"—makes students more aware of gender stereotypes, including what boys and girls are "allowed" to do (Hilliard and Liben).

After reviewing my presentation, my supervisor told principals to make sure students weren't around during the workshop because it contained inappropriate content. Afterward, some teachers approached me to say how much they had learned, but a few others scoffed at the idea of gender neutral pronouns: "How am I supposed to know what I should call them?" Still more would not give up lining their students up by sex, refusing to believe it actually had an impact on children's self-image. Many felt that discussing sexism, gender, and sexuality put them out on a limb.

That was a wake-up call for me. Although the world seems to be changing, many teachers still aren't able to address gender stereotypes and LGBTQ issues, or be "out" as supportive. I felt even more respect for the teacher-authors in this book, who have taken risks to make the work happen in their classrooms, schools, and communities.

Although I have met people unwilling or unable to give up on old ideas, young teachers and teacher education students give me hope. Recently, I have been teaching classes at a conservative, religious university; many of the students are from rural or suburban areas. Their attitude is that teaching gender, sexism, and sexuality is a "no-brainer"—of course they'll be addressing it in their classes! One student, Kellie, wrote:

> My sister always dressed like a boy, played with boy toys, and pretty much did anything that went against the typical girl stereotype. This was horrifying to me because I did not want to stand out or be judged because someone in my family was different. My school sent the message that if you were different, you were wrong. Unfortunately, that caused me to feel ashamed of my family and I was always reluctant to talk about them in school. Currently, my sister goes by the name of Alex and wants to be identified as a boy. I wish my early education had focused more on teaching tolerance because it could have been helpful to accepting this change in my family.

Kellie raises an important issue. Just as we cannot know with certainty if a child is gay or straight, we cannot tell who has a transgender sibling, a gay parent, or a gender-nonconforming neighbor. And freedom from sexism and gender roles is liberating for all children. Teaching LGBTQ issues isn't something to save for the year when a child in our class has lesbian parents or is visibly struggling with gender identity. It's part of building a nurturing classroom and school—every year.

One of the hot topics in schools right now is protecting our students from bullies: A "safe school" is a school that's a "bully-free zone." We've all watched bullies in movies and on television locking kids into lockers, calling them "weenies" and "creeps," and stealing their sandwiches. But talking about "bullies" makes it seem like an individual problem and glosses over homophobia, sexism, racism, Islamophobia—all the critical issues that underlie conflicts among children and adults. According to a recent California Healthy Kids Survey, more than 75 percent of students who are subjected to harassment on school property believe it is because of race, religion, national origin, gender, actual or perceived sexual orientation, or ability. Yet bullying programs don't typically work with educators to address these issues specifically.

In a liberatory school, teachers and school leaders do the work to build community based on social justice principles from the beginning. Then, they speak up when they hear homophobic or other discriminatory remarks, defend their students, and work with colleagues and families to increase understanding so that differences are not just tolerated, but celebrated.

Unfortunately, every school is not a liberatory school. We, the editors, are well aware of the disparate environments that educators find ourselves in. We hear about districts changing nondiscrimination policies to protect everyone on the LGBTQ spectrum. We hear about schools doing an amazing job of creating environments where faculty and staff welcome all families. However, many of us have worked in environments where this work is difficult and slow going, and our own classrooms may be the only places where we feel safe enough to approach topics of sexism, gender, and sexuality. There are many schools that remain stagnant in traditional ways. We want to acknowledge the courage behind finding some way to make a change, no matter what situation you find yourself in.

Our hope is that this book will nurture more and more liberatory classroom environments where students know they are allowed to come as they are, their families are welcomed, their opinions are heard, and their lives are built into the curriculum. We hope that every educator will take away useful new ideas and lessons to help liberate the spaces where they teach.

Resources

California Healthy Kids Survey. 2011. *Student Well-Being in California, 2009–11: Statewide Results*. WestEd Health and Human Development Program for the California Department of Education.

dePaola, Tomie. 1979. *Oliver Button Is a Sissy*. HMH Books for Young Readers.

Hilliard, Lacey J. and Lynn S. Liben, 2010. "Differing Levels of Gender Salience in Preschool Classrooms: Effects on Children's Gender Attitudes and Intergroup Bias," *Child Development*. 81: 1787–1798.

Hoffman, Mary. 2011. *The Great Big Book of Families*. Dial.

Kuklin, Susan. 2006. *Families*. Hyperion.

Richardson, Justin and Peter Parnell. 2005. *And Tango Makes Three*. Simon & Shuster Books for Young Readers.

Zolotow, Charlotte. 1985. *William's Doll*. Harper & Row.

10 Ways to Move Beyond Bully Prevention (And Why We Should)

BY LYN MIKEL BROWN

Lyn Mikel Brown is a professor of education at Colby College in Waterville, Maine. She is the author of five books, including *Girlfighting: Betrayal and Rejection Among Girls*. She is co-founder of the nonprofit Hardy Girls Healthy Women (hghw.org) and SPARK Movement (sparkmovement.org). A version of this article appeared in *Education Week*.

Some years ago, I helped found a nonprofit organization committed to changing the culture for girls. Our work is based on the health psychology notion of "hardiness"—a way of talking about resilience that not only identifies what girls need to thrive in an increasingly complex and stressful world, but also makes clear that adults are responsible for creating safe spaces for girls to grow, think critically, and work together to make their lives better.

> Bullying is a broad term that de-genders, de-races, de-everythings school safety.

As a result of this work, I've grown concerned that "bully prevention" has all but taken over the way we think about, talk about, and respond to the relational lives of children and youths in schools. So, from our group's strength-based approach, I offer 10 ways to move beyond what is too often being sold as a panacea for schools' social ills, and is becoming, I fear, a problem in and of itself:

I. Stop labeling kids.

Bully prevention programs typically put kids in three categories: bullies, victims, and bystanders. Labeling children in these ways denies what we know to be true: We are all complex beings with the capacity to do harm and to do good, sometimes within the same hour. It also makes the child the problem, which downplays the important role of parents, teachers, the school system,

J.D. King

an increasingly provocative and powerful media culture, and societal injustices children experience every day. Labeling kids bullies, for that matter, contributes to the negative climate and name-calling we're trying to address.

2. Talk accurately about behavior.

If it's sexual harassment, call it sexual harassment; if it's homophobia, call it homophobia, and so forth. To lump disparate behaviors under the generic "bullying" is to efface real differences that affect young people's lives. Bullying is a broad term that de-genders, de-races, de-everythings school safety. Because of this, as sexual harassment expert Nan Stein explains, embracing anti-bullying legislation can actually undermine the legal rights and protections offered by anti-harassment laws. Calling behaviors what they are helps us educate children about their rights, affirms their realities, encourages more complex and meaningful solutions, opens up a dialogue, invites children to participate in social change, and ultimately protects them.

3. Move beyond the individual.

Children's behaviors are greatly affected by their life histories and social contexts. To understand why a child uses aggression toward others, it's important to understand what impact race, ethnicity, social class, gender, religion, and ability has on his or her daily experiences in school—that is, how do these realities affect the kinds of attention and resources the child receives, where he fits in, whether she feels marginal or privileged in the school. Such differences in social capital, cultural capital, and power relations deeply affect a child's psychological and relational experiences in school.

4. Reflect reality.

Many schools across the country have adopted an approach developed by the Norwegian educator Dan Olweus, the Olweus Bullying Prevention Program. Described as a "universal intervention for the reduction and prevention of bully/victim problems," the Olweus program downplays those differences that make a difference. But even when bully prevention programs have been adequately evaluated, the University of Illinois' Dorothy Espelage argues, they often show less than positive results. "We do not have a one-size-fits-all school system," she reminds us. Because the United States has a diversity of races, ethnicities, languages, and inequalities among schools, bully prevention efforts here need to address that reality.

5. Adjust expectations.

We hold kids to ideals and expectations that we as adults could never meet. We expect girls to ingest a steady diet of media "mean girls" and always be nice and kind, and for boys to engage a culture of violence and never lash out. We expect kids never to express anger to adults, never to act in mean or hurtful ways to one another, even though they may spend much of the day in schools where they don't feel safe, and with teachers and other students who treat them with disrespect. Moreover, we expect kids to behave in ways most of us don't even value very much: to obey all the rules (regardless of their perceived or real unfairness), to never resist, refuse, or fight back.

It's important to promote consistent consequences—the hallmarks of most bully prevention programs—but it's also critically important to create space for honest conversations about who benefits from certain norms and rules and who doesn't. If we allow kids to speak out, to think critically and question unfairness, we provide the groundwork for civic engagement.

6. Listen to kids.

In her book *Other People's Children*, Lisa Delpit talks about the importance of "listening that requires not only open eyes and ears, but also hearts and minds." Again, consistent consequences are important; used well, they undermine privilege and protect those who are less powerful. But to make such a system work, schools have to listen to all students. It's the only way to ensure that staff members are not using discipline and consistent consequences simply to promote the status quo.

> If we allow kids to speak out, to think critically and question unfairness, we provide the groundwork for civic engagement.

7. Embrace grassroots movements.

There's nothing better than student-initiated change. Too many bully prevention programs are top-heavy with adult-generated rules, meetings, and trainings. We need to empower young people. This includes being on the lookout for positive grassroots resistance, ready to support and sometimes channel youth movements when they arise. We need to listen to students, take up their just causes, understand the world they experience, include them in the dialogue about school norms and rules, and use their creative energy to illuminate and challenge unfairness.

8. Be proactive, not reactive

In Maine, we have a nationally recognized Civil Rights Team Project. Youth-led, school-based preventive teams work to increase safety, educate their peers, and combat hate, violence, prejudice, and harassment in more than 150 schools across the state. This kind of proactive youth empowerment work is sorely needed, but is too often lost in the midst of zero-tolerance policies and top-down bully prevention efforts. Yet such efforts work. According to a study conducted by the Gay, Lesbian, and Straight Education Network (GLSEN), youth-led gay-straight alliances make schools safer for all students.

9. Build coalitions.

Rather than bully prevention, let's emphasize ally and coalition building, especially as activist Bernice Johnson Reagon defines it: work that's difficult, exhausting, but necessary "for all of us to feel that this is our world."

10. Accentuate the positive.

Instead of labeling kids, let's talk about them as potential leaders, affirm their strengths, and believe that they can do good, brave, remarkable things. The path to safer, less violent schools lies less in our control over children than in appreciating their need to have more control in their lives, to feel important, to be visible, to have an effect on people and situations.

Bully prevention has become a huge for-profit industry. Let's not let the steady stream of training sessions, rules, policies, consequence charts, and "no bullying" posters keep us from listening well, thinking critically, and creating approaches that meet the unique needs of our schools and communities.

Resources

Delpit, Lisa. 2006. *Other People's Children: Cultural Conflict in the Classroom.* The New Press.

Find out more about Maine's Civil Rights Team Project at maine.gov/ag/civil_rights/.

Simone Shin

4-Year-Olds Discuss Love and Marriage

BY A. J. JENNINGS

A. J. Jennings is a teacher at Park West Cooperative Nursery School in Chicago. Jennings is passionate about working with and advocating for LGBTQ young people and LGBTQ educators.

I teach in a play-based preschool on Chicago's north side, and I can accurately say that not a week has gone by in my decade-long teaching career when the topic of marriage has not come up.

It can be a part of a game: "You be the prince and I be the princess and we get married."

A child's story: "Then they danced and got married."

To taunt another child: "You're going to marry him!"

A declaration of infatuation: "I'm gonna marry her."

A subject of inquiry: "Are you married, Ali? Are you a mom?"

Even a hope for the future: "When I get big, I'm gonna be a dad and get married."

One day, Rory approached me during playtime, visibly shaken. "Those kids are telling me that girls can't marry girls and they can!"

"Well let's go and talk with them about it," I responded. When we reached the two girls, I told them that Rory was worried about the conversation they were having and asked what they were talking about. I learned that, just as Rory reported, the two girls had been discussing marriage and how girls couldn't marry girls. Rory had been insisting they could. He was certain of it. His mom had told him. The other two were skeptical. They all looked to me to clarify this point of contention.

I was delighted to be a part of the conversation and also struggled a bit with how to answer truthfully. Gay marriage is now legal in Illinois, but at that point, only civil unions were legal for lesbian and gay couples. Of course, this fine point has the potential to be lost on 4-year-olds. I generally feel that when talking about marriage most children mean adults loving one another, so I went that route.

"Well, two girls can be in love with each other," I responded.

"Yeah!" agreed Rory, vindicated by his teacher's affirmation of this point.

I continued: "And girls can love boys. And boys can love boys." The three children mulled this over.

> Through careful listening, we can identify the issues that kids in our classroom are grappling with. And, through conversation, we can model nonjudgmental behavior and challenge binary thinking.

"Like my mom and dad love each other," one of them answered.

"Right," I said. The kids continued their conversation of marriage and were no longer looking for my input. I listened for a few more minutes as they tossed around the idea that love might not be constrained to a mom loving a dad. Rory mentioned that he had a friend who had two moms who were married. The other two children were willing to accept this and incorporate the new information into their understanding of the boundaries of love and marriage.

Challenging Binary Thinking

As an educator (and a person), I value conversation as a way to build understanding and transform perspectives. It is an incredible curricular tool for addressing issues of identity (e.g., race, class, size, gender, sexuality, ability, religion). It can be especially meaningful when our students initiate the conversations. So I work to create a classroom environment where differing points of view can be addressed and explored. My goal is for the children to feel confident about articulating their point of view and safe enough to consider other perspectives. As teachers, through careful listening, we can identify the issues that kids in our classroom are grappling with. And, through conversation, we can model nonjudgmental behavior and challenge binary thinking.

This is especially significant in early childhood education. As young children develop their understanding of the world, they tend to rely heavily on binaries. If we understand the binaries a child is working within, we can encourage that child to think of counterexamples or introduce counterexamples ourselves into the conversation. These provide useful stumbling blocks that encourage them to expand their thinking.

For example, I have very short, sometimes dyed hair and it tends to be a common topic in my classroom. A child will look at me and ask, "Why do you have boy hair?"

"Do you mean why do I have short hair?"

This is often met with a quizzical look. "Yeah. It looks like boy hair."

"Well, this is how I like my hair to look. Do all boys have short hair?"

Usually at this moment in the conversation, that child or a peer will think of a boy they know who has long hair or a girl who has short hair. Even a simple conversation like this challenges children to expand their thinking.

> Many teachers prefer to plan ahead and address gender and sexuality with self-contained lessons. I'd like to challenge that desire.

If a parent witnesses their child asking me this type of question, I often sense nervousness about their child acting "rude." However, if I were to shut down the conversation by saying "It's not polite to say something like that about my hair," the interaction would be lost, and the child would continue to believe that only boys have short hair.

It's easy to feel vulnerable or overwhelmed when children ask questions about identity, but when we don't engage the issues involved, we are sending a message that the subjects are taboo. In terms of gender and sexuality, avoidance and silence can be particularly harmful for students who are or will later identify as LGBTQ or who come from families with LGBTQ family members. Silence is not a neutral response.

This is not a packaged curricular activity. I know that many teachers prefer to plan ahead and address gender and sexuality with self-contained lessons. I'd like to challenge that desire. Although there is a time and place for pre-planned curricular activities, I believe that setting up our classrooms so conversation is honored as part of the curriculum provides children with repeated opportunities to develop their critical thinking skills, empathy, and worldview. We can model active listening, teach the children to engage respectfully, and set up guidelines for what is and is not acceptable in a conversation. We cannot plan how conversations will unfold or what our students' experiences and perspectives will add. That means our perspective might be challenged and perhaps changed. Sometimes I realize later that a conversation didn't resolve in a way I'm comfortable with, but I know I can revisit it with the class in a day or two.

And Tango Makes Three

Of course, there are many resources to help initiate conversations and help frame our students' thinking. Because my class had been talking about same-sex marriage and love, we read *And Tango Makes Three* by Peter Parnell and Justin Richardson. This charming picture book is based on a true story of two male penguins in the Central Park Zoo. A zookeeper provides them with an egg to raise into a chick after he recognizes that they are mates and "in love."

As I was reading the story, a handful of kids chimed in that they knew two boys who loved each other or two girls who loved each other. Again the conversation turned to marriage. Some kids were insistent that boys could marry boys and girls could marry girls, others were sure that could not happen, and still others listened without sharing their ideas. The country's debate on gay marriage had reached the 4- and 5-year-olds in my class. The book prompted a conversation about an issue that kids were actively working to understand.

At this point, I felt a twinge of unease about potential parent responses. As I thought later about my nervousness, I realized I have never run into a parent who asked me not to talk about heterosexual marriage with their child. Why not? Heterosexual marriage is an acceptable part of dominant culture and is therefore not considered taboo. So it is seen as nonthreatening. Parents trust that, as a teacher, I can talk about heterosexual marriage without the conversation being dominated by sexuality. Heterosexual marriage is viewed through the lens of love. Same-sex marriage does not feel quite as benign because it is viewed by its opponents through the lens of sex. Gay sex, to be exact, which is perceived as inappropriate subject matter for young children. Based on religious beliefs about the immorality of "homosexual behavior," there are people who would rather that discussion of gay relationships be omitted entirely from their children's school experiences.

Too "Sensitive" for Class Discussion?

Some parents say they want to "save sensitive conversations for the home." Although I can understand a parent's desire to pass along their ideas and values to their children, the hope that those conversations will happen exclusively in the home is unrealistic. Students have a vast array of experiences and bring those to a classroom full of peers. For example, not many 3-year-olds have the experience of a parent dying, but when a child does, that tragic experience becomes part of the classroom dynamic. So even if teachers never initiate conversations about gender, sexuality, race, death, ability, religion, or any of the other "sensitive topics," those issues are present and affect the school environment.

I am acutely aware that my values may be different from those of families I serve. As teachers we live in a gray area—we each have our own ideas, biases, and values, often as varied as those of the children and families we serve. Regardless of any one of our ideological slants, a large part of our job is to help our students explore questions deeply and be able to think for themselves.

As the year unfolded, my students continued to play at themes of love and marriage. The conversations expanded and both the kids and I were able to introduce new and different stumbling blocks: one can be in love and not get married, not all married people are moms or dads, and not all moms and dads are married. The conversations shifted based on what information the kids had internalized.

For example, a table was full of kids working in their journals. Jack began to tease Joe:

Jack: "You're going to marry your sister!"

Joe: "But I don't have a sister. I have a brother."

Jill: "Boys can marry boys. Girls can marry girls."

Jack: "You're going to marry your brother (then)."

Joe starts to color in Jack's journal.

Teacher: "Joe, did you like what Jack was saying to you?"

Joe shakes his head.

Teacher: "You could tell him you didn't like it."

Joe: "I don't like that. I don't like it when you tell me that."

Jack: "I was trying to ask him who he was going to marry."

Joe: "No. I don't know who I'm going to marry yet."

Jack: "Well, when you're a teenager you can decide who you want to marry."

Teacher: "Does everybody have to get married?"

Jane: "When you're a grown-up you do."

Teacher: "I'm a grown-up and I'm not married. Not all people decide they want to get married."

Jane: "You can't marry someone in your family."

Joe: "You could when you get bigger. Like when I get big I could marry my brother."

Jane: "No. You can't. 'Cause then you'll lose your hand or your leg or something."

As this deeply layered conversation moved on, many points of view were stated, more questions were posed, and the children were able to articulate what they thought. I made a mental note to myself about topics to revisit, including finding a way to talk about inherited traits and Jane's ideas about the dangers of incest. There's always a new challenge!

Earlier in the year, the group of kids may have gotten stuck on the question of whether or not two boys could get married but, because we had previously engaged in full-class discussions and many smaller conversations about same-sex marriage, they were able to move further with the conversation. What started as one child's effort to tease turned into a conversation that many were involved and invested in. Even if I'd tried I couldn't have planned this conversation, but I'm glad there was time and space for it in the classroom. It left us with big questions and ideas that I hope my students will ponder and continue to revisit.

Resource

Parnell, Peter, and Justin Richardson. Illustrated by Henry Cole. 2005. *And Tango Makes Three*. Simon and Schuster.

It's OK to Be Neither
Teaching that supports gender-independent children

BY MELISSA BOLLOW TEMPEL

Melissa Bollow Tempel has worked as a bilingual elementary school teacher, teacher educator, and culturally responsive teacher leader. She has been a Rethinking Schools editor and is currently an organizer with the Milwaukee Educators' Network for Social Justice. Melissa and her partner live in Milwaukee with their two daughters and their menagerie of pets.

Allie arrived at our 1st-grade classroom wearing a sweatshirt with a hood. I asked her to take off her hood, and she refused. I thought she was just being difficult and ignored it. After breakfast we got in line for art, and I noticed that she still had not removed her hood. When we arrived at the art room, I said: "Allie, I'm not playing. It's time for art. The rule is no hoods or hats in school."

She looked up with tears in her eyes and I realized there was something wrong. Her classmates went into the art room and we moved to the art storage area so her classmates wouldn't hear our conversation. I softened my tone and asked her if she'd like to tell me what was wrong.

"My ponytail," she cried.

"Can I see?" I asked.

She nodded and pulled down her hood. Allie's braids had come undone overnight and there hadn't been time to redo them in the morning, so they had to be put back in a ponytail. It was high up on the back of her head like those of many girls in our class, but I could see that to Allie it just felt wrong. With Allie's permission, I took the elastic out and re-braided her hair so it could hang down.

"How's that?" I asked.

She smiled. "Good," she said and skipped off to join her friends in art.

"Why Do You Look Like a Boy?"

Allison was biologically a girl but felt more comfortable wearing Tony Hawk long-sleeved T-shirts, baggy jeans, and black tennis shoes. Her parents were accepting and supportive. Her mother braided her hair in cornrows because Allie thought it made her look like Will Smith's son in the remake of *The Karate Kid*. She preferred to be called Allie. The first day of school, children who hadn't

Katherine Streeter

been in Allie's class in kindergarten referred to her as "he."

I didn't want to assume I knew how Allie wanted me to respond to the continual gender mistakes, so I made a phone call home and Allie's mom put me on speakerphone.

"Allie," she said, "Ms. Melissa is on the phone. She would like to know if you want her to correct your classmates when they say you are a boy, or if you would rather that she just doesn't say anything."

Allie was shy on the phone. "Um . . . tell them that I am a girl," she whispered.

The next day when I corrected classmates and told them that Allie was a girl, they asked her a lot of questions that she wasn't prepared for: "Why do you look like a boy?" "If you're a girl, why do you always wear boys' clothes?" Some even told her that she wasn't supposed to wear boys' clothes if she was a girl. It became evident that I would have to address gender directly in order to make the classroom environment more comfortable for Allie and to squash the gender stereotypes that my 1st graders had absorbed in their short lives.

Gender Training Starts Early

Gender is not a subject that I would have broached in primary grades a few years ago. In fact, I remember scoffing with colleagues when we heard about a young kindergarten teacher who taught gender-related curriculum. We thought her lessons were a waste of instructional time and laughed at her "girl and boy" lessons.

My own thoughts about gender curriculum shifted when I became a mother. As I shopped for infant clothes for my first daughter, I was disgusted that almost everything was pink and there was no mistaking the boys' section of the store for the girls'. I refused to make my baby daughter fit in the box that society had created for her. "What if she doesn't like pink?" I thought. "What if she likes tigers and dinosaurs?"

> It wasn't until I had a child dealing with gender variance in my classroom that I realized how important it is to teach about gender and gender stereotypes.

As my two daughters grew, I talked with them about gender stereotypes. I let them choose "boys'" clothes if they wanted to (and often encouraged them because they are more practical). The first week of kindergarten, my younger daughter's teacher told me that she'd had a heated argument with a boy while they played dress up. "She insisted that boys can wear dresses if they want to," the teacher told me. I beamed with pride.

Unfortunately, it wasn't until I had a child who was gender independent (also called gender variant, and defined as "behavior or gender expression that does not conform to dominant gender norms of male and female") in my classroom that I realized how important it is to teach about gender and break down gender stereotypes. Why did I wait so long? I should have taken a hint from that kindergarten teacher years ago. As I thought about how to approach the topic, I realized that the lessons I was developing weren't just for Allie. She had sparked my thinking, but all the children in my class needed to learn to think critically about gender stereotypes and gender nonconformity.

We started off with a lesson about toys because it's a simple topic I knew my students thought they had clear ideas about. The class gathered on the carpet and I read *William's Doll*, which is about a boy who, against the wishes of his father, wants a doll more than anything.

After we read the story, I taped up two large pieces of paper and wrote "Boys" on one and "Girls" on the other. "Students," I said, "what are some toys that are for boys?" Eagerly, the students began to shout out their answers: "Legos!" "Hot Wheels!" "Skateboards!" "Bikes!" The list grew quite long. "OK," I said, "now tell me some toys that are for girls." "Baby dolls!" "Nail polish!" "Barbies!" "Makeup!"

When we had two extensive lists, I read both lists out loud to the class and then studied them carefully.

"Hmm," I said. "Here it says that Legos are for boys. Can girls play with Legos?"

"Yes!" most of them replied without hesitation.

"I wonder if any of the girls in our class like to play with Hot Wheels?"

"I do! I do!" blurted out some of the girls. We continued with the rest of the items on our "Boys" list, making a check mark next to each one as it was declared acceptable for girls.

Then we went on to the "Girls" list. We started with baby dolls. Because we had just read and discussed *William's Doll*, the children were OK with boys playing with dolls. "It's great practice for boys who want to be daddies when they grow up," I mentioned.

But when we got to nail polish and makeup the children were unsure. "There are some very famous rock 'n' roll bands," I said, "and the men in those bands wear a lot of makeup." Some of the children gasped.

Then Isabela raised her hand: "Sometimes my uncle wears black nail polish." The students took a moment to think about this.

"My cousin wears nail polish, too!" said another student. Soon many students were eager to share examples of how people pushed the limits on gender. Our school engineer, Ms. Joan, drove a motorcycle. Jeremy liked to dance. I could see the gears turning in their brains as the gender lines started to blur.

Supporting Gender Independence Every Day

I knew that broadening my students' ideas of what was acceptable for boys and girls was an important first step, but to make Allie feel comfortable and proud of herself, I was going to have to go further.

For example, as teachers, we often use gender to divide students into groups or teams. It seems easy and obvious. Many of us do this when we line students up to go to the bathroom. In one conversation that I had with Allie's mother, she told me that Allie did not like using public bathrooms because many times Allie would be accused of being in the wrong bathroom. As soon as she told me, I felt bad. By dividing the children into two lines by assigned gender, I had unintentionally made the children whose labels aren't so clear feel uncomfortable in more ways than one.

When we lined up to go to the bathroom, I kept my students in one line until we reached the bathroom, and then let them separate to enter their bathrooms. Allie usually said she didn't need to use the bathroom. The few times that she did, I offered the bathroom around the corner, a single-stall bathroom that was usually unoccupied. When the kids came out of the bathroom, they wanted to line up as most classrooms do, in boys' and girls' lines. Instead, I thought up a new way for them to line up each day. For example: "If you like popsicles, line up here. If you like ice cream, line up here." They loved this and it kept them entertained while they waited for their classmates. Here are a few more examples:

Which would you choose?

- Skateboard/Bike
- Milk/Juice
- Dogs/Cats
- Hot day/Snow day
- Fiction/Nonfiction
- Soccer/Basketball
- Beach/Pool

I also became very aware of using the phrase "boys and girls" to address my students. Instead, I used gender neutral terms like "students" or "children." At first, the more I thought about it, the more often I'd say "boys and girls." I tried not to be too hard on myself when I slipped, and eventually I got out of the habit and used "students" regularly.

Around the same time, another child's mother told me that her son had been taunted for wearing a Hello Kitty band-aid. She mentioned that his sister was also teased at school for having a lunch bag with skulls on it. I planned more lessons to combat gender stereotypes in our classroom.

"It's OK to Be Different"

In order to deepen our discussion of gender, I selected another read-aloud. Before we read, I asked my students: "I would like to know—how many of you like to dance?" Most raised their hands.

"How many of you have been told you can't do something because it was 'only for boys' or 'only for girls'?" Many hands went up.

Then I read *Oliver Button Is a Sissy*. In the book, Oliver is bullied because he prefers dancing to sports. The students quickly realized that this was not fair and empathized with Oliver Button.

The following day we read *It's Okay to Be Different* by Todd Parr. Parr's books are quite popular in the primary grades because they include an element of humor and simple, colorful illustrations. We read:

It's OK to wear glasses.

It's OK to come from a different place.

It's OK to be a different color.

As we read, I asked questions to empower the students: "Who used to live in a different place?" Students proudly held up their hands. "Awesome!" I replied. "My mom comes from a different place, too. She used to live in Hong Kong."

Then I guided the direction of the conversation toward gender. As a class, we brainstormed a list of things that students thought were "OK" even though they might challenge society's gender norms. Monica told us very matter-of-factly, "It's OK for a girl to marry a girl," and Jordan said, "My dad carries a purse and that's OK!" At that point I explained that my father and my friend Wayne both call their man purse a "murse." The children were fascinated.

> We teachers often use gender to divide students into groups or teams. It seems easy and obvious.

Toward the end of the discussion I explained: "People make all kinds of different decisions about gender. Sometimes, as we grow, we might not want to pick one or the other, and that's OK; we don't have to." I wanted them to begin to see that our lessons were not only about expanding the gender boxes that we've been put into, but also questioning or eliminating them altogether.

Afterward, I had the students do a simple write-and-respond exercise. I asked them to pick one activity that they associated with girls and one associated with boys to write about and illustrate. Monica drew two brides in beautiful wedding gowns. Miguel drew a man with a murse slung over his shoulder. I showed off the pictures on the hallway bulletin board around the words "It's OK to Be Different."

Although things were getting better for Allie, she still faced many challenges. At the end of the school year, Allie's mother told me a heartbreaking story. She said that for Allie's recent birthday party, her grandmother had bought her colorful, formfitting clothes and then demanded them back when Allie did not like them. "Does she know she is a girl?" she yelled, and announced she would never buy her clothes again.

It was so sad to hear this. I visualized Allie on her special day, excitedly ripping open gifts in front of her family and friends only to find, again and again, the gifts were things that she would never be comfortable with. As a mother, the feeling of extreme disappointment was unbearable for me to imagine.

I have just begun to empathize with the challenges that gender-independent children deal with. For some it may seem inappropriate to address these issues in the classroom. My job is not to answer the questions "Why?" or "How?" Allie is the way she is (although asking those questions and doing some research in order to better understand was definitely part of my process). My job is not to judge, but to teach, and I can't teach if the students in my class are distracted or uncomfortable. My job is also about preparing students to be a part of our society, ready to work and play with all kinds of people. I found that teaching about gender stereotypes is another social justice issue that needs to be addressed, like racism or immigrant rights, or protecting the environment.

Later in the year, I opened my inbox one morning and read: "Andrew says he wants a Baby Alive doll and he doesn't care if it's for girls. Thank you, Ms. Melissa!"

Resources

dePaola, Tomie. 1979. *Oliver Button Is a Sissy*. Sandpiper Books.

Parr, Todd. 2007. *It's Okay to Be Different*. Little, Brown Books for Young Readers.

Zolotow, Charlotte. 1985. *William's Doll*. Harper & Row Publishers.

For more information: acceptingdad.com/supportive-book-media-for-gender-variant-non-conforming-kids/.

Hello Kitty
A "boy teacher" takes on gender stereotypes

By Jay Weber

Jay Weber is a 3rd-grade teacher to the most wonderful students at Auburn Middle School in Auburn, Illinois. He lives in Mount Olive, Illinois, with his wife and cats and has completed his first novel, *Last of the Daydreamers*.

"Mr. Weber," said Tammy, a bright-faced 3rd grader, on the first day of school, "you are the first boy teacher I ever had."

"Thanks," I replied, flattered and amused at the same time. And then I thought about what that simple comment might imply about the gender expectations that my students had carried with them to 3rd grade. Beyond teaching 3rd graders the "standard curriculum," I also had the opportunity—and responsibility—to impact their visions of what is or is not "gender appropriate and acceptable." Children (and adults) are often pressured into fulfilling predetermined roles based on gender, and then are chastised if they do not adhere to those norms. When I viewed my position through that lens, I quickly realized that, as a male elementary school teacher, my actions and behaviors could go a long way toward helping my students redefine their gender expectations.

As I got to know my students at Auburn Middle School, located in a predominantly white, middle-class community in central Illinois, I learned that their gender stereotypes were even more ingrained than I had imagined. Anything out of the ordinary, even something as simple as a boy liking the color purple— as I mentioned that I did—struck them as weird. Against this unforeseen wall, I felt overwhelmed. If a boy liking a "girl color" caused my students to react so strongly, I didn't see much hope in reversing, or even tempering, the gender stereotypes of their young world.

But still, I tried. Together, we read "The Story of X," by Lois Gould, and had good class discussions about the problems with identifying items or activities as girl or boy specific. My students responded well to the story, with girls blurting out "I like football" and boys declaring "I like to bake." But when I posed the question "Should boys cook and clean?" the overwhelming answer was no, they never see boys doing that.

I wanted them to see the influence of media on their beliefs. So I brought in advertisements that we used to identify the gender stereotypes that are laid in front of us every day. We looked at ads directed at boys and girls, men and women, ranging from perfume ads to clothing ads, sports equipment to food. I asked the students to examine each ad and answer the question: What does this ad tell us about what men and women should do? This led to a much larger discussion about the stereotypes disseminated by the media, prompting the constant refrain from an animated Stephanie, "But that's just stupid!"

> My students had developed an academic knowledge of gender stereotypes, but were still just as likely to find it weird that a boy liked the color purple.

Aha! Had progress finally been made? Well, sort of. Students were able to identify examples of stereotypes in the ads. They agreed that those stereotypes did not in fact describe them or their mothers, fathers, brothers, or sisters. They stated emphatically that what boys and girls do should only be dependent on what they like, not what the stereotypes dictate.

However, I couldn't see much translation and application of these ideas to their lives. They had developed an academic knowledge of the issue, but were still just as likely to find it weird that a boy liked the color purple. I was disappointed.

Fortunately, I had discovered one of the worst-kept secrets of teaching young children: They are highly likely to be influenced by a teacher they like. I call this the "students will like it because I do" phenomenon. Although it's not universal, it is certainly true of many 3rd graders. I hesitate to take advantage of their positive bias because I am concerned that any manipulation, even the well-intentioned kind, is duplicitous. On the other hand, a teacher's persona, demeanor, and style are all transmitted to students every day. We are automatically role models, whether we think about it consciously or not. Like most teachers, I try to make sure that I am modeling tolerance, respect, and empathy toward others.

With this in mind, I racked my brain for a subtle approach to help my students diffuse their notions of gender stereotypes without beating them over the head with the issue. I decided to pick a stereotypically "girl" item, and make it my own. I chose a bright pink, highly decorated Hello Kitty lunch box. I knew my new lunch box would be in plain view for all students and members of the school community to see.

The first day I brought my Hello Kitty lunch box to school, I was inundated by girls telling me how much they liked it. As we were walking to lunch, a 3rd-grade boy from another class called out, "Mr. Weber! Why do you have a girl's lunch box?"

"Am I a girl?" I asked.

"No."

"Well, this is my lunch box, so I guess it's not *just* a girl's lunch box." The blank stare I received back told me that Hello Kitty was getting students to rethink what they thought they knew. That really was the best I could hope for. Change doesn't come all at once, and it doesn't come from telling someone, whether adult or child, what they should believe. It comes from the slow process of changing expectations through exposure, experience, and thoughtfulness.

I decided to pick a stereotypically "girl" item, and make it my own.

My classroom now contains many Hello Kitty items, several of which were presents from my students, who have embraced the fact that I love Hello Kitty (which is almost true in light of what she has helped me accomplish). I now get a round of thumbs up from boys in the hallway and a chorus of "nice lunch box!" When my students were selecting folders for a recent project, I was heartened to hear Matthew say: "I'll take purple. It's Mr. Weber's favorite color."

Although gender stereotypes are too pervasive to be easily eliminated, I am hopeful that gender expectations can shift, giving kids the opportunity to navigate life with the freedom to explore their gender identities absent the pressure of prevailing stereotypes. By bringing our "selves" into our classrooms and modeling acceptance, we can help our students grow into their best, most creative selves. It takes an effort from everyone, including a friendly, animated feline.

Resource

Gould, Lois. 1978. "The Story of X." Daughters Publishing Company. Text available at delta.edu/cmurbano/bio199/AIDS_Sexuality/BabyX.pdf.

Brent Nicastro

The Character of Our Content
A parent confronts bias in early elementary literature

By Jennifer Holladay

Jennifer Holladay has held strategic roles with two Colorado school districts, Denver Public Schools and Adams County School District 14, and served previously as the president of Highline Academy, an integrated public charter school in Denver, and as the senior advisor for strategic affairs at the Southern Poverty Law Center. She's proudest of her role as mom to Zoe.

A few years ago, my 2nd-grade daughter came home with an extra assignment—a worksheet she hadn't completed in class for a story called "The Selkie Girl." She brought the book home, too, and it was one I'd never seen before, a Junior Great Books anthology (Series 3, Book 1), published by the nonprofit Great Books Foundation.

As we settled in, I asked my daughter to tell me about "The Selkie Girl." Her rendition gave me pause, so I asked her to do her other homework first. She turned to a worksheet, and I cracked the book open.

"The Selkie Girl" is essentially about a magical seal-woman who is kidnapped and raped repeatedly during her long captivity. The man who holds her hostage proclaims early on that "I am in love" and "I want her to be my wife." When he kidnapped her, "She was crying bitterly, but she followed him." Later, the narrative tells us, "Because he was gentle and loving, she no longer wept. When their first child was born, he saw her smile." When her means of escape is discovered, however, she explains quite bluntly to the children she bore: "For I was brought here against my will, 20 years past."

It's like the modern-day reality of Jaycee Dugard (who was kidnapped at age 11 in California and held captive with her two children for 18 years), told in folklore for the consumption of young children. The white beauty norms in the story do not help, either:

> He went to look and, in wonder and delight, he saw three beautiful girls sitting on the rocks, naked, combing their hair. One of the girls had fair hair, one red, and one black. The fair-haired girl was singing. She was the most beautiful of the three, and Donallan could not take his eyes from her. He gazed and gazed at her gleaming white body and her long-lashed dark eyes.

When I asked our daughter about the "messages" of the story, she pointed to this passage and the accompanying illustrations as support for the idea that she—an African American girl—is "not pretty."

I was astonished, and I kept reading.

> # Nearly all women and girls are referred to as "wife," "mother," or "daughter," and that is understood to be the genesis of their power, standing, or importance.

Not all of the book's stories are horrible in an anti-bias sense, but the social norms conveyed by the text as a whole are. A third of the stories with human characters have female leads, but men—their virtue or their needs—actually dominate all of them. Further, nearly all women and girls are referred to as "wife," "mother," or "daughter," and that is understood to be the genesis of their power, standing, or importance. Men and boys, meanwhile, are presented in a multitude of ways. Finally, the volume's portrayals of poverty and its supposed causes—"[He] lived in the smallest hut of his village, and if he had been lazy he would have gone hungry at night"—are troubling, as is the recurring theme of obedience to the powerful.

Getting a Pass into Class

How could this book make its way into an early elementary classroom?

First, Junior Great Books easily pass the "research-based" test. On the publisher's website, you'll find a slew of studies about the series' positive effects. As summarized on the Great Books Foundation's 2011 990 tax return, "the K–12 program has significantly impacted reading levels in reading comprehension on state and national standardized tests." A pedagogical approach called "shared inquiry" that directs the accompanying teachers' guides also is backed by research: "Studies have also shown that the skills acquired by shared inquiry have transferred to other content areas, thus impacting achievement levels on tests in areas such as math and science."

Second, the series is aligned to individual state standards and to the Common Core. The state in which we live recently adopted the Common Core, and educators here are spending an untold number of hours realigning desired instructional outcomes to them. The Junior Great Books—marketed as "the cure for the Common Core!"—are more than welcome in this regard.

Third, the foundation promises access to "readings of high literary merit that are rich in discussible ideas" and touts selections from award-winning authors. My daughter's book includes a story by Anne Sibley O'Brien, who has received the National Education Association's Author-Illustrator Human and Civil Rights Award and the Aesop Prize, as well as a selection from storyteller Diane Wolkstein, recipient of the National Storytelling Association's Circle of Excellence Award.

Fourth, the series is marketed as appropriate for use with diverse learners. All images, videos, and samples on the foundation's K–12 website feature racially and ethnically diverse students, an important selling point for most public schools.

So it's not surprising that many schools are taking advantage of these offerings: "The K–12 program provides low-cost educational materials to more than 5,000 schools with more than 1,000,000 students."

What kind of values are likely to be promoted in school materials created by an organization whose board chair works for a rightist think tank?

Unfortunately, the adoption of these materials reflects a trend that extends well beyond Junior Great Books themselves. Concerns about the "narrowing of the curriculum" under No Child Left Behind (NCLB) often focus on the short shrift given to subjects like social studies, music, and art. The truth is that curriculum is also narrowing in language arts and math classrooms, where content increasingly is restricted to materials, like Junior Great Books, that are "proven" to boost test scores. School purchasing decisions have become highly dependent on products' alignment with standards and the presence of a "skill-supporting research base."[1] In the elementary context, 92 percent of teachers report that their districts have implemented "curriculum to put more emphasis on content and skills covered on state tests used for NCLB."[2]

Reflecting Conservative Norms?

I was unable to find any criticism of Junior Great Books in general or of "The Selkie Girl" in specific. (This latter absence may reflect the fact that the most recent copyright date for a story in my daughter's book is 1993.) That said, there were two things I discovered about the Great Books Foundation that might give someone pause.

> We—parents, educators, school leaders, and educational publishers—possess a collective responsibility to evaluate the character of the content as rigorously as we evaluate children's "learning outcomes."

The foundation was established in 1947 with the goal "to encourage Americans from all walks of life to participate in a 'Great Conversation' with the authors of some of the most significant works in the Western tradition." Its Junior Great Books program, launched in 1962, relied heavily on excerpts of selections—including *The Pilgrim's Progress* and *Adventures of Huckleberry Finn*—from the original adult program. Although the foundation's canon certainly has expanded over time, its genesis as an advancer of the male- and white-centric "Western tradition" raises a yellow flag.

The foundation's board of directors is chaired by Alex J. Pollock, who works at the American Enterprise Institute (AEI), one of the nation's most influential conservative think tanks. Mr. Pollock's expertise lies in financial policy issues, but, as the Southern Poverty Law Center has noted, "While its roots are in pro-business values, AEI in recent years has sponsored scholars whose views are seen by many as bigoted or even racist."[3]

For example, longstanding AEI fellow Charles Murray is best known as co-author of *The Bell Curve*, which infamously argues that whites are inherently more intelligent than African Americans and Latinas/os. He has argued forcefully elsewhere that the nation's interests are best served not by affording all children access to a quality education through college, but by focusing on the needs of "gifted" children. Meanwhile, AEI's longtime resident expert on gender issues is Christina Hoff Sommers, widely known for her scathing critiques of contemporary feminism. Hoff Sommers has strongly criticized what she sees as an anti-boy culture in schools, specifically the use of "feminized" literature.[4] More broadly, AEI exercised significant influence over the policies established under the second President Bush. As People for the American Way notes: "President George W. Bush appointed more than a dozen people from AEI to senior positions in his administration."

All of this prompted me to ask: What kind of values are likely to be promoted in school materials created by an organization whose board chair works for a rightist think tank?

Exactly the kind my daughter encountered in her Junior Great Book.

We Endorse What We Teach

In purchasing Junior Great Books as supplements for language arts classes, teachers and school leaders surely possess good intentions. They seek to provide students with what is described as engaging content while helping students build up their reading and writing skills.

As schools place greater and greater emphasis on documenting skill-based outcomes, I really do understand how and why a teacher might focus more on what a child writes on a test, rather than the content on which the test is based. I understand how problematic content might slip through, and I believe few, if any, educators would welcome a story like "The Selkie Girl" into an early-grades classroom if given the support and time to reflect on it first.

We—parents, educators, school leaders, and educational publishers—possess a collective responsibility to evaluate the character of the content as rigorously as we evaluate children's "learning outcomes." We must deliberately create space to reflect, because the material we place before children and thus endorse in our classrooms teaches much more than comprehension skills. The social messages and values children take away from the content—the *what* of their comprehension—matters.

At my daughter's school, raising these issues resulted in the text's immediate removal from classrooms—and a renewed commitment to evaluating the character of our content. A group of our teachers spent their summer taking a fresh look at our curricula, with eyes, ears, and hearts clearly focused on identifying bias and the broader communication of problematic social norms. These are needed steps within our school community, and they are steps other schools may need to undertake as well.

Footnotes

1   Market Data Retrieval. 2007. *Educator Buying Trends: How Teachers Make Buying Decisions, A National Survey.*

2   McMurrer, Jennifer. 2007. *NCLB Year 5: Choices, Changes, and Challenges: Curriculum and Instruction in the NCLB Era.* Center on Education Policy.

3   Berlet, Chip. 2003. "Into the Mainstream," *Southern Poverty Law Center Intelligence Report.*

4   Benfer, Amy. 2002. "Lost Boys," salon.com/2002/02/05/gender_ed. See also Hoff Sommers, Christina. 2000. *The War Against Boys: How Misguided Feminism Is Harming Our Young Men.* Simon & Schuster.

Artwork by students in Dale Weiss' class

Believe Me the First Time

BY DALE WEISS

Dale Weiss has been a public school teacher for the past 25 years and is a frequent contributor to *Rethinking Schools* magazine. Her passion is to help her students understand the world around them in all its intricacies and to know that when issues of injustice come to the fore, there is always something that one can do—regardless of age— to try to make our world a better place.

"I'm not a boy! I'm a girl! I'm a girl! I'm a girl!"

I followed the words echoing through my suddenly silent 2nd-grade classroom. There sat Alexis on the floor with Diego; puzzle pieces were strewn across the floor.

"What's wrong, Alexis?" I asked. "You sound upset."

"Every day someone asks me if I am a boy or a girl, and every time I answer that I'm a girl, but they just keep asking. Why can't they believe me?"

I thought back to the many conversations I'd had with Alexis about this topic since the beginning of the school year. Alexis is a bright, confident child who expresses herself with ease. Each time I heard someone ask her if she was a boy or a girl, I would check in: "How do you feel when your classmates ask you about your gender?"

And each time her reply was pretty much the same. "I'm ok. It's not really their fault. They just didn't know."

Several times I asked Alexis if she thought it would be a good idea to discuss this issue as a class—not to call attention to her but to explore in general the issue of gender. Each time she responded: "No, I don't think we need to do that."

"Why not?" I once asked.

"Because it's not that big of a deal."

I told Alexis that if she changed her mind, she should tell me. I felt tugged in two directions. As a teacher, I frequently explore the "isms" with my students (racism, classism, sexism, heterosexism, and so on) as a critical piece of teaching from an anti-bias perspective. At the same time, I wanted to respect Alexis' decision to hold off—though for how long, I was not sure.

Now I pulled Alexis aside. By this time she was in tears. "I tried to be patient with people. I said they were asking me because they didn't know. But I don't understand why they don't believe me when I say I am a girl. Why do they have to keep asking?"

"It's people not accepting that we're the experts on who we are."

As I gave Alexis a long hug, I thought about another student, one who'd been in my class two years prior. Classmates often expressed confusion as to whether Allie was a girl or a boy, too. And, as in Alexis' situation, classmates often did not accept her response. I flashed back to the time that year when we were discussing a story about children who wore uniforms to school. I'd asked my students if they would like to wear school uniforms. Allie's arm shot up in the air with fierce determination. "Yes! I would totally love it if kids wore uniforms in our school. That way all of us would be dressed the same and kids would finally stop asking me if I am a boy or a girl."

Alexis and I Plan a Teaching Unit

Back in the present, I said to Alexis: "I think it's time to deal with gender issues head-on with our class. Would you consider developing and leading a unit with me?" The tears were gone. "I sure would!"

The words spilled out of my mouth before I realized I'd offered to co-create a teaching unit with a student. I felt excited at the idea, but I'd never done it before. I often respond to issues and interests that emerge from my students by developing a unit—but collaborating with one of my students on creating and teaching a unit was definitely a first.

"How about if we meet after school on Wednesday? I'll check with your mom." "Sure!"

By this point in the year, we'd already had numerous and ongoing discussions about ways to build a supportive community in our classroom—and how, when we make a mistake, we can repair harm with one another. So we had a context for talking about gender in ways that would support Alexis. She was well liked by her peers and accepted as an integral part of our classroom community. I did not believe Alexis' classmates were intentionally trying to bully her—they were genuinely confused about her gender identity. However, I wanted my students to understand that consistently questioning someone about their gender identity can be experienced as bullying.

A few days later, we began our collaboration. "Alexis, why don't you first look through the books in our classroom library and pull out anything that addresses issues of gender and accepting people for who they are."

Twenty minutes later she brought over her book selections. I was excited to look at her pile until I realized it consisted of only seven books.

"Were there any others, Alexis?"

"Nope, this was it."

When I looked through the books she brought me and thought about the books we had, I realized she was right. "Wow!" I exclaimed. "This sure doesn't seem like enough books when the topic of gender is so incredibly important." Definitely one of those teacher moments when I realized I needed to do far better.

Alexis had already read each of those seven books. I asked her what she enjoyed—or perhaps didn't enjoy—about the books.

"There's nothing I didn't enjoy. But what I did enjoy is that when I read these books, I felt accepted for who I am."

A few days later, Alexis ran up to me when she arrived at school. "Ms. Dale, I thought I'd bring you one of my books from home in case you want to read it." The book was *Meet Polkadot,* by Talcott Broadhead.

"Tell me what the book's about, Alexis."

"This book is so cool! It's all about a person named Polkadot and how when they were born, they didn't get called any gender."

"And what do you like most about this book?" "

"I like that the book celebrates whatever gender someone feels they are, and that it's all really OK! You can borrow the book if you'd like to."

"I'd love to, Alexis. Thank you for sharing this book with me." Now I knew that Alexis viewed herself as an integral participant in shaping our unit.

Alexis Finds a 4th-Grade Mentor

In the meantime, I learned from a colleague that Allie, my former student, had been experiencing a lot of bullying from other 4th graders because of how she dressed. I wondered if I could help. I spoke with Allie's mom and asked her if Allie might be interested in the Peace Club I was running twice a week during recess and lunch. One of the Peace Club's topics was how to deal with bullying at our school. I asked Allie if she would like to be our 4th-grade mentor, and she agreed. Allie and Alexis' brother had also been friends since K5.

During Allie's first session of Peace Club, the students were making friendship bracelets. I sat down at an empty group of desks, only to be joined by two students who'd been up getting supplies: Allie and Alexis. I introduced them to each other. Alexis said: "I knew who you were because my brother is in your class. He told me you get bullied for the same things that I do." Then Alexis turned to me. "I have an idea! How about if Allie works on the gender project with us?"

I thought that was a great idea and asked Alexis to explain the project to Allie. And so our project expanded; we were now a group of three.

We met three more times before launching the gender unit in my 2nd-grade class. First we talked about different ways to approach the issue. After the brainstorming, both Allie and Alexis spoke about ways they had experienced bullying. Alexis began:

> Last summer I went to camp. On the registration form my parents said I was a girl. When I got to camp I waited in the check-in line with the other girls, but then this person who worked for the camp said I was in the wrong line. I tried to tell him that I was in the *right* line, but he kept arguing with me and showed me where they'd changed me to the boys' cabin. Finally it got worked out. But, in the meantime, all the other kids stared at me. I felt awful.

Allie listened intently, then shared her own story:

> One time I went with my mom to a store to get some new clothes. We were in the boys department because that is where I can find the clothes that I like the best. This saleslady came up to us and asked if we needed help finding something. I told her I was looking for some shirts and pants. She said "For you?!" so loud that everybody in the whole store could hear. I said, "Yes, for me." Then she kept telling me I had to go into the girls department because I was in the wrong part of the store. I felt really, really bad. And so did my mom. We left the store and went someplace else.

"That must have been really awful."

"Yeah, it was."

Soon we began to map out our unit. I said that I often found it helpful, when beginning a new unit with students, to find out their beliefs and thoughts about the subject. "Perhaps we could begin by giving students different categories to think about and comment on. Clothes, for example: Which clothes do students think of as 'girls' clothes' or 'boys' clothes' or clothes that are worn by both girls and boys?"

Alexis excitedly piped in, "We could do a Venn diagram!" Allie and I both thought that was a great idea. At first we talked about two interlocking circles—one labeled *girls*, one labeled *boys*—with the overlapping space in the middle labeled *both*. Allie paused for a second and then said: "But I think there will be a problem if we do the circles like this. Won't the space called *both* need to be larger?"

Alexis chimed in: "I get what you're talking about. If we make the *both* space larger, that would kind of give away what we're thinking." Alexis and Allie then decided to make three equal-sized circles on a long piece of butcher paper: girls on one side, boys on the other, both in the middle. We brainstormed the categories we wanted students to think about: sports, games, toys, animals, music, colors, songs, movies, hairstyles, clothes, shoes, and swimwear.

Meanwhile, our PTA announced mini-grants to teachers for classroom supplies, so I was able to purchase new children's books on sexism and gender. When I shared the new books with the girls, they pored through them excitedly.

"Oh, look at this book! It's all about a woman astronaut."

"*Jacob's New Dress*, that is so cool!"

"This book is about girl inventors. Did you know a woman invented windshield wipers?" We talked about ways to incorporate the books into our project and decided that after Three Circles Activity, students would choose a book to read and create a poster that addressed that book's main message.

A few days later, I ran into Allie's mom at school. She commented how happy Allie was being in Peace Club and how excited she was to work on our gender unit. Her words meant a lot. I also checked in with Alexis' mom several times. As we planned the unit, I asked myself more than once if discussing a child's experiences with gender so openly with her classmates was overstepping my bounds. I wondered if this was something that parents would prefer to do on their own. But Alexis' mom reassured me that the unit we were creating had her blessing and, in fact, was appreciated.

"I Want to Shout Out My Feelings"

As we worked on the unit, the girls deepened their relationship and shared more of their experiences. "One time my family was eating at a Mexican restaurant," Alexis said. "The waiter kept referring to me as 'el niño' and I had to keep saying, '¡Soy una niña! ¡Soy una niña!' But the waiter just didn't seem to really believe me."

"What do you say when someone treats you unkindly?" I asked. Allie explained that she often felt a lot of pressure to be kind, and that it was sometimes hard. "If someone bullies me, it's on purpose and so it's hard to be kind back. But if someone's just wondering if I'm a girl or a boy, it's easier to be nice because they're curious and don't know."

Alexis added, "Sometimes I want to shout out my feelings at the top of my lungs and tell people how I really feel."

"And what would you shout out?" I asked.

"I'm a girl! I'm a girl! Believe me when I tell you—I'm a girl!"

"Yeah, it's like people not accepting that we're the experts on who we are."

The next time we met, I began by asking if there was anything about our previous conversations that they wanted to discuss.

"I was thinking that the worst kind of bullying is not being able to use the bathroom because of the sign," Allie said.

"Say more about that," I suggested.

"Well, when we go to the bathroom, sometimes we're in lines—like a boy line and a girl line. And sometimes when I get into the girl line, then people say, 'No—you're supposed to be in the boy line.'"

In a quiet voice, Alexis added: "That happens to me, too. One time when I was taking a theater class, we had a bathroom break. A girl told the teachers, 'A boy went in the girls' bathroom . . . a boy went in the girls' bathroom . . . a boy went in the girls' bathroom.' I told her, 'I'm not a boy, I'm a girl.' But she kept arguing with me. The other kids know if I'm a boy or a girl. They just don't accept it."

Children need time and freedom to explore their own gender identification and to know that the choices they make do not have to be static.

I asked if there was anything else they would like to add before moving into the planning portion of our meeting. Alexis looked at Allie with sheer joy and said, "I am so glad I know you, Allie! It's like finally I feel someone really understands me!"

"Thanks," said Allie. "I was thinking the same thing."

We began to plan out the following day's lesson. I began by asking: "How would you explain to your classmates what this project is about? For example, a unit on. . ."

"I think I would say we are doing a unit about gender problems," said Allie.

"Gender problems," I echoed.

"No!" answered both girls.

"So what is it you want? You want gender. . ."

"Acceptance," Alexis said. Allie agreed.

I agreed as well. "I find it's often more powerful to say what we want instead of what we are against."

We created an agenda for the following day's project, I typed it up and made copies, and we were ready to go.

Alexis and Allie Lead the Class

The following day, my students gathered together in a circle on the classroom rug and Alexis started things off by introducing herself. After Allie did the same, Alexis explained that she and Allie often get bullied because of the clothes they choose to wear. "Lots of times we don't feel accepted for who we are," added Allie.

Alexis continued: "And so we are doing a project about gender acceptance and trying to let people know and understand that we are girls—no matter how we dress."

"What do you think gender is?" Allie asked the students.

Emma immediately responded, "If you are a boy or a girl."

Allie confidently explained: "Gender could be a lot of possibilities. Like if someone is born a girl or a boy and they felt that was the way they were supposed to be in their life. But gender could also be someone who is born a boy who felt like they wished they were a girl, or someone who is born a girl and wished they were a boy."

"Or maybe," I added, "someone feels like they're in the middle—they don't want to have to choose boy or girl. Whatever someone feels inside themselves, that's OK."

"Even if you feel like a girl and everyone knows you're a girl, you still might want to do things that some people think are boy things—like Power Rangers. Or you might be a boy and want to play with dolls or wear jewelry. So lots of people don't always want to have to choose between 'boy' or 'girl' when there are unfair rules about gender."

Alexis asked if there were any questions and then Allie explained the Three Circles Activity. Alexis described the 12 categories and gave everyone a copy of them, along with some sticky notes. I reiterated the instructions: "Let's start with the category Sports. Ask yourself: 'Can I think of a sport that only a girl would like—or a sport that only a boy would like—or a sport that both boys and girls might like?' Write the name of that sport on a sticky note and put it on the appropriate circle. Don't worry about spelling. Take your time to think before writing."

The room bustled for 20 minutes as the students explored ideas, wrote them down, and stuck them onto one of the large circles. Alexis and Allie then took turns reading through many of the Post-it notes, and then asked, "Were there some ideas you had an opinion about?" The room was alive with comments, questions, agreements, disagreements, and lots of thinking!

We Practice Peacemaking

As we talked about responses to the Clothes category, I asked: "Why do you think some people bullied Alexis and Allie for the kinds of T-shirts and pants they wore?"

Katie commented: "Maybe someone bullies someone else because they're thinking, 'You're not like me. If you're different from me, then you're not wearing the right kinds of clothes. So I'll bully you.' And, like Alexis said in the beginning, people keep asking if she's a boy or a girl. When they're not sure, they just bully her."

Emma slowly raised her hand. "I've been thinking about something. I've seen people stare at Alexis because they think she's a boy. And they make gross faces because they think she is a boy going into the girl's bathroom."

"Did you say anything to them?" I asked.

"One time I did. I said, 'Excuse me, she's a girl, so she does have a right to go in the girls' bathroom. So leave her alone.' And then they actually stopped bothering her. But the year before, I didn't say anything because I really didn't know if Alexis was a girl or a boy."

I explained that what Emma did was important because she was trying to interrupt the bullying behavior that was taking place. I added that if you see bullying and don't say anything, it's like sending the message that it is OK to treat people that way. "What you might do is say something to interrupt the bullying or, if that doesn't solve the problem, go ask an adult to help you. Who wants to act the problem out, along with a way to try to solve it?"

Many hands went up. Alexis wanted to play herself and Emma played the person who wouldn't believe Alexis. Katie interrupted the bullying by saying, "Excuse me, but she told you she is a girl. You should just believe her."

Reuben blurted out, "And you should believe her the first time!" followed by applause from several of the students.

I asked: "How many of you have heard someone asking if a student was a boy or a girl, not believing the answer they received, so they kept asking the question over and over again?"

All the students' hands went up. "And how many of you think you know what you might say if you overheard that type of thing again?"

All the students' hands went up again.

"And what you are doing is called?"

"Interrupt bullying!"

"Have any of you heard a boy being made fun of in a similar way?" No one had. "But is that something you could interrupt in the same kind of way?"

"Yes!"

"Think about the many ways we've tried to help each other within our classroom learn to make better choices about how we treat each other. A really important part of peacemaking is helping other people make better choices, and it takes a lot of courage to do that. Anything else anyone wants to say?"

The room was quiet for a moment and then a few students spoke.

"I feel sorry for you, Alexis and Allie, that you got bullied just for being yourselves."

"I am sorry for how people treated you. And I am glad you are my friends."

Diego was the last to speak. "I am sorry I didn't believe you were a girl the first time you told me that. I will always believe you now."

In the weeks that followed, students chose one of our new picture books. Most students worked in pairs, a few preferred to work alone. After reading their books and figuring out the book's central message, students created posters. Although the original plan was to take a proactive stance against bullying by displaying the posters in our schools' hallways at the start of the next school year, the posters were instead included in a multimedia exhibit on androgyny by a local photographer, Lois Bielefeld (see Resources).

Doing any classroom project for the first time always has an element of the unknown. I especially did not know how this unit would turn out with students sharing the helm for the project's development and implementation. What guided me more than anything was knowing that this unit evolved from the lives of two of my students and the incessant bullying they had experienced. It was their story that needed to be told, their experiences that needed to be understood, and their voices that needed to be heard.

Along the way, I learned how important it is to not put children in a "binary box." The traditional gender binary system is one that requires everyone to identify and be raised as either a boy or a girl—based on the sex one is assigned at birth. This rigidity forces some children to live out an identity that is not their own. And rigid gender stereotypes limit all of us in our thinking, creativity, and life choices. Children need time and freedom to explore their own gender identification and to know that the choices they make do not have to be static.

At the unit's completion I asked Alexis what these past few weeks meant to her. "I think everybody now accepts me for who I am." Raising both arms high in the air, she grinned and loudly exclaimed, "Finally!"

Resources

Archambault, John and Bill Martin Jr. 1989. *White Dynamite and Curly Kidd*. Illustrated by Ted Rand. Henry Holt.

Bang, Molly. 1999. *When Sophie Gets Angry—Really, Really Angry. . .* Scholastic.

Bielefeld, Lois. 2014. *Adrogyny: Girl Boy Both*. Available at loisbielefeld.com.

Blegvad, Lenore. 1987. *Anna Banana and Me*. Illustrated by Erik Blegvad. Margaret K. McElderry Books.

Broadhead, Talcott. 2014. *Meet Polkadot*. Danger Dot Publishing.

Campbell Ernst, Lisa. 1983. *Sam Johnson and the Blue Ribbon Quilt*. HarperCollins.

dePaola, Tomie. 1979. *Oliver Button Is a Sissy*. HMH Books for Young Readers.

Fox, Mem. 1998. *Tough Boris*. Illustrated by Kathryn Brown. HMH Books for Young Readers.

Gibbons, Faye. 1999. *Mama and Me and the Model T*. Illustrated by Ted Rand. HarperCollins.

Hoffman, Mary. 1991. *Amazing Grace*. Illustrated by Caroline Binch. Dial.

Hoffman, Sarah and Ian Hoffman. 2014. *Jacob's New Dress*. Illustrated by Chris Case. Albert Whitman and Company.

Howe, James. 1996. *Pinky and Rex and the Bully*. Illustrated by Melissa Sweet. Simon Spotlight.

Kiernan-Johnson, Eileen. 2013. *Roland Humphrey Is Wearing a WHAT?* Illustrated by Katrina Revenaugh. Huntley Rahara Press.

LaVigna Coyle, Carmela. 2003. *Do Princesses Wear Hiking Boots?* Illustrated by Mike Gordon. Cooper Square Publishing.

Leaf, Munro. 1936. *The Story of Ferdinand*. Illustrated by Robert Lawson. Viking Press.

Leone, Katie. 2014. *But, I'm Not a Boy!* Illustrated by Alison Pfeifer. CreateSpace.

Luenn, Nancy. 1990. *Nessa's Fish*. Illustrated by Neil Waldman. Atheneum.

Martin, Bill. 2001. *Little Granny Quarterback*. Boyds Mills Press.

Meltzer, Brad. 2014. *I Am Amelia Earhart*. Illustrated by Christopher Eliopoulos. Dial.

Parr, Todd. 2001. *It's Okay to Be Different*. Little, Brown & Company.

Rothblatt, Phyllis. 2011. *All I Want to Be Is Me*. CreateSpace.

Singh, Pushpinder. 2014. *The Boy with the Long Hair*. The Sikh Foundation.

Spinelli, Eileen. 1993. *Boy, Can He Dance!* Illustrated by Paul Yalowitz. Four Winds.

Thimmesh, Catherine. 2002. *Girls Think of Everything: Stories of Ingenious Inventions by Women*. Illustrated by Melissa Sweet. HMH Books for Young Readers.

Waber, Bernard. 1975. *Ira Sleeps Over*. HMH Books for Young Readers.

David Kamba

7th Graders and Sexism

By Lisa Espinosa

Lisa Espinosa taught in a Chicago public school for nearly 10 years. Since, she has supervised teacher candidates for Illinois State University and served on the advisory committee for the Annenberg Foundation's online resource *Essential Lens: Analyzing Photographs Across the Curriculum*. She is the author of the upcoming book *Answering Your Inner Calling*.

I began teaching in a predominantly Mexican neighborhood on the South Side of Chicago. As a daughter of Mexican immigrants, I feel a strong connection to this community. Teaching, for me, is an opportunity to help my students think critically about society's inequities.

I feel especially strongly about the injustices that living in a male-dominated society has created, especially for women of color. Part of my commitment to this issue has to do with my own struggles growing up with the strict gender roles in my family.

Early on, I realized there was a double standard in many families in my community: The expectations and responsibilities were different for boys and girls. Boys were expected to be independent and strong, to grow up to be heads of families, to be leaders. In preparation for this, they were encouraged, both explicitly and implicitly, to express their thoughts and ideas. Girls, on the other hand, were taught to cook, do chores, be nice, and not defy authority. We were strictly monitored and warned against having inappropriate encounters with boys.

I don't want to make it seem worse than it was. Girls were also encouraged to do well in school, and our parents wanted us to have a better life than they had. But the expectations were clearly different for us than they were for boys.

Perhaps not surprisingly, many of the girls I grew up with became teenage mothers while still in high school. I became pregnant when I was 18, during my first year in college. Even though it was difficult, I continued my education. It took me eight years to graduate, and by the time I did, I had four children.

> # I wanted my students to gain a deeper understanding of feminism and move beyond the common notion that feminists are a bunch of angry, bitter women who hate men.

Along the way, influential professors and works by authors such as Paulo Freire, Ronald Takaki, Gloria Anzaldúa, and bell hooks helped me become more politicized and broadened my understanding of issues of social justice, especially sexism. I read a lot about feminism and was frustrated to realize that men still earned more than women, that men still held most leadership roles, and that many women were still victimized by the men in their lives. I also realized that racism and classism intensified this problem for women of color.

When I became a teacher, I understood that I alone couldn't solve these problems in my classroom, but I felt it was my responsibility to address and discuss these issues with my students.

Why Study Gender Roles?

Problems that arose in the beginning of that first school year in my 7th-grade class prompted me to focus specifically on gender roles and sexism sooner than I had anticipated. Rivalries among girls erupted constantly, girls accused boys of touching them inappropriately, and students used the terms "gay" and "faggot" frequently when boys engaged in any activity that deviated from accepted male behavior.

I was also worried because, in answer to a question about their future hopes and dreams, several girls had responded "to find a guy to take care of me" or "to get married," although nearly all the boys named either an educational or professional goal. Although I tried to deal with these issues and incidents as they came up, I felt that exploring gender stereotypes in a more sustained way might be useful.

I planned a language arts gender unit for my homeroom class. Those were the students with whom I spent most of the day and with whom I had established the strongest connections. (I also taught science to the three 7th-grade classes in my school.) I wanted my students to understand that sexism is still a problem since many of them, I found, thought gender equality had been achieved. I planned for them to reflect on some common gender biases and to critically analyze the media's role in reaffirming these stereotypes. I wanted them to gain a deeper understanding of feminism and move beyond the common notion that feminists are a bunch of angry, bitter women who hate men. Finally, I hoped that both my boys and girls would incorporate the ideas and ideals of gender equity in their lives.

I wanted my female students to begin questioning why most of them continued to let the boys do most of the talking in class discussions, why many of them tied so much of their identity to their appearance, and why there was so much jealousy and competition among them instead of a sense of unity. I wanted my male students to begin asking themselves why many of them felt threatened by the idea of showing emotions such as caring and empathy, and why many of them used such homophobic language. I also wanted them to reflect on how they related to the girls in our class both verbally and physically. I wanted everyone to challenge their expectations of what they could strive for in life.

Taking On Gender Stereotypes

We started the unit by reading *An Island Like You: Stories of the Barrio* by Judith Ortiz Cofer. I also used the Spanish version, *Una isla como tú, historias del barrio*. These short stories deal with body image, peer pressure, and gender expectations—and are all told from the perspective of Latina/o teenagers.

Although the stories provoked discussions about gender issues, we had not explicitly discussed how and where we learn gender stereotypes. To facilitate that conversation, I did an activity originally developed by Paul Kivel of the Oakland Men's Project in Oakland, California.

Why is being called a girl so horrible?

I began by putting up two pieces of posterboard, one with "Act Like a Man" and the other with "Be Ladylike" as headings. I asked my students to brainstorm words and phrases they associated with these labels. Beforehand, I had gone over ground rules, explaining that although I wanted them to feel safe to share their ideas, I also expected them to do so in a respectful way.

At first, it was a slow process getting my students to participate. Many

David Kamba

seemed afraid of what reaction their peers might have to what they might say. Eventually, though, we had a lively class. Although it was tempting to interject, at this point I tried to just facilitate the discussion. As usual, the boys did most of the talking and I had to explicitly invite the girls to share their ideas.

In the end, both posters were full of the students' ideas. The list under Be Ladylike included: "be nice," "helpful," "have catfights," "gossip," "shop," "wear makeup," "talk on the phone," "like guys," "cry," and "do housework." The Act Like a Man list included: "don't cry," "like sports," "mature," "violent," "responsible," "serious," "tough," "work hard," and "fix cars."

I asked students to compare the two lists and to think about where these ideas come from. Although at first no one said anything, two of my most vocal boys soon spoke up.

"Because it's the truth," Rolando said.

"That's how it is," Fabian concurred.

Several other boys laughed.

The girls retreated and fell into silence. I encouraged them to contribute. Finally, Rita said, "From our families?"

Elena followed: "From TV?"

I noted, as I often had, that the girls offered their suggestions in the form of a question as opposed to the confident answers the boys tended to offer. Without singling out individual girls, I noted that it seemed to be harder for girls to share their thoughts. I wondered aloud if all those ideas on the Be Ladylike poster were connected to girls devaluing their own opinions.

Eventually, other students joined in with suggestions: music videos, tele-novelas (soap operas), commercials, songs, magazines, and billboards.

I then asked students to think about what happens when boys or girls defy these gender roles. Some of the boys, referring to the Act Like a Man poster, called out: "they're a sissy," "a wimp," "a fag."

"Boys aren't supposed to cry," someone said.

"So are boys never supposed to feel sad?" I asked them. "Are girls just more emotional?" Reminding them of what we had learned in our science class about the human body, I asked them if there was some physiological reason that prevented boys from crying. If not, then when—and why—did boys start believing that it was wrong to show certain emotions?

Several students pointed out that boys are told early on that they shouldn't cry like a girl—and being called a girl seemed to be the ultimate insult. "Why is being called a girl so horrible?" I asked, reminding them that when I talk to a group of boys and girls and refer to them all as guys (something I'm trying to stop doing), no one seems to mind. The students pondered these ideas but still seemed pretty skeptical.

Although somewhat frustrated, I realized that, at this early stage in our unit, students had done very little, if any, critical thinking about gender stereotypes. Still, it was a beginning, and it had allowed us to visibly explore their gender biases, even if they didn't yet identify them as stereotypes.

Finding Resources

In planning this unit, I knew that I was going to have to provide a lot of background knowledge that, unfortunately, was not in any of our textbooks. This was more complicated because five of the 31 students in my room were beginning English learners. My room was not a designated bilingual classroom but, because I was the only fluent Spanish-speaking teacher, I tended to get most of the students with the greatest language needs. Although I was not a trained bilingual teacher, I did the best I could, learning along the way. I incorporated a variety of methods, including gathering materials in Spanish, getting Spanish translations of the novels we were reading, translating resources myself, and pairing students with peer helpers.

The resources I gathered for the gender study included the introductory essay from *Feminism Is for Everybody*, by bell hooks; the short story "Girl," by Jamaica Kincaid; essays from *My Sisters' Voices*, edited by Iris Jacob; and a news article, "Latinos Redefine What It Means to be 'Manly.'" Unfortunately, I found there was not a lot written specifically for teenagers about this subject, and for most of the readings I had to provide extensive support. For example, several of the readings had challenging words, so I used those as the vocabulary words of the week. There was a lot of figurative language that had to be explained to the students in simpler terms. Because of this, we did most of the readings in class. When I assigned readings as homework, I added guiding questions to help them get through the text and pick out the important ideas. I supplemented the readings with videos that deal with gender issues, including *The Fairer Sex, What a Girl Wants, Benaat Chicago,* and *Tough Guise.* I wanted my students to learn about other teenage boys or young men who were trying to do something to change sexist behavior. This proved to be the hardest to find. One good resource was the website of Men Can Stop Rape.

Free Writing

In the beginning of our unit, I was often discouraged by what I interpreted as lack of interest and inner reflection from my students. Our discussions hardly included the type of deep critical thinking I had hoped would help them make connections to their own behavior and attitudes. It was out of frustration that I began incorporating free writing at the end of our lessons. These, I explained to my students, were not formal essays to be edited and graded, but rather a time for them to share freely what they were feeling or thinking about a particular topic.

It was through this writing that I saw the most evidence that the students were reflecting on what we were doing in class. On many occasions, students expressed things they hadn't felt comfortable sharing aloud.

For example, we watched the video *What a Girl Wants,* a documentary in which teenage girls are interviewed about the effects that depictions of women in music videos and movies have on their self-esteem. Afterward, I asked students to write about their reactions. Elena agreed with the girls in the video who said that media images influence the way they feel about themselves: "When girls see models or Britney Spears or Christina Aguilera [and] how nice and pretty they are and they have big breasts but they are skinny . . . it makes girls want to have breast surgery." Jose wrote about the pressure that many girls in the video felt to look perfect to get boys' attention: "I thought that is not fair for girls. A girl has to get the same rights like boys. What a girl wants is respect. A girl shouldn't be treated bad or called names by someone." Elena wrote: "This video made me think about how unfair a woman is treated. She is seen as lower than a guy." Claudia, after describing what she liked about the video, added that seeing the images of women "made me feel bad, because people always say I'm ugly and these people are boys in this classroom, in school, or in the street."

Some boys wanted to explain that not all boys disrespect girls. Cezar wrote: "I also think that there are a lot of guys that still do look for personality [in a girl]. I'd personally look for both looks and personality. But all the stuff the girls talked about was mostly right."

One of the most surprising pieces of writing came from a more formal narrative. The school required monthly compositions from each class and I tried to incorporate them into our current focus. When the narrative composition came due, I asked my students to write a story related to any of the issues we had discussed so far in our gender unit. We brainstormed a list together and came up with, among other topics, body image, gender roles, homophobia, and standards of beauty. I told them the composition could be fictionalized.

> It was encouraging to hear the students express frustration at the limited number of magazine images that countered gender stereotypes.

Rolando was one of the first to show me a draft of his writing. He had been one of the boys who seemed most resistant to the ideas we were talking about. He especially had difficulty accepting the idea that boys could express themselves in a variety of ways and was prone to angry outbursts in class. On more than one occasion, I had confrontations with him about his behavior or language.

As I read though his draft with some trepidation, I realized it was about a boy who was being harassed for being gay. In his fictionalized short story, he and a group of friends begin to suspect that one of their friends is gay. After some teasing, they finally ask him if he is gay. After he admits that he is, the boys laugh. The first-person narrator says: "I thought if I step up [and defend him] they will think I'm gay and they probably will laugh, and I looked down and left."

Then the narrator goes to his friend's house and finds him with a gun pointed at his head, ready to kill himself because of the despair he feels from the rejection of his friends. The narrator reassures his friend: "'Don't worry, a lot of people are gay.' He started to put the gun down and he got on his knees and started to cry. I said 'It will be all right, OK?'"

Although his story still contained some stereotypes and was a bit overdramatic, it was very encouraging to see Rolando addressing these issues.

Another telling piece came from Mari, one of my most reflective students. She titled it "A Part of My Life." Mari's story, like Rolando's, was fictionalized, yet written in the first person. The protagonist is a 12-year-old girl who is very "mature physically and emotionally" and looks like a girl who is 16. Mari writes about this girl's ambivalent feelings toward being harassed by men on the street and boys in school: "While I kept walking many guys kept looking at me. In some ways I felt bad, but in others I like to get their attention (all women like that)." She continues: "I'm a girl and this is why I get harassed like this. Some people tell me that if I don't take care of myself, I might be raped. I just hope nothing bad happens to me. Maybe I'm just going to have to cover up a little bit more."

This story seemed autobiographical. Mari was dealing with a lot of the same problems, especially harassment from boys. Several of the girls in the class argued that they should have the freedom to dress however they wanted and that the harassment was something the boys needed to work on. Although I agreed that the boys should be held responsible for their actions, I also wanted the girls to reflect on their self-worth and identity, and how much of it was tied into their appearance. Mari had never said much about this during class, so I was glad to see her reflecting on these issues. I realize these are small victories, but they showed a growing awareness on Rolando's and Mari's parts, and were signs that what we were doing in class was perhaps making a difference.

Analyzing Media

One of our final activities was making collages that either countered or reaffirmed common gender stereotypes. I decided to do this because I wanted my students to critically analyze the magazines they liked to read. I hoped they would see how the media perpetuates the gender stereotypes we had been discussing. First, I collected as many old magazines as I could, including those targeted to African Americans, Latina/os, and other people of color. Posting a sign in the office asking for magazine donations was helpful in getting all the magazines we needed.

I then arranged my class in groups of four or five. I assigned each group a specific task: creating a collage that either countered gender biases or one that reaffirmed them. For example, group one made a collage that countered male gender stereotypes, group two made one that reaffirmed male gender stereotypes, and so on. Each group was given a stack of magazines, a small poster board, and time to browse through the magazines, noting words and images they could use for their collage. A timer was useful in keeping them on track since it was easy to get sidetracked by the articles. I also provided a large manila envelope for them to keep their cutouts in order.

Although I pushed them to stay on task, I also encouraged the groups to interact, since some were finding images that would be useful for another group's collage. It was encouraging to hear the students express frustration at the limited number of images that countered gender stereotypes. Students excitedly called me over when they found a particularly positive image of a man or woman. There were also disturbing moments, like when I overhead Fabian say that he was in the "gay group" because he was looking for images of men in nontraditional roles. In the end, we had a thought-provoking set of collages to post and discuss.

It's hard to assess how successful I was in achieving my goals for the class. As I look back, there are things I would have done differently. For example, I would

David Kamba

have assigned more formal essays, and there were several readings and activities I never got to. I wonder how much my lack of experience affected what my students gained from these lessons. Since I was doing many of these activities for the first time, I didn't always anticipate the questions or problems that arose.

As the year went on, we continued to struggle with some of the problems that inspired the unit. In particular, many of the girls still didn't speak up nearly as often as the boys. On the other hand, my students often initiated conversations about the topics we discussed. When they saw an item on the news about youth being harassed because of their sexual preference, they brought it up for discussion in class. Periodically we analyzed their favorite TV shows—many of which, unfortunately, were very sexist.

One of the clearest signs that the students were reflecting on these issues came several weeks after our unit was over, during our elections for class representative. I was glad to hear the candidates being asked what they were going to do about sexism in the school and in the community. A student asked one of the candidates: "What would you do to end sexism in our neighborhood?" Before he could answer, another student exclaimed: "It'll never end. It's too hard. It's too much." Several students looked at me, hoping for a more optimistic reply. In some ways my student was right—the problem is too big. But I also believed and shared with my class that we could make things better, and that we could start with our classroom.

Resources

Benaat Chicago: Growing Up Arab and Female in Chicago. 1996. Available through Arab Film at arabfilm.com/item/20/.

Cofer, Judith Ortiz. 1996. *An Island Like You: Stories of the Barrio*. Puffin.

Cofer, Judith Ortiz. 1997. *Una isla como tu, historias del barrio*. Fondo de Cultura Económica.

hooks, bell. 2000. *Feminism Is for Everybody*. Pluto Press.

Jacob, Iris. 2002. *My Sisters' Voices: Teenage Girls of Color Speak Out*. Macmillan.

Kincaid, Jamaica. 1978. "Girl." *The New Yorker*, June 26.

Tough Guise: Violence, Media & the Crisis in Masculinity. 1999. mediaed.org/cgi-bin/commerce.cgi?preadd=action&key=211.

What A Girl Wants. 2001. mediaed.org/cgi-bin/commerce.cgi?preadd=action&key=214.

Wood, Daniel B. July 16, 2001. "Latinos Redefine What It Means to Be 'Manly.'" *Christian Science Monitor*. csmonitor.com/2001/0716/p1s3.html.

Dressing Up

BY CAROL MICHAELS FORESTA

Carol Michaels Foresta taught English and humanities in various public junior high schools for 25 years. In 1997, she became the founding principal of Bread & Roses Integrated Arts High School. She now works with the Progressive Education Network of New York and as the director of the Center for Collaborative Education of New York.

"How would you feel if I wore a dress to school?" the student sitting at the conference table asked me. I was the principal of his school, Bread & Roses Integrated Arts High School, a small, racially diverse public school in central Harlem, New York City, focused on social justice and artistic expression.

"Hmm. Why do you ask?" I replied.

"I just want to know."

"Is this something you are seriously considering or is it a theoretical question?"

"Well, I have been considering it, I just don't know if I'll be able to deal with the consequences."

"What do you imagine they might be?"

"Well, anything is possible. I might lose a lot of friends. Someone might get rough. Some of the adults might get mad. I might get kicked out of school because I have to defend myself."

"Miguel, what if your mother found out? After all, if you get suspended for fighting, we would have to call her and she would want to know why you were fighting."

"That wouldn't be good. I'd probably get thrown out of my house. Or, maybe my uncle would come over and beat me up and then I'd get thrown out."

"You're not responsible for the consequences of your actions, only the actions themselves. You have the right to wear anything you want. But, are you sure you want to wear a dress to school?"

"I think about it every day. I have some support from my friends, and there is a teacher or two who probably would have my back."

"What's the point?"

"I'm not sure yet, I just think there is one. I guess I have to do it and discover why as part of the process."

"I will support you, just let me know what you need. Also, be sure we check in every day, in the morning and again in the afternoon. You will need to be very patient. Most people won't understand what you're doing."

"I'm not sure I understand it either but I feel driven. There's something inside me that wants to come out. I can't think about homework, classwork,

92   **RETHINKING SEXISM, GENDER, AND SEXUALITY**

anything except wearing a dress."

Miguel got up from the conference table. I watched. I felt a bit nervous. I wanted to be more encouraging but couldn't find the right vocabulary. If I acted like a cheerleader, would it be more damaging in the end? After all, he hadn't decided definitely yet. I figured we had a few days to process his unusual request.

> "There's something inside me that wants to come out. I can't think about homework, classwork, anything except wearing a dress."

The next morning, Miguel arrived wearing a pink T-shirt that had a large "S" on it, a black pleated skirt, stockings, and heels. I saw him as he emerged from the staircase and made a brief stop on the second floor in front of my office.

"Nice Superman shirt," I volunteered lamely.

"Thanks, but it's Supergirl," he shot back with a big smile as he twirled around, showing off the Supergirl displayed on his back.

His face wore a big toothy smile. I smiled back and told him to keep in touch, as three of his best girlfriends emerged from the stairs behind him. They were giggling and chatting excitedly as they went off to class together. I flashed back on the days I would have laughed at the audacity of a friend who decided to challenge the norms. But as a principal, I thought of the violent acts that have befallen others with the courage to come out or dress up.

Miguel stopped by my office at the end of the day. He talked calmly about the various homophobic remarks he had fielded. He didn't seem shaken by any of the comments his classmates made. We spent more time discussing the best place for him to change his clothing when he arrived in the morning.

Katherine Streeter

The next day, Miguel's science teacher asked him to leave class. Miguel came to my office and was pretty angry about what happened in class. According to Miguel, some of the boys refused to work with him on a group assignment. The teacher lost patience with the situation and asked Miguel to leave the class. Based on our conversation, I decided to call an emergency staff meeting directly after school in the library.

There were 27 teachers and 10 support staff, including student teachers, school aides, and secretaries, seated promptly at 3 p.m. for our community meeting. I began the meeting by talking about students' rights. I thought it was important that everyone understood that in a school dedicated to developing activist citizens in a democracy, the rights of students were inviolable. This meant that if one of our most fragile students/citizens was unsafe, we were all unsafe. I said it was critical that Miguel not be asked to leave any class merely because his dress provided a distraction.

That day, four male teachers wore dresses or skirts to school.

We had an interesting meeting. Some staff members felt we should call Miguel's mother and tell her how he was dressing. We discussed whether we would be willing to take responsibility for finding Miguel a place to live if his mother threw him out of the house. We also questioned whether we could adequately physically protect Miguel if other members of his family physically attacked him. We agreed that we did not have the resources to support Miguel, to provide him with shelter and the love and nurturing that he could get from his parents and other members of his family.

Finally, we talked about the Civil Rights Movement and the lessons to be learned from the experiences of the first individuals to challenge the values of a community. Some African American teachers thought this situation was not analogous. Others thought there were direct parallels. I looked around the room; of the 37 people, 20 were women. Of the 20 women, not one was wearing a dress or skirt. I remembered a time not too long ago when female teachers were not allowed to wear pants to school. I wondered about the kind of courage it took women to move together to force that systemic change. That simple desire to be guided by your own sense of propriety rather than by societal values meant that some individuals had to create a small earthquake in the school system.

In the end, the teacher who expelled Miguel from class asked if I was ordering teachers not to do so. I said I was in order to protect Miguel's rights. But I also said I believed that, if the adults in our community showed real support for Miguel and his struggle to express himself, it would not be necessary to exclude anyone. Someone asked how he could show Miguel he supported him. I replied flippantly: "Well, perhaps some of the men here could wear a dress to school; after all, every woman in the room is wearing pants!"

The next morning I did not see Miguel when he arrived at school. Instead, I got a phone call from a staff member on the fifth floor about 20 minutes after classes were meant to begin. The staff member told me I'd better hurry upstairs because there was a crowd unwilling to disperse in the hallway. I asked if Miguel was at the center of things and she replied that she could not see much because the students were so thickly clustered. I took off and climbed the four flights like a mountain goat. When I hit the fifth floor, I saw immediately what had brought the alarming phone call. There was a large crowd of young people in the main hallway, peering into a classroom. When I got to the classroom, having dispersed most of the group, I asked one of the students what was going on.

She replied, "It is unusual to see a male wearing a dress, except for Miguel, who everyone expects to wear dresses."

I said, "So it's not Miguel that's disrupting things."

"Oh, no," came the quick retort. "It's Tim, and he doesn't know how to bend over when he's wearing a dress. Besides, he has hairy legs and he didn't bother to shave. At least Miguel has the good taste to shave."

I looked past her into the classroom to see a mustached, hairy Tim standing in front of his class, teaching, in a short, stylish, purple plaid dress borrowed from his wife.

That day, four male teachers wore dresses or skirts to school. They taught their classes. They marked papers. They went to lunch. They met with their advisories. There were no disruptions to the usual day after the initial surprised reaction to their choice of attire.

A few weeks later, Miguel visited my office early one morning. He was dressed in slacks and a shirt. He looked like a typical adolescent boy. I was concerned.

"Are you all right? Has anyone been bothering you?" I asked him.

"Not more than usual," he answered.

"Well, then why have you changed back to male clothes?" I asked as nonchalantly as I could manage. There was a long pause before he replied, "I think I've made my point."

After Miguel left my office, I reflected on the profound impact of his actions. I ordered pizza and called together a group of student leaders, including Miguel, for a meeting that day. We discussed what they felt were some of the most pressing issues confronting students. I asked them if they would be willing to organize a day dedicated to social justice so our school could struggle out a response in a series of ongoing workshops. We agreed that students had to be the initiators and take major responsibility for presenting the workshops. They would recruit teachers or outside facilitators to work with them. We all agreed workshops would reflect mixed grade levels, thus ensuring a lively conversation among students.

After two months of planning, the students taught the entire curriculum for a day. Two of the 15 workshops specifically discussed homophobia. Miguel taught one with the assistance of one of our special education teachers. Another student taught a workshop about heterosexism with the assistance of an outside facilitator. This day was so powerful that we all agreed it had to become a tradition and it had to happen at least two times a year.

The day Miguel revisited my office dressed in traditional male clothing, I reminded him that I would support him always and that I knew he had real courage. "That's interesting," he replied, "I thought Tim had real courage. He came to school wearing a dress and didn't shave his legs!"

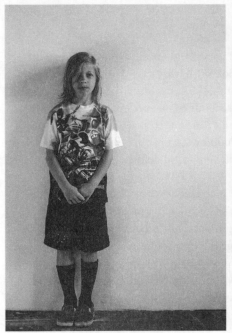

Lois Bielefeld

When the Gender Boxes Don't Fit

By Ericka Sokolower-Shain

Ericka Sokolower-Shain graduated from Wesleyan University in 2012. She works in film and theater in the Bay Area.

T he first day of high school is hard enough. Walking down the halls, trying to find my next class, surrounded by a sea of people who looked hundreds of years older, I felt like I had a red blinking sign over my head that flashed "freshman" every five seconds.

When I finally reached my classroom I was beyond relieved. I already knew my teacher, one of many perks of going to the same school where your mom teaches, and I was excited about her class, Identity and Ethnic Studies.

Our first activity was a game called Stand and Declare: The teacher reads a statement and students who feel the statement is true about themselves are instructed to stand silently. The idea is that the statements get deeper and more personal as the game progresses, but you have to start out easy. And what could be easier than the most basic aspect of human identity, the first question asked about a newborn baby? As my teacher read the first statement aloud, "Stand if you're a girl," my heart dropped.

What was supposed to be an easy question, a throwaway, a way to break the ice before delving into more personal issues, was for me a question I had been grappling with since elementary school. With what ease that teacher, herself a lesbian feminist, asked me to completely define my identity, something much more complex than standing for five seconds could ever express, something that I had been struggling with for years and continue to struggle with to this day. The simplicity of the question in her mind was apparent to me. Although I was unsurprised, having lived my entire life in a world defined by a gender binary system, I was still angry.

That an otherwise excellent and caring teacher could so quickly alienate some of her students is a reflection of the way gender identity is taught and viewed in schools: the first and ever-present question on any school form, the gendered bathroom system, boys vs. girls locker rooms and sports teams. Even without looking beyond high school, it is clear how sharply gender divides and defines student life. For many this division is simple and their place on one side of the gender line is clear, but not for me—and I'm not the only one in this situation.

Looking for Language, Looking for Community

For years I have struggled with finding my place in the gender binary. In elementary school I was constantly mistaken for a boy. I didn't feel comfortable in the girls' bathroom, so I would wait until after school, even if I was in agony. I always played on sports teams that were predominantly boys and, up until 4th grade, most of my friends were boys. By the time I reached middle school, I was pretty good at flying under the radar. Except for when I had to change for gym, I could manage to never be in a situation where I had to outwardly define my gender.

It wasn't until 9th grade that I found a language to put into words how I'd been feeling, as well as other people with similar experiences to my own. PISSR (People In Search of Safe Restrooms) met every other week at the San Francisco Lesbian Gay Bisexual Transgender Community Center. I always felt a sense of pride walking into the giant pink building. At my first meeting, we broke the ice by describing our ideal toilet paper. The humor was refreshing. Even though we came together to fight for a simple human right, a safe place to go to the bathroom, the meetings didn't have an atmosphere of life and death struggle. PISSR disbanded a few months after I joined, but my experiences with that wonderful group of people had a lasting impact on my life. They introduced me to a new vocabulary, words like genderqueer and gender variant, and to the idea that gender doesn't have to be so black and white. It's possible to see gender choices as open, fluid, even undefined. With a stronger sense of my own identity, I was able to live more freely in the gendered world.

> "Gender doesn't have to be so black and white. It's possible to see gender choices as open, fluid, even undefined."

Back at my high school, I tried to bring these new ideas to the Gay-Straight Alliance. My idea was to start a campaign to get a gender-neutral bathroom available to all students at my school. I was braced for a fight with the administration, but was unprepared for the reactions of other members of the club. What seemed like such a simple solution, a clear way we could work together for the rights of gender-variant students, became an internal struggle. A gender-neutral bathroom wouldn't be safe, some people said. I countered with the danger gender-variant students had to face daily in single-sex bathrooms, but my argument failed. I was shocked that a club whose purpose was to fight for the rights of all students could so bluntly let me down.

Katherine Streeter

Although I have grown into myself and become more confident, I can't forget the failures of my schools and the ignorance of well-meaning but misguided teachers. I can't blame that 9th-grade teacher for asking what many people believe is a simple question. Instead, I hope I can teach her something so she doesn't continue to alienate her students. What she needs is something the world needs: lessons and a language for the fluidity and complexities of gender.

As a Mom and a Teacher...

By Jody Sokolower

Jody Sokolower is a political activist, teacher, writer, and editor. She is the managing editor at Rethinking Schools.

How can we support children who don't feel comfortable identifying with the gender assigned to them at birth? I enter the discussion from two perspectives: first, as one of Ericka's lesbian moms. From the time she was a toddler, Ericka, now 25, struggled with defining her gender identity "both within and beyond the gender binary system," as she explains it. Second, I am a teacher who has tried, not always successfully, to support students who were struggling with similar issues.

Ericka was a bald baby, and she didn't grow hair for a long time. In the beginning, I thought that was why people said, "Oh, what a beautiful little boy." "Thank you, she's a girl," I would respond. By the time Ericka was 5, she had stopped wearing dresses and people on the street almost always assumed she was a boy. I almost always told them she was a girl.

One day as we drove through rush hour, she asked from the backseat, "When I grow up, can I decide to be a man?" While I framed an age-appropriate explanation of gender change options, the pit of my stomach turned to ice. I know young children see gender, like death, as changeable, but I also knew that for my child this was different. And that it was time for me to deal with my own issues so I could be there for her.

> It took me a long time to understand that freedom of gender expression isn't an attack on women's liberation.

As someone who had been part of the first consciousness-raising groups, and an activist for women's and gay liberation since the late 1960s, I was invested in believing that we fought so that women could be anything we wanted. When Ericka wasn't sure she wanted to be a woman, I took it personally—as a failure of everything I spent my life fighting for. It took me a long time to understand that freedom of gender expression isn't an attack on women's liberation. It makes more sense to see putting people in rigid gender boxes as one more aspect of sexual oppression.

Just as Ericka has struggled with defining herself in relation to gender, I have struggled to be supportive, to deal with my prejudices and defenses, and to bring what I've learned to the classroom.

Bias Against Gender-Variant Youth Runs Deep

Ericka went to an elementary school with an active lesbian and gay parents' group, which Karen, Ericka's other mom, and I joined. Every year parents went into each classroom to lead activities and discussions about nontraditional families and homophobia. But we didn't talk about transgender issues. Although we were confident that even very young children could understand gayness, somehow gender variance seemed too complicated, like one issue too many. Now I think we were just afraid.

I know from our reluctance, as a parent group committed to fighting homophobia in the schools, how scary it can feel to bring up issues of gender variance in the classroom. But opening up the discussion is a lifeline for youth like Ericka, whose struggles with defining themselves are so often hidden and silent.

Although schools and U.S. society in general are moving toward more acceptance and support of lesbian and gay youth, there is still enormous ignorance and prejudice about those who do not fit gender norms. The impact on these youth can be devastating. Forty-five percent of transgender youth in one study had thought seriously of killing themselves (Grossman, 2007). According to GLSEN's 2011 National School Climate Survey, 80 percent of transgender students reported that they felt unsafe at school because of their gender expression.

The Rocky Path to Support

So what can we do to nourish these kids? As a high school teacher, I brought discussions on gender variance into my social living class. I collaborated with two other teachers to make sure there were gender-neutral bathrooms available to students who were reluctant to use the single-sex bathrooms. But I also learned an important lesson about support from a mistake I made:

One year I had a student who told me before class the first day of 9th grade: "Don't call me Vanessa when you call the roll. My name is Ril." I agreed. For the first week everything was fine. The second week of school we had new attendance sheets from the office and I forgot to change Ril's name on the sheet. On Wednesday I was out sick and the substitute called Ril "Vanessa." Ril, who was using the beginning of high school as the opportunity to stop presenting as a girl, felt that his cover had been blown, and never forgave me. It seemed like a small, unavoidable slip to me, but it was huge to Ril. Ril's alienation was especially hard for me because I saw myself as an advocate. I went back and asked Ericka what she thought teachers could do to support gender-variant students.

"Don't you decide what kids need," she told me. "Remember when you always corrected people on the street and told them I was a girl? You thought you were standing up for me, but I felt like you were shoving me in the 'girl' box while other people were shoving me in the 'boy' box. I didn't want to be in either one.

"What gender-variant youth need are teachers who don't make assumptions, who ask lots of questions and then listen to the answers. Everyone is different. When a kid tells you what's important to them, that's what they want you to do."

References

Grossman, Arnold, and Anthony D'Augelli, A. 2007. "Transgender Youth and Life-Threatening Behaviors." *Suicide and Life-Threatening Behavior.* 37: 527–537.

Kosciw, Joseph G., et al. 2011. *The 2011 National School Climate Survey: the Experiences of Lesbian, Gay, Bisexual, and Transgender Youth in Our Nation's Schools*. Report by the Gay, Lesbian, and Straight Education Network. glsen.org.

Katrina Clark

Standing Up for Tocarra

By Tina Owen

Tina Owen is the lead teacher and a co-founder of the Alliance School in Milwaukee, Wisconsin. She teaches line dancing and participates in flash mobs whenever possible. She is the mother of two adult children and has been a foster or surrogate mother to many others. She lives in Milwaukee with her partner and their two adorable cats.

In the fall of 2005, a group of teachers opened the Alliance School of Milwaukee. Many of us on the planning team had witnessed the discrimination and homophobic harassment of LGBTQ youth in traditional schools, and it was our intention to create a place where it would be "OK to be Black, white, gay, straight, gothic, Buddhist, Christian, or just plain unique." What we didn't know was how far outside those doors we would have to go in standing up for our students.

Tocarra was one of my students at the high school where I taught before starting Alliance, and she was one of the reasons I felt so passionate about the mission of the school. A transgender student who was just starting to transition when I first met her, Tocarra was lucky to have great family support, and she was very proud of who she was. But at the large high school, she was being harassed and threatened every time she wore women's clothes to school. She would often come to my room between classes to take a "safety break" before moving on to her next class.

According to the administrators, they couldn't stop the students from harassing her. "If she would just stop dressing that way, she wouldn't have these problems," they said. Tocarra was on the brink of dropping out of school, but when she learned about Alliance, she hung on and transferred to the new school as soon as the paperwork could be turned in. And she played a key role in our final planning. Her voice influenced everything we did.

When the school opened, students came from all over to attend, and most of them didn't know each other before they walked through our doors. Some of the students who enrolled came for the mission, and others came because there were seats available or because Alliance started with the letter A so it was the first school listed in the school selection book. Our first year was an interesting one. There were students from every different background and ability group. There were students from the city and students from the country; Black students and white students; poor students and wealthy students; gay students, straight students, and everyone in between. We had to do a ton of work to build connections among the different groups of students.

Tocarra welcomed everyone and wasn't afraid to teach others what it means to be transgender, so she played a big role in bringing an understanding of transgender reality to the Alliance community. She was patient with those who didn't get it, teaching rather than chastising them when their words were hurtful, and she stood up for everyone who needed a defender, not just those students who were most like her.

> I wanted to cover the ears of my students so they wouldn't have to hear the fire-and-brimstone hate coming from his lips.

One day she was checking out my outfit (a long, princess-style coat with fur trimmed hat and cuffs) and she said, "Ms. Owen, when I become a woman, I want to be sexy like you—sexy classy, not sexy slutty."

Tocarra always knew just what to say to make someone feel beautiful, so it was no surprise that in a very short time she was well loved by the entire Alliance community. She became a mother figure for many of the students and a role model for some of the younger transgender students. She had a flair for fashion and a desire to be not just noticed, but adored, and adored she was.

Then, late one evening that first year, I received a call from one of the students. "Is it true?" she asked through her tears. "Is Tocarra dead?" She had received a text message, but I hadn't heard from anyone, so I told her I would call back as soon as I found out what was happening. I soon learned that it was true. Tocarra had suffered heart problems in the middle of the night and had passed away. She was 18 years old.

I called the staff together for a meeting at my house. We cried together, talked about how much we would miss Tocarra, and then made a plan for how we would talk to the students the following day. We decided to have a community meeting first thing in the morning and assembled a crisis team of social workers and support staff for any student or staff member who needed to talk. I knew I was going to need their support as much as anyone.

The students were devastated when they learned about Tocarra's death, and I spent much of that morning comforting students who fell apart in my arms. It just didn't seem possible. Tocarra had been fine just days before. She had even flown to New York two weeks earlier to tape a *Jerry Springer* show, one of those "my girlfriend is really a man" episodes with lots of silly fight talk and drama. Before she went, she had asked my opinion about participating. I told her she should do what she wanted, but to remember that people already perceive the transgender community in negative ways, so she should try not to reinforce stereotypes. She was not one to take her role in the community lightly, so she went back and forth about whether or not to be part of the show. In the end, her desire to be a star, if only for a moment, won out, and she headed to New York.

Most of Tocarra's family lived in Chicago, so it made sense that they would plan to have her funeral there. Many of our students and staff members wanted to attend, so we arranged for a bus to take us. More than half of the student body rode the bus that day to attend the service, including Tocarra's dearest friend Jade, who was also transgender. As she walked into the funeral parlor holding my arm, Jade looked like Marilyn Monroe in her blonde wig, black dress, and sunglasses. Despite the questioning looks from other people at the service, she walked into the room with all the pride, beauty, and anguish of a mourning widow.

We arrived just in time to fill up the seats of the small funeral parlor that had been reserved for Tocarra's service. It was a sad-feeling place, a room that didn't expect to have many guests for the likes of someone like Tocarra, and I couldn't help but wonder if it had ever been as full as it was that day.

The viewing was almost unbearable. The person who prepared Tocarra for the visitation must have looked only at what was between her legs to determine how to dress the body, and never considered what gender may have been in her heart. To our horror, when we walked to the front of the room, there was Tocarra dressed like an old man in a suit and tie, lying in the casket looking like someone we had never met.

Jade was furious. "What the hell?" she said, pointing at the casket and searching the room for who might have been responsible. Finding no answer in the line of people waiting to see the body, she stood up tall and walked angrily to the back of the room, where a few teachers and students stood, huddled in communal fury over what they had seen and discussing what Tocarra would have wanted instead.

When it was time for the service to start, we moved to our seats. My daughter and her best friend sat close to me, arms threaded through mine, tissues in hand, still in shock from the viewing and the loss of their sweet friend.

Things only got harder when the sermon began. The minister did not know Tocarra. He kept calling her by a boy's name that wouldn't have been correct even if Tocarra had wanted to be called by her boy name, and I cringed every time he said it. He was a traditional, homophobic, Baptist minister who preached a sermon that condemned Tocarra to an eternity in hell rather than raising her up for her family and friends. It was as if he was telling us, "I know what he was, and this is a warning for all of the rest of you."

I was outraged for Tocarra, and I wanted to cover the ears of my students so they wouldn't have to hear the fire-and-brimstone hate coming from his lips. Many of them had experienced that kind of religious condemnation personally; they knew exactly what was happening, and I could feel them crumbling inside. The more he preached, the more upset they became. Soon the ones sitting close to me, including my daughter and her best friend, started nudging me. "Do something," they whispered. "He can't talk about her like that. He's wrong."

They were right. I couldn't stand it any longer, either, so I did something I never imagined I would do—I raised my hand and asked if I could speak. The minister looked from me to Tocarra's family. I asked them directly, "May I speak?"

Tocarra's mother nodded to me, uncertain but hopeful, the weight of the minister's words too much for the young mother who had already lost her child in this world, and couldn't bear the thought of losing the promise of seeing her baby in the afterlife as well. "Please," she said, and the other members of her family nodded.

> I went up to the pulpit and started to talk about Tocarra as I knew her. I spoke about the young *woman* who was loving and accepting and funny, and who never gave up on anyone.

I went up to the pulpit and started to talk about Tocarra as I knew her. I spoke about the young woman who was loving and accepting and funny, and who never gave up on anyone. I spoke about the person who had helped to build our school with her great ideas and insights. She would never be forgotten by any of us. And, most importantly, I spoke about how Tocarra had earned her place in heaven with her loving ways, her joyful spirit, her commitment to helping others. I reassured her family and her friends that they need not worry, because we would all see her there someday. If anyone deserved a place in heaven, it was Tocarra.

When I was done, I invited her family and friends to come up and speak. Her mother came first, and then her brothers, and then friends and teachers lined up to share their memories. We laughed, cried, hugged each other, and sang her blessings to the universe. It was beautiful, and I've never felt as proud of anything I've done. So many people lined up that eventually the minister had to stop the line and ask people to save their stories for the burial, because there were other services that had to take place in that room. I think he was angry, but he didn't dare try to change the story that had grown, because people were emboldened now and they weren't about to let him pin the weight of sin back on the life of the young, beautiful spirit of a woman they had known.

That afternoon, I rode the bus back to Milwaukee in silent sadness, exhausted by the past several days of holding myself together for the students and staff. So many thoughts ran through my head as we traveled. I grieved for the loss of this young person who had become such a central figure in my life. I mourned for what the world had lost, someone who really could change the world and make it better. I wondered about the courage that had lifted my hand in that moment when I couldn't take the minister's words any longer. And I prayed for Tocarra and for all of the fabulous transgender souls who had gone to rest in less than fabulous fashion.

A few days later, the school community gathered in the community room to watch the *Jerry Springer* show that Tocarra had gone to New York to record. We were nervous but excited to see her alive on the television screen. I'll admit that I hadn't wanted her to be part of that show. But as we sat and watched that silly episode, where at one point one of her balloon breasts fell out of her shirt as she attempted to "fight" with her boyfriend's girlfriend, I couldn't help but laugh. Tocarra was such a great spirit—so bold, so funny, and so full of love. Although the show was as outrageous as expected, it was good to see Tocarra one last time as she would have wanted us to remember her—sexy classy, not sexy slutty—and beautiful to the core.

Creative Commons/ Jeffrey Beall

In Search of Safe Bathrooms

By Mia Cristerna

Mia Cristerna is a community youth activist. She wrote this article when she was part of a group of youth who gathered together with Curtis Acosta while fighting to maintain Ethnic Studies in Tucson (see "Young Women in the Movimiento: Chican@ Studies After the Ban," p. 175).

Most people probably never imagine how petrifying going to the bathroom can be in our heteronormative world. My best friend and I used to hold it all day long and wait for the school buildings to empty out before we would approach the eerie bathrooms. Sometimes, when we just couldn't hold it anymore, we would cross our fingers, hoping and praying that no one was in there as we made our way toward them. We would go in and out as quickly as possible. We always went together, because there's something about having someone by your side that makes you more courageous. And we knew that it was much worse when we went alone. Just imagine: After holding it for as long as possible, you scurry to the closest bathroom, hoping its empty, but when you turn the corner you're greeted by a crowd of girls. They glare at you, waiting for you to realize that this is girls' bathroom, not the boys'.

Now put yourself in my shoes: You're a 15-year-old Chicana. To others you might seem quiet, but thoughts and ideas are constantly racing through your mind. You have a brilliant smile and flourishing intelligence, but it's jaded. Because when the world looks at you, they get stuck looking at your short hair, loose jeans, big T-shirt, and the roughness of your personality.

When you don't turn around and, instead, continue walking toward them, they whisper to each other in disbelief, laughing at you in hushed tones. You enter the bathroom stall and hope that when you come out they're not there anymore. Sometimes you wait for them to leave, standing in the stall, pretending to fix your pants or fiddling with your shoelaces. You wait until you hear their giggles fade into the distance before you make your escape.

It wasn't the giggles or the whispers that were so intimidating. It was knowing that at anytime any one of those giggling girls could open their mouths and say something. We weren't afraid of them, we didn't fear their ignorant comments, we could defend ourselves quite well. We were just broken-down from having to constantly defend our gender. After always being questioned, always being stared at, we were tired of it, and so we tried to avoid the bickering as often as possible.

We weren't afraid of them. We were just broken-down from having to constantly defend our gender.

We didn't choose to be so different, to be lesbians. We don't really know why, or at least I don't. Maybe we were born like this. Maybe we just grew into it. Or maybe it was because of the time Daddy went too far—when the argument was no longer vocal, when it turned into broken bones, broken hearts, and black eyes. Maybe it was the fact that as children there was no time for sensitivity. After watching our moms hold back their tears, maybe we learned to do the same. Maybe it was because we were her rock, the one who could always manage to seem at ease in the midst of all the chaos. Or maybe we saw it all one too many times and knew that wasn't going to be us.

Whatever it was, after years of hoping for empty bathrooms and invisibility, we began to feel ashamed of hiding behind walls. We questioned our fear. Why did we feel such agony about this issue? We knew our life of short haircuts and dark baggy clothes was not easy, but we realized hiding was not the answer. After a while we stopped avoiding those daunting eyes, we stopped hiding, we stopped being silent.

Bec Young

Aren't There Any Poor Gay People Besides Me?
Teaching LGBTQ issues in the rural South

BY STEPHANIE ANNE SHELTON

Stephanie Anne Shelton is a PhD student and teaching assistant at the University of Georgia, where she is the principal editor of the *Journal of Language & Literacy Education*.

The halls were ringing with the squeaks of wet sneakers on linoleum as students rushed from lockers to classrooms. The hallways were marked with muddy red sneaker prints and bright yellow "Caution: Slippery When Wet" signs. School had been canceled the day before as a "mud day." We rarely got snow days, but if it rained heavily, there were enough students living on unpaved roads that school was cancelled because the buses couldn't bring them to school. One of the oddities of living in the rural South is that cell towers may reach students' phones, but asphalt doesn't always reach their driveways.

As my class wandered in, Joseph walked by, looking heartbroken. Because he was normally so energetic that he seemed to bounce even while sitting still, it alarmed not only me but his classmates as well. Several eyed him and then glanced at one another, looking for some explanation. Their shoulder shrugging and raised eyebrows told me that they didn't know any more than I did what was wrong.

The tardy bell sounded and the morning announcements started, ranging from yearbook sales to the athletic schedule. One reminded students that it was hunting season, so they needed to remove firearms and bladed weapons from their vehicles before arriving at school.

I glanced over at Joseph and saw a tear slide down his face as he kept his head down and wrote in his class folder. Concerned, I made up an excuse—my computer was not working—and asked someone to take the attendance to the office for me. I immediately had 30 volunteers, but I handed the paper to the one who hadn't raised his hand—Joseph.

Without looking up, he crumpled the paper and stood. As he reached the door, he quietly grabbed several tissues and walked out. By the time we had finished going over the warm-up, he hadn't returned, so I left a note on the door reminding him that we were going to be working in the media center and ushered the other 11th graders down the hall.

"Somebody Asked Him if He Was My Boyfriend"

As I watched the students working in their research groups, Joseph showed.

"You took a crazy long time getting the attendance to Ms. Morgan. I almost sent out a search party."

He tried to laugh and shook his head.

"What's going on? Why're you so upset, Joseph?"

He glanced around us, ensuring that no one could overhear. "Marcus is mad at me."

I looked over at Marcus, who was helping a shorter student pull a book from the top shelf. The idea of Marcus being angry about anything seemed strange to me; the idea of him being seriously mad at Joseph seemed impossible. They had been best friends for years.

"Why?"

Joseph hung his head and sniffled. "Somebody asked him if he was my boyfriend. He got mad, 'cause he thought I told them that."

Marcus and I were two of only a few people who knew that Joseph was gay. Both of us had been immediately supportive, but there were serious risks in our community for anyone who was openly gay. In one of my first years of teaching at the school, the local paper had printed a half-page editorial declaring that gay marriage was against God's will. In recent years, several people at the school had warned me that letting students know that I am a lesbian was a sure way to get fired, despite a successful teaching record. Only the day before I had driven to school behind a car with a bumper sticker referring to Leviticus 20:13 ("If a man also lie with mankind, as he lieth with a woman, both of them have committed an abomination: they shall surely be put to death; their blood shall be upon them," in the King James version).

The biggest concern for Joseph, though, was his father, an outspoken conservative pastor who had openly condemned what he termed "the gay lifestyle" for as long as I had known the family. In an area of approximately 5,000 people, if Joseph came out, news of his sexual orientation would reach his father in record time. It was probable that, like several congregation members, Joseph would be disowned.

"Did you tell someone that Marcus is your boyfriend?"

He shook his head, nearly in tears again. "I told my friend Carol at play practice that I hoped that I'd find a boyfriend like Marcus. What if Marcus never talks to me again?" He hesitated. "Or what if he starts talking about me to other people?"

I looked at Marcus, who seemed completely engrossed in the book he'd picked up, and then back at Joseph, whose bottom lip trembled. "Why don't you tell Marcus what you actually said and the two of you figure out how to move beyond this misunderstanding?"

Joseph nodded slowly, fully aware of how few options he had.

"Do you want to talk to the counselor?"

"I don't wanna hear that lady tell me about 'This is your choice, but I support you' like I just wanna be gay here in the stupid boondocks."

I patted him on the back and then watched him walk over to sit in Marcus' research group.

I Change My Teaching

Several days later, it seemed clear that Joseph and Marcus had resolved their problem, but I wasn't OK with me. I had fallen into a common trap for LGBTQ-supportive teachers: I professed my personal support while offering little or none in the curriculum.

Teachers love their students. Even in my extremely conservative community, teachers would express their support for students' "sexual preferences" at lunch. One of my fellow English teachers patted herself on the back each year when she made sure to tell her students that Oscar Wilde was gay, just before she continued on to his imprisonment and death.

But, however well intended, the cursory mention of a gay author does little if students aren't asked to consider how that element of the author's identity matters. Not a single teacher in the English department would have read Richard Wright without exploring racism or Kate Chopin without exploring women's rights. But canonized authors like Whitman, Wilde, and Woolf are generally taught with no discussion of their sexual identities (leaving students to assume they were heterosexual), or with their sexual identities mentioned so cursorily, or so associated with negative events, that students must assume that part of who the writers were is "wrong."

> I had fallen into a common trap for LGBTQ-supportive teachers: I professed my personal support while offering little or none in the curriculum.

As I reflected on my teaching and my own experiences as a student, I realized that I wasn't measuring up to either my professional or my teenage expectations. Because I remembered the feeling of being left out of the literature in my own schooling, I actively taught texts about poverty, race, and religion—often omitted issues that mattered very much to my students, too—but I had played it safe in terms of sexuality and gender. Besides Joseph, there was no telling how many other students had sat in my classroom and, just like me as a teenager, had wondered where they were in the assigned texts.

I went to the bookroom. After finding two spiders and tons of dust, I found Shakespeare's *The Merchant of Venice*. As we started reading the play in class, my stomach rolled as I weighed the consequences of talking about a possibly gay character. But before I could say anything, students began commenting on Antonio's behavior after Bassanio's appearance in Act I.

Bec Young

"The only way you're gonna give somebody who's that broke money, after they've already wasted all of the other money you gave them, is if you got it bad," one student said.

When I asked her to explain, another student rolled her eyes and said, "Man, Ms. Shelton, that fool's in love."

A few of the students were startled by and rejected their interpretation, but the text gave them a way to discuss a topic that had been taboo only the day before. By the end of the play, after many discussions and several essays, some students were sure that Antonio loved Bassanio, some thought the two men loved one another, and others decided they were just close friends. Regardless, the conversation normalized the topic of sexual orientation, allowing discussions then and later.

> "No matter how bad my mornings had been at home, or how many times I heard 'fag' or 'gay' in the hallway, I knew that in your classroom we were all safe. Not just me, all of us."

"They Turned All His Pictures to the Wall"

Despite how proud I was of my students and myself following the play, I did not want to limit their conversations to a couple of white men in a Shakespearean comedy. So we read a variety of informational texts that required conversations about sexual orientation and gender normativity (see Resources). One student brought in readings on transgender children after she'd watched a documentary. Marcus introduced a news report on a lesbian teen who was fighting to bring her girlfriend to prom.

When my student teacher's supervisor visited, she was stunned that several students were writing research papers on LGBTQ topics. After she'd chatted with one student who was writing about gay marriage, she told me, "I didn't know they even used the word 'gay' in small towns like this." All seemed to be going well. I felt like my teaching was honest now, and Joseph became more and more comfortable telling others that he was gay. Several months after his fear of losing Marcus, he now had many friends who knew what he described as "the whole me."

And then one morning Joseph wasn't there when I took attendance. I asked

Marcus, who shrugged and said: "I thought he was gonna be here. Me and him are supposed to be doing a presentation in history today."

Another student lightly slapped his shoulder. "Man, you and him are supposed to be best friends. Who's gonna keep up with him if you don't?" She laughed and Marcus shrugged again.

"I don't know," he said. "Maybe he got sick or something."

The next day, there was no Joseph, and still Marcus was unsure of what was going on. I used part of my lunch period to call his house and left a message for his parents to call me. No one did.

On the third day Marcus came in and said, "Ms. Shelton, I gotta talk to you." We walked into the hallway as the other students started their warm-ups.

"Ms. Shelton, they turned all his pictures to the wall."

Unprepared for this beginning, I replied, "Huh?"

"His pictures. I called his house last night and his mama wouldn't let me talk to him, and when I called his cell phone, it just went to voice mail. So I knew something wasn't right, you know? I told my mama that I thought he was in trouble, so she called his house and Joseph's mama told her, 'You can just come get him! I don't want this filth in my house! If you wanna take it to yours, that's fine, and I'll pray for you and yours.' So me and Mama went and got him and brought him to our house."

He stopped and took a deep breath, as if he had stopped breathing while he'd been talking. Something Marcus had said still didn't make sense.

"What about his pictures, Marcus?"

"I guess somebody told Joseph's parents about him or something, 'cause when he got home on Monday, they knew. They knew he's gay. He said they yelled, they screamed, they prayed, and then they sent him to his room. When he got up the next morning to come to breakfast, every picture that they had of him had been turned to the wall. Like he didn't exist anymore. He just went back to bed and cried."

In that moment I felt a lot like I had as a small kid trying to stay afloat in the deep end of a pool. No part of my teacher education or my years of experience had taught me what to do for Joseph in this moment. "Marcus, how long is Joseph going to stay at your house?"

"My mom is taking him home today, and she's gonna talk to his mom. Make sure he's gonna be safe there."

It saddened me that Joseph was going back to his parents so soon, but I understood. All of the students at the school qualified for free breakfast and lunch, and there was no way that Marcus' mother could afford an additional person in her household. In addition, because of Joseph's father's position in the community, few adults in Joseph's neighborhood would be willing to support Joseph rather than his father. One of the difficulties of living in a rural area is that the schools have many of the same issues as those in urban settings, but with fewer resources and little outside awareness. Plus, the resources that are available are often tangled with community politics and conservative church connections.

For Joseph, there was no food bank or shelter, and probably no local family that would take him in. Joseph would have to go home. He would have no choice.

"How Come They're All Rich?"

Joseph's classmates and I started looking for free resources that could help him. One day a student came in and said, "Y'all know about some online stuff that has people talking about things that happened when they told folks they were gay, and they're OK now?" She looked at Joseph. "Some of them sound kind of like you. You ought to look online."

One of the other students snorted and laughed: "Girl, you are so stupid. You know he hasn't got internet where he stays, just like I don't. How's he gonna look online?"

I said, "Well, if some of you want to help Joseph find this online stuff, I can write a pass for you to use the school computers during lunch." A group of three agreed and, for the first time in a while, Joseph looked hopeful.

The next day, as students wandered in from the locker room, I asked Joseph, "Did you find the websites yesterday?" He nodded and then paused, looking puzzled. "What is it?" I asked.

"Well," he began, "some of those folks were kind of like me. I mean, they had parents who treated them real bad, too. My folks just ignore me, but some people talk about way worse stuff."

"Then what's wrong?"

"How come they're all rich?"

"How do you know they're rich, Joseph?"

"Ms. Shelton, most of them are talking on their computers in their houses, and the stuff behind them in the room is really nice, and they're all wearing name-brand stuff." He paused and then continued, "Aren't there any poor gay people besides me?"

Class Counts

There are plenty of teacher resources and scholarly articles detailing strategies for teachers to create more inclusive and socially just classrooms, but the issue in my rural Southern school was that those resources did not acknowledge the inevitable community resistance that I, and other teachers like me, would face for introducing LGBTQ topics in their classrooms. Although I was very proud of my students, there were community complaints about me, including a call to my administrator from a local pastor, who claimed that I had "dismissed the Bible." If I had been a novice teacher, I probably would never have mentioned anything beyond the textbook in my classroom again, and I would have lived in daily fear of losing my job. As a teacher educator now, I am very aware of the limitations that particular communities and schools present for teachers and students who want to discuss sexuality and gender within the context of academic curriculum. Knowing what to do and wanting to do it are not the same as being supported in doing so, or even allowed to do so.

What is more, the pop culture visibility and online existence of LGBTQ characters and "survivors" can be contradictory, or even damaging. There are promising signs of LGBTQ acceptance on a national level, but that acceptance is not all-inclusive. Almost every openly gay character on a prime-time show is an economically stable white male, and many online testimonies by LGBTQ adults and youth who have survived trauma offer the same demographics, or slight variations.

Joseph and other LGBTQ students I have supported since do not look at these people and see themselves. They are fully aware that the background sets of these television shows suggest middle-class comfort. They hear that the online testimonies are delivered without my students' pronounced Southern drawls. They understand that the options in the plot lines and real-life testimonies are not available to them.

All Is Not Lost

However, it is important not to underestimate the power of the school experience in supporting LGBTQ students. Ultimately what got Joseph through high school were not television programs or online promises of a better future. The community of friends and learners that had formed in my 11th-grade classroom was his lifeline until he graduated. That there were at least one adult and a few dozen peers who knew him, who accepted him, who loved him, was essential for Joseph.

Several days before graduation day, I walked into my classroom to find a carefully folded note under my door. I opened it to find a four-page handwritten letter from Joseph.

He thanked me for all that he had learned, for all of the essays that I had made him write, and for all of the times that I had listened when he had drama. The end of the letter was what sent me in search of tissues:

> I know you're probably tired of reading all this stuff I'm writing, and
> you always fussed at me about not being able to read my handwrit-
> ing, but I want to end by saying that you saved me. You saved all of
> us. Every single day when I walked up the bus ramp to come into
> this school, no matter how bad my morning had been at home, or
> how many times I heard "fag" or "gay" in the hallway, I knew that in
> your classroom we were all safe. Not just me, all of us. You always
> joked about how we're gonna be in charge of the world some day and
> you're just hedging your bets and trying to make us a little smarter,
> but you did more than that—you helped make us kinder. We will

leave the world a better place, and you were part of that. Thank you.

It is not for the thank-you notes or the tear-inducing moments that we teach. We teach so that both our students and we know that the world will be a better place. For all of us.

Resources

Bouie, Jamelle. Feb. 13, 2014. "Anti-Gay Jim Crow Comes to Kansas." *The Daily Beast*. thedailybeast.com/articles/2014/02/13/anti-gay-jim-crow-comes-to-kansas.

Denizet-Lewis, Benoit. Sept. 23, 2009. "Coming Out in Middle School." *The New York Times*. nytimes.com/2009/09/27/magazine/27out-t.html?pagewanted=all&_r=0.

Hutchinson, Bill. Feb. 9, 2014. "Missouri Football Player Michael Sam Says He Is Gay, Aims to Be First Publicly Gay Player in NFL." *New York Daily News*. nydailynews.com/sports/football/missouri-sam-aims-openly-gay-nfl-player-article-1.1607997.

Sancya, Paul. 2010. "Michigan Teacher Suspended Over Anti-Gay Punishment." *USA Today*, Nov. 16. usatoday30.usatoday.com/news/nation/2010-11-16-michigan-teacher-suspended-gay_N.htm.

Walsh, Michael. Dec. 29, 2013. "School Staff Bullies Lesbian Student with Anti-Gay Slurs, Calls Her 'It': Lawsuit." *New York Daily New*. nydailynews.com/news/national/school-staff-bullies-lesbian-student-anti-gay-slurs-calls-lawsuit-article-1.1560922.

Untitled

By Deanna Gao

Deanna Gao is a queer, gender nonconforming Chinese American woman who grew up in Ann Arbor, Michigan. She is in pursuit of a justice that is rooted in practices of love and healing. For the past few years she has worked with youth of color in Los Angeles and, in more recent years, with Asian youth in San Francisco and Oakland. She is passionate about political education with young people as a means of individual and collective transformation.

"um. excuse me, you're in the wrong bathroom"

always a statement of well-intended policing

it's spoken so effortlessly like maybe i have no cultural reference to understand the
difference

between the slim waisted stick figure and the one wearing a feminized triangle

that combined with my accented Asian features dulls my masculinity

to something benign.

something confused.

something nonthreatening. something to be corrected and born meaning

through consumption by white imperialist benevolence.

something weak, passive, and . . . wait. this sounds familiar.

something . . . feminine.

like the ways my eyes squint in grimace gives people permission to assume

i wandered into the wrong bathroom.

like even if i wandered into the wrong bathroom people must fulfill their patriotic duty

to show me how things are done in this country

like even if I find myself on the other side of the drinking fountain staring into the deep
abyss of a urinal

I am insulting what it is to be a "man"

like citizenship is as simple as standing phallic and erect and peeing all over everything

i can only ONLY imagine if i was darker

if my bathroom experience was the cumulation of centuries of other people's violently
socialized

exercise of power, fear, and entitlement projected onto my body

if me sitting on the toilet trying to pee invoked the threatening images of black people assimilated to the likeness of king kong

gorillas are supposed to be tamed, disciplined, and caged but not potty trained

it's no wonder that well-intended policing sits in irreconcilable contradiction

that well-intended policing is actually code for "i don't see you as human"

"I can't see you as human"

"I won't see you as human"

"um. excuse me, you're in the wrong bathroom"

today when those words assault me with familiar intention a part of me wants to shrink

and a shrinking part of me does

a part of me returns to eighth grade when the cost of my haircut was the loss of my
     dignity

a part of me travels to summer in China where it was my Mandarin teacher who,
     assuming my

blossoming manhood, was responsible for my humiliation

a part of me tightens to remember feet hitting cold pavement, running
     towards imagination, away

because I couldn't bear the threat of my family's disdain and haircuts forbidden

a part of me goes weak at the knees to think of all those girls I lusted for, who brushed
     my arm with too

much suggestion, and eventually and always and inevitably went to prom with John
     White

a part of me blames my mom

because why didn't she try to understand what it felt like, when I begged her

to design an independent study to replace mandatory gym class

to avoid the misery of the girl's public high school locker room

and then a growing part of me keeps my feet planted squarely on tile

a growing part of me stares back with determination

knowing that my expression upsets expectations of gender and sexual conformity

racialized assimilation

a phrase that strikes a chord of confidence in knowing that

my gender confuses, complicates, and challenges

"um. excuse me, you're in the wrong bathroom"

and all I can do is smile

CHAPTER 3

Favianna Rodriguez

Our Curriculum: Introduction

By Jeff Sapp

Jeff Sapp (jeffsapp.com) has been a teacher, writer, and activist for 36 years. He began his career as a middle and high school math and science teacher and is currently professor of education at California State University, Dominguez Hills. Jeff lives in Long Beach with his husband, Sino, and 6-year-old daughter, Helena. They spend their time gardening, renovating a 100-year-old bungalow house, and having lots of conversations about feminism.

When those who have the power to name and to socially construct reality choose not to see you or hear you, whether you are dark-skinned, old, disabled, female, or speak with a different accent or dialect than theirs, when someone with the authority of a teacher, say, describes the world and you are not in it, there is a moment of psychic disequilibrium, as if you looked into a mirror and saw nothing.
— *Adrienne Rich*

As a young gay boy growing up in a religious home in a small Appalachian town, I had the classic experience of fearing that I was the only gay person in the entire world. I never once saw myself reflected in the world around me. I thought isolation and loneliness would consume me. But then, suddenly, I found books.

I remember the first gay novel I ever stumbled upon. It was *The Front Runner*, by Patricia Nell Warren, and I saw it on a drugstore bookshelf. Buying that paperback novel was one of the bravest things I've accomplished in my life. I hid it under my mattress, sneaking to read it chapter by chapter, desperate to know that I wasn't alone. Many years later, I read Paul Monette's *Becoming a Man: Half a Life Story* and then Andrew Tobias' *The Best Little Boy in the World*, both accounts of growing up gay in the United States. Literature saved me.

I remember the day I found out that Plato and Socrates were gay. That James Baldwin was gay. Walt Whitman and Gertrude Stein. All kinds of authors and historical figures were contextualized in my high school classes, but never for sexual orientation. Queerness was invisible.

As a nerd, I read a lot of books on gay and lesbian history before I came out. The first one was Eric Marcus' *Making History: The Struggle for Gay and Lesbian Equal Rights,* and I was riveted by the story of Sylvia Rivera, the drag queen who threw the first stone of resistance at police brutality and started the Stonewall Riots. Reading Marcus' book made me mad. Where had these stories been? I had looked into the mirror of schooling and seen nothing.

So curriculum matters. Not only as a mirror, as Rich so beautifully explains, but as a window to the world as well. Unfortunately, too often the folks writing "big curriculum" work for corporations like Pearson, and liberatory mirrors and windows are the last things on their minds.

I read an article recently about scholars who were reviewing social studies textbook content in Texas. They found that the textbooks included statements that portrayed Muslims inappropriately and negatively, largely ignored Native American peoples and culture, and gave undue legitimacy to neo-Confederate arguments about states' rights and the legacy of slavery. They also found a number of government and world history textbooks that exaggerated the Judeo-Christian influence on the nation's founding.

Social justice curriculum is both a mirror and a window to the world.

Olive Earley

The challenge for progressive teachers, of course, is how to deal with the corporate curriculum we're handed. I teach a graduate-level course on curriculum development. I asked the students—all of whom were student teaching in the Los Angeles Unified School District (LAUSD)—whether they were using the required textbooks in their classrooms. I had them write about their own practice and then ask their colleagues at the schools where they were teaching. What they found is that, in fact, most of the teachers either completely ignored the required textbooks or used them sparingly as resources. Like the authors in this book, these teachers were, instead, writing their own curriculum, day after day after day, a much more difficult and time-consuming task. Why? Because the mandated textbook didn't engage or meet the needs of their diverse student populations. As one eloquent and insightful educator concluded, "It's boring shit."

The one exception to teachers ignoring the textbooks was the sex education class. LAUSD mandated the sex education curriculum and required attendance at a training where teachers were told to never deviate from the scripted lessons. This was an "abstinence-plus" curriculum: That means emphasize abstinence but include information about contraception and sexually transmitted diseases (STDs). The curriculum focused on teaching young girls to avoid pregnancy and STDs. Queer students were invisible, their issues ignored.

According to one student: "It made sense why they told us 'don't ever leave the script' because they didn't want queer issues addressed in schools."

"It is a misogynistic, disease-based model, plain and simple," wrote another. "It's as if this curriculum is saying that 'girls are sluts and will get pregnant and diseases, and boys have nothing to do with it whatsoever!' What is that actually saying to young women?"

Curriculum is not an "it" but a "Thou."

The articles in this book, and particularly in this chapter, confront this backward approach by providing sex-positive, gender- and sexuality-inclusive curriculum. For articles that address sex education specifically, see "Sex Talk on the Carpet: Incorporating gender and sexuality into 5th-grade curriculum," by Valdine Ciwko; "Elbow Is Not a Sexy Word: Approaches to Sex Education," by Jody Sokolower; "Teaching Sex Positivity: An interview with Lena Solow," by Annika Butler-Wall; and "7 Tips for Teaching Sex Ed," by Ericka Hart.

Progressive content is important, but not sufficient. I had a professor once who taught a course on democratic education, but he was a tyrant in the classroom. Trust me, no one learned anything about democratic behavior in that class. He may have been teaching John Dewey, but what we learned (not for the first time) was that teachers have the power.

The truth is that curriculum doesn't stand by itself. It is always deeply, intimately connected to the personhood of the teacher. The teacher and the curriculum are one, forever entwined in the eyes of students. This is why I love the work of Parker J. Palmer in *The Courage to Teach* and his focus on the "who" question:

> The question we most commonly ask is the "what" question— "What subjects shall we teach?" When the conversation goes a bit deeper, we ask the "how" question—"What methods and techniques are required to teach well?" Occasionally, when it goes deeper still, we ask the "why" question—"For what purpose and to what ends do we teach?" But seldom, if ever, do we ask the "who" question—"Who is the self that teaches? How does the quality of my selfhood form—or deform—the way I relate to my students, my subject, my colleagues, my world? How can educational institutions sustain and deepen the selfhood from which good teaching comes?"

As critical, reflective, self-aware educators we, as Maxine Greene says, are always to be on a "search for freedom" and to inspire that search in our students. Teachers who have a rich sense of self and can draw freely from that pool build tremendous, appropriate relationships with their subjects, their methods, and their students. These deep, intersecting relationships are what create community inside a classroom. That's when students say things like "You know, we were a family in that classroom." This is the kind of transcendent atmosphere that leads to authentic conversations that transform lives.

And that brings me to the last thing that really matters.

Subversion.

Herbert Kohl says:

> Don't teach against your conscience. Don't align yourself with texts, people, or rules that hurt children; resist them as creatively and effectively as you can, whether through humor or developing alternative curricula. I don't believe there is a single technique or curriculum that leads to success. Consequently, pick and choose, retool, and restructure the best of what you find and make it your own.

There you have it. Curriculum, if it is anything, is the lifelong process of the teacher's intellectual life and integrity alongside the deep desire to dialogue with students about content that thrills us with possibilities. Curriculum is not an "it"—an object to be mastered, but a "Thou"—a subject so deeply and intimately connected to the teacher that students see them as one.

Christiane Grauert

Disarming the Nuclear Family

Creating a classroom book that reflects the class

By Willow McCormick

Willow McCormick is a 2nd-grade teacher in West Linn, Oregon. She is an Oregon Writing Project consultant and a Library of Congress Civil Rights Institute fellow.

I have more than 1,000 books in my classroom library, cobbled together from garage sales, used bookstores, and the collections of former students who have outgrown their picture books. As a social justice educator, I try to fill my primary classroom library with books that feature characters from a variety of cultures, traditions, classes, and backgrounds. And yet, despite my efforts, I'm dismayed by how many of the thoughtful, well-written books in my collection feature the nuclear family unit, be it human or animal. Even my favorite authors default to the nuke.

Kevin Henkes is a perennial favorite in primary classrooms across the country. The mice that populate his books cope with universal struggles of young children—separation anxiety, teasing, loneliness, empathy. Unfortunately,

Henkes' books present something else as universal as well: a doting mother and father plus a sibling or two waiting at home to soothe and support the struggler.

Trudy Ludwig has written an excellent collection of books, including *Trouble Talk* and *Sorry!*, that dig into the power dynamics among children and offer strategies on how a child can transition from being a target to a self-advocate—with a little help from mom, dad, and brother in a tidy, suburban home. The message of empowerment is a noble and essential one, which is why I read these books to my class every year. But another message is being conveyed as well when these books are read back to back: two-parent heterosexual families are the norm.

When a book does acknowledge the existence of other family structures, the difference is often the focus of the story—how Addison has two fancy houses instead of one in Tamara Schmitz's *Standing on My Own Two Feet: A Child's Affirmation of Love in the Midst of Divorce*. If you want to read a story featuring children in foster care, you'll have to look long and hard for anything other than guides for making the transition in or out of care. It takes a lot of work to find books that include same-gender parents, step-parents, foster or adopted children, or other nontraditional families as background in an adventure tale, a friendship parable, or a holiday romp.

When two-parent, heterosexual families are presented as the norm in story after story, year in and year out, an insidious message is conveyed: Families that don't conform to this structure are not normal. And, of course, the message is reinforced in the majority of movies and television shows geared toward children. Shame, secrecy, and evasion can result from this incessant messaging.

I see it play out in my classroom. Two years ago, I had a student with divorced lesbian moms, step-siblings, half-siblings, and a close-knit extended family. I doubt any children's book out there includes a family like hers. They were a loud and loving family, and Marie was a loud and loving girl. Yet she rarely divulged that she had two moms and, in fact, fabricated an absentee dad at one point early in the year. Another boy, Andrew, didn't want anyone to know he was adopted, afraid they would think he was "weird." He said it was hard enough having brown skin when his parents and most of his classmates were white; he didn't want kids to think of him as different in another way, too. I pride myself on having an accepting and appreciative classroom community, but the undermining effect of the dominant family system in children's books and media slips into our snug community like toxic smoke.

What is a 2nd-grade teacher to do? Dispose of all Kevin Henkes books, and deprive 7-year-olds of the pleasure of repeating "Chrysanthemum, Chrysanthemum, Chrysanthemum" as they root for the main character to embrace her unusual name and accept herself? Give periodic rambling qualifiers before read-alouds, trying to explain the heteronormative paradigm in kid-friendly language? Build a library where every family structure is represented equally, thus ensuring a library of 100 books or fewer? I've considered all of these scenarios in moments of exasperation, but nothing seems realistic.

Susan Kuklin's *Families*

Luckily there are resources out there that shine a light on a path forward. A few years ago I discovered a beautiful book by Susan Kuklin simply titled *Families*. Kuklin puts family structure in a larger context of diversity of all types. To create the book, she interviewed children aged 4 to 14 from a variety of family structures, mainly in New York City, but also in rural communities. She then worked with the children to select a page's worth of text describing their family members, religious traditions, household, hobbies, and studies. A family portrait accompanies each page; the children themselves chose the location, clothing worn by all family members, pets, and props. The net effect is a refreshingly matter-of-fact look at 16 very different families. Ella is a summer camp aficionado who was adopted by her two fathers as a baby. There's also Kira and Matias, biracial children who live beside a creek and love catching fish for dinner. Yaakov, Leah, Miriam, and Asher are Orthodox Jews who make themselves laugh with goofy invented languages. Chris, Louie, and Adam are close-knit brothers whose parents come from Puerto Rico and the Dominican Republic; they discuss food and language, only mentioning in passing that Louie has Down syndrome.

We Make Our Own Book

Families has all sorts of potential for classroom use. I use it as a mentor text for writing our own class book of families. Each day I read aloud one family story to the class. The straightforward tone of the book leads easily to a straightforward discussion afterward. I ask the kids to make connections between the family we just met in the book and their own families, or the families of their friends or neighbors. What do they have in common? What are some differences? The class often starts with the goofy languages—they make up silly words, too!—or the hobbies or study habits they share with the children in the book. But it's not long before the conversation gets more personal. Finn mentions his gay aunts, two children of divorced families compare how they split up—or don't—their time between households, devout Christian Isaiah notices that he and a Muslim boy in the book both consider themselves servants of God.

Over time, we begin to craft our own narratives. First we brainstorm themes that come up again and again in the book—food, religion, traditions, sports and hobbies, descriptions of family members—and the kids start to make lists from their own lives that fit into these categories. Then they write, each in their own style. Ramona tells how her cousins came to live with her family as foster children. "My mom wanted to know how long they would be staying, but now we're all glad they came." Isaiah tells us that religion is the biggest part of his family's life. Marie writes about her two moms, and Rory explains that he doesn't have a dad or siblings, but his uncles and pets fill in, and he and his mom have an extra special relationship because it's just the two of them. Andrew, after a few fretful conferences with a couple of trusted peers and me, decides to include his adoption in his narrative:

> Hi, I am Andrew. I am 8 years old. I have one sister and no brothers. I live in Oregon. I was adopted because my birth mom could not take care of me. My dad was at work when the phone rang. Somebody said into the phone, "Jon, do you want to be a dad?" "Yes!" After one day my mom and my dad came to the place where I was. My new mom and dad took me home.

The undermining effect of the dominant family system in children's books and media slips into our snug community like toxic smoke.

Once the narratives are crafted, the kids bring in photos to use as illustrations, or direct me to photograph them doing things they love at school. They paste their narratives and photos on oversized construction paper to create their own page in our classroom edition of *Families*.

To draw the project to a close, I host a writing celebration in the classroom. The children lay their pages out carefully on the tables and we spend the hour rotating from desk to desk, reading stories and leaving notes of praise and connection. "My family goes hiking on Easter, too!" "You have two moms?! You are sooo lucky!"

At the end of the day, I collect all the pages and bind them together. Now there's at least one book in our classroom library where all of my students can find themselves. When I think about how intently the majority of my students read and respond to the writing of their peers, I realize that, even if my classroom were fully stocked with high-quality literature featuring a complete spectrum of family structures, I'd still want this book, our book, at the center of my library. It is satisfying for the students to see themselves reflected in the books and other media that surround them. But it is also powerful—and comforting— for children to see and be seen by their own peers. Ultimately I want both for my students: a world in which they feel they belong, and a classroom community in which they feel known.

Sex Talk on the Carpet
Incorporating gender and sexuality into 5th-grade curriculum

BY VALDINE CIWKO

Valdine Ciwko became a teacher after working in the performing arts for more than 15 years. In the late 1980s she was on the board of AIDS Vancouver, where she first began thinking about the importance of discussing sexuality in public. She currently teaches grades 5, 6, and 7 in Vancouver, B.C.

My grade 5 students are gathered at the carpet area. I am dressed as a giant purple bell with a tinsel wig and sparkly *Wizard of Oz* shoes. There are cats and pirates and ghastly ghouls. It's Halloween Day, and we are exploring the metacognitive power of asking questions while you read.

I read aloud from Christopher Phillips' *The Philosophers' Club* (a wonderful book for kids about how to ask big questions in a meaningful way) and we generate questions: Which came first, the chicken or the egg? What is philosophy? What is violence? These kids are fantastic at wondering about the world they are beginning to enter as preteenagers. Big ideas spark more questions and the kids call out all kinds of questions. I read: "Is it possible to be happy and sad at the same time?" and a voice asks, "Can you change from a boy to a girl?"

Maybe it's the tinsel hair, the otherworldliness of the day, but there aren't gales of laughter. Suddenly my morning is a whole lot more interesting. I could ignore the question, but it is a fair and important question, and deserves a fair and important response.

As teachers we make choices every day. What we leave in a lesson, what we take out. What we make time for, what we make disappear.

"Why, yes, a person can change from a boy to a girl, but it's not like someone just wakes up one morning and says, 'Hey, I think I'll become a girl today.'"

Opening a Discussion About Transgender People

And so begins our discussion about transgender people. We begin to talk about what a serious decision that would be, how hard it must be to be in the wrong body, and how we hope that there would be people around who can

Carrie Neumayer

accept you for who you really are. I have a good friend who first entered my life as a woman but who is now a man and very active in transgender politics. I mention that, if my friend was to come visit, the students would have no idea he had not always been a he.

There are no girl-only or boy-only questions.

We talk about how long the process can take. My friend didn't make the decision overnight. Life as a teenager had been hell. He'd left home early, attempted suicide, and lived a pretty transient life. It wasn't until he was in his late 20s and ended up in Vancouver that he finally made the transition.

Suddenly a small pirate in the group pipes up that she, too, knows someone who used to be a girl but is a boy now—a family friend back in her home country of El Salvador. In still-hesitant English she explains that the biggest problem he had was his boobies, and that he had to bind them. What is most astonishing at this moment is that not one of my 9- and 10-year-olds giggles at the term "booby," which under usual circumstances could have had them rolling on the floor. Instead they ask:

"What did he have to do?"

"Did it hurt?"

"Was it hard?"

"Did his friends still stay his friends?"

"What did his family say?"

"Can you tell?"

"Does he have a penis?"

"What about a beard?"

And what started as a language lesson became a life lesson.

Getting Comfortable Teaching About Sexuality and Gender

Could a discussion occur like this just out of the blue in any classroom? Certainly the question could, but I would argue that the discussion might not. And that is a shame. It is a shame for the students in our classes who are questioning, trying to figure out who they are, and how they fit in this world. We need to open up the doors to talk about gender, sexuality, sexual identity, and acceptance of people for who they are.

But there are many barriers that get in the way: fear that a parent will make a complaint, fear that we are crossing some boundary of religious beliefs, fear that we don't know all the answers, fear of straying from the plan for the day, fear of straying from the curriculum.

One reason I was able to lead this discussion was that a year earlier, a group of educators working with the Vancouver Board of Education developed teaching materials to address new curriculum learning outcomes around puberty. It's called *Growing Up: Teaching Sexual Health*. When a flier advertised a two-day professional development for grade 5 teachers, I signed up. I was in the pilot group to test-drive the materials in my class.

It was an interesting year. I invited two volunteers from Options for Sexual Health (a nonprofit that was part of the curriculum planning process) to come work with me and my students. I jumped at the chance to have them help teach a section of the curriculum on reproductive body parts. During our time in small groups, a student asked how the penis and vagina meet. Tara, one of the volunteers, addressed it matter-of-factly and succinctly, and the group work continued.

The next day my principal approached me. A parent had called with concerns about what the "nurse" had told the kids the day before. I reported what had happened and reminisced about what I learned when I was in grade 5, growing up in Winnipeg. Or, more to the point, what I didn't learn. In "sex ed" we heard how babies are made by the meeting of the egg and the sperm, and that once you got your period, you could get pregnant. Unfortunately, they left out that key detail—how do these tiny little things meet in the first place? I am sure I was not the only little prairie girl confused about pregnancy and wondering if it happened from kissing, or a man touching you while you had your period, or what.

My principal, a woman of a similar age and schooling, had similar memories. After we had a good chuckle about the ignorance of it all in our day, my principal agreed to respond to the mom. I was lucky. I had a supportive principal who believed in what I was doing with my students. More importantly, what was being taught was within the curriculum, so there was no ambiguity about whether these kinds of discussions should occur. Here in British Columbia, parents can choose to have their children sit out these lessons, but they must provide a scheduled plan of how they will teach this aspect of the curriculum.

For me, it was significant that this student had gone home and talked about what he had learned that day, something that his mom lamented rarely happened. Yet the stigma surrounding talking about sex meant that this parent, who didn't hesitate to ask me how to help her son in math or reading, could not cross the boundary to talk with me directly about this particular aspect of his learning.

Moving Past "the Nurse's Puberty Talk"

Because I incorporated sexual health education into my weekly planning instead of inviting the nurse to come one fine spring day and have "the talk" with the girls while the boys have "the talk" with some brave male teacher on staff, my students developed confidence in asking questions about things they wanted to know or were fearful about. They also developed a healthy attitude toward talking about sexual issues in a whole-class setting.

For example, a word-sort of terms and definitions for male and female body parts turned into a rigorous class activity. The school nurse had given me a good bit of advice: When doing activities with sensitive words or images, it's helpful to have students working together on the floor. Maybe it's the shift of focus from a screen or board, maybe it's the ability to work closer together than tables or desks allow that eases the task, but it seemed to work. The students were divided into groups and given some time to match words with definitions. They settled right into the job at hand and no, they could not use the dictionary, they had to discuss and settle on their best guesses. In true grade 5 style, competitive spirit won out over any embarrassment about the words. I admit that I slipped over to close my classroom door, realizing that shouts of "clitoris . . . clitoris . . . clitoris . . . yes!" might be misinterpreted by an uninformed passerby.

> If students never hear the words *gay*, *lesbian*, *transgender*, and *questioning* from us when we are talking about sexual development, what message do we send?

Throughout that year, I made it clear that there were no girl-only or boy-only questions, that it's important for each to understand what is happening to the other. I invited students to anonymously write down questions and deposit them in the question box and we went through them weekly. Mostly, at this age, the questions came from girls. There were the obvious ones like "How do babies get formed?" "Will it hurt to get your period?" "Is it OK to have periods when you are 10?" and then one that stood out: "Are movies on YouTube a good place to learn about puberty?"

What I learned from that year of piloting the curriculum was how much kids want to know and need to know. And how afraid both teachers and parents still are about talking about sex. Sadly, many teachers still leave the puberty talk to the nurses. If we, as educators, are not yet willing to have open and frank discussions about puberty and body changes and sex, how can kids ever begin to talk about sexuality?

And if the puberty talks only focus on procreation within heterosexual activity, what happens to our students who are already beginning to realize they might not fit that mold? If "family life" and sexuality are only presented within the confines of heterosexuality, if we do not open up our language to include the possible feelings of all of our students, by omission we are saying everything else is not normal. If students never hear the words *gay, lesbian, transgender*, and *questioning* from us when we are talking about sexual development, what message do we send?

So how did my class the following year end up ensconced in a serious discussion about gender in October? I hadn't yet started up my formal, slotted health lessons. My letter to parents explaining my plans for teaching sexual education was still in draft mode on my computer. I was surprised we were in the midst of such an open conversation so early in the year, but I was prepared, too. The questions our students have are not compartmentalized into strictly math or social studies, science or health. Their questions come when they come. And my experiences from the previous year had left me confident and ready for this conversation. Maybe that's why it happened.

Students of this age are hungry to learn new things. The days that "health" was integrated into the shape of the day were some of my best days of teaching. The conversations we had were honest and heartfelt. For many, these were things they weren't likely to be talking about at home. And the "everydayness" of it meant that issues of gender and sexuality could arise at any possible moment in the day, like that Halloween morning in an ordinary language arts lesson.

2nd Graders Put On a Gender-Bending Assembly

BY MARGOT PEPPER

Margot Pepper is a bilingual educator, poet-teacher, and journalist whose work has been published internationally by *Utne Reader, Common Dreams, Counterpunch*, the *San Francisco Bay Guardian, Monthly Review, Rethinking Schools*, City Lights, Hampton-Brown, and others. She is author of a memoir, *Through the Wall: A Year in Havana*; a book of poetry, *At This Very Moment*; and a dystopian science fiction thriller, *American Day Dream*.

"That's so girly!"

As a 2nd-grade teacher, I'm inclined to address sexist and transphobic comments on the spot. I see it as an opportunity to dissuade bullying and educate my students about tolerance, empathy, civil rights, and gender identity. In my early years as an elementary school teacher—before the eras of No Child Left Behind, Race to the Top, and Common Core—I'd launch my women's unit on March 8, International Women's Day. The goal was to challenge Barbie-doll stereotypes about gender. The unit included Amelia Earhart, Helen Keller, Frida Kahlo, Harriet Tubman, Rosa Parks, and Sor Juana Inés de la Cruz.

But with the growing testing craze and standardization of curriculum, I've found myself reprimanded by the administration more than once. I've learned that critical pedagogy—exploring the violence in children's television shows or having students read poetry on Univisión to bring attention to the wrongful deportation of a classmate—is not always embraced by parents and administrators. A few years ago, when a new principal suggested that my language lab enrichment class present an assembly on "open-mindedness," I seized the opportunity.

Not all students in my language lab class at Rosa Parks Elementary School in Berkeley, California, are on my homeroom roster. Each afternoon, our school groups children by language ability and level, regardless of grade, to tailor instruction to their specific language development needs. Spanish learners in two-way Spanish immersion work on developing Spanish vocabulary and grammar; those learning English do the same. Students who are at grade level in writing and reading receive "enrichment."

Keeping It Simple

"Open-mindedness is learning about what you don't know," Samantha commented after listening to the story my class loved best: Marcus Ewert's picture book *10,000 Dresses*. The story is told from the viewpoint of Bailey, a child assigned the male gender at birth, who dreams of dresses. The narrator refers to Bailey with the feminine pronouns "she" and "her." When Bailey tells her parents that she wants to wear dresses, they become angry and tell her she's a boy. Her older brother calls her "gross," and threatens to hurt her. Eventually Bailey meets Laurel, an older girl who lives nearby and who is accepting of Bailey's love of dresses and gender identity. Laurel explains that, although she longs to sew, she can't think up any design ideas. Together, Bailey and her new friend set to work making dresses. Delighted with their creations, Laurel asks Bailey if she can dream up any future designs. Bailey responds: "I can dream up 10,000 dresses."

Illustration by Rex Ray from *10,000 Dresses* by Marcus Ewert.

> ## "People get closed-minded when they don't know about something."

The students decided they wanted to re-enact *10,000 Dresses* for the school assembly.

"All right. Who wants to play Bailey?" I asked. A third of the students' hands went up.

"Shouldn't it be a boy?" a female student inquired.

About half the hands went down.

"The leading actor gets to wear a dress in the final scene," I noted. The rest of the hands disappeared.

I could see it was time for stories about gender fluidity. I told the class about a former student, who would dash across the playground like a shooting star with his mane of long, blonde hair flying. Although he identified as a boy, he was often mistaken for a girl. But he shrugged it off; he was confident of his own identity. I recounted my own triumphs over gender: strolling the school halls as Astro Boy in my red squeaky rain boots, polyester pants, and cape; surfing an 18-foot face over jagged Waikiki coral; skating the high blacktop hills of Paul Revere Junior High with the now-famous Dogtown Z-Boys gang.

"You know how to skateboard and surf?"

"Yeah, remember? She showed us!" The students recalled the first days of school, when their "femme," eye-liner-and-lipsticked teacher got on her skateboard in a mini-dress and boots, slalomed around some desks, and pulled off a 180 on the rug.

"I want to play Bailey. I love wearing dresses!" Benjamin volunteered.

"Me, too!'" Alex chimed in.

"Me, too!" José asserted.

I chose Benjamin, explaining he was the first to volunteer.

A second star emerged as we filled the roles; Emily volunteered to play Laurel. The story was near to Emily's heart. "My older sibling is transgender," she confidently explained during our discussion.

"You mean your sibling is the opposite gender on the inside to what they look like on the outside?" I asked. Emily nodded, smiling because I understood.

I felt prepared for the discussion, thanks to a training at my district by Welcoming Schools, a Human Rights Campaign Foundation project to prevent the bullying of LGBTQ students. "Keep it simple," their website suggests, and that's what I tried to do: "A transgender person is born with the physical anatomy of a boy or a girl but deep inside they feel like a different gender. For example, someone may have been born with the physical body of a boy but deep inside she feels like a girl and wants to live her life as a woman."

"My older sibling is transgender," Emily confidently explained during our discussion.

"But my parents say that's wrong" is a comment I've sometimes heard during this type of discussion. Now, thanks to Welcoming Schools, I feel empowered to say, "Then you have a real opportunity to explain to your parents, don't you?"

I could see the conversation liberating students who didn't fit neatly into the prefab box designated for their gender; one in particular was Ofra. Although she often didn't contribute to conversations, Ofra listened attentively as her classmates and I talked.

"People get closed-minded when they don't know about something," Domo noted.

"And they don't want to find out about it," Inácio added.

"Because they're afraid," Samantha said.

"So you think closed-mindedness is about being fearful?" I asked.

The students nodded enthusiastically.

"Maybe open-mindedness is learning about things you're afraid of so that you're no longer afraid."

"Yeah!" they agreed.

The next day, my students spontaneously re-enacted *10,000 Dresses*, staying remarkably true to the original. I was impressed with how they brought out the repetition. As director, I suggested a few gestures: "Slap your hands together when you repeat 'Bailey, you're a boy. Boys don't wear dresses and that's that!'"

I gave the audience a role, too: When they heard the characters being closed-minded, they were to cover their eyes dramatically and say "Closed-minded!" When the characters were open-minded, they opened their palms in an arc over their faces, looked skyward, and said: "Open-minded!"

Other situations that came up in the discussion were also turned into skits for the assembly. We wanted to have lots of examples of open-mindedness.

The Open-Mindedness Assembly

One morning, midway through our project, a colleague mentioned that television reporters might want to film our class as backdrop for a news story on schools. I was apprehensive. The student groups were about to perform for the class for the first time; cameras might put them off. I was starting to doubt they'd be able to pull off a performance in time for the school assembly. Itai, our narrator, still stumbled over the *10,000 Dresses* text. Ofra, acting as the mother, kept distracting Itai, her best friend, and being silly. And Greta, who was playing Bailey's father, was painstakingly soft-spoken. Benjamin, who ordinarily had to work double-time at keeping out of trouble, tried hard to refocus his colleagues. At his suggestion two days earlier, the group demanded copies of *10,000 Dresses* to practice at home. I figured it would take them at least a week to show progress.

After lunch, my language lab students entered, eager to practice their performances. To my amazement, with just two days of home practice, the *10,000 Dresses* troupe enacted the entire story from memory. Benjamin was magnificent as Bailey. He recalled almost verbatim Bailey's lines in the story. His dress for the last scene was made from a white mosquito net. With some glitter, it wrapped around his trousers like fancy ballerina netting. Itai read beautifully, without missing a word. Ofra stayed in character and remembered all her lines. When each family member scolded Bailey for preferring dresses, the seated students acting as the audience said softly, "Closed-minded!" It gave me goose bumps.

So I was delighted when the two reporters entered the room.

"They're ready for you!" I announced.

"How long will this take?" one reporter inquired.

"Five minutes."

The kids began their play. The reporters began talking loudly over the student actors.

"Wait, wait, wait," I stopped the kids. Turning to the reporters, I inquired: "You're not going to film them?"

"No."

They left, apparently to film elsewhere.

"Closed-minded!" the students said spontaneously as the door slammed shut. We all burst out laughing.

Alone again, we got down to business. I shared a prop: a Groucho Marx mask with wind-up, wiggling eyebrows and mustache so the school audience would have an easier time recognizing Greta as the father. When Greta had trouble winding the mask, Anurm suggested that Bailey say, "Oh, father, you have something on your nose. May I wipe it?" while winding the knob. "Oh, I can't seem to get it." Greta tried hard not to laugh as she recited her lines, and the eyebrows and mustache took on a life of their own.

Although our dress rehearsals went smoothly in class, rehearsal on the multi-purpose room stage the day before the school assembly was another matter. "Remember what you learned about improvising," I reminded them. "You're magicians. You distract the audience so they don't notice what you're really doing when you make a mistake. You fool them into thinking that's how it should be. They don't know."

The reporters left. "Closed-minded!" the students said spontaneously as the door slammed shut.

And this is precisely what they did the morning of the assembly. One of the microphones broke, but Alex, David, and Harry were masters of improvisation. Alex used his charisma to elicit laughter from the audience as he swapped mics and put David down for a poor game of invisible wall ball. "Closed-minded," the audience chimed on cue. It was wonderful having involved the audience from the outset because now all 400 were drawn in, giving my students immediate feedback, which made them perform better than I ever imagined. Sarah filled in seamlessly for a student who suddenly got stage fright. Benjamin and Emily convincingly delivered their lines without a pause. Greta didn't so much as giggle as the audience roared at her twitching eyebrows and mustache. The applause at the end of the show was enthusiastically raucous. My 7- and 8-year-old actors glowed.

After the performance, one of Emily's parents introduced herself. "You know how dear this subject is to our hearts," she said, referring to Emily's older sibling Randy.

The following day, I asked my class what they thought about our play and our class discussion on gender.

Ofra said the best part of our project was learning that there were lots of children testing and breaking through the limits of their gender. "Girls can play with cars and basketball and that kind of thing, just like it's OK for boys to play with dolls. It's OK for them to be different."

"I feel relieved," Emily offered. "People aren't asking me about Randy's gender anymore. Now I know there are other people in the same situation, that Randy's not the only one. From all this I've learned that we can be whoever we want to be."

It has been a few years since our play. Thanks to increased push from more teachers, new awareness has begun to germinate at our school. I've been able to bring back some of my critical lessons addressing gender and race. A couple of Halloweens ago, for the first time in my nearly two decades at Rosa Parks, more than a dozen girls dressed up as male heroes. Conversely, there were a few boys dressed as females. And this year, our school launched its first gender-neutral student restrooms.

If students are comfortable testing the confines of gender, they will be more capable of thinking outside the box to solve the complex challenges confronting their generation, like global warming and inequality. And isn't this dream of unlimited potential what all teachers wish for their students?

Bec Young

Of Mice and Marginalization

By Michelle Kenney

Michelle Kenney teaches language arts at Madison High School in Portland, Oregon.

"What novels will you study?" It was Back to School Night at Madison High School in Portland, Oregon. My old job at Marshall High was over. After an emotional year of contentious debate, protests, and tears, the district had finally done it. They closed the building and the students were farmed out to other schools. I received a position at nearby Madison.

"And what exactly is *A Long Way Gone*?" Meredith's mother peered at me over her copy of my syllabus. Like many of the parents at Madison's Back to School Night, Meredith's mother was white, middle class, and well educated.

Back at Marshall, where many parents were bogged down by making ends meet and other obligations, we were lucky to see a handful of parents show up at Back to School Night. At Madison the room was packed. I wasn't used to this kind of crowd.

"*A Long Way Gone* is a memoir of a boy's experience as a child slave during the civil war in Sierra Leone," I explained, trying to project an aura of professional self-confidence. It was difficult to maintain since my room was still in a state of chaos from the move. Every corner was stuffed with boxes. "It's a part of my commitment to incorporate social justice themes throughout my curriculum. I've actually had a lot of success teaching this book as part of my unit on the International Rights of the Child."

"It sounds a little violent to me."

"It doesn't sound like it would challenge my daughter at all. Will this prepare her for an AP class?"

"We read *Lord of the Flies* in 10th grade. Can you teach *Lord of the Flies*?"

"Well, to tell the truth, I don't really like *Lord of the Flies*. It's overly pessimistic about human nature, and all of the characters are—"

"*Lord of the Flies* was the best book I ever read," Meredith's mother interrupted, looking at me steadily.

I tried to mentally gird my loins for a good fight to defend my curriculum. In Portland, high school English teachers have a great deal of choice in designing our own units. At my previous school, we enjoyed substantial autonomy, and many of us used it to collaborate on multicultural units around issues of race and social justice. Instead of teaching our diverse student body canonic books like *Lord of the Flies* or *The Old Man and the Sea*, stories written by white men about male relationships, I created challenging units on food and civil rights. After the earthquake in Haiti, I collaborated with colleagues on a unit around Haitian history. As a result, my students read books that weren't necessarily on the usual core books list. They read *Fast Food Nation* and *Alligator Bayou*. They read *Fences* and *Always Running* and *Mountains Beyond Mountains*. They did not read *Lord of the Flies*.

All of this I should have explained to Meredith's mother. But instead of fighting the good fight, I gave in to pressure and nerves, and I caved.

"On the other hand," I continued, "if a lot of my students have already read *A Long Way Gone*, I could always substitute another reading. I could always teach. . ." My mind searched for an alternative that would please the crowd and not compromise my principles too much.

"Why not *The Old Man and the Sea*?" someone suggested. Heads nodded across the room.

"Actually, I was thinking about trying *Of Mice and Men*." The words came out in a desperate squeak—I still have no clue where I got the idea, except for a dim memory of reading it in 10th grade myself. But it did the trick. The atmosphere in the room lightened immediately. Folks were smiling, the bell rang, and the crowd went home.

The next day, I re-read John Steinbeck's *Of Mice and Men* and fell in love. It was a beautiful read, one of those classic novels that bring a smile to people's faces whenever they hear the title mentioned. No wonder the parents at Back to School Night had approved. I couldn't put it down, and I couldn't wait to teach it. So many things made this book perfect for a 10th-grade classroom. First of all, it was easy and short. There would be none of the groans I used to hear about longer, more difficult texts. Plus, it was engaging. The characters were vividly drawn, and the plot was simple but interesting. The themes of friendship, loneliness, and the cruel nature of the world were clear and readily accessible to adolescents. Also—and to my relief—the novel contained unmistakable social justice themes: the oppression of the poor and the weak in a capitalist economy; the way that racism and sexism weaken and erode the characters. Crooks, the African American stable hand, and Curley's wife, a neglected and abused woman, are characters with spirits so beaten down that, instead of fighting back against their oppressors, they can only fight each other. It was perfect. In fact, you couldn't order up a novel more suited to introduce literary terms, character development, foreshadowing, theme, setting, mood, the school of naturalism. And yes, I cried at the end, just like I did in high school.

> I was teaching on the instructional equivalent of cruise control for the first time in 12 years, and it was fun.

I let myself be seduced by my new Steinbeck unit. I couldn't have been happier, even though I had to keep it a secret from a couple of colleagues at other schools who never taught *Of Mice and Men* because "the only woman in that book is a dead woman."

Many of my students thought it was the best book they had ever read. My classes worked on chapter questions and theme posters and literary essays. In a departure from my usual habit of writing all of my materials by myself (or using a trusted colleague's curriculum), I blithely printed off worksheets from the plethora of materials available online and in my district. I told myself that I deserved the break. What my colleagues didn't know wouldn't hurt them.

I was teaching on the instructional equivalent of cruise control for the first time in 12 years, and it was fun. To tell the truth, back at Marshall, the social justice angle had occasionally been a hard sell: "Why are we studying Haiti? This isn't a social studies class." "Why do we always read so much about Black people?" "Who cares about high fructose corn syrup?" "Why can't you just give us worksheets like our English teacher last year?" For many of my students, reading *Of Mice and Men* was an expected 10th-grade rite of passage. Their parents and older siblings had read it, so no one was complaining.

"She Was Sort of a Slut"

But when we were three chapters into the novel, a lot of my Latina/o students—mostly girls—stopped coming to class. I coaxed many of them back, but could never persuade more than a few to read the book. "What's the matter?" I would ask. "Is it hard?"

"No, it's not hard," Marisol told me. "I'm just not that into it, I guess."

I also noticed that my African American students' interest was dropping off. We had started the year reading and writing poetry and short stories that celebrated all of the students' backgrounds and identities. My African American students enthusiastically participated in every activity; they produced and performed work that earned them the highest grades in the class. But as we got into *Of Mice and Men*, their interest flagged. "Is it the use of the n-word?" I asked Terrell, who hadn't been to class in two weeks. Before reading the book, we had discussed the history of the n-word, watched footage of the NAACP's symbolic funeral for the word in Detroit, debated its use in rap music, and agreed as a class that, although it was important to understand the historical context for the use of the n-word, we would not read it out loud or use it in class.

"No, I just don't like Crooks. He's a weird guy."

"Is it the violence, the murder of Curley's wife?" I asked Katie, who had been hiding a small graphic novel inside her copy of the novel during class reading time.

"No, I don't like her anyway," Katie replied.

"Don't you feel a little sorry for her, though?" I asked. "Back in those days, women were so dependent on men for support. Her only power is in her sexuality, maybe her race. We talked about what the times were like back then."

"I think we understand that it was a sexist time, Ms. Kenney," Meredith interjected. "But she was sort of a slut."

I re-read the book over the weekend, and I had to agree with Katie. I didn't like Curley's wife much, either, even after Lennie kills her. Despite understanding her situation, despite knowing the sexism of the times, the tears that my students and I shed at the end of the book were not over the murder of the only female character, but over the demise of the male friendship Steinbeck so lovingly developed throughout the novel.

The more I thought about it, the more I realized that the problem with *Of Mice and Men* wasn't limited to the fact that the only woman is a dead woman. The only woman in the book was one of the least sympathetic characters: a dimwitted, spiteful femme fatale who takes delight in using her looks to manipulate men, particularly vulnerable men like Lennie.

No one could argue that her murder isn't wrong. Nevertheless, it is "sort of accidental," as some students noted, and everyone's sympathy ends up with Lennie and George, two buddies who have been together through thick and thin, only to be brought down in the end by a woman. No wonder some of the girls weren't enthusiastic about *Of Mice and Men*.

The corrupting influence of women on men is a theme that creeps into many high school reading lists. There are many offenders, titles that I'd successfully minimized in my teaching, including Arthur Miller's plays *The Crucible* and *Death of a Salesman*, and Ken Kesey's novel *One Flew Over the Cuckoo's Nest*. In Miller's plays, women are rarely portrayed as anything but passive wives or destructive sluts. Kesey's most well-known work similarly portrays women, like the infamous Nurse Ratched, as predators bent on destroying men's spirits. In discussions, many of my colleagues downplayed the sexism, argued that the female roles are metaphors, or insisted that the other themes in these novels and plays have so much socially redeeming value they are still worth teaching. After all, Arthur Miller takes on McCarthyism in *The Crucible*, the myth of the American Dream in *Death of a Salesman*. These are classics of American literature, classroom staples, and indispensable texts for many high school English teachers. Who was I to even suggest that we stop teaching them?

When Students Check Out

I realized that I was also doing an injustice to my African American students. Although Steinbeck certainly acknowledges the racism of the times, his one African American character, the stable hand Crooks, is so embittered by racism, so disempowered, physically twisted, and miserable that he is incapable of fighting back against the society that keeps him down. An adult reader might see Crooks as a symbol of the destructive effects of racism; most of my 10th-grade students, still struggling with the concept of metaphor, see a pathetic, embarrassing character with few redeeming qualities and no means to fight back.

But I didn't understand this right away, and I finished more than one school day frustrated by the change in behavior I noticed. African American kids who previously led class discussions decided to check out. They stopped reading and complained that the novel was boring. Eyes glazed over with teenage ennui while thumbs got busy texting under desktops. A surge of extended trips to the bathroom left my two hall passes missing or in shreds. Heads were down on desks. Small groups loitered in the hall until an administrator brought them back to my room or sent them to the office. Even though I knew these kids and had seen the amazing work they could do, it was easy to interpret the texting and side conversations as defiance, and very hard to resist writing referrals and sending kids to the dean.

It wasn't until the end of the unit that I asked myself if the African American students' behavior wasn't a clear signal that something was wrong with my teaching. I started to realize that the behaviors that I had interpreted as apathy or just downright naughtiness—the attendance issues, the lack of engagement—were a more conscious refusal to engage in a novel and curriculum that didn't speak to them. If Crooks, the only African American character in the book, lacked the ability to fight back for himself, these kids were more than ready to act on his behalf by texting, napping, or hijacking my bathroom passes and voting with their feet.

Finally, the unit was over and I sat down to grade essays. The assignment was to explore a theme in the novel, a typical 10th-grade essay. Normally, I love reading student papers, but these nearly put me to sleep. My progress grading them slowed to a death march because I needed so many breaks between essays to work up the courage to return. The writing was skimpy and dry, as if my students had treated this as just another academic hoop to jump through. Plus, I realized that five essays out of 75 contained whole sections lifted from the internet, something that had rarely happened to me before.

After a little detective work and a few tough conversations, I came to the conclusion that plagiarism is just what happens when you open a can of curriculum and assign 60 15-year-olds a generic essay subject. What did I expect? The internet is not only a great place for teachers to mooch free lesson plans; it's also a great place for students to find trite essays on *Of Mice and Men*, *The Crucible*, or any other reading in the high school canon. It was too tempting to copy and paste. Before the essays came in, I felt guilty about marginalizing the girls and African American students, but the uninspired writing I got about *Of Mice and Men* convinced me that this unit had done a disservice to all of my students. I learned my lesson and decided to move on.

A Raisin in the Sun

Our next reading was *A Raisin in the Sun*, Lorraine Hansberry's famous play about an African American family struggling against racism and poverty in the 1940s. I chose it partially because it is a play often read in high school, one I knew parents would accept. I also chose it because Hansberry, an African American woman, shapes her characters and their conflicts in a way that I believed my students could relate to. In *A Raisin in the Sun*, the characters confront many of the same obstacles as Crooks and Curley's wife, but they are drawn as complex people and they respond very differently to their circumstances. For example, Beneatha, the daughter in the family, is a strong, bright, optimistic girl determined to become a doctor, despite the odds against her as an African American and a woman. Instead of succumbing to the racism and sexism prevalent in her day, Beneatha fights back.

Right away, I noticed that this agency on the part of the character opened up possibilities for my curriculum. Not only were we discussing racism, we were discussing resistance. As the characters developed, there were more questions to ask and answer, more discussions to have, more writing to do, more connections to make to my students' lives, and to the history and demographics of our own city, Portland, once notorious for keeping African Americans in certain neighborhoods and out of others.

The students who had tuned out the Steinbeck novel perked up. Everyone was eager to listen to the play and read it out loud. This time, instead of assigning essay topics, I had the students keep dialogue journals following a theme or character of interest. I let them choose their own topics to write about based on their notes and commentary.

The corrupting influence of women on men is a theme that creeps into many high school reading lists.

The essays I received at the end of the unit were a far cry from the previous batch. This time students of all races and ethnicities were performing to a higher standard than before, instead of jumping through hoops to get a grade. They wrote about *A Raisin in the Sun* with the passion, depth, and the intensity that was missing from the previous essays. They wrote about Beneatha's struggle to overcome the stereotypes holding her back, about Walter's dream of going into business, about Mama's steadfast love and support for her family and their dreams. They saw that, although these characters were facing many of the same roadblocks as Curley's wife and Crooks, they were fighting back with the courage and dignity Steinbeck's two-dimensional characters lacked. My students understood the weaknesses of this all-too-human family—Walter's gullibility, Beneatha's temper—but admired their struggles and found many parallels between the characters' experiences and their own.

At the beginning of the next school year, I confronted the dilemma I had been avoiding for nine months: Do I teach books that a narrow but vocal segment of the community promotes, or do I return to teaching equally challenging novels, plays, poems, and nonfiction works that speak to all students in terms of the themes and characters they introduce? I began the year prepared to have conversations about the suitability of the literature some parents expect to see on my syllabus. I decided to trust myself, my education, and my own experiences when making critical decisions about what will work for everyone in our increasingly diverse school, not just those whose parents are able to show up for Back to School Night.

Alaura Seidl

Elbow Is Not a Sexy Word
Approaches to sex education

BY JODY SOKOLOWER

Jody Sokolower is a political activist, teacher, writer, and editor. She is the managing editor at Rethinking Schools. Thanks to Anne Peacock, who introduced her to several of the activities in this article, and to the original team of Identity and Ethnic Studies teachers at Berkeley High.

"We're going to start out today with a contest," I told my 9th-grade students at the beginning of our unit on sex education. I put them in groups of four or five, and had each group divide a piece of paper into four large rectangles.

"I'm going to give you four words," I explained, "one at a time. You'll have two minutes to come up with as many synonyms—as many words that mean the same thing—as you can. They can be in English or any other language; they can be nice words or not-nice words. Anything goes. The group that comes up with the most synonyms wins. Got it?"

Once everyone was clear and each group had a scribe with pen in hand, we started.

"The first word is *penis*."

After a few seconds of shocked silence and then giggles, the groups got busy. I walked around, encouraging individuals and groups that were having trouble getting past their shyness or embarrassment. "How do you say *penis* in Urdu?" I asked one group. "What did your family call penises when you were little?" I asked another.

At about two minutes, I told everyone to stop. "How many did you get?" I asked. "Who wants to read their list?"

Then we moved on to the next rectangle. "Are you ready for another? The next word is *breast*."

We repeated the process and then moved on to the third word: *vagina*.

After the groups spent two minutes on vagina, I said: "Are you ready? Here's the last word: *elbow*."

It took a little while for the students to realize how few words there are for elbow. Some groups wrote elbow in another language or two, but that was about it. One group broke into laughter as they realized they had skidded to a halt.

After finding out how many words the groups had for each square and asking for volunteers to read their lists, we moved to some broader questions. "Look at your lists," I said. "What do you notice?"

"There are lots of words for breast, penis, and vagina, but hardly any for elbow."

"Why do you think that is?" I asked.

"Because people like to talk about sex?"

"Because our society is kind of obsessed with that stuff?"

"Because elbows are boring!"

"A lot of the words for breast and vagina are nasty," Sonja said. "Like put-downs of women. The words for penis aren't like that."

"'Wiener' isn't that nice a word," Jeremiah objected.

"No, but it doesn't feel as bad as 'cunt,'" Michael suggested. "Maybe it's the way people use those words."

"Why do you think that might be?" I asked. A few students made connections to the ideas we had discussed during our unit on sexism several months earlier.

Then I asked: "So why do you think I started our sex ed unit with this game?" We spent a few minutes teasing out the goals for the activity: to help them feel comfortable talking about sex in class, to clarify why we would be using clear but neutral terms for body parts and sexual acts, and to inject a little humor to lighten the mood.

Those aren't far off from my goals for this article. It's not a rounded look at our unit. It's just a few ideas for how to approach sex education in ways that are inclusive, sex-positive, and encourage participation and growth.

Building on Community

I was teaching sex education at Berkeley High School in Berkeley, California, in the context of a yearlong Identity and Ethnic Studies class. In the fall, we had worked on building community and completed units on racism, immigration, and sexism. So the students were already experienced at discussing personal and controversial topics with each other. Supportive community is critical for sex education that will empower and enlighten. It was important that we had explored the history and current reality of sexism (including homophobia and transphobia) before we started talking about sex.

I also wanted to make sure that the students were already thinking about their own values. I often taught Erik Erikson's stages of life before we started the sex education part of the curriculum. Although Erikson was homophobic and that's reflected in his writings, I have found his description of the challenges at each life stage helpful to adolescents. I discussed each stage with the class, then had them make drawings or create written or acted vignettes to show that they understood each.

According to Erikson, the developmental challenge for teenagers is identity vs. confusion. That provided a chance for me to talk about this as a time in their lives to think about their own values as distinct from those they grew up with in family and community. I see acting consciously on your own values as central to sex ed and returned to it at many points during the unit.

I also distributed an opt-out permission slip for students to take home to their parents—according to district policy, parents could ask that their students not participate in the sex education curriculum. I never had a parent send back the form. One year a student told me he wasn't comfortable learning about sex in a mixed-gender classroom; he and I arranged an alternative program for him on those days and he went to the library.

"How do you say *penis* in Urdu?"

After the synonyms game, I laid the groundwork for the unit by teaching the anatomy and physiology of sex, starting with female bodies and then moving on to male bodies. Before we started, I briefly reviewed the difference between anatomy and gender. We were going to be reviewing sexual anatomy, which is not necessarily the same as how individuals define their gender.

I distributed blank outlines of female sexual and reproductive organs, handed out colored pencils, projected the outline onto the whiteboard, and dimmed the lights. Then, starting with the ovaries and working our way through to the clitoris, we labeled, colored, and described the function of each organ. I welcomed and answered questions. Along the way, I added details that paved the way for later discussions of birth control and safer sex. I explained the menstrual cycle and its implications for fertility. I talked about routine gynecological visits and preventive healthcare. Something about the dim lights and coloring in an outline makes students more relaxed; they ask questions that wouldn't come up in other situations.

When I got to the external sex organs, I said: "You know, guys know what their sex organs look like just by looking down. For women, it's a little harder, but it's something you want to know. So pick a day when you have some privacy at your home, grab a mirror, lock the door to your bedroom or bathroom, and take a look at yourself." This was greeted by giggles and groans. "Just think about it," I added. "We want people we're intimate with to know, love, and respect us and our bodies. That starts with knowing, loving, and respecting ourselves." Then I moved on. I was just planting the seed of an idea.

The next day, we did the same with male anatomy. Once again, I laid groundwork for an understanding of birth control and safer sex. For example, when we looked at the vasa deferentia, we talked about the difference between sperm and ejaculate. I explained what a vasectomy does and we talked about why that was a decision a male probably wouldn't make until later in his reproductive life. "What questions would you ask yourself," I said, "before you would decide to have a vasectomy? Why might you decide that was a good idea? Why might you decide it was a bad idea?"

At the end of the male anatomy lesson, I showed the segment "What Happens During Ejaculation" from Woody Allen's 1972 movie *Everything You Always Wanted to Know About Sex (But Were Afraid to Ask)*. It's a fantasy of what's happening at "command central" during a sexual encounter. It's funny, but pretty accurate, so it makes kids laugh but also reinforces their understanding.

Journaling

I had students write almost every day in their journals to ensure that they were reflecting on what we were discussing. I wanted to stay in close touch with what they were thinking and feeling. By this point in the year, my students had lots of experience with journaling. When I first introduce journals in the fall, I explain that they can always fold a page over if they don't want me to read a particular entry because it's too personal. I also explain that if their journal reveals that they might be hurting or thinking about hurting themselves or others, or if they are being hurt by someone, I have to do something about it, but I'll always talk to them first.

Here are a few examples of prompts that I used during the sex ed unit:

- When did you first learn about sex? Who told you? What did they say? What were your first reactions?
- What experience have you had with sex ed—at school, at home, elsewhere? What happened? What were your thoughts and feelings about it?
- What are the rules in your family about "going out" or dating? What rules do you agree with? What rules don't you agree with?

- How do you think teenagers should decide whether they want to be sexually intimate with someone they like or love? What questions should they ask themselves? What should they talk about with their partner?

We usually did journal writing in the beginning of class as an opener for the day's lesson. I would read and explain the prompt, then give students 10–15 minutes to write. If most students were still writing, I would give extra time. If students stopped writing and turned to other things after five minutes, I would repeat my standard mantra about journal writing: "When you think you're done writing, when you put down your pen and start looking around at everyone else, twiddle your thumbs for awhile, and then pick up the pen and start writing again—that's the real journaling. The heart of journal writing is when you go deep under what's on the surface, what you write after you think you're done."

After I'd given everyone a two-minute warning and asked them to finish up, I'd ask if anyone wanted to share or talk about what they'd written. I've almost never had a class where at least some students weren't eager to break the ice and share what they wrote.

Talking About Sex

Berkeley has a sex education program that starts in elementary school. By the time students get to 9th grade, there are usually volunteers ready to demonstrate how a condom goes on a model penis. At the high school, there is a peer education project that operates out of the health center. Peer educators have a planned curriculum in which they show and discuss various forms of birth control and safer sex protection. That made my job much easier.

To prepare for their visit, I opened up a discussion of birth control and safer sex. "Birth control is just about pregnancy," I explained. "Its only goal is keeping sperm from meeting up with an egg until the right time in everyone's lives for having a baby. Safer sex, on the other hand, is about preventing the spread of sexually transmitted diseases in addition to preventing pregnancy. For example, let's start with birth control pills. What do they do?"

"Girls take them. But if you forget, you get pregnant. That's what happened to my cousin," Lila said.

"That's right. Birth control pills change the environment in the uterus so that even if an egg is fertilized it won't nest in the uterus and begin to grow. So birth control pills, just like their name says, work as birth control. Do they work as safer sex? Do they protect you from sexually transmitted infections (STIs) like gonorrhea or HIV?"

"No," a chorus of students responded. They explained that you need a physical barrier—a condom or a dental dam—to prevent STIs.

"What about if two males are having sex?" I asked. "What about two females?"

The next day, the peer educators had a series of games that reinforced the differences between safer sex and birth control. They had a volunteer demonstrate how to use a condom and explained how students could get condoms at the health center (which has its own sex education process). They split the students into roving small groups so they could see different kinds of birth control and ask questions. After the peer education presentation, I reviewed what we had learned and asked for questions again.

The mechanics of safer sex and contraception are useless without communication. Talking about safer sex is difficult for all of us, and especially for youth. I wanted to make the point that communication is at the center of relationships, and that communicating about safer sex is a subset of this. So I had students do another activity. I asked them to brainstorm all the things you might want to do with someone you feel attracted to. I threw out a few ideas to get things rolling: compliment them on their clothes, text them, have oral sex, bake them a cake, hold hands. Soon students were calling out ideas from all over the room. I wrote them all on the board in no particular order. In general, I keep an eye out to make sure that our list is LGBTQ-inclusive. If students are shy to name "anal sex" or "intercourse," I'll say it. On the other hand, if there aren't lots of lighter options like "going to the movies" or "kissing," I'll suggest those.

Once the board was covered with ideas, I counted them and wrote the number—31—on the board. I reminded students that we had used continuums frequently over the course of the year. "So what is a continuum?" I prompted.

"It's putting things on a line from the least to the most," someone volunteered.

Some students talked about the contradiction between what they have heard at church or at home— that abortion is murder—and what they actually think would be the right thing to do.

"Exactly. Now take a piece of paper and turn it sideways. Draw a long line all the way across the paper. Label the left end 'least intimate' and the right end 'most intimate.' Now look at all the ideas on the board. Think about how well you would need to know someone, how close you would need to feel to them, to want to do each one. Then write the ideas on the line in the order of how you feel about them in terms of intimacy. For example, for me, if I liked someone but didn't know them very well and I wanted to start flirting, I might say I liked their clothes. I'm going to put that first. Write the ideas sideways across the line so you have enough room to fit them all in."

"Once you have all the ideas in order, start numbering them from left to right, No. 1 to No. 31. If there are some ideas you don't think you would ever want to do, just leave them off. And remember, this list is just for you. We're not going to share the lists, and you're not going to turn them in. Just go with how you feel."

When the students had finished putting the ideas on their continuum charts and numbering them, we debriefed. "Can someone tell me," I asked, "what they have for No. 13?"

"Necking," Jesús volunteered.

"Did anyone else have necking for No. 13?" A few hands went up.

"Anyone want to volunteer something else they have for 13?"

"Meeting my parents."

"Oral sex."

"Going to the movies."

"Could someone tell me one thing they have for one of the last three numbers?" I asked.

I was careful not to push anyone to share more than they wanted to, but soon we had amassed enough information for the students to realize how different their lists were. I said: "Wow, from what you all have volunteered, it's clear that your continuums are really different. For example, take oral sex. For some of you, that's something that takes a lot of intimacy. You probably wouldn't want to have oral sex with someone until you had been in a relationship for a while and had built up a lot of trust. For other people, it's no big deal."

"So what does that mean? If you feel attracted to someone, how are you going to know what they want to do, and what will make them feel like running in the opposite direction?"

"I guess you have to talk them."

"This is weird. I had no idea it would be so different."

"Can't you just kind of tell what a girl wants?"

I used this activity as the entry point for lots of discussion and role playing: What kind of problems could you run into if you make assumptions about what someone wants to do sexually? What constitutes "consent?" What does that look like? How does it sound? How might you talk about taking the next step? How might you talk about safer sex?

Then, I started our unit on pregnancy with a journal entry:

> Imagine that you find out that you or your partner is pregnant. What is your first reaction? How do you feel? Who would you talk with about it? Who wouldn't you tell? What do you think you might do?

We explored the options—abortion, adoption, and raising the child—working in small groups to generate possible advantages and disadvantages for each path. In their journals and in class discussion, some students talked about the contradiction between what they have heard at church or at home—that abortion is murder—and what they actually think would be the right thing to do. I tried to create space for them to think about the difference between what their church and/or community might say, and what they might feel and need in that situation. I included quotes from a range of youth who decided to have abortions, those who are raising their children, and those who decided to have their babies placed for adoption.

The historical and political context often gets ignored in sex education classes, and this is something that I try to include in one way or another. In some classes, we have spent a week or two studying the history of reproductive rights, including the videos *When Abortion Was Illegal* and *If These Walls Could Talk*. Angela Davis' seminal book *Women, Race, & Class* has an excellent section on the racist contradictions of the early reproductive health movement.

I always teach basic information about HIV/AIDS, but some years I expand that to study the history of the epidemic (watching *And the Band Played On* and/or *Philadelphia*), explore the science, research the impact of HIV/AIDS in Africa and other parts of the world, invite someone living with HIV to the class, and so on.

What Will Fly at My School?

Not every school has a health center with a program for educating students about condoms and making them available. Not every school has peer educators. In some schools, an open discussion about the advantages and disadvantages of having an abortion could get you fired.

I understand, and I realize that many of these activities might have to be modified depending on the school climate. But I believe that the basic principles can be successfully adapted to many situations. The first is building a classroom community where students feel safe exploring their own developing thoughts and feelings, in journal writing and class discussions. It is also helpful to lay groundwork by studying sexism and homophobia earlier in the year. That could take the form of critiquing popular culture for views on women and gay people, focusing on women's history and/or literature, talking about recent changes in laws and popular ideas about gay marriage, and so on. I don't want the first time I talk about sexism to be in the context of a discussion of what constitutes consent, or the first time I mention lesbians to be in the context of dental dams. Then, I think the watchwords for building a unit are: include lots of information, perspectives, and youth voice; be careful not to make judgments; and approach sexuality as part of the joy of life.

Finally, this is a fairly new and rapidly developing field. How I teach sex ed—particularly in terms of trans inclusion and not assuming a gender binary—has changed a lot in the past decade or so. So I try to keep my ears, my heart, and my mind open.

Teaching Sex Positivity
An interview with Lena Solow

By Annika Butler-Wall

Lena Solow is the sex education program coordinator for Just Ask Me (JAM), a peer education program at the Women's Housing and Economic Development Corporation in the Bronx, New York.

Annika Butler-Wall is an editor of *Rethinking Sexism, Gender, and Sexuality* and an editorial intern at Rethinking Schools.

Annika Butler-Wall: How did you get involved in sex education?

Lena Solow: I've been doing sex education practically since I came out of the womb. There's a story about me learning what sex was when I was 4 and then telling my younger sister about it really loudly in a public bathroom. I was the one who taught all my friends about puberty.

When I was in high school, I was trained as a peer sex educator at the Young Women's Project in Washington, D.C. I continued this work at Wesleyan University, where I was the director of a program that taught sex education workshops at local high schools. I was a dance major at Wesleyan, and I think the messages of dance and sex education are similar: celebrating our bodies, being comfortable and empowered in our bodies, and working together to make something beautiful.

Now, at Just Ask Me (JAM) I have a team of high school students who I work with and train, and then they teach a comprehensive sex education curriculum to middle schoolers in an after-school program.

ABW: What does sex positive education mean to you?

LS: A sex-positive education means coming at conversations about sex, sexuality, gender, and bodies in ways that affirm and celebrate a variety of bodies, relationships, types of sex, and ways of feeling about sex. It's about sharing honest and complete information. It's understanding that many variations exist in the world and going beyond "let's not judge" to "let's celebrate!"

Sex positivity is bringing a sense of the possibility of joy and pleasure to sex and sexuality. Sometimes that makes people anxious, especially when we're talking about younger teens. But the truth is that youth are exposed to violent images of sexuality all the time—they hear stories about rape, they see *Law and Order: Special Victims Unit*. But they often don't have examples of what it means to have a good sexual experience. All sexual activities should be consensual and pleasurable. It's empowering and exciting to give young folks that perspective.

> Youth are exposed to violent images of sexuality all the time, but they often don't have examples of what a good sexual experience looks like.

I was having a conversation with some 7th graders about sexual assault and they were asking a lot of victim-blaming questions: "Was she drinking?" "What if they were making out before they went up to the bedroom?" "Why did she take off her pants in the bedroom?" Of course, partly they were saying: "Well, it was her fault. She was asking for it." But they were also asking: "What does it look like to have a consensual sexual experience? No one has ever told me what that would be like." All they know are stereotypes like "girls say 'no' when they mean 'yes.'" They need to see and talk about alternatives, see and talk about positive sexual experiences.

In practice, this means talking about a variety of sexual activities. If you tell a middle school class what a blow job is, people get upset. But the truth is, when you do sex education in the classic way, you talk explicitly about vaginal intercourse because you're talking about pregnancy. Teachers say, "The pull-out method doesn't work," or "Here's what happens when semen goes into the vagina." But when you want to talk to young people about blow jobs or anal sex or kissing, it freaks people out. And that's because you're talking to teenagers about sex as pleasure.

When you talk about pleasure, you're giving young people a model for what sex is supposed to be like. If you only talk about reproduction, you're also leaving out gay people and the sex they might have. You're leaving out talking about women's and trans people's pleasure, because you're only talking about ejaculation and not about how a person with a vulva might experience pleasure.

Of course, especially in 6th, 7th, and 8th grade, there's such a wide range of experience and comfort levels—from kids who haven't started puberty to those who are having sex. So we tell students: "This is information for your whole life. It may not be relevant right now and it may make you feel weird. That's OK. But we want you to be ready for when it is relevant. That may be tomorrow, it may be in five years, it may be in 10 years, and some of it may never be relevant. But the more you know, the better prepared you'll be."

ABW: Do you talk about the gender binary?

LS: Sex positivity definitely means being inclusive of all genders and sexualities, and not just talking about this on the LGBTQ day. So much of what we hear about gender and the way that sex education is taught assumes that people with a certain gender have certain body parts and certain hormones. It's hard, for example, to find a worksheet for labeling anatomy that says *vulva* as opposed to *female external genitalia*. I actually haven't found one; I made my own.

It's hard to be consistent, but you can't have a lesson in which you explain that everyone's gender is totally valid, the gender you're assigned at birth is not necessarily the same as your gender identity, and there are people who identify as men and have vulvas—and then the next day say, "When a *woman* gets pregnant. . . ." If you do that, you're negating everything you just said and making trans folks invisible. The same is true for sexual orientation. If you have a day when you say, "We love and support gay people and they're great," and then every time you talk about sex you only talk about vaginal intercourse, the message is not that you support gay people and their sexual relationships.

It's taken me a lot of practice to change to more inclusive language, and we talk about it explicitly in our peer education training. Every lesson we ask ourselves: "Are there ways this might not be inclusive? What changes do we need to make?" It's not going to happen by accident—we have too many internalized messages about gender and sexuality. You have to be explicit and careful.

For example, I love using gender-neutral names in scenarios. We will be reading a scenario about consent and the kids will ask, "Jessie and Taylor—wait, which one's the boy, which one's the girl?" Then I'll say, "Well, anyone in the scenario could be any gender." Usually they just say "Oh, OK," because they're focused on the story. We're having a conversation about consent and everyone, no matter their gender, needs to get consent from their partner.

Teaching Enthusiastic Consent

When we talk about consent we're always talking about enthusiastic consent—consent is not just the absence of "no," it's the presence of a really excited "yes!" Getting and giving enthusiastic consent requires communication, and I think sometimes teachers have a hard time talking about communication. We'll tell kids "You need to communicate" and leave it at that, which is not very helpful. I did a workshop the other day, and we had an interesting conversation about how in movies people never talk about or during sex. That makes it hard to imagine what that would be like, so teachers need to give young people the tools to communicate with a partner and to understand what enthusiastic consent looks and sounds like.

This could be reading through scenarios and thinking about what each partner might say to each other. Or it could be examples of things a partner might say and discussing whether or not those things indicate "yes," "no," or "you need to check in."

One reason to have these conversations earlier is that middle schoolers are far more likely to get on board with ideas about enthusiastic consent than high schoolers. By high school, unfortunately, more youth have had messed-up sexual experiences or heard about messed-up sexual experiences, and they tend to normalize them. They say, "Nobody would ever ask 'Hey, how are you feeling?'" because no one has asked them. But when you ask middle schoolers "What would you say to your partner?" they say "Oh, you would just ask if they were OK." They know that you wouldn't want to do something if the other person didn't want to do it. That clicks for them.

Consent is not just the absence of "no," but the presence of a really excited "yes!"

Then we talk about how you get enthusiastic consent and why that might be hard. So, for example, I give everybody a red, yellow, and green piece of paper. Red means stop, green means keep going, and yellow means check in with your partner. Then I read a list of phrases like: "I really like that," "That hurts," "OK, I guess so," "Sure, that's fine," and "I think my parents are going to be home soon." As I read each phrase, students hold up their red, green, or yellow piece of paper. We talk about each answer, and I ask questions: "Why might it be hard for someone to say 'no' directly to their partner?" "If you're not sure if you should keep going, what can you do?"

The next step is talking about checking in. I put up a big sheet of paper titled "Let's Talk" and we brainstorm checking-in phrases: "Are you comfortable?" "Is this OK?" "Can I touch you there?" "I want to do this," "I don't want to do this." Then I'll give them different scenarios. For example: Jesse is in a relationship with Andy; they usually make out when they go on a date, but tonight Andy doesn't feel like it. Or: Alex and Cat are hooking up at a party; they go into a room and Cat starts to take off Alex's pants.

The students' job is to come up with things to say, ways to talk about the situation and make sure they and their partner are on the same page. I ask: "Does taking off someone's pants always mean the same thing?" "Do you ever owe someone a sexual activity?"

ABW: JAM is a peer education program. How does that work?

LS: JAM was started by some young women who said: "Everyone we know is getting pregnant. They don't have information about how not to get pregnant or information about how to avoid sexually transmitted infections (STIs). We have to do something." So it was started by teens and young people are still driving what happens. The high school peer educators are mostly pulled from the middle school program, so everyone is really part of the same community.

I think the model is incredible. Young people are brilliant, and we need to be working with them. Not telling them, "Here's how it's going to happen," but asking, "What do you think kids need to know, what do you have questions about?" As one of my peer educators said, "We can give them straight-up answers, student to student, a luxury that teachers may not have."

Like all teachers, peer educators need good training. We do work on both the content and the facilitation, including a lot of practice facilitation. We'll pretend to be a "bad" class, and they practice facilitating in situations where there are issues or problems.

During the training and once they start teaching, I do a lot of check-ins: "How are you feeling?" "What do you need to understand better?" "What do you need more practice on?" Having them involved in the process of curriculum revision is important, too. For example, we recently revamped our STI lesson. First I asked them: "What are our goals? What are the main things we want kids to know?"

They were very clear: "We want them to know how to stay safe. We want them to know the basic information about STIs: that STIs can be treated, some can be cured, and they can have long-term consequences if you don't deal with them. We want them to know how to get tested and what that is like."

So they created a skit about two friends talking about getting tested. One of them says: "I really want to have sex with my girlfriend, but I'm thinking we should get tested first. I'm worried about it." Then the other friend says: "No, it's totally fine. I'll go with you and here's what it's going to be like. . . ."

They also came up with an idea for a gallery walk. We put poster paper up around the room with statements like: "You can only get an STI if you have a ton of sex" and "Testing is painful." Then participants write suggestions for responses on each poster.

During the training we have big-picture conversations. One day we had an intense and challenging talk about rape culture. To decompress from that difficult conversation, we brainstormed how we visualize an ideal sexual situation. We created a beautiful list: Everyone communicates. Everyone feels good. Everyone's pleasures are valued equally. No one is judgmental about anyone's body.

Then we talked about what we need from the world to make that possible. The students mentioned access to healthcare, conversations about sex and sexuality without blaming, valuing all different types of relationships. So, we said, this is what we're working toward.

It's important to have conversations about what we can imagine, what we are excited about, and what kind of world we are trying to build. It's easy to get focused on the problems: "You might get syphilis," or "You might get pregnant," or "Everyone bullies gay people." It can get very negative. It's important to teach sex ed in a positive way and make space for conversations that young people aren't having anywhere else.

ABW: How does race come into the conversation?

LS: Often people think that sex education is somehow separate from race—that we can remove race from the conversation. But it's important that we understand how white supremacy impacts every part of our lives, including sex education. This means, especially for me as a white sex educator, looking to sex educators of color for guidance. It also means understanding how our own attitudes about race may be coming into play in the classroom. For example, are we assuming that certain communities are more likely to be homophobic or less likely to be able to avoid unwanted pregnancy? We need to challenge those assumptions.

> A reproductive justice framework says that you have the right to have and parent children in a world where they're going to be safe from harm.

We also need to be thinking about reproductive justice as opposed to reproductive rights or "a woman's right to choose." In 1994, a group of women of color who formed the SisterSong Collective coined the phrase "reproductive justice" to reference a framework for what it means to have a world that is safe and healthy for everyone (not just white people) to have reproductive freedom. Often when we talk about reproductive rights we mean the right to birth control, the right to abortion. That is obviously important, but for women of color, there's a long and horrifying history of forced sterilization that we need to include in the picture. A reproductive justice framework says that you have the right to have and parent children in a world where they're going to be safe from harm. In that context, we have to talk about the connection between reproductive rights and racism, police violence, economic injustice, healthcare, the criminal justice system, and all the other factors that get in the way of people having children when and how they want to.

ABW: How do you teach about HIV/AIDS from a sex positive outlook?

LS: It's about setting the groundwork. If the first time you bring up gay people is when you talk about HIV, that's a problem. If the first time you bring up anal sex is when you talk about HIV, that's also a problem. So I make sure that, long before we get to HIV, we've had conversations about gender identities and sexualities, we've had conversations about different sexual activities and the reasons why people might engage in them. So learning about HIV becomes more information in a larger context.

In terms of sexual transmission of HIV, a lot of the stigma is based on assumptions about the kind of sex gay men are having and stigma about anal sex. The first time you say "anal sex," kids are going to say "ewww!" That just happens. So I don't wait until the HIV day to say, "No, no, we're not judging." As soon as "ewww" happens, I say: "Hey, listen, here's the thing about sexual activities—you don't have to be into any specific sexual activity. That's totally fine, everybody has different ideas and boundaries. But we're not going to judge what anybody is interested in or make comments about certain activities, because you wouldn't want anyone to say something about what you're interested in."

For right now, I teach HIV and other STIs in the same lesson. I'll tell a 7th- or 8th-grade class: "OK, we're going to be talking about sex so let's get a big list of sexual activities up on the board." I make sure there's a wide range of things, from masturbation to kissing to oral sex—we're always normalizing the different ways that people may choose to be with each other's bodies. Then I ask them to make a list of reasons why people may or may not engage in certain sexual activities. We come up with reasons like culture, comfort with your partner, protection, health, pleasure. It's important to establish that risk for STIs is just one of the many reasons people may choose not to engage in a given sexual activity. Then we have time for individual reflection about boundary setting, with an understanding that those boundaries may change at any time.

> No one thinks that telling kids to wear their seat belts makes them more likely to get in a car crash.

Then we talk about which of the activities are higher and lower risk for specific STIs, and how to make an activity lower risk (by using barriers).

We also talk about getting tested for HIV and other STIs. We discuss why it can be challenging to get tested, and what is involved in the various tests. We have a list of nearby clinics. In New York City, testing is free and confidential. If it's not free and confidential for young people, it's much more complicated

Kristina Brown

because teens don't want their parents to know and they often don't have money to pay for it.

I'd like to go into more depth around HIV/AIDS. I'd start with the historical context, including the racism and the homophobia in the government's response to the rising epidemic in the 1980s and '90s. We'd look at the activism of ACT-UP and other organizations. I'd want to talk about HIV/AIDS internationally, and why some people have access to antiretroviral drugs to manage their HIV/AIDS and others don't.

ABW: Have you experienced administrative or parental backlash?

LS: I've had some. One way to address it is to explain that sex education is education for life—we don't suddenly learn at age 18 how to stay safe, how our bodies work, how to communicate with a partner, so we need to get this information earlier, hopefully before it's necessary.

I like to use driving as an example. We teach kids that driving is a positive thing, it can make you more independent. But it's also potentially dangerous, so you need to obey the speed limit, you need to wear your seat belt, and you need to pay attention to other drivers, pedestrians, and bike riders around you. No one thinks that telling kids to wear their seat belts makes them more likely to get in a car crash. Giving people information to be safe doesn't make them do unsafe things.

I also tell parents and schools that I really believe that a sex-positive model for sex education is the most effective way to ensure that young people have the tools and knowledge they need to have happy and healthy sexual lives. My goal is not to stop young people from doing any sexual activities; my goal is that they only do things they want to do, when they feel comfortable and excited about doing them, in a safe way. An abstinence-only model says, "Sit on either end of the couch and never touch each other." Even a fear-based comprehensive model says: "If you have sex, you're probably going to get an STI or get pregnant. But, if you insist, at least use condoms." A sex-positive model says: "OK, maybe you want to have intercourse. If both of you want to, that's totally fine, and here are conversations you might want to have with your partner about it, here's how to use protection effectively, here's how to keep communicating. But if don't or you're not sure, there are lots of other things you can do that might be exciting and fun." If you're a horny teenager, that resonates with your life a lot more than "never touch anyone!"

Sometimes people defend comprehensive sex education by saying, "Kids are going to have sex whether you want them to or not, so we better prepare them." That's true. But thinking about the big picture again, we can also say: "When we talk about sex and sexuality, what do we want for everyone? We want everyone to have information about their bodies. We want everyone to have information about their health. We want everyone to feel empowered to choose pleasurable and consensual sexual activities. So, then, what is the information we need to give young folks to help make that a reality?"

7 Tips for Teaching Sex Ed

By Ericka Hart

Ericka Hart is Black, queer, Sagittarius, cancer warrior, activist, sex educator, and performer. She has taught sex education to elementary-aged youth to adults across New York City for the past seven years. The catalyst for her work in sex education was her service as a Peace Corps volunteer in Ethiopia. She has been featured in *Cosmopolitan* and the *Huffington Post*.

The focus of comprehensive sex education is helping young people choose if they want to be abstinent or have sex, and helping them protect themselves. My touch on comprehensive sex ed is sex positivity—talking to students about what works for their bodies and what feels good for their bodies, no matter what age they are. Is this something you want to do? Is this something you don't want to do? For youth, adding the aspect of pleasure is important because often there's nothing about pleasure in sex education.

Teenagers want to know that they're normal. They don't want things to be secret; they want information out in the open. That's across the board. They are in a period of huge social development, so if their friends are all having sex in certain ways, they are probably going to want to be a part of that. As educators, it's up to us to guide them.

I. Know Who You're Teaching

Research the community and the climate of the school. Ask yourself: Where are the students are coming from? Do they have guardians in their lives? What's happening after school? Often when people work with youth they think "kids are just kids," but it's so much more than that. A group of kids on the Upper East Side might operate very differently from a group of kids in Brooklyn. You have to be responsible to that before you teach.

Sex education tends to get hyper-focused on genitals, sexually transmitted diseases, and pregnancy. Recently people have started having more conversations about consent and healthy relationships. That is important, but we also need to ask: What is the culture of the community? What do healthy relationships look like for that particular community? How does the community impact how young people are going to operate in their romantic relationships? It's important to bring in all those intersections before you teach a sexuality program so that you can deliver a curriculum that is actually going to work for that particular audience. Of course no teacher is an expert on every community, but it's important to be committed to learning, to be respectful and open-minded, and to listen to your students and their families.

2. Establish Ground Rules

For sensitive subjects like sexuality or sex, it's incredibly important to put in ground rules or group norms for your class, and to have the group agree to them. One of them should be "Don't yuck my yum." One way I like to introduce group norms is by dividing students into groups or pairs and asking them to draw a group norm they want for the space. They present the group norm and then, every week that I return, I bring those pictures so there is a visual reminder of what we agreed to.

3. Address Stereotypes

In terms of race and what is "normal," I hear: "Black people don't do that." As a person of color, I said things like that when I was young, so I can understand where it's coming from. If we're talking about ostracized communities, like LGBTQ communities, and someone says "Black people don't do that" or "Black people are not going to have anal sex," I say: "Wait a minute, you're applying a race or a particular group of people to that behavior and that doesn't make any sense. You've gotten that from somewhere and it's not true."

Many communities, particularly African American communities, have been so sexualized that now there's a protective coat. With sex education, you have to acknowledge that history and its impact. Then it's a matter of talking about what people like and what they don't like. Because you're Black, it doesn't necessarily mean you're not going to enjoy anal sex, or you're not going to enjoy vaginal penetrative sex, or you're not going to be a lesbian. It's just not true that everyone experiences sex in the same way.

4. Be Aware of Your Own Assumptions

If you teach a same-gendered class of female-bodied students who identify as she, you might assume all of them have boyfriends, but that's not necessarily true. You need to be mindful of your assumptions and what you say—maybe some of the students you assume have boyfriends are asexual or queer. Maybe someone in your class who identifies as lesbian has sex with boys. Sexuality is fluid and language around it is ever-changing.

5. Use Gender-Neutral Pronouns

To start out a session, I explain what gender-neutral pronouns are—sometimes I have to explain what a pronoun is. I say: "Generally, you look at someone and then you decide if they are a he or a she, but that is not always true. If you don't use someone's preferred pronoun, that can hurt their feelings." We look at examples of gender-neutral pronouns (e.g., the singular they/their, the person's name instead of a pronoun, zie/zir). Then I ask the students to take out a book and I say: "Read two sentences from this book to your partner only using gender-neutral pronouns."

Sometimes when you ask people their pronouns they can feel outed, so I always invite youth to share their pronouns only if they wish to. I use nametags with names and preferred pronouns to help people remember what to say.

6. Make Space for Questions

In addition to leaving lots of space for questions and discussion in class, every week I ask students to write down whatever they want to ask me about sex and sexuality. I'm queer, so I'll talk about myself. I think it's important in a room of predominately youth of color. I don't always come out, but I think it makes a difference if they have someone to relate to.

7. Keep It Consistent

Reinforcement is huge. I don't know that teachers always acknowledge the difference that we make and the influence that we have. What we say at the front of the room is generally what the student is going to believe. If one teacher says something like "masturbation is a great opportunity for self-love," and then another teacher says "masturbation is wrong," there's a disconnect. The school has to be in alignment with common principles. That's definitely something that teachers should fight for in their schools: guiding principles around gender and sexuality that are based in sex positivity and respect.

Intersectionality: Gender, Race, and the Media
An interview with Liza Gesuden

By Jody Sokolower and Annika Butler-Wall

Liza Gesuden is a second-generation Pinay educator and organizer. She has taught English in Southern California and the Bay Area for the past 13 years, and is currently the lead humanities teacher at California College Preparatory Academy in Richmond, California. Gesuden is co-chair of the People's Education Movement Bay Area. She is pursuing her master's in interdisciplinary education at San Francisco State University.

Jody Sokolower interviewed Gesuden in 2013 about her work at Oakland School for the Arts, a culturally and economically diverse charter school in downtown Oakland, California.

Jody Sokolower: Tell us about your Gender Studies class.

Liza Gesuden: A few years ago, I started teaching Gender Studies, an elective for 11th and 12th graders. It's an introduction to gender, sex, sexuality, and the way we're socialized to understand them in our society.

I do an introductory unit and then I give the students a list of themes and topics, and I let them choose. Last year they chose to focus on pop culture, media, and misrepresentation; violence, prisons and policing; health; and childhood and socialization. This year it's similar, but they're really interested in intersectionality, so we've been talking more about the intersections of race, class, gender, and sexuality.

Intersectionality in the Classroom

JS: What do you mean by intersectionality and how does it come up in class?

LG: Oppressions don't exist in isolation from each other; they're always intermeshed, reinforcing and contradicting each other. That's intersectionality. For instance, we were just talking about the movie *Fruitvale Station*, which is about the murder of Oscar Grant, a young African American man, by a BART policeman here in Oakland. We were talking about gender and masculinity in the movie, but we can't talk about Oscar Grant and his life without talking about him as a Black male.

This was part of our media unit, so we were talking about how important it is for us to have many images of people. Students said the point of *Fruitvale Station* is to humanize Oscar Grant because so often there are polarizing views of Black males in general, and of Grant in particular. He is either villainized—seen as this bad person who was on parole and dealt drugs, and therefore had this coming to him—or portrayed as a saint or a martyr. The film portrays him as a real person, which is not a depiction of Black males that you often see. You see gangsters wearing hoodies or you see people wearing hoodies who you are supposed to assume are gangsters.

After they saw the film, students said, "Oscar's just a regular guy, with his flaws and with his potential." *Fruitvale* resonated for them because you see Grant as someone who had a family. He was someone's son, he was someone's dad, he was someone's significant other. Students talked about the scene with the dog. [In the movie, Grant befriends a stray dog that is killed by a car that doesn't even slow down.] We read an article that said director Ryan Coogler chose a pit bull to symbolize African American men. Pit bulls are seen as vicious and aggressive, which is how African American males are depicted in the media. One student said she saw symbolism in the film when the car drove away as if the driver took no responsibility for what he had done, in the same way that, when Oscar Grant was killed, the BART policeman who shot him got a light sentence and no one took any real responsibility for his death.

JS: What terms do you use in the class and how do you teach them? Do students see words like *intersectionality* or *patriarchy* as relating to their own lives?

LG: The introductory unit focuses on terms, concepts, and definitions, so we develop a working vocabulary early on. For example, we work to understand patriarchy as a system. We talk about the idea of systems, and institutions that are part of systems. When I ask, "Who do you think is in a position of power?" students typically answer, "The government."

Then, because we're an art school, I ask about power in the art world: Who is famous? Who is recognized? Who is an acknowledged leader? The students brainstorm a list, and the overwhelming majority are men. I ask, "Why do you think that is?" Some students say that men have more opportunities. Some say that they work harder. I wait for that comment and then I ask: "Do men work harder than women? Is that your experience when you look at your family, the school, the people you know?"

People often think that gender studies is about women. But patriarchy affects everyone. On a basic level, I talk about it as a system of oppression—a system where men are dominant over women. The boys say, "I don't feel dominant." But then we bring up examples: who's in power, how much money men make compared to women, the media's portrayal of men and women. We look at how patriarchy functions at school and in families.

Once we've established some ideas about patriarchy, we complicate it. How is this power dynamic complicated if you are a woman of color? If you are a lesbian or trans woman? We end up constructing a power pyramid. This is when I introduce the idea of intersectionality. Obama is the most powerful elected leader in the United States. But how does that relate to the lives of the majority of African Americans? And how does the fact that Obama is Black affect how he is portrayed and viewed—by those who support him and by those who oppose him?

We talk about how patriarchy affects young men. Sports is a good way to do that. Men are socialized to be aggressive and want to play sports. But what happens when a group of men who are seen as stronger dominate a group of men who are seen as physically weaker? What does it do to you when you aren't viewed as a strong man? What if you don't like sports or you're not good at them? How is the impact of patriarchy different if you are a heterosexual man or if you're gay? How is it the same?

One activity I did this year to help students think about power and representation was showing white rapper Macklemore's Grammy performance of "Same Love" while Queen Latifah officiated at a wedding ceremony for 33 couples. I asked the students: "What do you see? Who do you see? Who is missing?"

One of the students said: "It's interesting that a straight white, cisgender male is doing this in support of gay people. It's sad, but people will only listen to people who are the same as them. They listen to him because he represents the dominant society. But if no one listens to us when we speak for our own communities, how are we going to create change?"

Teaching Media Literacy

JS: Can you give examples of some of the materials you use? How do you make them accessible to students at different reading levels?

LG: If it's a challenging text, we'll read it together, or I'll have them read it on their own and we'll go over certain parts again in class.

For example, in the media unit we read excerpts from Laura Mulvey's "Visual Pleasure and Narrative Cinema," an important text from the 1970s. Mulvey was one of the first to talk about how movies have trained us to see, particularly how to view women's bodies. The text is college- or graduate-level work. So I excerpt it and then we read it together in class, line by line. I have students annotate what they read. Then students share their notes, and we discuss them, defining words as we go along.

We also look at Chris Hedges' *Empire of Illusion: The End of Literacy and the Triumph of the Spectacle*. I ask the students to read different excerpts in groups; I put one or two people in each group who can help the students who might be struggling. Groups report on their section of the reading and then take notes on what the other students share.

Oppressions are always intermeshed, reinforcing and contradicting each other—that's intersectionality.

In the Hedges text, we look at degradation and humiliation in the media as entertainment, and also the concepts of escapism and voyeurism—how there's this fantasy world that the media tries to create for people and how the media teaches us to value deception and lying. For example, in reality TV shows like *Survivor,* you get points if you can get people to your side by telling lies about other groups. In *The Bachelor* and *The Bachelorette*, contestants hide how they really feel. These are seen as good things.

We read excerpts of Stuart Hall's "Encoding/Decoding" and talk about dominant and resistant readings, and who encodes and decodes. We watch *Miss Representation*, about how women are portrayed in the media and how that impacts their roles in terms of leadership. That's their introduction to the Bechdel Test [invented by feminist cartoonist Alison Bechdel]. A film passes the Bechdel Test if it includes two or more women with names, and they talk to each other about something besides a man. We discuss the test, apply it to a number of examples, and explore what the test reveals about systemic issues in the media.

We also watch the Belgian movie *Ma Vie en Rose*, which students like a lot. The main character, Ludovic, was assigned as a boy at birth but identifies as a girl. His father loses his job and the whole neighborhood blames Ludo for the disruption around him. Students talk about what it means when a community struggles so much to deal with a young child who's just trying to be herself.

We also watch clips from *Hip-Hop: Beyond Beats & Rhymes*, especially the part about misogyny. It's dated but useful for exploring misogyny, homoeroticism, and hip-hop. Other helpful videos include *Invisible War,* about women and rape in the military; *On the Outs,* about three women of color in the juvenile justice system; and *Pariah,* about a young queer woman of color in Brooklyn.

When I teach media literacy, the students are engaged because they're relearning things they already know. They watch and listen to a lot of media—they're well versed in it. It's about giving them tools to deconstruct and understand it so they're not passive viewers anymore, but see things beneath the surface.

JS: How do you view the relationship between course content and building skills?

LG: Sometimes when we think about social justice education, we don't think about skills. It's about content or organizing. Those are important, but I think teaching skills is very much a critical social justice act. We need students to develop skills so they can use those skills to fight all the forms of oppression that they're experiencing.

For example, the final project for the Gender Studies class is a teaching project. It has two stages: First students teach our class, and then they teach 9th graders or 10th graders.

Teaching skills is a critical social justice act.

Before they begin, I write out a lesson plan and teach that lesson so they can see how a lesson plan turns into something that happens in class, how you need a clear sense of what you want the students to achieve. For my sample lesson, I show part of *Orange Is the New Black*, using the focus question: "Is this a positive portrayal of a trans woman in the media, or is it a stereotype?"

Then, working in groups of one, two, or three, students pick topics and develop objectives for their lesson. I tell the students they can take a concept we studied or suggest something new, with my approval. This year, one group's objective was to analyze the depiction of Black women in the media. Another group looked at queer-baiting in the media. Yet another focused on gender roles in *Star Trek*. One student in the *Star Trek* group showed how, despite the fact that women's uniforms in the old *Star Trek* series were more overtly sexy than in the remake, women had stronger roles in the '70s version of the show. She also demonstrated how the Bechdel test could be undermined. She found an episode in which two named women were discussing something other than a man, but the whole time they were talking, they were undressing!

Each group teaches our class a 25-minute lesson. Afterward, we discuss what went well and what they could improve. Then they revise their lesson plans and teach a 45- to 60-minute lesson for a different class. I offer their lessons to my 9th graders as extra credit workshops during finals week—that ensures a willing and cooperative audience. Some groups teach in 10th-grade classrooms.

One student used the Hedges text to talk about moral nihilism in *Bad Girls Club*, a popular reality show that puts a group of women in a house together and turns the camera on. My students pointed out that the women, the "bad girls," are provoked to fight through alcohol and sleep deprivation. The show preys on young women with mental health issues and, when they tear each other apart, it becomes a form of entertainment. Many students questioned why there isn't a bad boys club. When my student taught this lesson to 10th graders, they asked, "Should we stop watching?" My student responded: "We're not telling you not to watch, but think about what this show is doing, think about what you're participating in when you watch it."

Beyond the Classroom

JS: What kind of impact do you think the Gender Studies class has on your students?

LG: One of the biggest changes I see this year is that students are talking to their families about what they're learning. I think the class is very real for students; it's something that they can share with the people in their lives.

I had a student tell me recently about her experience regarding our lesson on preferred gender pronouns. We read a couple of articles, and I told a story about a friend of mine who doesn't use gender pronouns. It was the first time most of the students had thought about this. When this student was talking with her mom about someone's gender presentation, her mom said: "What is that?" Is it a he-she?"

The student was able to talk to her mom about how dehumanizing it was to call someone "that" or "he-she" because you don't know how the person identifies. If you really want to know, she said, you should ask them. She felt empowered to say something, and now she has language to talk about it. Students are being allies to people in the community and sharing their knowledge with people they love in a caring way. I see that as powerful because it's often hardest to talk about these issues with our families.

I also see students teach each other. Ideas can come from me, but the most powerful things happen when they're sharing things with each other or challenging each other. Last year there was a student who sometimes made slightly inappropriate comments, maybe something that others were thinking, but no one else wanted to voice. In a lot of ways, what he said represented the voice of dominant society. When we were talking about harassment, he told us that he had approached a girl on the BART train and told her she was "sexy chocolate"; he said he knew she liked what he was saying to her because she talked to him. As the class listened, one of the women said: "You say you talked to this woman on the BART, but you can't even tell us her name. How can you call her 'sexy chocolate' if you don't even know her name? You're objectifying her." If I had said it, it would have been different.

JS: What would you say to other teachers about teaching subjects like this?

LG: I'm always in a place of learning, too. Sometimes we don't want to teach this kind of class because we don't have all the answers. And there have been moments when I've had to apologize or correct myself. Just recently, I was talking to students about how I wanted to get a boy haircut and the students corrected me: "You mean a pixie cut, because there's no such thing as a boy haircut."

That's a small thing, but I make a lot of mistakes. I want to encourage other teachers to be in that place, too, because we need to do this work. We need to figure out how to do it. It's hard; there are times when I don't know how a class is going to go. That's scary, but there are huge rewards for taking the risks.

Resources

Bechdel, Alison. 1985. "The Rule." *Dykes to Watch Out For* (comic strip). dyke-stowatchoutfor.com/the-rule.

Fruitvale Station. 2013. Dir. Ryan Coogler. Produced by Forest Whitaker.

Hall, Stuart. 1980. "Coding/Decoding." *Culture, Media, Language*. Hutchinson.

Hedges, Chris. 2010. *Empire of Illusion: The End of Literacy and the Triumph of the Spectacle*. Nation Books.

Hip-Hop: Beyond Beats & Rhymes. 2006. Dir. Byron Hurt. Independent Television Services.

Ma Vie en Rose. 1997. Dir. by Alain Berliner. Sony Pictures Classics.

Mulvey, Laura. 1975. "Visual Pleasure and Narrative Cinema," *Screen* 16.3:6–18.

Ricardo Levins Morales

Young Women
in the Movimiento
Chican@ studies after the ban

BY CURTIS ACOSTA, ALANNA CASTRO, AND MARIA TERESA MEJIA

Curtis Acosta is a former Chican@ literature teacher in the Mexican American Studies program in Tucson, Arizona. He now works with teachers throughout the United States with the Acosta Latino Learning Partnership and Xican@ Institute for Teaching and Organizing.

Alanna Castro is currently finishing her bachelor's degree in business administration at Eller College of Management. She was recently recognized as one of the college's Top 50 Hispanic Scholars of the Year. On graduation, she plans to attend graduate school.

Maria Teresa Mejia is in her 4th year at the University of Arizona studying to become a midwife. Her father, mother, and family have inspired her to be an activist and fight for the education of others, regardless of class, race, gender, or sexuality.

Curtis Acosta Speaks:

After the dismantling of Mexican American Studies (MAS) in the public schools of Tucson on Jan. 10, 2012, a group of students and I began meeting on Sunday afternoons at a local youth center to continue our study of Chican@ literature and other voices pushed outside the margins of traditional public school curriculum. We named ourselves Chican@ Literature After School Studies (CLASS). Our meetings centered on student empowerment, education for liberation, and our banned *cultura*, history, and *cuentos*.

Students ranged in age from 15 to 21 years old. Some were alumni of the MAS program; others had been students during the state takeover of our spaces and felt that they were robbed of the experiences of our MAS classes; still others came because they never had the opportunity to take an MAS class.

Once I made the commitment to start a Sunday freedom school and recruited a class of youth, the hard part began. It is one thing to make class in a public high school setting culturally and socially responsive and engaging; it is an entirely different prospect to create an academic space that students are inspired to attend on a Sunday afternoon. Fortunately, through my 18 years of teaching, especially the Latin@ literature classes at Tucson High School (THS), I had developed a plethora of units that our MAS students loved—but I needed to narrow and adapt these to the new teaching context. I decided to bring in the feminist literature that had inspired the most dialogue in my Chican@ literature classes at THS, then add new content focused on gender roles, sexism, and heterosexism in hip-hop.

I had always felt that our Chican@ literature classes were opportunities to heal cultural and social trauma through academically rigorous content. My teaching practices are grounded in rehumanizing academic spaces through indigenous principles such as *In Lak'ech* (you are my other me) and the *Nahui Ollin*, which evoke a sense of empathy, self-reflection, and will to act toward personal and social transformation. I believe it is essential to model awareness of our own human flaws and examine our privilege, starting with my own, as a way to cultivate trust and love in the academic space.

Our Chican@ literature classes were opportunities to heal cultural and social trauma through academically rigorous content.

We read stories by *maestras* Ana Castillo, Sandra Cisneros, and Gloria Anzaldúa, who overtly speak to the sexism, fear, and violence experienced by Chicanas/Latinas both within our own Chican@/Latin@ community and the larger culture of the United States. These stories provided a foundation for sharing and community building through literary analysis.

I took a backseat as a male and tried to cultivate a classroom climate encouraging the young women to serve as leaders. Sometimes silence is used as a power grab or a place to retreat from ideas or dialogue that challenge the status quo. I have been in so many situations as a Chicano where individuals of

European descent sat quietly during discussions of racism and discrimination and did not engage. Silence can be a way to exercise privilege. I did not want the young women in my class to doubt my engagement. I wanted them to know that I heard them, empathized, and was learning from them—because I was!

For example, Cisneros' vignette "Woman Hollering Creek" focuses on Cleófilas' reaction to being abused by her husband. Cleófilas does not react the way she had always expected to when watching such incidents on her favorite telenovelas. Instead of immediately fleeing from her home with her son, she remains with her husband, even consoling him as he cries for forgiveness "this time and each."

The young women in CLASS took the lead in our discussion and raised a variety of different perspectives and questions about the violence and the main character's reaction: Should Cleófilas leave and head back to her father with her young son? Should she stay and find resolution with her abusive husband? What are the ramifications of leaving or staying? Is Cleófilas in a position to liberate herself and thrive on her own?

It became clear to me that the young women had significant insight into the myriad of reactions, choices, and limitations facing Cleófilas. There was no consensus about what was the "right" thing for a woman to do in her situation. However, one thing that was revealed by the discussion was that there were many factors that I, as a man, hadn't considered.

Our discussion of the story illuminated the many ways the young women in CLASS navigate violence, objectification, and sexism in their daily lives. They talked about how Cleófilas does not have the means to leave her husband and his abuse due to traditional gender roles rooted in patriarchy. The young men in our group noted that they are expected to be employed and to have a car or other means to get to work; these social expectations ensure a level of independence that Cleófilas does not have.

The voices of the young women became our guide to obtaining *Quetzalcoatl*, precious and beautiful knowledge.

As we turned our attention to LGBTQ themes, we were able to build connections to the feminist struggles that we had already analyzed, while pushing toward new insights revealed through powerful lesbian, gay, bisexual, and transgender characters.

> I wanted to make sure we didn't end up with a flat, stereotyped, or over-romanticized view of LGBTQ people.

Popular recording artist Frank Ocean's revelation that he is bisexual in the album *Channel Orange* served as an organic transition. The song "Bad Religion" was a particularly engaging work for the students of CLASS. The lyrics are ambiguous about what religion represents, but the pain Ocean experiences from his unrequited love for another man is very clear:

> he said "Allahu akbar"
> i told him don't curse me
> "Bo Bo, you need prayer"
> i guess it couldn't hurt me
> if it brings me to my knees
> it's a bad religion
> this unrequited love
> to me it's nothing but a one-man cult
> and cyanide in my Styrofoam cup
> i can never make him love me

Short stories by Manuel Muñoz and Ramón García helped us explore the dehumanizing homophobic status quo within the Chican@ community alongside a vision of what respect and love for our LGBTQ comrades would look like. In "Lindo y Querido," Muñoz portrays a Chicana mother dealing with the loss of her gay teenage son after a motorcycle accident that also claimed the life of his boyfriend. In García's story "La Llorona: Our Lady of Deformities," a transgender woman who is revered within California's Central Valley migrant community seeks justice for parents who watch their newborn babies suffer and die from pesticide poisoning.

Looking at all these works was important; I wanted to make sure we didn't end up with a flat, stereotyped, or over-romanticized view of LGBTQ people. I wanted the students to see the depth, diversity, and humanity of the characters. Queer characters in these stories were out and in love, in the closet from their parents, and fierce warriors for social justice. As a Chicano, I am often frustrated at how mainstream society portrays Chican@s/Latin@s as a monolith, so it is crucial for me to honor the diversity and intersectionality of my students' cultures and identities.

For one of my students who self-identifies as a Chicana lesbian, these stories were the first time that she experienced any academic unit of study that reflected the complexity of her identity. Since the majority of our class identified as heterosexual, we had the opportunity to practice *In Lak'ech* and defer to her, in much the same way that the young men and I approached the Chicanisma unit.

We wanted to create some type of *Huitzilopochtli* (will to act) by developing plans that would transform the inequalities and injustices we had unearthed. We began with building the leadership of the students, who each took over the class space and became the teacher for a day, developing learning objectives and interactive lessons.

The following essays by Alanna Castro and Maria Teresa Mejia, two brilliant young scholar-activists, show the work they did, respectively, on gender roles in hip-hop and domestic abuse. I hope you will learn, as I have, from their insights.

Alanna Castro Speaks:

As a high school student, I was given the opportunity to receive a culturally diverse education through my MAS classes. We read literary works by LGBTQ writers, immigrants, feminists, philosophers, and theorists. My senior year, my literature class was given an assignment to interview people in the Tucson community who were living counter-narratives. As a class, we transcribed the interviews, turned them into monologues, and performed them. I chose to be a performer and I chose the monologue of a transgender woman. Her story spoke to me in ways that I am still unable to explain. The education I received in the classrooms of Curtis Acosta and Jose Gonzalez has been unmatched in my four years of college.

After the MAS program was destroyed, I began working on an after-school project with Curtis. His vision was to bring elements of the MAS program to students outside the institutionalized public school space. We decided to create CLASS. He would be the teacher, and I would be an organizer and yet again his student. We began the journey of bringing back the love of education to students who were being denied that in the public school system.

When we were asked to conduct a class session on our own, I volunteered to go first, with no idea what I would teach. For weeks, I stumbled through ideas. I knew I wanted to do something with hip-hop. But what exactly could I teach? What did I know that I could I share with my classmates?

We had mentioned sensual hip-hop in CLASS, and I liked the challenge of finding men in hip-hop culture who were sensitive and nurturing rather than just macho.

So my lesson "Men, Love, and Hip-Hop" was based on songs that portray men as not only sensual, but also loving and heartbroken. I chose the songs "Love and Appreciate" by Murs, "Fuck You Lucy" by Atmosphere, and "Mind Sex" by Dead Prez.

> The display of emotion and love in hip-hop is what makes it real, what makes me love it.

Murs talks about putting his machismo aside to buy the woman in his life what she needs during her period: "Buy some flowers/open up some doors/she needs some tampons/homie go to the store/vitamin water/a bottle of motrin/ teddy bear, candy bar something/A token of affection a step in that direction/ cause love is about progress not perfection." I put this song under the Sweet

Love category.

"Fuck You Lucy" is about a man ravaged by a breakup: "Hunger for the drama, hunger for the nurture/Gonna take it further, the hurt feels like murder/Interpret the eyes, read the lines on her face/The sunshine is fake, how much time did I waste?" This song fell into the Sour Love category.

Unlike most mainstream hip-hop, which is all about hitting it and quitting it, Dead Prez's "Mind Sex" taps into a broader sensuality: "It's time for some mind sex, we ain't got to take our clothes off yet/We can burn an incense, and just chat/Relax, I got the good vibrations/Before we make love let's have a good conversation." I put this song in the Sensual Love category. Each example was a way for me to show that there is more to men than what is commonly acknowledged in popular culture.

Instead of having every student analyze each song, I split the class into three groups. I had each group pick one of the categories—Sweet Love, Sour Love, or Sensual Love—without telling them the song that went with that category. Once each group had chosen a category, I gave them the lyrics to all three songs and asked them to follow along as I played the music. At the end of each song I gave a few minutes for open discussion: What category does this song belong to? What textual evidence supports that?

I wanted the students to see that there isn't any difference between analyzing a hip-hop song and analyzing a poem or a short story. It was obvious to the students which category each song fit into. They drew examples from the lyrics as we had done with previous literary analyses.

Next I asked each group to analyze the song that went with the category they had chosen. I asked them to focus on three questions:

In what ways does the song contradict or perpetuate typical male gender roles in love or relationships?

What are the artists trying to express about the characters in the song?

How is the song relevant to the different stages of a relationship?

The songs were ambiguous about men's roles and feelings; they were filled with internal contradictions. For instance, Murs talks about treating women right and that's how you keep them, yet he also implies that he keeps women around for sex: "I love my dudes but imma pick a girl anytime I gotta choose/I like mad . . . but I love orgasms and I'm not trying to have the same problem you're having." The students saw examples in all the songs that exemplified what men are "known" to do, and other examples that expressed more vulnerability, love, and nonstereotypical feelings.

My goal with this lesson was to show my students that, in a society where there is a constant battle of the sexes, it doesn't have to be that way. I wanted to convey that men can be just as sensitive as women, that men love and hurt like other humans. As a woman, I wanted to deliver the message to the young men in the class that it's OK to love and to be heartbroken, that showing sensitivity will not make you any less of a man. Men showing emotion in mainstream culture is often frowned upon, yet the display of emotion and love in hip-hop is what makes it real, what makes me love it.

Maria Teresa Mejia Speaks:

I walk on thin ice. I am an educated *mujer* who has grown up in a male-dominant world, where my needs are seen as not as important as a man's. I may only be 18 years old, but my personal experiences make age just a number. The education system is flawed. I have rarely heard a women's perspective or seen material in the curriculum to make a woman feel like she is equal to a man. So I have taken it upon myself to release a woman's voice out into society.

Domestic abuse happens often and is hidden from others because it is seen as shameful, and no one wants to hear the truth of what happens behind closed doors. I've seen so many women who let their husbands drown them in pain, women who are stronger than words can explain but who look so small when they are within arm's length of their husbands.

As a child I remember peeking around the corner of my grandma's house and watching my cousin's husband grab his children by their ears and force them into the back of the car. I was scared to death watching him, wondering why she did not leave him, wondering how you could love a man who pushes you and your children around and torments you with his words. But my cousin's husband had power. Being the man he was, with fists of steel, he had the last word. She would never talk back to him. She lived in a small town where there wasn't anywhere else to go. She was stuck in this life with no other choice.

My freshman year, I attended Tucson's University High School, where I was taught to be blind to inequalities. The Anglo students were ignorant about the racial slurs that made them laugh and uneducated about the inequalities between men and women. We were told we were all the same, yet the students whose skin was lighter than mine got help from teachers, and I was pushed aside as if I had no reason to be in school. Being a Chicana meant you got looked up and down in the halls as if you were a species that was rare and exotic. Are you surprised I felt inferior?

> So many women are stronger than words can explain but look so small when they are within arm's length of their husbands.

As the youngest girl in my family. I was not allowed to go to the movies at night or on a date unless a family member came, too. I understood that those rules were in my best interest because women are victims. Watching different women in my life and the women on TV, I started to think that love was not real, that it was an illusion that led women to be in the arms of someone who could kill them.

But then I changed high schools and joined the MAS class. I had the chance to read literature written by women, about women. Reading stories of strong women with hearts of gold and spirits with the strength to change the world, I realized that we are not fragile.

After my senior year of high school, I attended a workshop with Ana Castillo, who is now a banned author in the Tucson Unified School District. During her workshop she expressed how hard it is to be a woman—having to live up to standards, living each day trying to break stereotypes, and dealing with our enormous hearts that let everyone in.

We did an exercise where all the students taking the workshop switched a picture they had brought with the person next to them. We were to analyze this new picture and determine what was going on, figure out the importance of the picture. I had a picture of my mom, my sister, my brother, father, and me, which I passed to the woman next to me. She looked at the picture for a long time. When she shared what she saw, she said that she saw a strong woman. I told her my mother was dealing with stage four cancer. At that time, she was not yet in remission.

The next day Castillo read her poem "I Ask the Impossible." As she read, my eyes were opened to the idea of a love so true that it can conquer the hardest times.

> Love me when you're bored—
> when every woman you see is more beautiful than the last,
> or more pathetic, love me as you always have:
> not as admirer or judge, but with
> the compassion you save for yourself
> in your solitude.

Castillo's poem made me believe in love, believe in partnerships where you never stop loving, where you work to your last breath to make things work out. It was the love that my mom had to recover from the cancer, the love that many women have, to fight for what we want. As women, we love so much because loving someone comes easy for us. It is a risk we take because we are stronger than anyone ever thought.

A month later, I joined CLASS. When we were asked to teach the group, I knew right away I wanted to teach about domestic violence. I was no longer that 5-year-old hiding behind the wall, watching my cousins cry as they were shoved into the car. Now I had the chance to speak out and educate students on an issue our society faces. The women in my life inspired me to focus my lesson on abuse toward woman—emotional, physical, and mental.

Castillo's book *I Ask the Impossible* is filled with poems about women who struggled, who loved, and who were hurt. As I planned my teaching experience, I re-read the poems and marked the ones that matched my agenda. I wanted to open up the students' perspectives about the challenges facing women who are thinking of leaving a man. I chose three poems:

"How Does It Feel to Be Cruel to a Woman?" revolves around physical abuse. In addition to the physical abuse, the woman is emotionally abused by being called a bad mom for letting the abuser into her life: "Say: she doesn't care about her children/for letting you in in the first place,/for trying to love and be loved."

"She Was Brave to Leave You" tells about a woman on a train who carries a journal that holds the secrets of the pain she has endured. She is escaping: "She imagined him later/running at night/with wild rage and drunk."

"I Decide Not to Fall in Love" is about being left brokenhearted so many times that there is no hope for love anymore, it is better to just not feel: "and I, wrapped in wool/without you, slept alone again, I decided then not to,/not to, not to."

I decided to have the students break into three groups; each group read one of the poems. I asked them to read and interpret their poem. If we had more time and a larger group, I would have asked them to create a skit or scenario of a related life event or some other response to the poem.

When I asked the students what they learned from the poems about why

Alec Dunn

women are with men who hurt them, they talked about how challenging it can be for women to leave: Some men have connections with authorities who could find the wife and hurt her for leaving. The woman might have no place to go. Some women believe getting married means they are committing themselves to whatever lies ahead, no matter how bad. Others have children they would not be able to support without the husband. Still others are worried that if they leave they will get killed.

Teaching the class helped me to examine what I was thinking. I got ideas from the students that I would not have thought about on my own. I believe that the poems helped some students think twice before they judge a woman for not leaving an abusive situation.

I hope to educate more people about domestic violence. As a Chicana, I want to talk with other women about the limitations society has placed on us, and ensure that we can break those barriers and be as successful, independent, and strong as we want to be.

Resources

Atmosphere. 2002. "Fuck You Lucy." *God Loves Ugly* (studio album). Fat Beats Records.

Castillo, Ana. 2001. *I Ask the Impossible: Poems*. Anchor.

Cisneros, Sandra. 1992. "Woman Hollering Creek." *Woman Hollering Creek and Other Stories*. Vintage.

Dead Prez. 2000. "Mind Sex." *Let's Get Free* (studio album). Loud Records.

Garcia, Ramón. 2000. *La Llorona: Our Lady of Deformities*.

Muñoz, Manuel. 2007. "Lindo y Querido." *The Faith Healer of Olive Avenue*. Algonquin Books.

Murs and 9th Wonder. 2006. "Love and Appreciate." *Murray's Revenge* (studio album). Record Collection.

Ocean, Frank. 2012. "Bad Religion." *Channel Orange* (audio CD). Def Jam.

Ethan Heitner

When Emma Goldman Entered the Room
Dealing with the unexpected in a role play

BY BRIAN C. GIBBS

Brian C. Gibbs taught history and government at Theodore Roosevelt High School in East Los Angeles for 16 years. He is currently an assistant professor of education at the University of North Carolina, Chapel Hill.

T he room was awhirl: students dashing in and out, noisily planning strategy, silently reviewing questions, rehearsing their speeches. Most were already in costume—making adjustments to headbands, scarves, ties, and jackets—when José arrived. He was a football player, 6 feet tall, dressed in women's clothes complete with makeup, an ample bosom, a smile on his face, and an accentuated swish of the hips. His entrance was greeted with laughter, whispering, and catcalls, especially from the female students. He walked the length of the room as though it were a catwalk, hips swinging and eyelashes batting.

Ignoring José, I called my students together, had them take their places as character teams in a large circle, and began to introduce our role play. The unit was thematic and focused on the fears and political sacrifices of the 1920s, 1950s, and 2000s. In all three time periods, there was something feared. They were to some extent justifiable fears, but exaggerated and exploited by those in power. During the 1920s, it was the Russian Revolution and communism; during the '50s it was communism, Stalin, and the atomic bomb; and during the 2000s, Islamic terrorism. The effects of these exploited fears included the increased surveillance of U.S. citizens, the rollback of fundamental rights and freedoms, and racist attacks and expulsions (even of citizens). I asked students to use the essential question "What are we willing to sacrifice to feel safe?" to compare the three time periods in order to put the use of torture, the prison at Guatanamo Bay, extraordinary rendition, and the U.S. Patriot Act in historical context. Students examined primary source documents, including letters, speeches, and newspaper articles; read excerpts from several secondary history sources; watched film of Joe McCarthy and the House Un-American Activities Committee; and analyzed excerpts of the 9/11 Commission report.

"Emma" stood center stage, cleared his throat, and readjusted his fake breasts, to the complete delight of the crowd.

I then assigned teams of students to roles from the three time periods (e.g., ACLU founder Roger Baldwin, Supreme Court Justice Oliver Wendell Holmes Jr., President Woodrow Wilson, Socialist leader Eugene V. Debs, President Harry S. Truman, blacklisted screenwriter Dalton Trumbo, broadcast journalist Edward R. Murrow, Sen. Russ Feingold, and President George W. Bush). From their historical figure's perspective, students wrote speeches, developed questions, and framed an argument to answer the essential question. José and his team represented Emma Goldman—anarchist, free speech advocate, feminist, and all-around rabble-rouser.

José spoke for his team during the opening of the seminar portion of the role play. He was third up and followed strong and well-rehearsed speeches delivered in the characters of Baldwin and Holmes. As I introduced Goldman, José strode to the middle of the room. The giggles and catcalls re-emerged. He stood center stage, cleared his throat, and readjusted his fake breasts, to the complete delight of the crowd. He began speaking in a forced, fake, and high-pitched voice, continuing his comic charade. The voice distracted everyone at first, especially when he began to work the room, walking back and forth, pointing at different historical characters in the room, gesticulating to emphasize his points.

However, his arguments as Emma Goldman were spot on, well thought out, detailed, and complete, with several well-placed quotations from Goldman herself: "No real social change has ever been brought about without a revolution. . . . Revolution is but thought carried into action." "The demand for equal rights in every vocation of life is just and fair." "The history of progress is written in the blood of men and women who have dared to espouse an unpopular cause." Some were from speeches we'd analyzed in class, others were from the group's own research. As Goldman, José asked several rhetorical questions: "What and who are we afraid of? Who says we should fear them? What's the source of the information?" He argued that the fear was misplaced: "The world is made of workers who are oppressed and exploited. Through this we are all united." He finished his speech with a crescendoed call to action and resistance that Goldman herself might well have been proud of. His bow was greeted with thunderous applause.

The role play continued. Other speakers delivered such strong performances that the project engaged us for three full days.

> "The history of progress is written in the blood of men and women who have dared to espouse an unpopular cause."
>
> —Emma Goldman

Role plays and other forms of experiential learning always carry a risk. There is an emotionality to them and a stretching of oneself that generally garners strong academic and intellectual results, but can also carry students to places that surprise them, and sometimes surprise me, too. Taking on a role allows students to move beyond themselves; this can include women as male characters, men as females, Latinas/os as whites, African Americans as Native Americans, and so on. Although it is not necessary, I find that having students dress in character in some way, from something as small as creating a nametag to creating a full-on costume, can help them find the voice and nuance of their person. I give students the choice of playing either the character or someone who was close to and supportive of the character's positions. This allows everyone to participate at their own comfort level.

When "Boys Will Be Boys" Isn't Good Enough

As our activity developed over the next few days, the students engaged the issues and each other. Questions were asked, arguments made, passions raised, and content invoked. There was laughter, outrage, and argument in this serious intellectual endeavor. Students seemed to have forgotten José's swagger that first day.

But it bothered me still. José's exposition of Goldman's life, experiences, and opinions was correct, clear, and well argued. It was his performance that was troubling. I'd been experimenting with adding costumes to role plays for several years, but hadn't run into this negative aspect before. José's rendition of Goldman was stereotypical, overly sexualized, distorted, and generally inappropriate. His continuous touching and shifting of his "bosom" and provocative walk combined to create an insulting caricature of a heroic historical figure. By not engaging the issue, I had given my tacit approval to the portrayal.

This was a realization that I didn't come to until the end of my second sleepless night. For the three days of the seminar, I let it ride. As a teacher I'd learned that it is sometimes simpler to let some things go. A note from a substitute teacher about how badly my classes acted while I was gone—let it go, they won't act that way now that I'm here. A ridiculous excuse for why a student is late—let it go, she's here now and she knows I know. The role play had been a success, students had demonstrated intellectual and academic skill. No one had registered anger or revulsion at his behavior, so why not just let it go?

Sometime during that second sleepless night, I remembered the presentation that the Gay-Straight Alliance had made at the opening faculty meeting. "You would never allow the words *nigger* or *bitch, chink or spic*, so why do we allow the word *fag*?" The student speaking wasn't using defiant language. No hands on her hips, no fierce look in her eye. Really, she had been asking. "It's not the students who are using the word you need to worry about," she continued. "It's the quiet students in the back of the room who will never reveal themselves by asking you to make it stop." I realized that, for all my feminist intent, I had allowed sexism space in my classroom.

The next day, I approached several colleagues, both male and female. The general consensus was "Boys will be boys" and "Don't make a mountain out of a molehill." I wanted to agree, but I couldn't.

What Would Emma Do?

I knew I needed to approach the issue in a way that didn't undercut the successful role play we'd had. I was also concerned about isolating José, who certainly wasn't alone in his compliance with misogynistic stereotypes. I asked myself: Do I engage José alone first, then the whole class? The whole class first, then José individually if needed?

I decided to raise the issue with the Emma Goldman team: Ysenia, Sade, Michael, and José. They agreed to meet me after school and arrived all together in a bustle on a bright Thursday afternoon. They were still excited about their victory. Goldman and like-minded individuals from the 1950s and 2000s had carried the day by arguing that rights and freedoms should never be rolled back. They agreed that fear itself—of other cultures, languages, ethnicities, political systems—was the problem We discussed the role play for a bit, sharing the most provocative and powerful moments.

The conversation shifted when Ysenia asked, "Do you have the pictures yet?" She was referring to my habit of snapping pictures during role plays and printing them out, one for the student photographed and one for the "museum," my classroom walls that were covered with years of student photos. I did have the photos, and we spent some time looking at them. In preparation for this discussion, I had removed all but two of the photos of José. When we arrived at the first one, he smiled and the group began to laugh.

"What do you think of the photo?" I asked.

"Hilarious."

"He was a good-looking woman."

Then all eyes turned toward José. "You got my good side," he said.

"What would Emma Goldman think of this?" I asked.

"We rocked it, man," Sade argued emphatically. "We represented her hard-core."

"We left it all on the field," added Michael.

"I felt like I knew her, like I was her, you know what I mean?" José said, as the other three nodded their heads in agreement. "I think that she would be outraged by what's happening now, she would be in the streets, giving speeches, organizing. She was wrong in some ways, especially for today, but she'd be proud of us and I totally respect her spirit, her zeal."

"It was the selections of her autobiography that really helped me get to know her," added Ysenia.

"So you represented her well?" I asked.

"We did everything on the criteria chart and did it well," Michael said. "Even Ysenia spoke. Her conclusion at the end of the seminar was right on." He patted her on the shoulder.

"We not only represented her well, we defended her well," Sade continued.

There was a pause, but only for a moment.

"It was the costumes wasn't it?" Ysenia ventured.

"What about the costumes?" I asked.

"It was disrespectful, wasn't it?"

"We were just having fun and we did everything on the criteria chart," Michael insisted.

José said nothing.

"It wasn't the costume so much, it was the acting, right?" Ysenia was still digging, still processing. "It was José. When he did that walk and all. You know, the. . ." She pantomimed his hip-swinging sashay.

"Really, was that disrespectful? I mean come on. . ." Michael's "really" came out defiantly, but the rest struck a reflective tone.

"Yes, it was!" This was Ysenia with a fierceness I'd never credited her with.

"I can see it, I get it," José said. "But for reals, I was just messing around, I've seen people do way worse stuff."

"In this class?" Sade asked.

"Nahh, in the quad, the street, television, movies, you know, out there." He pointed out the door for emphasis.

Making It Right

We talked some more, Ysenia absolutely convinced that it was disrespectful, Sade agreeing that it was disrespectful but not that bad, and the two boys agreeing that it was disrespectful but not really a big deal.

José asked me, "If it was so bad, why didn't you stop it?" I didn't have a clear answer, but I tried: "I didn't want to embarrass you. You and your team did a great job on everything I asked you to do. I didn't have the words then, it took a while for it to bubble to the surface. It just nagged at me, I knew something wasn't right, but I wasn't sure. . ."

I went on. I shared what I learned from the Gay-Straight Alliance. I spoke about my wife, my daughter, my secret crush on Emma Goldman, and the world I tried to create within the walls of my classroom. I also said that I had an idea what José was thinking—it seemed like a good way to get through having to perform a female role. But that wasn't good enough. We need a world ready for Sade, Ysenia, and my daughter—a place where women, their struggles, and their contributions are respected. Real learning comes with laughter and buffoonery, or at least it should, but humor has its place, and I didn't think that making fun of Goldman that way was the right place.

> "If it was so bad, why didn't you stop it?"

"Why wasn't this part of the criteria?" asked Ysenia.

So we talked about what was good about the criteria chart, how it allowed them to self-reflect, know what was expected, and earn a grade for the performative aspect of the role play, for "bringing it all to life." But it left open the possibility of disrespect. The openness of the criteria was freeing. Did we want to end that with a bunch of rules over what Michael called a "little thing like this?" This led to a long argument. Finally José joined in. "If we want females represented fairly and accurately, and we all agreed we do, then we need to add something."

They wanted to leave the flexibility, but force my hand, because they all thought I should have done more to intervene in the moment. After two more meetings, we all agreed to add this language to the criteria chart:

> All historical characters will be presented as close to reality and with as much respect as possible. Any intentional or unintentional disrespect will result in a lowered grade and an intervention meeting with the teacher.

When the writing was finished we were a bit exhausted but buoyant, feeling we had done some good.

"So now what? Is this it?" asked José. He had come around to an understanding and wanted more.

Yesenia rescued us. "Why don't we present this to the class?"

"Why don't you present it to all the classes?" I asked.

And so they did. With some assistance from me, they created a discussion-based presentation that opened with a photo of José as Emma Goldman projected on a large screen in the front of the room and my opening question: "What do you think of this photo?"

In each class it led to a spirited discussion of deep and difficult things. In each class there was resistance, with some arguing that the new criterion was too restrictive, but there were countervailing voices as well. Staying silent for most of the classes, facilitating a bit here and there, I did speak at the end. I talked about the world I wanted for my daughter and for all of us, how it was my responsibility to use my positional authority if necessary to push reflection and a larger understanding of gender stereotypes, feminism, and historical accuracy.

I have never had a student act that way again. All the sexism in the world, my school, and my class did not disappear, but we did make a dent. And a dent is a beginning.

Is She Your Bitch?
Confronting sexism on the fly

By Deborah Godner

Deborah Godner has taught social studies and English as well as been the Gay-Straight Alliance (GSA) teacher coordinator at King Middle School and Berkeley High School for more than 20 years. She co-founded and co-led a small learning community, the School for Social Justice and Ecology, at Berkeley High.

"Obama made Romney his bitch!" a student exclaimed as we were summarizing *The Daily Show*'s episode on the second presidential debate. My ears perked up: an opportunity for an on-the-spot teachable moment.

I wanted to be careful how I responded to the comment and how I framed the issue—to keep the focus on the societal issue and not on the person who blurted out the comment. I didn't want the male students in my class to feel attacked and defensive, as if they were the "bad guys." I wanted them to be open to examining how sexism limits and hurts everyone, including them. I said: "I want to talk about what Sam just said, but I want to make sure you know this is not about Sam. Any one of us could have easily made this comment. We *all* learn and internalize ideas—from the media, from the people in our lives. I am really glad when someone brings these issues up, so thank you, Sam!"

Then I grabbed my marker and my ball, ready for the lively discussion I knew would ensue. I wrote the statement on the board, scrapping the planned lesson on the presidential debates. I told my students a brief story from when I taught at a middle school, where I often heard boys calling out to each other in the hallways: "Is that your bitch?" One time, I approached a boy I didn't know, smiled, shook his hand and introduced myself. Then, I asked: "Do you see any dog owners in the halls?" He looked at me with a puzzled expression. "I was just curious," I told him, "because when you ask your friend if a girl is his bitch, it sounds like you are talking about someone's dog. Do you understand what I mean?" The student was silent. "Just think about it, OK?" I shook his hand again and moved on.

After sharing the hallway story, I wrote three questions on the board and asked students to think-write for 10 minutes:

- What does being someone's bitch mean? (either Romney being Obama's bitch or the girl being her boyfriend's bitch)
- How do you feel/what do you think about this comment?
- How might it be offensive, oppressive, or disrespectful to women and men?

After everyone finished writing, we passed the ball around the classroom—whoever has the ball has the floor to speak. I charted the conversation on the board so students could add to their writing if they chose:

"It's all about ownership and no girl wants to be owned."

"It's different when girls call other girls bitches from when a boy calls a girl a bitch."

"It's like the n-word, loaded with history."

"Boys use it to call other boys pussies—girls."

Trying to push their thinking, I asked for explanations and examples. Is it really different when a boy calls a girl "(my) bitch" than when another girl does it? Why? How is "bitch" historically loaded like the n-word? What do those two words have in common historically? What's different? I asked students to talk through the questions with a partner and then bring their insights back to the class.

Is it different when a boy calls a girl "(my) bitch" than when another girl does it?

At the end of the school day, one student stopped by to tell me that some of my 10th graders had continued the conversation throughout the day. That night, I decided to switch my curriculum around and pursue the issues that had been raised.

Hip-Hop: Beyond Beats & Rhymes

The next day, I introduced Byron Hurt's video *Hip-Hop: Beyond Beats & Rhymes* (see Resources). I emphasized that sexism, violence, gender roles, and misogyny are found in all parts of society, not just in hip-hop.

I asked students to set up a Take Notes (quote or paraphrase main ideas and details)/Make Notes (questions and reactions) T-chart in their notebooks. I set up the same T-chart on the whiteboard to model note-taking and to capture essential and provocative quotes from the "text." We watched the "Introduction" and "Everybody Wants to Be Hard" sections of the video, in which Hurt lays out his thesis: Violent and aggressive images of manhood in our culture (he focuses on hip-hop culture as an example) teach boys to act hard; this conflicts with who boys and men really are. This "box" or "prison" in which boys/men are trapped creates violence toward other men and women.

Students quoted and paraphrased main ideas and details as we watched. Then students wrote their questions and reactions, and we discussed them. I listened to make sure the main points got raised: the manhood "box" of prescribed masculine stereotypes, the gap between who men really are versus the image they feel the need to project to the world, hypermasculinity as an integral part of American identity, how society limits the range of emotions men are allowed, and the use of the word *bitch* to express domination, humiliation, and control.

Over the next two days, I showed the other sections of the film: "Shut Up and Give Me Your Bone Marrow," "Sistahs and Bitches," "Bitch-Ass Niggas," and "Manhood in a Bottle." We continued to take notes and write and share our reactions. I tried to make explicit connections back to the original "his bitch" comment.

Gender Stereotypes

The next day, students worked in same-sex pairs to brainstorm gender stereotypes. The students who identified as young women filled in boxes with descriptions of how girls and women are "supposed" to be and act, and what happens if they step out of the box. The students who identified as young men did the same thing for boys and men. For example: Men are supposed to be "hard," "tough," "ready to fight," "in control," "have lots of girls," and "not cry." If they step out of this box, they get called "pussy," "faggot," "bitch." The girls talked about when and why girls get called "bitch," "ho," and "dyke."

Students wrote their responses in large boxes on the board and we brainstormed some more. Then I had them rotate via "musical chairs" to talk about how they felt about the activity in mixed-gender pairs—I again reminded them that however they identify is OK. We shared out a few responses as whole class.

Next, in same-sex groups of four, students collected media images of the "manhood" and "womanhood" stereotypes we had listed on the board from magazines and online movie, TV show, and music advertisements. Each group created a poster of gender stereotypes with words and images. Then we put the posters on the walls and did a gallery walk. Students read the posters and wrote their one strongest reaction and their one most confusing question on sticky notes next to an image or words. We all gathered around the poster gallery to read the reactions aloud and discuss the questions.

Writing Essays

Then students wrote essays responding to a quote from the film:
- "Hip-hop videos have taken a view of women of color that is not radically different from the views of 19th-century white slave owners." (Professor Jelani Cobb)
- "We live in a society where manhood is all about conquering and violence. . . . That kind of definition of manhood ultimately destroys [us]." (Kevin Powell)

- "We are playing a role from the time we're 7 years old. We walk down the street and somebody calls us a sissy, a sucker, church boy. We start playing that role." (Rev. Conrad Tillard)
- "Generally speaking, Black people do not believe that misogyny and sexism and violence against women are urgent issues. We still think that racism, police brutality, and black male incarceration are the issues that we need to be concerned about." (Dr. Beverly Guy-Sheftall)
- "I jokingly say that I'm in recovery from hip-hop. It's like being in a domestic violence situation. Your home is hip-hop and your man beats you." (Toni Blackman)

I asked students to use evidence and examples from the film, their own lives, and the gender stereotype posters to support their arguments.

> ## "Hip-hop videos have taken a view of women of color that is not radically different from the views of 19th-century white slave owners."
> ### —Jelani Cobb

To share our essays, we gathered in one big circle for a "read-around." I always review the rules for feedback before we start: Paraphrase or quote passages you like and say why. Write down a moment in the piece you connected to and say why. The read-around is a great community builder; I work to keep it safe for kids to take the risk to share. And I always read my own piece as a member of the circle.

I reminded students that they could either read or pass. I gave everyone strips of paper. As each person read their piece, everyone, including me, wrote specific feedback about the content and the style.

Students talked back to gender stereotypes in their essays. One student shared: "I learned a lot about myself . . . that I am not a stereotypical guy. I am a scrawny cat person. I cannot bench press a fighter jet. I am proud of not being the stereotype."

Another wrote: "Men and boys get worse punishment for stepping out the box than girls do. We are so scared to step out and girls have more freedom to step out."

Another shared: "Sometimes I act like a princess, wearing lots of color, sophisticated clothes, and makeup. Then people think of me as an intelligent woman. They smile at me. But when I am in my other girl mood, wearing colors of the night, hoodies, no makeup, listening to loud rock, people look at me as the girl whose life is messed up."

And yet another: "I used to feel ashamed of myself because I have some things about me that might seem "feminine," like jump-roping or just being nice and smiling. I am not ashamed anymore because I don't want to be the kind of man who is only hard and mean. Men fight each other too much. They are supposed to have lots of women and cash and not be scared to die. That's really hard for us."

To wrap up, I asked students to think about the original comment: "Obama made Romney his bitch." Students talked about how their thoughts and feelings about the comment had changed. I reminded them that on-the-fly comments we all make are sometimes loaded; it is important to unpack them so we don't continue to add to oppression.

Conclusion

As an educator, parent, woman, and genderqueer lesbian, I have had to live and breathe activism around issues of sexism, gender, and sexuality in order to keep my own pride and help middle school and high school students feel freer to be themselves. I love the transformations and liberations I have witnessed through the year: boys feeling comfortable hugging each other and being "sweet," girls speaking up a bit louder about how they want respect from boys, a gay and a trans student each coming out—seemingly nonchalantly—in the middle of a discussion.

My students have not stopped calling each other "bitch," but I have noticed some of them more carefully choosing the words they use and challenging each other. When we challenge ourselves to examine the impact of our statements, we open up the possibility of living in a more thoughtful, accepting, and just world.

Resource

Hip-Hop: Beyond Beats & Rhymes. 2006. Dir. Byron Hurt. Independent Television Services.

Seneca Falls, 1848
Women organize for equality

BY BILL BIGELOW

Bill Bigelow is the curriculum editor of Rethinking Schools. This article was originally written for the Zinn Education Project website (zinnedproject.org), where you can find the sources for the historical information.

T he first organized gathering of women to demand their rights *as women* took place during two days in July 1848 in Seneca Falls, New York. The manifesto they produced provided a blueprint for feminist organizing for decades to come. The most "radical" demand—at least the only demand not passed unanimously by the assembly—was for universal suffrage. Not all attendees were women. In fact, it was the most prominent African American abolitionist, Frederick Douglass, who seconded Elizabeth Cady Stanton's motion for female suffrage. However, the large majority of those present were women and many, perhaps most, were veterans of the abolition movement. Some of those in attendance were working-class, but most came from privileged backgrounds. Their *Declaration of Sentiments and Resolutions* proclaimed that "the history of mankind is a history of repeated injuries and usurpations on the part of man toward woman, having in direct object the establishment of an absolute tyranny over her." But, as the feminist scholar Gerda Lerner points out, the authors of this denunciation "did not speak for the truly exploited and abused working woman. As a matter of fact, they were largely ignorant of her condition and, with the notable exception of Susan B. Anthony, indifferent to her fate." Nor did the document address the plight of women who were not white.

This role play is designed to simultaneously honor the accomplishments and explore the limitations of the women of Seneca Falls. The activity includes roles for the upper-class and middle-class white women who organized the convention, but also for women who were not in attendance: poor, working-class white mill workers; enslaved African American women; Cherokee women 10 years after the Trail of Tears; and Mexican women in territory newly conquered by the United States in its war with Mexico. This is not the entire rainbow coalition that would have been in attendance at an assembly fully representative of this country's women in 1848. But it's representative enough to give students a chance to imagine the additional demands that might have been raised that summer had the meeting's attendees not been so limited in terms of race and class.

Suggested Procedure

1. The more students have read of Chapter 6, "The Intimately Oppressed," in Howard Zinn's *A People's History of the United States*, the better. However, it's best if they don't read the final paragraphs, which deal with the Seneca Falls declaration of principles, as this may give away one of the "punch lines" of the lesson.

Review the handout "The Rights of Women: Laws and Practices." Questions for discussion:

- How do you think the laws making divorce so difficult affected women? How might women have been forced to respond? How were children affected?
- How were women of different social classes affected differently by the divorce laws?
- Until 1848, women in the United States had not gathered in a large meeting or demonstration to protest their lack of rights. Why not?
- Do any of these laws help explain why women were active in the temperance movement, which wanted to outlaw the consumption of alcohol? How could a man's addiction to alcohol be a threat to his family's physical and financial health?
- Why do you think women weren't allowed to attend college?
- How did lawmakers and other men justify women's lack of legal rights?
- What underlying attitudes about women led people to pass and/or tolerate laws like these?
- What groups of women did these laws not apply to? What laws governed their lives and rights?

2. Divide students into five groups of relatively equal size and have students sit with their group. Explain that each of them will represent a woman in one of the five groups: New England mill workers, enslaved African American women, Cherokee women living in Oklahoma, middle-class and upper-class white reformers, or Mexican women in the recently conquered territory of New Mexico.

My experience is that male students may have some difficulty with being asked to portray women. And yet, I've not generally encountered young women having a difficult time portraying male characters in role plays. My friend Sorca O'Connor, who taught at Portland State University, would ask her sociology students to look around the classroom to see how many students were "cross-dressed." "What do you mean 'cross-dressed?'" they would ask. Once they understood she was asking how many males were wearing dresses or skirts, and how many females were wearing pants, they saw where she was going: Male/female hierarchies are still with us. It's OK for women to "move up" and adopt men's attire, but not OK for men to "move down" and adopt women's attire. If male students are resistant to taking female roles, O'Connor's approach can be a useful entry point to discussion.

3. Review with students the three-part assignment on the handout "Seneca Falls Women's Rights Convention." Emphasize that in writing their resolutions, students can use whatever information they have available, but the resolutions must be based on the perspective of the group that they represent. For example, enslaved African American women are going to be much more concerned with abolishing slavery than with abolishing the divorce laws that affect women—mostly white women—in the North.

4. In their groups, have the students read and discuss their roles, and then create their lists of demands. Circulate from group to group to make sure that students stay in role and write appropriate resolutions.

5. Explain to students that, in preparation for the large convention, they will have a chance to talk with members of other groups. Remind them that the information in their role descriptions are not included in other groups' role descriptions, so they will have to teach each other about their life conditions. Also tell them that their challenge will be to try to reach consensus on prioritizing their demands: "Naturally, you can come up with as many demands as you like, but it's likely that the newspapers and even your supporters will pay closest attention to your top three demands."

It's this requirement to narrow their demands that creates the dramatic tension in the role play. The negotiating session is an opportunity for individuals from different groups to build alliances and to get support for their resolutions in advance of the Seneca Falls convention. Ask students to choose half their group as traveling negotiators. Have travelers rotate from group to group in roughly 10-minute intervals. For example, all the travelers from the African American women's group meet with the Cherokee women's group, and then move on to the New Mexican women's group, and so on. You'll only need two rounds for every combination of groups to meet. Remind students that this is not a competition, but an effort to build unity among different groups of women in the United States.

As an alternative, you could redivide the groups so that each new group has at least one representative from the five social groups. Then, still representing their roles, the students can share experiences and compare resolutions.

6. Have students reconvene in their original groups and begin the convention. The goal here is to decide as a convention on the three most important resolutions. When I've done this role play, I've introduced myself as a longtime abolitionist and women's rights supporter, and have run the meeting using a very loose version of Robert's Rules of Order. I ask students to propose a resolution that they think should be one of their top three and speak to why they believe that resolution is essential. We only discuss the resolution that is on the floor. After discussion, I call for an up or down vote. Students propose and discuss resolutions until we've agreed on three, and then I ask them to rank

these in order of importance. This is not how the Seneca Falls Convention was structured—which I'll let them know later—but having to select just a few resolutions forces students to articulate which are the most urgent grievances that must be addressed.

7. Ask students to turn to the handout "Declaration of Sentiments and Resolutions: Seneca Falls Convention, July 1848." Obviously, there are numbers of ways to handle the comparison between the students' declaration and the original. As with the entire lesson, the broad aim is twofold: to alert students to a U.S. tradition of courageous feminism, and to encourage them to critique this early feminism in terms of its inclusiveness. Depending on the skill level of the class, you might read aloud the list of indictments that precede the formal resolutions. Ask students if they recognize the document that the Seneca Falls Declaration is patterned after: the Declaration of Independence. (I added numbers to the resolutions to facilitate discussion. The original resolutions were not numbered.) Questions for discussion:

- What clues can you find to the writers' class and/or race backgrounds—e.g., "He has withheld from her rights which are given to the most ignorant and degraded men—both natives and foreigners."
- In your own words, list the criticisms that the authors of the declaration are making about U.S. society.
- According to the document, who or what makes women fully equal to men?
- Is there anything that confuses you about the document? What questions does it raise for you? What more would you need to know to decide whether you agreed with all the criticisms included in the declaration?
- From your group's standpoint, what is left out of this list of complaints about the status of women? Why do you think the authors of the document didn't address these issues?
- What actions do the women say they will take to win their demands? Are there actions that they might have included, but left out?

8. Ask students to pair up. Assign each pair one of the 12 resolutions and ask them to translate it into their own words. Someone from each pair should write their translation on the board. Review these one by one, keeping the above questions in mind.

9. Ask students to write a critique of the Seneca Falls Declaration from their group's standpoint. Remind them that a critique does not mean that they are just to criticize. A critique can also be an appreciation. Obviously, exactly how appreciative they are of the declaration will depend on which group students belong to.

The Rights of Women:

Laws and Practices

The following are some of the laws and conditions affecting many women in the United States in 1848:

It is extremely difficult for a woman to divorce her husband in most states. In New York, adultery is the only grounds for divorce. Other states allow divorce for bigamy, desertion, or extreme cruelty. Most courts grant custody of the children to men. Alimony is sometimes awarded to women, but they are not allowed to sue in court to make the ex-husband pay up.

It is considered improper for women to speak in public.

Until 1839, women were not allowed to own property anywhere in the United States.

In almost every state, the father can legally make a will appointing a guardian for his children in the event of his death. Should the husband die, a mother could have her children taken away from her.

In most states, it is legal for a man to beat his wife. New York courts ruled that, in order to keep his wife from nagging, a man could beat her with a horsewhip every few weeks.

Until 1837, no college in the United States accepted women as regular students.

Women cannot vote in any state in the union.

A woman cannot sign a contract even if her husband lets her.

Some women teach school, but they are paid only 30-50 percent of what men are paid for the same job.

New England Mill Workers

You are young white women who were born on farms throughout New England and have come to Lowell, Massachusetts, to work in the textile mills. Most of you are single, but some of you left bad marriages. Married women often must change their names because, according to the law, whatever money a woman makes belongs to her husband. Many people stereotype factory jobs as male jobs. But in 1848, almost a quarter of the people working in factories in the United States are women.

People say that at one time, conditions were pleasant in the mills, but no more. Summer hours of work in the mills are from 5 a.m. to 7 p.m. Young women work an average of 75 hours a week, with only four holidays a year. You get about 35 minutes for meals, but this includes travel time between the mill and your boarding house in the neighborhood. For this, you're paid anywhere from $20-25 a *month*.

But it's not only the long hours and the short time for meals. The conditions of the work itself are terrible. The air in the factory is polluted with flying lint and fumes from the whale oil lamps that hang on pegs from each loom. The overseers regularly spray the air with water to keep the humidity high so the cotton threads won't break. The windows are all nailed shut. The long hours in the bad air mean that you and your friends often get sick. It's common for workers to get tuberculosis—"the white death," as you call it. The owners don't have clinics for the workers, and there are no hospitals for the poor. Young women with breathing problems just go home to die. Add to this the terrible speed of the work. All workers must tend more than one loom, and the male overseers harass slower workers.

Living conditions are very crowded. It's common for young women to live six to a room with three beds.

In response to these conditions, you've joined with other young women in the "10-hour movement" to reduce hours from the current 12 or 13 a day down to 10. Some people say that women should do as they're told, but women in the mills have gone on strike a number of times to protest the long hours and bad conditions. Thousands of you have signed petitions demanding shorter hours. During strikes, owners fire strikers and hire "scabs," people who take the place of striking workers.

Enslaved African American Women

You are enslaved African American women living in the South. No one can imagine the horrible conditions of your lives, but here are some brief details. The most basic fact of slavery is that you have no control over any aspect of your life. As a woman, this lack of control is especially harsh. You are often sold away from members of your family. Or your children are sold away from you. This may happen, for example, when a white owner wants money to pay a debt or he dies. A master can do anything to you. If an owner wants to beat you, he beats you. If he wants to whip you, he whips you. If he wants to rape you, he rapes you. Your body is owned by another person.

You have no right to vote, to own property, to an education, to travel, to marry, to protect your children. Enslaved African American women have no rights—period.

Most enslaved people do not live on huge plantations, but on smaller estates with just a few slaves. This means that contact with an owner is almost constant. Some owners make you sleep on the floor by their bed to attend to their needs. Not only do enslaved women do the housework, but also you often do most of the field work. Enslaved African American men often do blacksmithing, carpentry, or other skilled work while women are sent to the fields to pick cotton. Whether you work in the field or in the house of the white owner, women perform double duty. You still must cook for your family and take care of your own children.

Forty years ago, in 1808, sexual abuse of black women became even worse. The African slave trade was outlawed. So now all new slaves have to be "bred" on the plantations. Many women are treated as breeders. One Texas woman was sold four times as a breeder, but did not get to keep any of her children. If a white man rapes a Black woman, the woman's child is a slave. So white owners profit from rape.

One way enslaved women and men fight against slavery is by trying to escape and make their way to freedom in the North or Canada. Some, like Harriet Tubman, then help others escape by becoming part of the Underground Railroad, a series of safe houses and routes along the way. Other enslaved women and men have joined rebellions like those led by Gabriel Prosser or Nat Turner. Some people who have escaped from slavery, like Sojourner Truth and Frederick Douglass, are becoming important voices for women's rights as well as the rights of African Americans.

Cherokee Women

Life for Cherokee women has changed dramatically in the last 100 years—for the worse. Today, in 1848, you live in Oklahoma, where the United States Army moved you by force. But there was a time when you had more power, respect, and happiness. Your homelands were in what is now Virginia, North Carolina, Tennessee, and Georgia.

In Cherokee culture, women historically had great influence. It was the man who went to live in the house of the woman's family. As John Ross, principal chief of the Cherokee, explained to a white U.S. general: "By the laws of the Cherokee Nation, the property of husband and wife remain separate and apart, and neither of these can sell or dispose of the property of the other." If a couple "divorced," the women kept the children and her property. The men were the main hunters and women were the main farmers. The Cherokee, like other Native Americans, did not believe in private property. Anyone could use unoccupied land, and cultivated fields were controlled by large families, led by the women. No individual or family could own land.

As contact increased between white settlers and the Cherokee people, women lost more and more power. The Europeans wanted to deal only with men. They had no use for the women. Meanwhile, the white Protestant missionaries who came into your territory wanted Cherokee women to act like white women. They wanted you to convert to Christianity, wear dresses, and let the men head the households and own the property. Whites also pushed Cherokees to give up your traditional approach to the land.

Then, 30 years ago, whites in Georgia and other nearby areas came onto Cherokee land and attacked your people. You did everything you could to stay in your homelands, but Georgia law even prohibited Cherokees from testifying in court. Many Cherokees tried to appeal to the whites by adopting their ways. In fact, in 1826 the Cherokee government adopted a law that no woman could vote or hold office.

Ten years ago, in 1838, the U.S. government took all the Cherokee land and forcibly moved you to Oklahoma. About 15,000 people were marched west; 4,000 died on the trip that was later named the Trail of Tears. An eyewitness reported that "even aged females, apparently nearly ready to drop in the grave, were traveling with heavy burdens attached to the back." At least 69 Cherokee women gave birth along the Trail of Tears. One observer said that troops forced women in labor to continue marching until they collapsed and gave birth "in the midst of the company of soldiers."

After removal to Oklahoma your people had to totally rebuild. Now, in 1848, the divisions among the Cherokee have been healed and new schools are under construction, including a college for Cherokee young women. You worry that white settlers and the U.S. government will once again steal your land and kill your people. In places like Kansas Territory, just north of Oklahoma, white settlers are beginning to move in and take Indian land. You don't want another Trail of Tears. You don't want your children and families attacked once again.

Middle- and Upper-Class White Reformers

The first thing you discovered you had in common with each other is your opposition to slavery. Even though all of you are white, you believe that slavery is a terrible wrong. You are all abolitionists—people who want to abolish (end) slavery. So what does wanting to end slavery have to do with wanting rights for women? The more you spoke out against slavery and for the rights of Black people, the more you saw your *own* lack of rights. In many ways, women are the possessions of their husbands. As with slavery, you want this inequality and injustice to end.

Almost all of you are from upper-class or middle-class backgrounds. Elizabeth Cady Stanton's father was a prominent lawyer, judge, and former congressman who served on the New York Supreme Court. Lucretia Mott's father was the master of a whaling ship and her mother ran a store. Sarah and Angelina Grimké's family was one of the wealthiest slaveowning families in South Carolina. Despite your privileged backgrounds, your lives have been limited by women's lack of rights. There is only one college in the United States that will accept women. There is not one woman doctor or lawyer. Women are rarely allowed to speak in public, never allowed to vote or be elected to political office. In 1838, when Angelina Grimké delivered antislavery petitions and spoke before the Massachusetts state legislature, it was the first time a woman had ever spoken before a legislative body in the United States.

The idea of the Women's Rights Convention in Seneca Falls was born eight years ago in London. Lucretia Mott and Elizabeth Cady Stanton were attending the World Anti-Slavery Convention. Even though they were active abolitionists in the United States and Mott was an elected delegate, they were not allowed to participate. They could only be spectators.

Now, eight years later, the time has come for women to speak about our needs, speak about our rights. Women's lives are too hard. It isn't right for us to speak up for freedom and against slavery, but to remain silent about the need for freedom for women. We are educated women. If we won't stand up for women's rights, who will?

Women in the Newly Conquered Territory of New Mexico

Two years ago, in 1846, the United States went to war with Mexico. That summer, U.S. Col. Stephen W. Kearny marched into Santa Fé to take control. Up until that moment, you had been Mexican women. Since that moment, you have been *conquered* Mexican women. There are about 25,000 to 30,000 of you in New Mexico. Your lives have been changed for the worse by the U.S. conquest. You worry that things will continue to go downhill now that the United States has won the war.

The white male conquerors have contempt for all Mexicans, especially women. As one of the politicians in the North said: "The mass of the people are Mexicans, a hybrid race of Spanish and Indian origin, ignorant, degraded, demoralized and priest-ridden." If this is what U.S. leaders have to say in public, think about how this encourages the soldiers to treat people in private. Even the commander of the U.S. troops in Mexico, Gen. Winfield Scott, admitted that his troops "committed atrocities to make Heaven weep and every American of Christian morals blush for his country. Murder, robbery, and rape of mothers and daughters in the presence of tied-up males of families have been common."

These are hard economic times for all Mexicans. For women it's even worse. Half the women of Santa Fé live in poverty. The only people with cash are the Anglo (white) soldiers and the Anglo businessmen who are arriving. If you are lucky, you make some money washing, sewing, or being a domestic worker for Anglos. A woman domestic worker might make 50 cents a day, a seamstress as little as five cents a day. Mexican men who work as laborers make twice as much as Mexican female domestic workers; Anglo men make 30 times as much as Mexican seamstresses. Women have to work two jobs just to feed their families.

The Anglo Easterners arrive with so many dollars that it drives up prices. Food costs more these days. But that's not the worst of it. The Anglos are buying up land to mine for copper and silver. The Treaty of Guadalupe Hidalgo, which ended the war, guaranteed that all Mexicans in the conquered territories could keep their property and have all the rights of U.S. citizens. But a treaty is just a piece of paper unless it is enforced. Anglos are taking Mexican lands by trickery and theft.

Traditional Mexican communities like yours were not perfect, but everyone had rights to land and water. As a woman, you could own property in your maiden name, and sell or give it away without your husband's signature. You could farm your own land apart from your husband's land or land you owned together. You've heard that Anglo women in the East don't have these rights. If becoming a U.S. citizen means that your husband will control your property, you say, "No, thank you."

With the conquest, you are hurt because you are women, you are hurt because you are poor, and you are hurt because you are Mexican.

Seneca Falls Women's Rights Convention

Women from all over the country have been invited to a convention in Seneca Falls, New York, to discuss the plight of women and to propose a number of reforms to make life better for women. All of you are delegates to this convention.

1. In your group, read the role describing some of the conditions that you face. Based on what you know and information from chapter 6 of *A People's History of the United States*, the handout "Rights of Women: Laws and Practices," and your role handout, brainstorm a list of all the conditions and laws that you want changed. Not all of these changes need to apply *only* to women. You may want to change conditions that also apply to men who face similar conditions. Remember to stay in your role.

2. Then, as a group, make a list of your most important demands. You should have at least five. Begin each demand with "Resolved that . . ." For example: "Resolved that it should be against the law for a man to beat his wife." Possible categories include:
- slavery
- divorce and children
- working conditions
- personal property and land ownership
- wages
- voting/political participation
- ability to speak out and participate in organizations
- sexual abuse
- language
- cultural rights

3. Put your demands in order of importance to your group: Resolution #1, most important; Resolution #2, second most important; etc.

Declaration of Sentiments and Resolutions

Seneca Falls Convention, July 1848

When, in the course of human events, it becomes necessary for one portion of the family of man to assume among the people of the earth a position different from that which they have hitherto occupied, but one to which the laws of nature and of nature's God entitle them, a decent respect to the opinions of mankind require that they should declare the causes that impel them to such a course.

We hold these truths to be self-evident: that all men and women are created equal; that they are endowed by their Creator with certain inalienable rights; that among these are life, liberty, and the pursuit of happiness; that to secure these rights governments are instituted, deriving their just powers from the consent of the governed. Whenever any form of government becomes destructive of these ends, it is the right of those who suffer from it to refuse allegiance to it, and to insist upon the institution of a new government. . . . The history of mankind is a history of repeated injuries and usurpations on the part of man toward woman, having in direct object the establishment of an absolute tyranny over her. To prove this, let facts be submitted to a candid world:

> He has never permitted her to exercise her inalienable right to the elective franchise.

> He has compelled her to submit to laws, in the formation of which she had no voice.

> He has withheld from her rights which are given to the most ignorant and degraded men—both natives and foreigners. . .

> He has made her, if married, in the eye of the law, civilly dead.

> He has taken from her all right in property, even to the wages she earns.

> He has made her, morally, an irresponsible being, as she can commit many crimes with impunity, provided they be done in the presence of her husband. In the covenant of marriage, she is compelled to promise obedience to her husband, he becoming, to all intents and purposes, her master—the law giving him power to deprive her of her liberty, and to administer chastisement.

> He has so framed the laws of divorce, as to what shall be the proper causes, and in case of separation, to whom the guardianship of the children shall be given . . . the law, in all cases, going upon a false supposition of the supremacy of man, and giving all power into his hands.

After depriving her of all rights as a married woman, if single, and the owner of property, he has taxed her to support a government which recognizes her only when her property can be made profitable to it.

He has monopolized nearly all the profitable employments, and from those she is permitted to follow, she receives but a scanty remuneration. He closes against her all the avenues to wealth and distinction which he considers most honorable to himself. As a teacher of theology, medicine, or law, she is not known.

He has denied her the facilities for obtaining a thorough education, all colleges being closed against her.

He allows her in Church, as well as State, but a subordinate position.

He has created a false public sentiment by giving to the world a different code of morals for men and women, by which moral delinquencies which exclude women from society, are not only tolerated, but deemed of little account in man.

He has usurped the prerogative of Jehovah himself, claiming it as his right to assign for her a sphere of action, when that belongs to her conscience and to her God.

He has endeavored . . . to destroy her confidence in her own powers, to lessen her self-respect, and to make her willing to lead a dependent and abject life.

Now, in view of this entire disfranchisement of one-half the people of this country, their social and religious degradation—in view of the unjust laws above mentioned, and because women do feel themselves aggrieved, oppressed, and fraudulently deprived of their most sacred rights, we insist that they have immediate admission to all the rights and privileges which belong to them as citizens of the United States.

In entering upon the great work before us, we anticipate no small amount of misconception, misrepresentation, and ridicule; but we shall use every instrumentality within our power to effect our object. We shall employ agents, circulate tracts, petition the State and National legislatures, and endeavor to enlist the pulpit and the press in our behalf. We hope this Convention will be followed by a series of Conventions embracing every part of the country.

Resolutions

Whereas, the great precept of nature is conceded to be, that each person "shall pursue his own true and substantial happiness" . . . therefore,

1. **Resolved**, that such laws as conflict . . . with the true and substantial happiness of woman, are contrary to the great precept of nature and of no validity.
2. **Resolved**, that all laws which prevent woman from occupying such a station in society as her conscience shall dictate, or which place her in a position inferior to that of man, are contrary to the great precept of nature, and therefore of no . . . authority.
3. **Resolved**, that woman is man's equal—was intended to be so by the Creator, and the highest good of the race demands that she should be recognized as such.
4. **Resolved**, that the women of this country ought to be enlightened in regard to the laws under which they live, that they may no longer publish their degradation by declaring themselves satisfied with their present position, nor their ignorance, by asserting that they have all the rights they want.
5. **Resolved**, that inasmuch as man, while claiming for himself intellectual superiority, does accord to woman moral superiority, it is pre-eminently his duty to encourage her to speak and teach . . . in all religious assemblies.
6. **Resolved**, that the same amount of virtue, delicacy and refinement of behavior that is required of woman . . . should also be required of man, and the same transgressions should be visited with equal severity on both man and woman.
7. **Resolved**, that the objection of indelicacy and impropriety, which is so often brought against woman when she addresses a public audience, comes with a very ill-grace from those who encourage, by their attendance, her appearance on the stage, in the concert, or in feats of the circus.
8. **Resolved**, that woman has too long rested satisfied in the circumscribed limits which corrupt customs and a perverted application of the Scriptures have marked out for her, and that it is time she should move in the enlarged sphere which her Creator has assigned her.
9. **Resolved**, that it is the duty of the women of this country to secure to themselves their sacred right to the elective franchise [voting rights].
10. **Resolved**, that the equality of human rights results necessarily from the fact of the identity of the race in capabilities and responsibilities.
11. **Resolved**, that being invested by the Creator with the same capabilities, and the same consciousness of responsibility for their exercise, it is . . . the right and duty of woman, equally with man, to promote every righteous cause by every righteous means. . .
12. **Resolved**, that the speedy success of our cause depends upon the zealous and untiring efforts of both men and women, for the overthrow of the monopoly of the pulpit, and for the securing to woman an equal participation with men in the various trades, professions, and commerce.

Christiane Grauert

A Midsummer Night's Gender Diversity

BY LAUREN POROSOFF

Lauren Porosoff is a middle school teacher, curriculum design consultant, and author of *Curriculum at Your Core: Meaningful Teaching in the Age of Standards.*

W e'd diagrammed the love quadrangle. We'd laughed at Bottom's word choices. We'd recited Titania's speeches. We'd played games to help us understand Shakespeare-speak and subtext, and we'd written lines with scansion marks to see the rhythms. We'd acted out Puck's tricks and reviewed Shakespeare's colorful insults, and it seemed like the class was having a grand old time. Then David approached me after class.

"Ms. Porosoff, are we going to do anything with this book? You know, besides read it out loud and have you translate it for us?"

Stab. I knew just what he meant: Instead of the deep dig into a text's ethical and societal questions that I usually bring to my English class, we were acting out a shallow story about lovers, fairies, and donkey-headed bad actors, with some iambic pentameter thrown in. As defensive as I felt ("But it's Shakespeare!"), I knew David was right. I wanted to meet his challenge—to approach *A Midsummer Night's Dream* more critically and in a way that felt more relevant to the students' lives.

> "Interesting how the characters we find most likeable are the ones we put in the middle of the gender expression spectrum."

As if Puck himself had magically contrived it, that same week I attended a workshop where Jennifer Bryan presented her New Diagram of Sex and Gender (see Resources), which offers a way to think beyond binaries by using a set of continuums for biological sex, gender identity, gender expression, and sexual orientation. At the workshop, I came up with a new way to approach *A Midsummer Night's Dream* with my 7th graders at Ethical Culture Fieldston, a private pre-K–12 school in New York (about 35 percent of the 1,700 students identify as students of color, and 22 percent receive financial aid).

Three Adjectives

For the first day of the lesson, I broke the students into four groups and assigned each group a set of characters: the lovers (Hermia, Helena, Demetrius, and Lysander), the Athenians at court (Egeus, Theseus, and Hippolyta), the mechanicals (Bottom, Quince, and Flute), and the fairies (Oberon, Titania, and Puck). Working together, the students in each group had to agree on three adjectives that defined each of their characters. The students described Helena, who rats out her best friend in an attempt to get attention and later gets her man through fairy magic, as desperate, jealous, and self-conscious. Her beloved Demetrius, who went after Hermia even though she was in love with someone else, was stuck up, narrow-minded, and persistent.

Next, the student groups switched character lists and had to revise the adjectives, keeping at least one and changing at least one adjective per character. I wanted them to negotiate meaning and return to the text for evidence to support their claims about their characters. So even though proud, beautiful, and seductive all seemed fitting descriptors for Titania, the group that was working on her cut proud (they reasoned: "Just because Oberon called her proud doesn't mean she was!") in favor of independent-minded (citing how she refuses to spend time with Oberon or give him the changeling boy). I pushed that group, asking them how they knew Titania was beautiful when there's no description of what she looks like. Caroline said, "She's the *fairy* queen."

The next day, I told the class that we'd be discussing a theme that interested Shakespeare: gender. I showed them Bryan's diagram and went over the concepts of biological sex characteristics, gender identity, gender expression, and sexual orientation—and how these don't necessarily "line up"; a heterosexual woman can have masculine characteristics, and a person can be born with XY chromosomes but present as a girl. (The students had studied genetics in their life sciences class, so they knew what XX and XY meant. Still, they were surprised to learn that XX doesn't equal girl.)

I asked the students what messages they get about how girls and boys are "supposed to" look and act, and what happens when people challenge those assumptions. Some students tentatively mentioned labels for those who defy gender expectations—tomboy, metrosexual, and homo—and for relationships that fall outside societal comfort levels—bromance, manny, and girl-crush.

"But a bromance doesn't mean you're gay," Nick protested. "It's the opposite."

"Right," Caroline said, "but why do you need a label at all? There's no term like that for girls."

"Because it's different for girls."

"Why? Girls are allowed to spend a lot of time with their best friends, but guys aren't?"

"Guys are, too. It's not like if I hang out with another guy all the time, everyone starts saying we're gay."

"I don't think when people call it a bromance anyone thinks the two guys are actually gay. It's as if you're making fun of the idea of guys spending so much time together."

I jumped in: "Caroline, it sounds like you're saying that the word 'bromance' reveals a cultural conflict between gender identity and gender expression. In what we call a bromance, two guys are very close friends."

"But having close friends isn't gay," Nick said.

"But is it considered feminine? I think what we're getting into is how gender identity, gender expression, and sexual orientation all get lumped together. Why is a very close friendship between two straight, masculine guys a problem?"

"It's not a problem."

"Then why do we label it a bromance?"

Class was over. I left them with the question.

"Is Puck Bi?"

The next day, I wasn't sure whether I should pick up the discussion about labels and bromances—and the sexism and heterosexism that limit our views of what friendship can look like—or return to *A Midsummer Night's Dream*. Motivated by pressure to keep on with the curriculum and hoping there would be more teachable moments, I opted for the latter.

I drew a line all the way across the board, labeled the ends "masculine" and "feminine," and asked the students to get back into their small groups and place the characters from *A Midsummer Night's Dream* on the gender expression spectrum. Listening to the students' negotiations was amusing and enlightening:

"No, Hermia's not more masculine than Egeus. Egeus is her dad!"

"Yeah, but she went against what he wanted. Plus, Egeus has to listen to Theseus."

"So then Theseus should be more masculine than Egeus."

The big reveal came when I wrote the adjectives from the previous day under each character's name. The adjectives for Helena, who they'd deemed very feminine, were *insecure, jealous,* and *whiny.* For Titania, who they considered more masculine, the adjectives were *aggressive, stubborn,* and *powerful.* What did this tell us?

I can't save discussions of gender and sexual orientation for when we read texts by women and LGBTQ authors.

Some students acknowledged that gender stereotypes affect their readings of characters: "Demetrius and Helena are basically in the same position. They both like someone who doesn't like them back. But when Demetrius chases Hermia, we call him persistent, and when Helena chases Demetrius, we call her desperate. That's not right."

Others protested that guys and girls "aren't really like that," and I reminded them that we weren't talking about individual behaviors—how actual women or men act—but about how we expect women and men to act. As one student deftly summarized it: "We expect girls to have close friendships. We don't assume they're lesbians just because they hang out a lot and give each other hugs. But if guys do that, and we know for a fact that they're not gay, maybe we call it a bromance. As if it's not normal to be at the straight end of sexual orientation and the masculine end of gender expression, and still have a close friendship. So we label it."

"Exactly."

Then I asked: "Which characters do we like the best?"

"Puck! He's funny."

"Bottom."

"I respect Hermia for not listening to her dad."

"I wish Helena would've just listened to Demetrius. Who'd want to marry some guy who only loves you because of a flower? A flower!"

"Interesting how the characters we find most likeable are the ones we put in the middle of the gender expression spectrum."

"Ms. Porosoff, is Puck supposed to be bi?"

"Remember, we're talking about gender expression, not sexual orientation. We don't see Puck having a love life of his own, so we don't know if he's gay, straight, or somewhere in between. But we did say he's somewhere in between masculine and feminine. Why?"

"'Cause he's a fairy and he's a guy? Aren't fairies supposed to be girly?"

"Oberon's a fairy, too, and we put him all the way over here," I said, pointing to the masculine end of the spectrum.

"Yeah, but Oberon's the boss. Look—it says right here—"

"Tell us where you are."

"Act 2, scene 1, line 44. When Puck is talking to that other fairy he meets in the woods, he says, 'I jest to Oberon and make him smile.' Oberon is the king, and Puck is his jester."

"True. So are you saying we think Puck is less masculine because he's subservient? And that, since Oberon is the boss, he must be more masculine? Is it possible to be feminine and the boss?"

"Titania's the queen. She's a boss, too—that fairy Puck meets works for her. And we put her way on the feminine side."

"Yeah, but not as feminine as Helena."

"Whatever," Caroline said. "I can be as feminine as I want and still be a CEO."

Beyond "Diversity Books"

I can't say the lesson radically changed the students' worldviews. They still sometimes confuse gender expression with sexual orientation. They still use words I wish they wouldn't. They, and I, are still in the process of accepting gender as a set of spectrums. But we did think about gender diversity—and a canonical text—in a way that helped us explore societal expectations and our own assumptions.

Amid all the jargon about 21st-century skills and multicultural competencies is an important question: How can we honor students' real experiences, help them bring their real concerns to class, and teach them how to critically read the real world?

At first, my response was simply to alternate between classics like *A Midsummer Night's Dream* and relatively contemporary texts with a greater diversity of voices. This approach is what James Banks and Cherry A. McGee Banks would call "additive": "[the] addition of content, concepts, themes, and perspectives to the curriculum without changing its basic structure, purposes, and characteristics . . . usually accomplished by the addition of a book, a unit, or a course to the curriculum" (see Resources).

But I know I need to do more than add a few more diverse literary works into a curriculum composed largely of texts by straight white men. At the same time, I don't want to just dismiss the classics as outdated. For one thing, the classics are classics for a reason: They were constructed with a sophistication and creativity worth studying, and they contain universal truths about the human experience that still feel relevant to students' lives. For another, all books should be "diversity books." I can't save discussions of gender and sexual orientation for when we read texts by women and LGBTQ authors—any more than I can save discussions of race for when we read texts by authors of color.

Instead, I'm beginning to change how I define reading. Reading still includes examining texts for authors' devices and motifs. But it also includes looking at how identity is constructed in texts, and applying those understandings to how we "read" media, current events, and each other. This approach is more like what Banks and Banks call the "transformational" approach, which "changes the basic assumptions of the curriculum" so that students learn multiple ways to see the world.

So, yes, I need to update my reading list, and I also need to change my basic assumptions about how we approach literature. I haven't yet taken my English course to that level of transformation, but as diversity practitioners often say, "That's the work."

Resources

Banks, James A., and Cherry A. McGee Banks. 2009. *Multicultural Education: Issues and Perspectives*, 7th Edition. Wiley.

Bryan, Jennifer. 2012. *From the Dress-Up Corner to the Senior Prom: Navigating Gender and Sexuality Diversity in PreK-12 Schools*. Rowman & Littlefield Education.

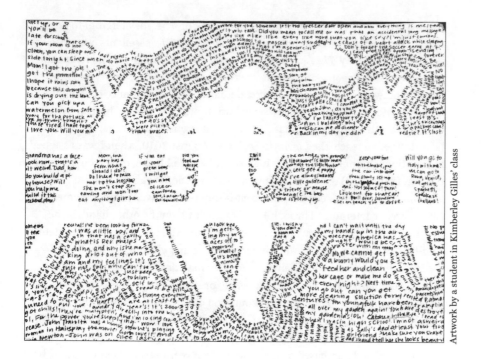

Artwork by a student in Kimberley Gilles' class

Teaching *The Laramie Project*

By Kimberley Gilles

Kimberley Gilles has been teaching for 30 years in high schools and middle schools, urban schools and suburban schools. She won the California Teachers Association 2012 Human Rights Award "for exemplary contributions in the area of human and civil rights" and was named the 2014 National Education Association's National Teacher of Excellence. Gilles lives in Oakland and teaches at Monte Vista High School in Danville, California.

"'Live and let live.' That is such crap. . . . Basically it boils down to: If I don't tell you I'm a fag, you won't beat the crap out of me. I mean, what's so great about that? That's a great philosophy?"

—*Stephen Belber, interviewed for* The Laramie Project

Created from interviews with more than 70 people in and around Laramie, Wyoming, *The Laramie Project* tells the story of the murder of Matthew Shepard, a University of Wyoming student, and the aftermath. Two young men, Aaron McKinney and Russell Henderson, abducted Matthew on Oct. 6, 1998, and smashed in his skull because he was gay.

After tying him to a buck fence on the Wyoming prairie, they left him to die. The crime, Matthew's death and funeral, and the trials of his assailants comprise the narrative of the play. *The Laramie Project* is a portrait of a town and its inhabitants. We see the people of Laramie as cruel, compassionate, brave, and everything in between. *The Laramie Project* demands that its audience confront one question: What is there about the sexual orientation of another human being that calls forth so many personal and public passions?

I decided to teach *The Laramie Project* in August 2010, when I was assigned two sections of English 12. At the high school where I teach, on the outskirts of the San Francisco Bay Area, students who are passionate about English generally choose an English elective that excites them—Creative Writing, Women's Literature, or Literature Through Film. English 12, on the other hand, is the province of seniors who have never liked English, AP burnouts, varsity athletes fulfilling graduation credits, and refugees from other classes.

I cruised the bookroom shelves, searching for titles that might entice this mix of students to read, think, speak, write, or simply care. There, standing in perma-bound splendor among well-thumbed classics like *Macbeth* and *The Catcher in the Rye*, I discovered two class sets of Moisés Kaufman's *The Laramie Project*. They had never been used. Jackpot! The book had been approved by the school board and purchased by the school seven years earlier, yet no teacher had touched it.

The Laramie Project is a great play. It draws readers in emotionally and offers a broad range of humanity to examine. Readers respond—and recoil. Furthermore, *The Laramie Project* is based on source documents, making it of particular value to English teachers trying to deal with the demands of Common Core. It is an astonishing "two-for-the-price-of-one" pedagogical option: nonfiction text within the aesthetic framework of a powerful play. I added the title to my list of texts for the following year.

Imagine my surprise when I was unable to discover any curriculum available online. Apparently, high school drama classes across the nation are producing *The Laramie Project*, but English classes aren't touching it. Determined to move away from fill-in-the-blank, scantron-bubble thinking, I wrote my own curriculum, keeping in mind the philosophy of educator/activist Maxine Greene. She believed that reading literature is valuable because it nurtures empathy. Empathy is, in literature and in life, an act of imagination.

I decided to design an arts-based curriculum that focused on imagination more than analysis or evaluation. The arts demand two elements: First, the artist must see—not look, not glance, but see. Then, the artist must use the imagination to express what is seen. It is no accident that we say we *see* something as a way to express that we understand. Seeing and saying would be the fulcrum of my curriculum. I wanted to send young people into the world who had practice seeing, imagining, empathizing, and reflecting.

Centering my curriculum on empathy came as a response to a thread in student conversations that disturbs me. The put-down, particularly the sexual put-down, is often students' wisecrack of choice. Students use a put-down to tease a friend: "Give me the pencil, faggot!" "What?" "Oh, yeah. But Ms. G, he's a friend of mine. Sorry, Ms. G."

They use a put-down to describe an adversary: "What a douche!" "What?" "Yeah, I do know what it means. Sorry, Ms. G."

They use it to marginalize a person: "She's a slut." "What?" "Oh, sorry, Ms. G. It's just that she really bothers me!"

Homophobic and sexist casual cruelty run rampant in the conversations of my students. Homophobic casual cruelty resulted in the death of Matthew Shepard.

How could I help students raised on *Call of Duty* video games and the nightly news see murder as the ultimate act of silencing?

I knew that the play would provide the opportunity to explore many issues, including capital punishment, the role of religion in American life, and the parent-child relationship. But an undeniable fact remains at the center of the play: Matthew Shepard was gay. Around that fact a range of issues buckle and swirl: the Westboro Baptist Church and its hateful web address—godhatesfags. com, the nature of hate crimes, homophobia, HIV/AIDS, gay rights, the pain of remaining "in the closet," the pain of "coming out," the place of LGBTQ people in their churches, their communities, and their families.

Before we began the play, I asked students to create a "spectrum." Working in pairs, they created long posters with a horizontal line reaching from one end to the other. One end of the line was labeled Intolerance/Homophobia/Misocainea (hatred of new ideas). The other extreme was labeled Tolerance/Activism/Solidarity. Neutral/Unknown was the midpoint.

As we read, each pair had to decide where the dozens of individuals quoted in the play "stood" on the spectrum of homophobia and write their names on the spectrum line. I told them it was fine to move the characters if they changed and grew throughout the ordeal of Matthew Shepard's murder and burial, and the trial of his murderers. I wanted my students to pay attention to what actions the characters took, and to consider what characters said and left unsaid. Discrepancies between words and actions were rich areas for discussion. Looking across the room, I would see a head shaking vehemently or partners bending over a spectrum with fingers pointing to two different points on the line.

Reflecting on the spectrum assignment, I see room for improvement. Why? The goal I had assigned myself was to move beyond "yes/no" thinking, yet here

I was demanding exactly that! For example, Father Roger Schmidt, the Catholic priest who led the first public vigil for Matthew Shepard, defies placement on a particular point of the spectrum. Human sexuality, human behavior, and human beings are far too complicated to pigeonhole on an imaginary line. I can improve the conversations and thinking my students engage in by insisting they take nuances into consideration.

"Knocking In" Conversation

One of the most important parts of teaching *The Laramie Project* was reading the entire play aloud during class. Conversation was a pedagogical goal, so I invited students to "knock in"—rap on their desks—whenever they chose to comment on a moment that struck them as confusing, noteworthy, or appalling.

The two most thunderous knocks occurred in Act III. Students audibly gasped when they read Aaron McKinney's epiphany during his interrogation by Det. Sgt. Rob DeBree. After a pause, McKinney says, "I'm never going to see my son again." Knocks resounded across the classroom.

"You mean, McKinney is a dad?"

"How could he kill Matthew if he's a dad?"

"Man, he wasn't thinking like a dad when he bashed in Matthew's brains; he was thinking like a jerk!"

"Oh, my God! That means his kid has to grow up knowing what his dad did!"

"You'd think becoming a dad would change you. You know, grow you up."

"Becoming a father isn't the same as becoming a dad."

"True that." Heads nodded all across the room.

Within five minutes of this conversation, knocks again exploded across the desktops.

"Whoa! Are you tellin' me that Dennis Shepard (Matthew's father) does *not* want Aaron McKinney to die?"

"Is he asking the court *not* to give the death penalty even though he would love to see Aaron McKinney dead?"

"That's not right!"

I had to interject. "Whoa! Whoa! Let's ask, 'Why?' Why does Dennis Shepard ask the court to set aside the possibility of the death penalty?"

Heads ducked as faces turned back to the pages open before them. One girl answered tentatively, "I think Mr. Shepard wants Aaron McKinney to suffer. I think Mr. Shepard thinks that McKinney having to live with what he did is worse."

"Yeah, but could you do that?"

"I'm not saying it's right. I'm saying it's what he did."

Voices erupted around the room. Eric, who is usually quiet, said: "Know what I think? I think the death penalty is wrong."

We never did get back to reading the play that day. We speculated about

Dennis Shepard's possible motives and the morality of the death penalty. Fathers and sons. Life and death. These issues matter to young people. Not one student packed up to leave before the bell rang.

Negative Space

At the heart of the play is a death. Matthew Shepard was silenced—absolutely and eternally. I was stumped. How could I help students raised on *Call of Duty* video games and the nightly news see murder as the ultimate act of silencing? Every marginalized group is silenced in some way. How could I lead students to confront questions of who is being silenced and who is doing the silencing? Who suffers from silencing? Who benefits?

Matthew Shepard was forever silenced because he was gay. How could students "see" this terrible silence? The answer came from the realm of art: negative space, the rendering of what is not there.

> School climate committees and workshops on sexual harassment aren't going to dent the casual and constant homophobia that permeates teen culture and the larger U.S. culture.

I began by asking them to get out a sheet or two of paper. We were going to write. I asked students to consider something that they were looking forward to, an event perhaps. Prom featured prominently in their conversations. Then, I asked them to consider the lives that lay before them, to consider the decades: 20s, 30s, 40s, up to 80. What did they anticipate that they might say in each of those decades? I asked them to write down their thoughts. I told them they needed to generate lots of text. The atmosphere was jovial, cheerful, the walls echoed with chatter and laughter. "I got the job!" "The honeymoon was perfect!" "It's a boy!" "No, we cannot get a bunny. Would you feed her and clean her cage or make me do it every night?"

Then I asked my students to start including the difficult things they might have to say as those years passed. They grew quieter. "My joints hurt." "I was fired." "They think it has metastasized." The options became more serious. The pages filled.

I asked my students to put down their pens and pencils. I said: "Matthew

Shepard died in 1998 at the age of 21. He and his family and his friends will never experience the joys and complications of any of those lines you just wrote. They were savagely torn away from him and from all who loved him. All he was left was silence."

You could hear my students breathing. No one stirred. I sent them back to their pages, but this time I asked them to consider the life stages snatched away from Matthew. I asked them to write all the declarations and questions and exclamations that Matthew Shepard was never permitted to express. "I encourage you to think of all the challenges, heartbreaks, triumphs, satisfactions, failures, joys, and complications that life will send us—if we are given enough time. McKinney and Henderson stole that time, that life, from Matthew Shepard."

Again, students wrote—silently, sincerely. When they had written for another 15 minutes, I interrupted to show them two examples of "figure–ground reversal." This technique uses the art concept of negative space. One example was a pear rendered in white against a black background, the other was the white shape of an airplane against a black background. *Layers Magazine* has a clear explanation of negative space:

> When composing a piece of artwork, we generally work with three elements: the frame, the positive space, and the negative space (also called white space). The frame is the bounding size of the artwork, the positive space is the subject, and the negative space is the empty space around the subject. (Cass, 2009)

I asked students to decide on an image to create with negative space—leaving what would have been positive space as blankness. The missing image would represent the emptiness that was left when Matthew was killed, the emptiness where Matthew should have been. Students would create that silence by creating a background of all that should have been—a lifetime of declarations, questions, stories, experiences. Once they had decided on a central image, I taught them how to enlarge a smaller drawing (see Resources).

The space they created was a pair of Doc Martens, shoes that had been removed from Matthew's feet in an attempt to make the murder appear to be a robbery gone wrong. The space was the gun used to bludgeon Matthew into a coma. The spaces were weeping angels and broken hearts and tears flowing. The space was a boy tied to a fence. They took their pieces of paper home and came back to class with art. I could tell that they had spent hours and hours depicting the silence.

I jettisoned the next lesson plan and decided that we needed a gallery walk. Students placed their pieces on the centers of their desks along with a piece of blank paper. They then circulated among the art, sitting at a desk to study the image and read the background of text. When they had finished, they wrote a note to the artist, quietly rose, and went to another desk to sit and see again. The room was quiet except for the rasp of pens on paper and the shuffling of feet as students moved from desk to desk. After about 20 minutes, I asked them to return to their desks. My students read their classmates' responses to their art in silence. It was eerie and yet completely appropriate.

Students then chose their two most powerful lines—one negative and one positive—that Matthew would never express. They rose, one by one, using a Quaker meeting format and speaking as the spirit moved them. I released control of the flow of ideas. As students felt moved, they stood, spoke their truths, and then sat again. No one agreed or disagreed. Each student's truth hung in the air: heard, understood, and accepted.

By far the most frequently spoken phrase was "I love you."

> If educators want to tackle one of the critical civil rights issue of our day—the rights of the LGBTQ community—we cannot relegate that discussion to the margins.

Acting with Empathy

When we finished reading the play aloud, students staged selected moments in 10-minute productions. The scenes were polished and daring. The children of Danville became the people of Laramie, the best opportunity I can imagine to practice true empathy. Cross-gender casting was common. Role-doubling was necessary.

Students who habitually sped through their assignments no longer aspired to efficiency. Instead, they aimed at truth. I particularly remember Hassan, a senior whom I had first taught three years earlier. Hassan was a manipulator, a cutter of corners, and a charmer. I expected superficiality from him, but I was wrong. He played both the outraged judge who sentenced Henderson and McKinney, and McKinney as he was interrogated by a detective. In both scenes, Hassan revealed the humanity of his characters. All the students did. Matthew Shepard was a complicated young man who caused his parents to worry. Russell Henderson was an Eagle Scout raised by a devoted grandmother. Aaron McKinney was the father of a young son. The true horror of *The Laramie Project* is that there are no monsters. We are the people of Laramie. Human beings. Murderers and advocates. Bigots and heroes.

So what makes me so hopeful? A different silence.

As the school year ended and my seniors prepared for graduation, I became aware of a remarkable shift in the culture of the class. The language in Room 310 had changed. Students still needled one another, but the words had changed. ("Hey, loser! Who are you taking to the prom? Um, yeah, I know, Ms.

G. Sorry.") There were still occasional epithets and put-downs in my class, but the habit of using sexual identity to insult others disappeared. Did that disappearance occur because I wouldn't abide that form of hate speech? Partly.

But I have come to believe in something much more substantive.

Curriculum, Not Just Climate

If educators want to tackle one of the critical civil rights issue of our day— the rights of the LGBTQ community—we cannot relegate that discussion to the margins of education. "Character education," school climate committees, and workshops on sexual harassment aren't going to dent the casual and constant homophobia that permeates both teen culture and the larger U.S. culture. We need to take a page out of the playbook of the Black civil and human rights movements of the 1960s. As a student in the '60s and '70s, I learned that racism was institutionally and culturally unacceptable when we studied *Black Boy* and *A Raisin in the Sun*. I knew that African American culture was valued when its music showed up in the pieces our choir sang. I recognized its heroes when they showed up in the persons of Benjamin Banneker, Phillis Wheatley, and Malcolm X. African American music became my music. African American heroes became my heroes. We shared an undeniable humanity.

> One of the main ways students decipher what society values is by mastering the content that is presented in schools.

Classroom teachers must include the LGBTQ experience in the story we construct about life through the curriculum we present. Why? Because one of the main ways students decipher what society values is by mastering the content that is presented in schools. Students don't look to their schools' mission statements, inspirational posters, or posted classroom rules for guidance. They look to instruction.

When that instruction occurs, behavioral shifts will follow. Fewer and fewer students will be subjected, directly and indirectly, to verbal sexual abuse. All sexual orientations will become socially accepted as our young people develop their adult identities. Our LGBTQ youth will be better protected. As a result, I hope they will suffer less abuse, self-loathing, fear, violence, and—the most tragic possibilities—murder and suicide.

Until the contributions of LGBTQ peoples are included in all the disciplines of modern American curriculum, we educators will be guilty of trivializing, marginalizing, and bigotry. I cannot live with that. So, I teach Shakespeare's sonnets to a mysterious young man and to a dark lady, the poetry of Sappho, and *The Laramie Project*. Authors and characters who are lesbian, gay, and bisexual have a place in the canon presented in my classroom. Why? Because the literature is good. Because teaching literature is about teaching the human story. Because LGBTQ people are contributing creators of that story. To exclude them is to deny the truth.

And I won't do that.

Resources

Cass, Jacobs. 2009. "Negative space," *Layers*. layersmagazine.com/negative-space.html.

EHow. "How to Enlarge a Drawing Using a Grid." ehow.com/how_12732_enlarge-drawing-using.html. Worksheet example: pinterest.com/mimififi/art-class-worksheets.

Greene, Maxine. 1995. *Releasing the Imagination: Essays on Education, the Arts, and Social Change*. Jossey-Bass.

Kaufman, Moisés. 2001. *The Laramie Project*. First Vintage Books Edition.

The Laramie Project. 2002. Prod. Declan Baldwin. Screenplay by Moisés Kaufman. Gabay Productions. DVD.

Pear in negative space: marynewman.net/images/Negative%20Space%20-%20Photogram.jpg.

Colin Matthes

Creative Conflict: Collaborative Playwriting

BY KATHLEEN MELVILLE

Kathleen Melville teaches English, Spanish, and playwriting at a public high school in
Philadelphia. She advocates for teachers as a founding member of Teachers Lead Philly.

T he conflict in my classroom was explosive: defiant teenagers, raging
parents, broken promises, betrayal among friends. Students were on
their feet, shoving furniture, glaring menacingly, raising their voices.
As I surveyed the room, part of me was very pleased.

In some ways, the project this class had undertaken—creating collaborative
plays about issues important in students' lives—was going well. The students,
20 high school seniors, seemed engaged and invested in the work, from brainstorming and improvising to writing and revising. The class had read and
watched a variety of dramatic pieces, and students had already written and
performed some excellent monologues and short scenes. For this unit, we had
started by generating an exhaustive list of themes and issues that interested
students in the class. In the end, the students narrowed the list down to three
topics—peer pressure, sexuality, and domestic abuse—and formed collaborative

playwriting groups to explore each issue and create original plays.

The students were also proving that they had a clear understanding of one of the foundational concepts in playwriting—conflict. For the purposes of playwriting in our class, I had defined conflict in this way:

Conflict = want + obstacle

In order for an interesting conflict to develop, a character must have a want or need (for example, a young woman wants to play basketball), and there must also be something or someone standing in the way (for example, her grandma forbids her to leave the house). Students agreed that conflict is what makes drama interesting, and they quickly learned to incorporate it into the scenes they wrote in class.

The Conflict

In the midst of this creative process, however, I was troubled. Many of the scenes being enacted in the room were scenes of violence, and it was hard for me to watch my students play this out. Some of the violence I saw in students' work was physical violence taking place between characters. In one scene, two young women attacked each other in a dispute over a young man; in another, a mother beat her teenage daughter. I also noticed some vicious verbal abuse among characters who were spouses, siblings, and classmates. Given the topics students had chosen to explore, including peer pressure and domestic abuse, the violence was not surprising. I was committed to giving students authorial and creative control, but I still worried about the impact of these representations of violence, both on my student playwrights and on a potential audience of community members. What would it say about my students if they wrote and performed plays full of verbal and physical violence? Wouldn't it reinforce some of the most pernicious stereotypes about urban youth?

The first and simplest answer that occurred to me was to censor their work. I knew that if I tried this, they would lose some of their passion for playwriting, and we would all lose some of the integrity of the creative process.

As a teacher, I was facing an important conflict. My "want" was for my students to experience the power of creative, collaborative work. I hoped that writing plays would give them an opportunity to develop their voices and explore complex issues with one another. I imagined plays that could provide a more nuanced, authentic view of my students' lives than a media that often portrays urban youth as reckless and destructive. The "obstacle" in my way was that their work, in fact, resembled many of the TV shows and movies that I hated for their flat, negative portrayals of young people. How could I push their thinking beyond the stereotypes they saw in the media? How could I bring this conflict in my teaching to a productive resolution?

The Want

In playwriting, the most powerful wants are those with high stakes. High stakes means there is a lot to gain and also a lot to lose. This is how I felt about my "want" for the playwriting class. It was my third year teaching this class, an elective that I designed in collaboration with Philadelphia Young Playwrights, a local arts education organization. My prior experience had taught me that playwriting could evoke powerful responses from my students. In creating characters and settings, students shared their perceptions of the world—what they found admirable, despicable, exciting, ideal. In crafting dialogue, they found a safe haven for the rhythms and vocabulary that best portrayed their realities; because plays often employ dialect, I was able to take a break from policing their writing and embrace the rich nuances of nonstandard English. And finally, in performing each other's work, students built community and confidence as artists.

Standing before a group of 20 restless seniors, I wanted all of this and more. I also wanted to give my seniors a space to address some of the issues that were on their minds as they contemplated the end of high school. Just as playwriting can create a safe space for students to express themselves in nonstandard English, it can also create a space to explore the issues that are rarely discussed in school. In class, we looked at examples of plays that take on complex topics like race, sexuality, violence, and identity. We studied *Fences, The Laramie Project*, and the work of Anna Deavere Smith. We looked at ways playwrights draw on multiple sources (history, memory, interviews, music, news) to create a meaningful whole with a powerful message. I wanted my students to be able to harness this same creative power in their work.

The Obstacle

In playwriting, the obstacle is what gets in the way of the want. It's the forbidding parent, the envious sibling, the mountain that must be climbed. For me, it was the violence being acted out all over my classroom. Students were enacting not only physical and emotional violence, but also a kind of violence of representation. The caricatures they put on stage—from the obnoxious, aggressive mother to the single-mindedly promiscuous young woman—stood in the way of my vision of a more authentic, nuanced portrayal. And instead of provoking thought, these caricatures elicited guffaws and groans from our class audience. My students and I had seen these characters before: on TV or in movies. Re-enacted in our room, the stereotypes seemed familiar and amusing to some, predictable and boring to others.

I was confronting what Marsha Pincus refers to as "a moment of dissonance." My desire to promote real artistic control and a real creative process had led to stereotypes that made me cringe. How could I redirect my students toward creating more nuanced characters? How could I support them in teasing out more authentic portrayals?

> # What would it say about my students if they wrote and performed plays full of violence? Wouldn't it reinforce some of the most pernicious stereotypes about urban youth?

Luckily, thanks to the partnership with Philadelphia Young Playwrights, I shared this class with a brilliant teaching artist, John Jarboe. John and I talked together about our concerns and tried to address them with the class. We led a discussion about stereotypes and brainstormed a list of stereotypical characters from TV and film. Then, we challenged our students to go beyond the stereotypes, to dig deeper for more complex, realistic characters.

Our students were attached to the characters they had created. Exaggerated stereotypes are funny, they contended. And in some ways, they were right. In the case of a play about sexuality, seeing the "whore," the "player," and the "virgin" parade across the stage *did* elicit laughter from the class in rehearsals.

Another group argued that they had already defied a stereotype in their play on domestic violence. They had cast the abuser, a role typically filled by a man, as a woman, an aggressive mother who incessantly insulted her husband and daughter. Although I applauded them for exploring a new angle and their classmates rewarded them with hearty laughter during rehearsals, I still felt that their portrayal was more of a caricature than an authentic imagining of a real problem.

I realized that my challenge now was to prove to my students that there could be a more gratifying response to drama than just laughter. I believed that if they were willing to leave the relative safety of stereotypes, they could move audiences with their work. I just wasn't sure how to get them to believe.

Resolution and Final Product

Every great conflict in a play must end in a satisfying resolution. The question must be answered, the tension dissolved. The resolution of the conflict in my practice was not neat or easy, but it was deeply satisfying—certainly for me, and I hope for my students as well.

It began when I found a way to invite my students to bring their own experiences into their work. Initially, this proved difficult. Students had intentionally chosen controversial topics because they wanted to use their plays to raise questions about "things that don't get talked about." Many students had selected issues that were important to them for personal reasons, but very few were willing to share their personal experiences with sexuality, domestic abuse, and peer pressure. Without their authentic experiences informing the plays, however, we were left with empty caricatures and recycled stereotypes.

I talked with the students about the importance of taking risks in their work, and we agreed that the best way to make the plays more powerful and authentic was to incorporate real, lived experiences. For each play topic, I developed a set of writing prompts that I hoped would elicit a broad range of reflections and experiences. I realized that there were some assumptions in the class about whose voices mattered. For example, only those who had had sex could really speak meaningfully about sexuality; only those who had been abused could really speak meaningfully about domestic abuse. To counter these perceptions, I was careful to frame questions that everyone could answer. Writing prompts on the topic of sexuality, for example, included: How did you learn about sexuality? When? Where? Write about a time that you learned about sexuality in school. Write about someone you know who has been given a label (for example, player, whore, fag) that has to do with their sexuality. Why do you think this person was labeled? How do you think he or she feels?

I posted the sexuality questions at the front of the room and gave students time to write. I asked that they write anonymously so we might be able to use the writing to develop and revise our plays. Then I collected all the student writing into a packet. I told the class that I planned to give the packet of writing to the collaborative playwriting group that was working on the play about sexuality and that I hoped that the writing might help them weave more authentic experiences into the fabric of their play. I made a point of including my own writing in the packet, and I asked if anyone wanted their writing removed from the packet. Surprisingly, no one did.

We went through the same process for both domestic abuse and peer pressure. By the end of class, we had three packets of writing, each filled with student reflections on the play topics. The next day, students gathered into their collaborative playwriting groups, and I distributed each packet to the corresponding group. I passed out highlighters and asked the groups to pass each piece of writing around their table, reading silently and highlighting words or phrases that stood out to them. Inevitably, there was some speculation about the authors of different pieces of writing, but for the most part, students were engrossed in reading and respectful of their classmates' honesty and willingness to take a risk for the sake of improving the plays.

Once everyone had finished reading and highlighting, I asked the class to create "mash-up" poems made up of the highlighted words and phrases. Each group worked collaboratively to piece together their classmates' words into rhythmic chains of impressions and reflections. The next day, members from each group performed the poems for the rest of the class.

The poems were not cohesive or neat, but they were drawn from real voices—our voices.

The performances were powerful, in part because many of us heard our own words echoed back to us as poetry. There was also a shared sense of working together to paint an authentic picture around these important issues. The poems were not cohesive or neat, but they were drawn from real voices—our voices.

After the poetry performances, the playwriting groups revised their plays. One group used their mash-up poem as the final scene in their play. Another used vignettes from the writing activity as transitions between the scenes in their play. All of the plays became richer and more nuanced.

The group that had chosen sexuality as their topic decided to name their play *As Told by Teens*. It includes a scene that I find particularly moving; it represents the resolution that my students and I were seeking:

(Jerry, Sean, and Jahlil are walking into the locker room; all guys begin to get changed.)

> **Jerry:** Yo, fellas, I gotta tell y'all something important and it has to stay between the three of us, OK?
> (They all stop. Sean and Jahlil turn around and give Jerry a concerned look.)
> **Jahlil:** Uhh, OK, what's up?
> **Jerry:** So it's like this, y'all remember that time we was out and I was talking to the dude who I said owed me money?
> **Sean:** Yeah, what about him?
> **Jerry:** Well, the thing is that he didn't really owe me money . . . I was kind of . . . sort of . . . getting his number.
> (There is a pause as all three boys look at each other.)
> **Jahlil:** So you're telling us. . .
> **Sean:** That you. . .
> **Jerry:** Yeah. . .
> **Sean:** How long have you known?
> **Jerry:** For about a couple years.
> **Jahlil:** (Harshly) So all these years we've been together, chilling and shit, you suddenly have these thoughts that damn, I think I wanna be gay from now on!?
> **Sean:** Yo, dude, chill.

Jerry: It's not even like that. It's nothing that you can just decide like, oh, I feel like wearing sneaks today or flip-flops tomorrow. I didn't know. I wasn't sure.

Jahlil: Naw, you know I don't play that gay stuff!

Sean: Yo, Jahlil, you way outta pocket right now, like what is your problem? That's our friend right there.

Jahlil: My problem is that this is someone we be hanging around. (Turns his attention to Jerry)

And if you think to even try to come at me with that gay stuff, then best believe that it will be a problem. Without second-guessing, I will knock you out.

Jerry: Really, though!? I told y'all this in 100 percent confidence because I thought that both of y'all was my friend. And then you snap on me like this. Some real friends y'all are.

Sean: (Getting between both of them)

Will both of you shut the hell up for a minute!

(The room gets silent for a moment then Sean continues to speak.)

Now listen, Jerry's gay . . . who the hell cares? He's been our friend since we was in grade school, he's had our back throughout the most difficult days that we had.

Jerry: So why the hell—

Sean: Shut up.

(Jerry gets quiet again.)

Nothing about him changed . . . other than his sexual interest.

Jahlil: Sean, you know I don't associate myself with those kind of people.

Jerry: (Hitting his boiling point) Those people?

(Trying to get past Sean but is stopped.)

You know what, fine, I got you. Oh, I got you.

(Picks up his stuff and walks out.)

Sean: Dude, what the hell is wrong with you?

Jahlil: Nothing is wrong with me. I'm not going to sit around and wait for Jerry to try and pull some gay stuff on me. You know what, forget this. I'm leaving.

(Picks up his stuff and begins to walk out.)

Sean: Where are you going? We have to get changed for practice.

Jahlil: I'm going home. I ain't gonna be around that gay stuff. Peace.

(Jahlil exits. Sean picks up his things and leaves, shaking his head as he exits.)

Reaction and Reflection

This scene, and many of the other scenes in the plays, show my students as they really are: passionate, thoughtful, complex, working hard to navigate the changing terrain of their relationships and their world. Jerry and Sean defy the stereotype of the homophobic black male, and by the end of the play, so does Jahlil; his loyalty to his friend Jerry triumphs over his initial discomfort.

Still, I worried about how the play would be received. We had planned to perform it for an audience of family, friends, students, and teachers. I worried that parents and teachers might think these topics had no place in school. I worried that students in the audience might laugh or call out during some of the tenser scenes. I was worried that my student-performers might be disappointed if they didn't garner the applause and plaudits I thought they deserved.

I stood nervously in the back of the auditorium as *As Told by Teens* unfolded. As the students performed what we called "the coming out scene," I held my breath, anticipating some kind of explosion from the audience. There were gasps and a few giggles, but nothing extreme. Mostly, the audience seemed enthralled by the conflict on stage. In the scene directly following this one, Jerry delivers a monologue in which he claims his right to be open and feel comfortable about his sexuality. After his final words, the audience exploded into applause.

> In creating characters and settings, students shared their perceptions of the world—what they found admirable, despicable, exciting, ideal.

The success of the plays is a testament to the brave creativity of the playwright-performers and to the warm acceptance of our school community. I thought about the students in the audience who were gay, lesbian, or bisexual. How did it feel for them to hear that applause? To know that not just a few of their teachers, but a whole audience of peers and community members applauded the decision to come out? This message of acceptance was a unique and powerful result of the students' work. It was not something that a teacher or a guest speaker or a school policy—no matter how great—could deliver. It was made possible only through the original work of students, writing and performing for and with their own community.

In the end, both the plays and the conflict in my practice came to satisfying resolutions. But neither one ever felt like a foregone conclusion. Most days during the semester I felt overwhelmed by how many things could go wrong. I often felt like I was in over my head or that I had opened a Pandora's box that I couldn't shut. But I'm glad I stuck with it, and I hope to do this type of work with students again in the future. I know that there will be new conflicts—in the playwriting and in my practice—but I have a lot more faith in the process of working through them with my students. Freeing students to pursue the creative process and address controversial issues felt scary and even dangerous. Acknowledging and embracing the conflict in my practice felt risky and destabilizing at times. But the conflict and questions opened the door to real learning and creation for both me and my students. And working alongside them in that process is what makes my teaching feel vital, authentic, and important.

Resources

Harris, Sean, Nafis Pugh, Savon Goodman, Lynnae Edwards, Laborah Myles, Jordan Reese, and Oriana Principe. Jan. 24, 2012. *As Told by Teens*. Unpublished play. Performed at National Constitution Center, Philadelphia.

Pincus, Marsha. 2005. "Playing with the Possible: Teaching, Learning, and Drama on the Second Stage." *Going Public with Our Teaching: An Anthology of Practice*. Carnegie Foundation for the Advancement of Teaching.

Alec Dunn

500 Square Feet of Respect
Queering a study of the criminal justice system

By Adam Grant Kelley

Adam Grant Kelley holds a BS in elementary education from University of Wisconsin–Madison and an MA in social studies education from Teachers College, which named him one of 20 educators "Most Likely to Change the World." His experience is rich, whether as a Peace Corps education volunteer in Uganda, an American history teacher in a Brooklyn transfer school, or a grade 4 teacher at Battery Park City School in Lower Manhattan, where he presently works.

A backpack striking the ground signaled the intersection of identities in the hallway of our Brooklyn transfer school. Shouts echoed against the walls and down to the lounge: "Hit her like the boy she wants to be." Teachers exchanged nervous glances—another fight. I jolted from my seat and sprinted down the hallway. Rounding the corner, I found Stormy, a butch lesbian student, unleashing frustration on Ty, a Black male student who divided his time between our hallways and the juvenile detention center at Riker's Island. Blow by blow, I could see the tears dripping on the tiles, mixed with blood.

"She tries to be like the rest of us. Puttin' on a tough face when she has no idea what it means to be tough. The need to be tough. To survive." Ty sat in the corner of the counseling suite, arms crossed, staring at the ground.

"Don't tell me what I know, what I've been through," Stormy retorted, arms sailing through the air as a demand that everyone acknowledge her presence.

"People don't see you as a threat. Cops don't stop you because of how you look. They didn't drop you in Queens last night at 3 a.m. after an hour in the back of the squad car without a reason. They don't do that to women. They do that to people like me."

"People don't harass you because you don't look or act like they expect you to. Cops don't stop you and curse at you until you stand up for yourself, which only gets you cuffed."

This exchange continued a while longer, both students refusing to acknowledge the other's words, holding fast to the idea that they had nothing in common. Almost as if their experience made them more worthy of the punches thrown at one another and the rage they felt for the world. It was impossible to mediate an end that would cultivate empathy within Ty and Stormy. We concluded with an armistice: Stormy and Ty agreed to avoid one another.

The altercation consumed me for days, raising questions about the community of respect I tried so hard to create within my room. After many contemplative subway rides, I decided to create a course that would allow kids like Ty and Stormy to hear one another and take action against their common experience: entrapment, disenfranchisement, and targeted criminalization.

When Trying Harder Isn't the Answer

The impact of the criminal justice system on students became a glaring issue for me the moment I entered a New York City transfer school. The city created these schools as alternative pathways for overage, under-credited students who end up within the juvenile justice system. Our institution offered smaller class sizes, a trimester system for increased credit accumulation, and the extra support of advocate counselors to navigate conflict. Despite progressive accommodations, many students entered with little trust in adults. New York's militarization of schools exacerbated our students' constant preparation for confrontation.

> I came to understand the importance of integrating LGBTQ people and issues consistently in everything we looked at.

Our population reflected the statistics: mostly Black and Latina/o youth, mostly male. However, the more I communicated with students, the more I realized the presence of queer kids in the school. In discussion, many shared stories of harassment in previous schools, citing lack of administrative support as one reason they turned away from education. My heart ached for their educational abandonment. However, it did not bring me to activism; instead, I followed the culture of the school, focusing on graduation as the solution. In New York, graduation preparation became code for heavy exam prep.

After Stormy and Ty's hallway episode, I faced the reality: students cannot focus on content mastery when faced daily with the threat of battle against police and one another. Furthermore, my students would never identify with academics if it was not immediately connected to their experience.

Shaken from my haze, I immersed myself the next few months in weekly teacher inquiry groups organized by the New York Collective of Radical Educators. The first group of seminars I attended dealt directly with the prison-industrial complex (PIC)—the rise of incarceration rates in the United States, its connection to private corporations and, most startling, its infiltration of public education. In this group, I learned of targeted student arrests—largely African American and Latino boys and men—and the rise of police presence in schools. We explored activist efforts against the system and discussed ways to create awareness around the topic.

Although the PIC inquiry group touched on the experience of queer kids, it was not enough for me to feel secure in presenting it to others, so I tried to find an activist group that was looking at the disproportionate number of queer kids in the American penal system. I did not find a group dedicated to this specific topic, but I did find a group of educators who wanted to engage in discussions of queering the curriculum. Our conversations challenged the narrow scope of what I believed "queering" to be: including examples of LGBTQ individuals and groups to increase awareness and potentially cultivate a more respectful community. Now my perspective on queering the curriculum expanded to include challenging heteronormativity: the assumption of heterosexuality in studying and discussing academic topics. I came to understand the importance of integrating LGBTQ people and issues consistently in everything we looked at.

As I continued to reach out for resources and perspectives, these education activists became a sounding board for curricular ideas and a support system for navigating the politics of school.

Making Theory Accessible

Working with students who missed entire grades meant the course had to serve multiple functions. In addition to exploring issues of oppression, we needed to build basic literacy skills. Early on, I decided I wanted to sell the class to the kids as an experience they might encounter in a college setting. Thus, I included texts in a reader, complete with a syllabus. I excerpted the specific parts of the texts I wanted them to concentrate on. Then I wrote focus questions at the beginning of the day's reading for students to consider and respond to in their notebooks, helping them build active reading and comprehension competences. To promote independence in decoding, I underlined words I believed they might struggle with and wrote definitions in the margins. I knew these supports would assist most students, but not all. To ensure all kids felt prepared for class discussions, I offered a guided reading group at lunch, where the kids would read together. This provided me an opportunity to teach basic literacy skills explicitly, modeling "practices of good readers."

Planning the course took the most time. Finding authentic text and differentiating for the levels of my students consumed evenings and weekends; however, it allowed students to interact with interesting, age-appropriate writing. Remaining true to the idea of queering the curriculum, I wanted to find a range of texts that addressed the PIC while also challenging the idea that only straight people found themselves within the confines of the penal institution. We read selections from *The New Jim Crow: Mass Incarceration in the Age of Colorblindness* by Michelle Alexander, *The New Abolitionists* by Joy James, *Captive Genders* by Eric Stanley, studies by the New York Civil Liberties Union addressing the incarceration of school-aged youth, and Wesley Ware's study *Locked Up & Out: Lesbian, Gay, Bisexual, & Transgender Youth in Louisiana's Juvenile Justice System*. The hard work was worth it when students said how accomplished they felt reading texts that college kids study.

The feeling of hopelessness often pervaded our course.

Some of my most successful learning experiences were cross-curricular. For example, to help students understand the term "disproportionality," I reached out to math teachers and asked them to come in and work with the kids on the inclusion of mathematical models to support an idea. After a week of providing examples and making pie charts and bar graphs of the racial breakdown in our school district versus the national population, the class created visual representations of the population of women, men, Latina/o, African American, and queer individuals in the prison system. I decided to assign students a group that did not reflect their identity to help them take multiple perspectives. Kids analyzed disproportionality by comparing the population of a specific group and the statistics of the same group within the prison system.

Recognizing a System

King, a straight male student with a reputation for high-ranking gang affiliation, had a visible moment of reflection as he looked over his data. Presenting his pie chart on transgender youth, he explained that researchers estimate that less than 2 percent of young people in the United States identify as transgender, yet 15 of every 100 young people in the juvenile justice system identify as transgender. When the classroom erupted into laughter, King stifled his classmates: "That's crazy. I didn't know this was a thing. An issue. All these people running into cops on the street. Like me. Like all y'all."

"People call us criminals or dropouts. And we turn on one another in anger. But now we know what is going on."

This kind of moment of emotional clarity allowed the class to engage in discussion that brought common experiences to the surfaces. The statistics did more than challenge students' thinking, they offered proof that their circumstances were more than a set of unfortunate choices. They were part of a system that unfairly targeted specific groups of people. The clearer this became, the more active the students became in class.

Another activity provided more examples. In my PIC inquiry group, we had participated in an activity that showed how quickly kids at school fall into suspension. Modifying this activity, I created a set of situation cards that I laid face down on the floor in a fashion similar to hopscotch. As students moved from square to square, they were forced to make choices. For example, one card stated:

> You are a homeless lesbian teen, turned out of your home after coming out to your family. You're currently on probation after multiple arrests for soliciting drugs, which you sold to fend for yourself. In addition, you've been suspended from school multiple times for fighting after classmates harass you for being a lesbian. In school, someone whispers a homophobic comment and takes your phone. This is your only way to find housing with friends each night.
>
> CHOICE:
> 1. Report the incident to school safety officers—MOVE RIGHT.
> 2. Confront the student directly—MOVE LEFT.

Both choices have consequences. In the first option, the school safety officer refuses to take action against the verbal harassment; instead, he confiscates the phone, making it even more difficult to find housing for the evening. Arguing with the school safety agent gets the student arrested for disorderly conduct, violating the terms of probation. The second choice may lead to a fight, which results in suspension and also violates the terms of the student's probation.

The act of making the choices and seeing the consequences allowed students to see the workings of a system. Stormy testified to the added pressure of being harassed for being gay. "When people want to throw razors at your face, you have to stick up for yourself," she shouted as she moved to the left. As we debriefed the activity, students confronted a chilling truth: No matter what you do, chances are you'll end up in the same place. "That's crazy," Ty whispered.

Confronting Hopelessness

The feeling of hopelessness often pervaded our course. I saw faces fall and heads slump into crossed arms on the tops of desks. Rather than feeling uncomfortable and ignoring the emotions within the class, I'd begin a discussion, re-emphasizing why it was important to study these topics. Allowing the kids to verbalize that education is better than ignorance often brought them back from the brink of giving up. However, directing the course toward the study and creation of alternatives became imperative the longer we studied difficult issues. After a few weeks of analyzing the system, we read excerpts from Angela Davis' *Are Prisons Obsolete?* Davis argues for the eradication of prisons in favor of alternative approaches to justice. She challenged the students to think about restitution and forgiveness. We watched *The Interrupters*, a documentary that follows a group of grassroots activists in Chicago as they work to stop acts of violence before they happen. Addressing the pull toward hopelessness and providing opportunities for students to consider alternatives to the system kept us from feeling defeated.

Taking It to the Community

After months studying prison abuse, discussing unfair targeting of oppressed populations, and working with teaching artists to create and distribute hip-hop beats to the community about the PIC, my kids needed another outlet to voice their experiences and new knowledge, and to offer the alternatives we had discussed. I wanted to bring together a range of people with different roles and experiences related to the criminal justice system. I reached out to civil rights lawyers, local city council members, school safety officers, prison abolitionists, parole officers, and formerly incarcerated activists. I invited them to meet with my students, knowing this would challenge my students to synthesize everything we had learned and discuss it in organized, clear ways.

By this point in the year, the kids took risks in their learning without fidgeting as they did in the first few weeks. However, as I enthusiastically shared the good news about our community meeting, I could feel the kids recoil into their jackets and hoods. We would need to build confidence before the big day to ensure they could share their understandings. Over a few weeks, the students compiled talking points. Together, we created a list of the main issues we wanted to discuss at the meeting. One example was alternatives to incarceration. From our readings, videos, and discussions, the students outlined what they thought were feasible alternatives, including a schoolwide commitment to restorative justice. At the meeting, they would present their ideas, then ask the attendees what they thought were feasible alternatives. The point was to open up communication.

Together, we wrote and revised speaking notes. They practiced their public speaking, offering suggestions to help each other improve ideas. As a class, we brainstormed potential questions that guests might ask and developed possible responses. This explicit preparation for the community panel allowed the students to bring their focus slowly away from their audience and onto the ideas they had formed through our study.

The day of our panel, I looked around the classroom. Kids no longer self-segregated; instead, they distributed themselves around the room. As the discussion commenced, students used terminology and statistics from our course discussions. Issues faced by queer students were no longer left to stew in the air; they were integrated into the presentations and conversations. Students referenced one another's presentations, encouraged classmates to share their hip-hop beats, showed solidarity when speaking. Paramount was the respectful silence in the room, signaling that they recognized the importance of their common experience.

Although I was proud, I noticed Ty remained quiet, looking detached from the discussion. Then, toward the end of the panel, he raised his hand. Ty spoke in short sentences, his eyes pointed directly at the ground. Everyone listened intently. "Look around. We are trapped. Some of us are Black. Others Latino. Some are gay. We are being thrown together. People call us criminals or dropouts. And we turn on one another in anger. But now we know what is going on. Others will find out. We will tell them."

"Word," Stormy echoed, throwing her arms in the air, knocking her backpack to the ground. This time, the adults didn't exchange nervous glances. No one sprinted down the hall. No blood spilled on the ground. And the only tears in the room were those in my eyes.

As an openly gay teacher, I consistently try to build classroom community and engage homophobic comments with dialogue. But creating 500 square feet of respect proved insufficient. It did not protect Stormy in the hallway. It did not provide Ty with a context to connect with people different from himself. I had to challenge my comfort level and my students' perspectives to validate the queer experience within the authority of the curriculum. This showed itself to be as essential to queer kids as straight kids. Stormy puts it best in her track:

> You can't make me live in shadows for no one to see.
> Gotta stop trying to chain me, contain me.
> Gotta set *your* eyes free.

Resources

Alexander, Michelle. 2010. *The New Jim Crow: Mass Incarceration in the Age of Colorblindness.* The New Press, pp: 52–84, 105–130.

Davis, Angela. 2011. *Are Prisons Obsolete?* Seven Stories Press, pp: 106–115.

James, Joy. 2005. *The New Abolitionists: (Neo)slave Narratives and Contemporary Prison Writings.* SUNY Press, pp: 161–169.

Smith, Nat and Eric Stanley. 2011. *Captive Genders: Trans Embodiment and the Prison Industrial Complex.* AK Press, pp: 77–85, 323–355.

The Interrupters. 2011. Dir. Steve James. Kartemquin Films, Available at interrupters.kartemquin.com.

Ware, Wesley. 2011. *Locked Up & Out: Lesbian, Gay, Bisexual, & Transgender Youth in Louisiana's Juvenile Justice System.*

Teaching *Angels in America*

By Jody N. Polleck

Jody Polleck is currently a full-time associate professor in adolescent literacy at Hunter College–CUNY and a part-time literacy intervention teacher and coach in New York City. Her research focuses on differentiated and culturally responsive instruction and curriculum with urban youth. Many thanks to Melissa Schieble from Hunter College, who helped videotape class discussions and contributed to the first drafts of this chapter.

It is an unusually warm May afternoon in New York City, and the last place most adolescents want to be is stuffed in a cramped classroom with no air conditioning. As a 10th-grade English teacher in a small, progressive high school, I have been working steadily to keep my students motivated and critically engaged for the past nine months. The energy, however, is different these last few weeks of school: My students have been excited about our new text, Tony Kushner's *Angels in America*.

Angels in America: A Gay Fantasia on National Themes is a seminal play that provides a complex view of what life, society, and politics were like in the 1980s during the height of the AIDS epidemic in the United States. Kushner presents a world of chaos, mixing historical and fictional characters, juxtaposing realistic experiences with magical realism. He enmeshes his audience in the struggles and stigma of coming out and of being HIV-positive, as his characters search for connection, meaning, and acceptance.

Although *Angels in America* is grounded in politics and ideologies, it is the characters themselves that my students connect to. The play revolves around two couples: Louis and Prior, Joe and Harper. Prior suffers from AIDS-related diseases and his partner, Louis, is not strong enough to handle it. Joe is a closeted gay man married to Harper, who struggles with mental health issues. Joe and Louis have an affair while their aggressive boss, Roy Cohn (a historical figure known for his role in prosecuting Julius and Ethel Rosenberg and as Senator Joe McCarthy's right-hand man), hides his homosexuality and dies from AIDS.

Throughout the unit, my students are riveted by the characters' complex behaviors and emotions, their entangled relationships, and the realistic dialogue. On this particular day, Greg bursts into class just before the bell rings and declares: "We should do nothing else today but read *Angels in America*. That's it! No independent reading—no writing—let's just read. I can't wait to see what happens next."

A few more students beg "please" in agreement, while others dash to the board to write their names next to a character in the play. Manuel and Robert argue over who will be Roy, Robert convincingly arguing he makes a much better "bad guy." Lorena and Anastasia negotiate who will take Harper or Belize; they cannot decide which character they love the best. Meanwhile, I prod students to find their seats.

I have been at the school for more than a decade in different roles: literacy coach, English teacher, and literacy specialist. Our demographics are similar to other schools in New York City: 400 students, of whom 63 percent are Latina/o and 31 percent are African American; 77 percent qualify for free or reduced lunch; 25 percent are designated special needs; and about 60 percent read below grade level.

For more than 10 years, Shakespeare's *Othello* was the 10th-grade play, but this year I decided a change was needed. For many years, I felt an intense discomfort with the overemphasis on Shakespeare. I decided to select a text that would challenge students and also challenge the status quo, which has favored Eurocentric texts with heterosexual characters. I wanted my students to understand how literature can advocate for equality and promote change, and that's one of the many purposes that *Angels in America* has served for the LGBTQ community.

Setting the Scene

The first days of the unit are about exposing students to the larger questions and big ideas in the play. Although eventually students will select their own central themes, I present four essential questions to frame our unit: How do we make progress? How do people persevere in the face of suffering? How does sexual orientation impact the way people are treated? What does it mean to live in "America?" Introducing these essential questions provides students with a purpose before they read so they can collect textual evidence for literary essays at the end of the unit.

For example, I tell the students: "Let's look at the last question—what does it mean to live here? What does it mean to be 'American?'" I ask them to write in their journals and then we open the questions to class discussion.

John volunteers first: "It means to socialize, to have fun, but also to watch your back all the time, and there's lots of judgments."

I (Jody) ask: "Who agrees with John's responses? Why don't we list responses in two columns: the positive and the negative? Keep these in your notes so we can continue to add to them as we read the play."

Julie: "We have rights and free education."

Nicholas: "Lots of opportunities."

Jody: "Does everybody have the same opportunities?"

Nicholas: "No, but if you work for them, you can."

Jody: "Good, Nicholas. Who wants to respond to that?"

Ronald: "Can I read what I wrote? I said: 'To live in America can be the best thing ever if you have come here with not a lot of stuff. However, if you really live here, it's not. How can you have freedom without truly being free? All of these rights mean nothing, and the Constitution is really just full of lies.'"

Jody: "What I hear is that to live in America is to live within contradictions. As we read the play, we're going to look at those contradictions in the 1980s, which is the time period of the play, and reflect on how much things have and have not changed. This essential question would work as a powerful essay topic when we finish the play."

In addition to introducing some of the essential questions in the play, I open discussions of homophobia and heteronormativity. Because of the sensitive nature of the play, I want students to self-reflect on their own assumptions about sexuality before engaging with the text. Heteronormativity is the silent, yet pervasive, notion that heterosexuality is normal and natural. This can be a challenging concept for teenagers, but without addressing heteronormativity, discussions of homophobia can remain an examination of an "other" that only reinforces stereotypes. To start them thinking about this, I distribute copies of "The Heterosexuality Questionnaire" (see Resources). Here is a sample of the questions:

- What do you think caused your heterosexuality?
- When did you first decide you were heterosexual?
- If you never slept with someone of your gender, how do you know you wouldn't like that?
- Who have you told that you are heterosexual?
- Given the problems that heterosexuals face, would you want your children to be heterosexual?

The initial written and verbal reactions from students are diverse. Some students tear through the questions—reading "heterosexual" as "homosexual"—and then have to redo their answers after clarification. Others immediately catch on to the purpose of doing the survey and respond candidly in writing and with each other.

"I get what you're doing here, Jody!" announces Lorena. "This is cool."

"This is messed up," retorts Ivan, a recent immigrant from Russia. Ivan is immediately offended by the questions. "This is not appropriate for the classroom," he says.

"So why do you think I've given you this questionnaire to fill out?" I ask.

"You want us to feel like how gay people might feel," explains Lorena.

"That is exactly the purpose, Lorena. Do heterosexual people have to defend themselves in this way?"

"No," chime in several students simultaneously.

"Not really, right? If you are not heterosexual, do you have to defend your sexuality?"

"Yes!" Lorena shouts.

"Often times you do. That's the point of this questionnaire—to flip it upside down. For those of you who are heterosexual, this may help you understand what it's like to have your sexuality questioned. Tony Kushner is a gay man who has experienced homophobia his whole life, and it is one of the major themes of this play."

After class, Ivan and I have a personal conversation to discuss his feelings of discomfort. I want to honor his emotions—and I also want to make sure Ivan understands the purpose of the questionnaire.

Next, as a class, we talk about HIV. As a woman born in the 1970s, I am old enough to remember the enormity of the AIDS epidemic—and society's fears, confusion, and misconceptions about the disease. In the 1980s, discrimination toward those living with HIV/AIDS was severe and debilitating. Before effective treatments were discovered, deaths from the AIDS epidemic had a devastating impact on the gay community and many others as well. In 1990, for example, AIDS was the second largest killer of men between the ages of 25 and 44 in the United States.

I put the students into small groups to take an HIV/AIDS myth vs. reality quiz so they can discuss what they know and assume about the disease. To my surprise, most of them are knowledgeable about how HIV is transmitted. Then we build additional background knowledge for issues covered in the play. I ask the students to select topics for research. Choices include gay hate crimes, Ronald Reagan, Republicans and Democrats, 1980s, the AIDS epidemic, and Mormons. In small, interest-based groups, students conduct internet research and then present their findings to the class. The mini-presentations help students understand the time period and why Kushner felt impelled to create this brilliant work.

Diving In: Critical Analysis

I want students to think critically about the text and its impact when it was first performed in the early 1990s—and also about ways in which members of the LGBTQ community continue to experience homophobia. Most importantly, I want them to understand how Kushner used his writing as a platform for change, resistance, and advocacy. At the same time, I know I have to cover our mandated Common Core standards. These two seemingly disparate goals do not clash in this instance because critical analysis (a Common Core standard) is central to understanding and interpreting the play.

As a way to scaffold textual analysis, we begin our work by analyzing clips from the HBO film staging of *Angels in America* as way to introduce the central themes and characters (see Resources). Using the video clips, students are able to "see" Roy as he gets ill; they visually experience Joe's pain when he comes out to his mother.

Once students have a grasp of the main characters and the context, we are ready to begin reading the play. I post the essential questions on the wall. As we read, we collect and analyze significant quotations (textual evidence) that support these themes. I model how to do this and then students practice as a whole class, in small groups, and individually. Below is part of one of our first analytical conversations:

Jody: "What does it mean to have a critical lens?"

Lorena: "To think about what the author is trying to teach us."

Jody: "Yes, and that is exactly what we are going to do as we read this play together. We are going to read it with a critical lens, look at what Kushner is trying to get us to see, and explore what we think about that. Julie, can you read this aloud?"

Julie: "In a murderous time, the heart breaks and breaks and lives by breaking.'"

Jody: "Let's paraphrase first. What does this mean? Work with your partner and then let's come back together. . . . How would you paraphrase this, say it a different way?"

Jose: "We continue to thrive despite the pain we experience."

Nicholas: "In times of turmoil, emotions are rough but people need to do that so they can get over it and move on and grow."

John: "In a chaotic time, the soul crumbles, but continues to live on."

I went on to ask the students questions like: What do you think about what Kushner is saying here? Do you agree or disagree? Does it remind you of anything in your own life? Or another piece of writing or art?

"We should do nothing else today but read *Angels in America*. I can't wait to see what happens next."

Constructing meaning together is an important part of the process so that students can begin to analyze deeply on their own and think about how lines in the play reinforce Kushner's larger themes. In addition to discussing passages and themes, students analyze key characters in the play, looking at their personalities, actions, dialogue, relationships with others, and positions of power. We discuss how the characters themselves reinforce Kushner's themes. Each week, students choose a character to follow, which helps them think about different perspectives throughout the play.

I distribute organizers as frameworks for analyzing passages, themes, and characters, and then give written feedback on the work as a way to push their thinking (see Resources). Students keep their organizers and my feedback so they have evidence and analysis for their final literary essay. These organizers also help generate discussion in the classroom.

For example, many students choose Louis as a character to follow. They are angered at his treatment toward his partner, Prior, but sympathize with his struggles. Ronald says: "Louis was super upset that Prior was dying, so he went to Central Park and just found another gay guy and they did it. While they were doing it, the guy said, 'I think the condom broke.' But Louis didn't want to stop. That was really messed up."

Julie: "I know, right! I just don't get it. Prior wasn't dying. He was just in the hospital. Why would Louis do that?"

Robert: "You have to understand that he's under a lot of pressure. He's stressed out. He doesn't know how to deal, so he just does the complete opposite of what he should be doing."

Amanda: "I can't believe what he was shouting. He kept saying, 'Infect me, infect me.' It was a really hard part to read for me."

This particular scene is one of the more graphic and intense in the play; I am proud to see the students deal with the content in a mature manner and thoughtfully analyze the reactions and behavior of the characters.

As we continue with the play, we create a list of one-word themes: sacrifice, love, power, responsibility, deception, survival, struggle. We add these themes to the wall with our essential questions.

I also ask students to track and analyze literary devices. One element that we discuss frequently is magical realism. One day, after we read a scene in which Prior and Harper enter a dream together, I ask: "Why would Kushner include magical realism in a play that is so realistic and true to life?"

Amanda: "Harper goes to Antarctica, right? I think Kushner put that there to show how she abuses drugs, how that brings her to a different world."

Ronald: "Yeah, but why would he put in that dream between Harper and Prior, when Prior doesn't even use drugs?"

Jose: "That scene was crazy and really funny."

Amanda: "I think it was to show how they are alike. To show their connection, their common pain and unhappiness. They both had partners who were betraying them and that's why they met each other."

Jody: "What about the angel?"

Greg: "Is she supposed to be gay? She kissed Hannah."

Ben: "I think that the angel herself was bisexual. That's symbolism, because in those days people thought that if you like your own gender, it's a sin—you won't be accepted into heaven. She's an angel and she is bisexual, so it shows that it doesn't matter what you are or what you like, you still will be accepted into heaven."

Jody: "Excellent analysis here. Now, what one-word theme could we connect this moment to?"

Students suggest the words *acceptance* and *tolerance*, and we add these to our wall of essential questions and one-word themes. Later, we turn the one-word themes into thematic (or thesis) statements to help students with their final essays. These include the following:

- Discrimination makes people behave in ways they don't want to. They are forced to act mainstream so as not to be abused.
- Being homophobic is like being racist and it is another way to discriminate.
- There are different types of love; some people need masks to hide who they are or who they love.

> "In a murderous time, the heart breaks and breaks and lives by breaking."
>
> —Tony Kushner,
> *Angels in America*

Staging Critical Discussions: Socratic Seminars

We have Socratic seminars on most Fridays. I use the seminars to encourage student-centered learning. Students write their own questions before we begin and use their organizers to support their analytical contributions. Students call on each other while I stay in the background, taking notes and clarifying when necessary. The students take notes and then, for homework, use these to write about what they learned from their peers. At the end of the session, students reflect on the experience to think about what worked—and to set goals for our next discussion. Below is a snippet from our final seminar:

John: "Do you think Joe was holding Harper back from progressing?"

Jose: "I think so a little bit, because after she left him, that's when she started to become sane. She knew when she was in Prospect Park, she started knowing that she was doing crazy stuff like biting down trees with her teeth."

Lorena: "Why does it have to be that Joe was stopping Harper from progressing? Maybe it was her stopping him from progressing, because he said that he didn't want to be with her, and she kept on trying to get back with him. Why couldn't she just let him go on and be happy with somebody else?"

Jose: "They both held each other back from progressing. She wanted to leave him, then he wanted to leave her. She needed him—and he needed her. He needed her to 'be straight.' To keep that mask."

John: "I have a new question: Why do you think Prior didn't stay in heaven? Was he the true prophet?"

Fungai: "Yeah! Remember what he said when he confronted the disciples? They were like 'You can choose to live with us,' and he was like 'I wouldn't want to live here. I want my problem to be solved, so I'm going back to my weak state and continue living until it is solved.'"

John: "I feel the same because he chose to stay and die. He had a responsibility to his people."

Final Productions

As our unit comes to a close, it's time for students to synthesize and demonstrate what they learned from *Angels in America*. I ask them to complete two different summative assessments. For the first assessment, they write their own plays, modeled on Kushner's work. These are drafted and revised over a six-week period—and eventually performed for the students by several professional actors in our school's theater.

The second assessment is either an essay or an analytical letter to Kushner about the impact of his play. The only requirements are length and that the paper be critical in nature. Returning to our essential questions and themes, students analyze the message of the play, as portrayed through Kushner's writing and use of literary elements. For example, Fungai, one of my English language learners, elects to write a traditional essay—a challenge she has not taken previously during the school year. Here's a paragraph from her essay:

> In the book *Angels in America*, many of the characters have huge fears. Some of these fears don't let them be who they really are. It makes them pretend to be something else so the rest of the world won't judge them. One example would be when Louis went to his grandmother's funeral, he was saying his name was Lou, not Louis, because [Louis] made him seem gay. Also, Joe is gay but afraid of what others will say. It's against his religion and he feels it's wrong. When his wife asks him, he replies by saying, "I think we ought to pray. Ask God for help." He feels it's wrong being who he really is, but it's the total opposite.

Moved deeply by the play, Lorena chooses the letter to Kushner and writes:

> Your play teaches people to be comfortable in their own skin, to become a better person, how to handle things better, and to know that when making mistakes and hurting people you love, forgiving and taking responsibility are the right things to do. So for you writing this amazingly helpful, life-changing play, Mr. Kushner, I say thank you with the most honorable smile on my face.

Making the choice to teach and converse with students about heteronormativity and homophobia is not an easy one. I do not pretend that every day was democratic and smooth—in fact, many days were spent in difficult discussions about difficult issues. The journey, however, was worth it. By the end of the unit, every student, including Ivan, enjoyed the text and learned powerful messages about the impact of social norms. Monika, who began the unit wanting her "kids liking the opposite gender," reflected at the end of the year that the play taught "people to always be themselves, no matter what anybody thinks of you. Don't change for no one."

Critical, culturally relevant literature like *Angels in America* offers a rich opportunity for students to interpret text and our world. Kushner's play is a powerful opportunity to analyze text and to foster conversations with our students about heteronormativity, homophobia, and LGBTQ equality—both within the historical context of the play and as it relates to contemporary times. In the words of 16-year-old Jose: "[Kushner] wanted to teach us about the ignorance that people have. He taught us about how people deny themselves and others like them for the sake of their image. This play can help young minds to develop and understand others, homosexual and otherwise. It can break barriers that have been set in our society."

Resources

Angels in America. 2003. Avenue Pictures Productions. HBO Television.

"Heterosexuality Questionnaire." www4.csudh.edu/Assets/CSUDH-Sites/Safe-Space/docs/handout-heterosexual-questionnaire.pdf.

Kushner, Tony. 2003. *Angels in America: A Gay Fantasia on National Themes.*

Angels in America

Thematic Analysis Organizer

Essential Questions	Textual Evidence	Analysis: How does it connect to Kushner's message?
How do we make progress?		
How do people persevere in the face of suffering?		
How does sexual orientation impact the way people are treated?		
What does it mean to live in "America?"		
Choose your own:		

Angels in America

Character Analysis Organizer

Who is your favorite character in the play right now? Explain why.

Track them throughout Act II:

Personality Traits	Important Dialogue	Relationships with Other People
Example: *Joe is quiet, Republican, conservative, Mormon, not out yet, in denial*	Example: *"buddy kiss"* *"I'm not gay."*	Example: *Strained relationship with wife. Becoming close with Louis—flirting with him. Comes out to his mother—but she denies his sexual identity.*

Bec Young

Baby Mamas in Literature and Life

BY ABBY KINDELSPERGER

Abby Kindelsperger is a PhD student in curriculum and instruction at the University of Illinois at Chicago and a graduate teaching assistant in the English Education program. She is a former alternative high school English teacher.

From folders emblazoned with "Jojo's Mommy" to name tattoos on necks and arms, hints of my students' children have always been present in my classroom. Without directly asking, by the end of the first week of school I know the parenting status of nearly all of my students. In the alternative school where I teach on Chicago's West Side, between one-third and one-half of the students, depending on the semester, are pregnant or parenting. Although comments about parenting frequently wove their way into our classroom conversations, it wasn't until I became pregnant that I realized the potential richness and importance of bringing this theme into the curriculum.

When I announced my pregnancy to my students in the spring of my fifth year of teaching here, I was expecting excitement, questions, and newfound opportunities to bond. I was not anticipating, however, the ways that my transition to motherhood would change my identity as a teacher and my relationship with my students. Sure, there were unsolicited daily comments on my changing body and suggestions for names. But, more surprising to me, students also showed extreme concern for my well-being, both physical (offers to carry materials) and mental ("Don't stress her out!"). A believer in the reciprocal nature of learning, I had already noticed ways my students educated me about the world, but now many of them took on the expert role and filled me in on what I had to look forward to—both joyous and gross—about having a baby. Even students without children were very involved, as most of them lived with or frequently cared for young children. Perhaps it was because of the role reversal on this topic, but I started listening and responding to my students differently during this time.

I realized that parenting—specifically adolescent parenting—was what Paulo Freire called a "generative theme" of my students' lives. Fraught with contradictions and controversy, this topic is generally excluded from the official curriculum of schools, except in the context of abstinence-only sex education. What, I wondered, would happen if schools embraced the messy realities instead of the usual deficit model? As an English/language arts teacher and believer in critical pedagogy, I decided my students and I should try. I designed an instructional unit with two essential questions in mind: How are stereotypes of parents, especially teen mothers, presented and countered in fiction and nonfiction texts? How do race, class, and gender intersect in discussions of parenthood? My learning goals focused on citing textual evidence to support claims about the representation of school-age mothers in U.S. culture, and analyzing texts of different genres and mediums for the portrayal of parents of different ages, races, and socioeconomic backgrounds.

Maya Angelou's *Letter to My Daughter*

My school is part of a larger network of alternative high schools that enrolls 17- to 21-year-old students who have been kicked out, forced out, or dropped out of traditional high schools. Students attend for one semester, a year, or longer, depending on the number of credits they need to earn a diploma. The English courses are not organized by grade level or even skill level; instead, they are semester-long courses that resemble electives, with great teacher freedom to choose a genre or theme of focus. For several years, I have been teaching variations of "Women's Literature," focusing primarily on texts by African American authors. I organize the course thematically; "motherhood" is the second major unit. Drawing on some of the lessons from previous years, I reframed the first half of the motherhood unit to specifically explore adolescent motherhood.

We began the unit by journaling about birth. Students were invited to write about their own birth, giving birth, being present for a birth, or a story about someone else's birth. Everyone had something to share, and we spent some time in a read-around. We listened as Shakira shared that she was a "miracle baby," born extremely prematurely. Brandon made us laugh with his account of being born at home in the bathroom. Adrienne read aloud: "June 5, 2011, was the day I met my baby, the happiest day of my life. . . . She makes me so happy to be a teen mom. This is the first time I can say I did something good with my life." Alisha described her niece's birth as "disgusting but beautiful."

When schools address single parenting at all, it is inevitably linked to moralizing about "good choices."

The first text of the unit was chapters three and four from Maya Angelou's *Letter to My Daughter*, which describes her unplanned pregnancy at the age of 16. I chose to start there because it immediately presents a contrast to the common deficit-based narrative of teen parenting; Angelou was an extremely respected and successful woman, not identified by her status as a teen parent.

We began with a casual K-W-L (*know, want to know,* and *learned* brainstorming activity) about Angelou. I had not yet explicitly shared that we were focusing on adolescent parents, and none of my students knew this part of her story. Then we began reading the text aloud. As we read, students completed a double-entry journal (see *Reading, Writing, and Rising Up*, a Rethinking Schools book by Linda Christensen). Students selected exact quotations to copy down and then responded using starters: This reminds me of. . . , I can picture. . . , I wonder. . . , I agree/disagree because. . . , This is important because. . .

This strategy invites students to use a range of reading strategies but, not surprisingly, many focused on personal connections. The most commonly selected quotation was "There is no reason to ruin three lives; our family is going to have a wonderful baby." Students shared their agreement with this statement and their approval of how Maya's mother handled finding out about the pregnancy. For example, Deanna wrote, "This reminds me of when I thought my mom was going to be so mad when I told her I was pregnant, but she was actually really happy." Although students completed their double-entry journals independently, we paused along the way to share passages we were marking and how we were responding. *Letter to My Daughter* was my springboard into the topic of adolescent motherhood, making it clear that I was committed to approaching the theme from a nonpunitive angle. When we returned to our K-W-L, students were enthusiastic about filling in details they learned about Angelou in relation to her pregnancy, her personality, and her relationship with her own mother.

Although the passage is fewer than 1,200 words, it is rich with ideas, vocabulary, and style to analyze—enough to challenge even the most sophisticated readers. Her chapter on becoming pregnant is called "Revelations," and this biblical reference serves as an anchoring metaphor. After we read, I directed students to the title and asked, "Where have you seen this word before?" Latisha was quick to respond that it was a church word, and Jamal was able to summarize the Book of Revelation as part of the New Testament in the Bible that talks about the end of the world.

I then asked, "Why would Maya Angelou choose this title?"

After a long pause Shakira inferred, "Well, I guess having a baby was like the end of the world as she knew it."

Marquita added, "Yeah, or maybe even just losing her virginity, because then that changed everything."

I asked if they thought the title had a negative or positive connotation, and Bianca used her personal experience to answer: "It's kinda both. Like for me when I got pregnant, it felt bad for a minute, but then it turned out really great."

The class agreed that any big change is difficult and often seems negative at first, but obviously Angelou considered this to be a positive change in the end.

I ended the class period with students working in small groups to answer open-ended and multiple-choice questions. For example, I asked students to use context clues to infer the connotation of the term "enormity" and the possible meaning of "recalcitrant." I also asked students about genre conventions: "How do you know this is a memoir?" "How would you describe the narration?" In a class with a wide range of ability levels, my students benefit from cooperative learning time and do quite a bit of teaching and learning amongst themselves. Listening in, I heard a student challenge his peer's assertion that "enormity" was obviously positive because it related to being big; another group criticized my answer choices for "recalcitrant," but that created a chance to discuss the shortcomings of multiple-choice assessments.

Imani All Mine

To set up a contrast with the genre, style, and content of *Letter to My Daughter*, I selected the first chapter of the young adult novel *Imani All Mine*, by Connie Porter, as the second text. About a 15-year-old narrator whose mother is not supportive of her pregnancy, *Imani All Mine* is written in a conversational style, with consistent features of Black English. The reading level made it accessible to all my students to read independently, and they completed another double-entry journal, along with individual and small group discussion questions. I was struck by the tensions that student responses revealed, from joy over a baby's birth to the challenges that come later. In response to the line "I wasn't expecting nothing for my birthday this year," Marquita wrote: "I don't be expecting nothing for my birthday ever again because I have a child." In response to the narrator's mother saying she had it easy, Deanna reflected: "I disagree. Things be hard on us. Having a baby young ain't easy. At all." When I read through their work, I knew we had some interesting points for the next day's discussion. Even the students without children were sympathetic toward the narrator and critical of her mother's lack of support.

Starting with the text, I asked: "Do you think the narrator is being a good mother? Explain, giving specific evidence from the text." All the students adamantly agreed she is a good mother, citing lines about how much she loves her daughter and how she takes care of her without help. This theme of responsibility echoed again and again as our discussion moved from this text to comparisons with Angelou to stories from our own lives. I typed up some of the most provocative responses from the double-entry journals, including Deanna's and Marquita's statements. The students, parents and not, articulated the double-edged nature of teen parenthood. Tiana candidly shared that even though she initially planned to get an abortion, now she would probably kill herself if something happened to her baby: "She's my whole world." The conversation turned to how students would handle it if their children or younger siblings became teen parents. Most students agreed that better parenting would prevent the likelihood of unplanned pregnancy, often blaming mothers for not talking honestly with their daughters, and fathers for not setting good examples. Despite the frequent assertions that becoming a parent was an entirely positive life change, my students still considered pregnancies like mine, later in life and with a supportive partner, to be the ideal. They—not I—pointed out the difference between us. This conversation probably would not have happened in a previous semester, but my new pregnant identity made it easier. My classroom was a place where we could be honest and allow what was potentially uncomfortable to be embraced, rather than avoided.

Is there a difference between being called a *baby mama* and a *mother*?

Imani All Mine ended up being students' favorite text of the semester. I gave out all eight of my copies of the book after we read the first chapter for class, and I heard back from many students about finishing the book later. In retrospect, I wish I had included more of the book in order to provide a more complex picture that could have pushed the discussion deeper into issues of poverty and violence. Both of these themes came up in our discussions, but we did not pursue them with as much attention as they deserve.

There are many other texts that could have easily been added into my unit or replaced the ones I chose. Later in the semester we read *The Women of Brewster Place*, by Gloria Naylor, which features more than one example of an adolescent mother. I like *The First Part Last*, by Angela Johnson, for its focus on an adolescent father. I worry that only focusing on African American characters perpetuates racial stereotypes, so in the future I might bring in *Make Lemonade*, by Virginia Euwer Wolff, or *Slam*, by Nick Hornby, to explore teen parenting in different racial and cultural contexts.

Baby Mamas and Babies' Mothers

With some topics, I would not have started with literary texts, but would have chosen a more creative anticipatory set for the theme. However, this theme was already alive in my classroom and already present in my students' lives, so I felt that we would be best served by rooting our study in a shared text. As we read, the stories of my students' lives came into the curriculum through discussion and shared writing.

Next, we were ready to move to a more critical and political approach. I decided to start by unpacking some of the language about adolescent parents that came up frequently in my classroom.

I passed out an anticipation guide with the following statements:

1. Is there a difference between being called a *baby mama* and a *mother*?
2. When you hear the term *baby mama*, do you associate it with a certain race?
3. Is *baby mama* a negative term?
4. Do you use the term *baby mama* to refer to yourself, members of your family, your close friends, or your girlfriend?

Students could choose *yes, not sure,* or *no* for each statement, with a box for answering at the beginning of class and a separate one for the end of class. We tallied our initial yes and no votes, and the discussion was lively from the very beginning.

A few outspoken students were adamant that they were mothers, not baby mamas. Brittney explained: "To me, a baby mama is someone that just has a baby. A mother is someone that cares for their child, is responsible." Others disagreed, saying it was all the same thing. Tyrone argued that he uses the term in a positive way to differentiate his child's mother from other females. Tiana's opinion was that baby mama referred to unmarried mothers, and some students agreed that maybe age mattered. No one argued that the term was racist. I let the initial discussion go on without giving much input, although students pointed out that they would not call me a baby mama, leading a few students to question their initial reaction to the race difference, since I am a white woman and all of my students are Black. Brittney identified the difference as class, saying that maybe you would call a poor white woman a baby mama, but not someone like me.

Then we listened to the song "Baby Mama," by Fantasia Barrino, and used highlighting and annotations on the lyrics to find statements we agreed with, disagreed with, or were confused by. Many of my students knew this song by heart and sang along with the lyrics:

> This goes out to all my baby mamas
> I got love for all my baby mamas.
> It's about time we had our own song
> Don't know what took so long
> Cause nowadays it's like a badge of honor
> To be a baby mama
> I see ya payin' your bills
> I see ya workin' your job
> I see ya goin' to school
> And girl I know it's hard
> Even though ya fed up
> With makin' beds up
> Girl keep ya head up.

Although students primarily agreed with Fantasia, they were struck by the definitions of baby mama offered in Gregory Kane's commentary on Black America Web, which basically states that a baby mama is a woman who got pregnant by a loser. Kane compares embracing baby mama to calling yourself a thug, gangsta, or pimp: "The fact that so many of us embrace [these terms] shows the cultural shift that has occurred among Black Americans. You wouldn't have heard Black radio stations playing a song like 'Baby Mama' 50 years ago. Black folks wouldn't have tolerated it." The class certainly did not reach a consensus, but a few students did start to question the term's connotations. Donetta suggested: "Maybe in the beginning, like back in the day, baby mama was a more negative thing. And maybe when older folks say it, they mean it bad."

To address the potential racial implications of the term, I offered a second example: a video clip from Fox News in which Michelle Obama is referred to as "Obama's baby mama." "Bogus" was my students' common refrain, with many pointing out it seemed purposefully disrespectful.

Tony spoke up. "You know, I think it can be racist. I think Fox was being racist." Some of his classmates agreed.

I often find that students do not share my belief that language is political. As in the beginning of the "baby mama" lesson, students push back on the power of specific words, even derogatory terms. This lesson, however, elicited the most meaningful consideration of different viewpoints and even some changes in opinion. In the column for responses at the end of class, more than one-third of the students changed at least one opinion.

There are many more layers to this issue that could be explored, from consideration of Black English (*baby mama* versus *baby's mama*) to the similarities and differences with the term *baby daddy*. Later in the unit, we looked at hip-hop songs about mothers, and certainly a class period could be spent considering the contradiction between how some rappers talk about their own mothers versus the mothers of their children. It would be worth specifically exploring how mothers of different races and cultures are portrayed in literature and popular culture (the MTV shows *Teen Mom* and *Sixteen and Pregnant* offer a potentially rich opportunity for exploration). In previous classes, I have addressed adoption by pairing *The First Part Last* with a *Sixteen and Pregnant* episode.

While teaching this mini-unit, I was struck by a series of *New York Times* articles reporting on a $400,000 anti-teen-pregnancy ad campaign New York City launched on buses and in subway stations. I showed my students an example featuring a crying toddler (who is not white) and the text "I'm twice as likely not to graduate high school because you had me as a teen." I asked the students to respond in writing about how they felt.

Tiana wrote: "If I saw one, I would try to rip down the sign. . . . The ad is a stereotype, and it's disrespectful to young mothers."

Tony, who is not a parent, responded: "I think the ads are not a good idea because you shouldn't down someone. You should reach out and help somebody." He also pointed out that his mother had been a teen mother, but he was going to graduate from high school.

The students were unanimous in finding the ads offensive and a waste of money that could be spent in a positive way. After the semester ended, I noticed that Chicago started a similar campaign on buses; I hope that when my students see these ads, after their initial anger they will be reminded of the conversations we shared this semester.

Reflections

After our consideration of adolescent mothers, we moved into motherhood and parenting more broadly, and many of the same themes re-emerged. One thing I learned from my students was that being a parent, regardless of your age or marital status, brings with it universal emotions and experiences. Every school-age parent in my classroom was trying to be a good parent in spite of the dominant discourses telling them they would not succeed.

Although the teen fathers in my classroom brought their perspectives to our dialogue, our discussions showed me I need to reshape this entire unit with more attention to school-age fathers. In one class, I had four fathers of young girls who sat near each other and humorously bounced stories off one another. They often spoke from the parental role about how they will talk to their daughters about young men and prevent them from becoming teen mothers. The nature of the curriculum this time did not always push them to consider the contradictions in their positions or reflect on the meaning and portrayal of young fathers. I know there are more important conversations we need to have about male-female relationships and the role of fathers; next time I will be sure to foster them.

When schools address single parenting at all, let alone teen parenting, it is almost inevitably linked to moralizing about "good choices" (Kelly 1998). As social justice educators, we need to recognize how the voices and identities of school-age parents are being silenced and denigrated by the curriculum and reframe the issue as part of an investigation of the complexity of life and the web of power, gender, race, and class.

References

Angelou, Maya. 2008. *Letter to My Daughter*. Random House.

Christensen, Linda. 2009. *Reading, Writing, and Rising Up*. Rethinking Schools.

Freire, Paulo. 2000. *Pedagogy of the Oppressed*. Continuum.

Kane, Gregory. April 20, 2005. "Commentary: What Exactly Is a 'Baby Mama?' It Depends on How You Define Yourself." *BlackAmericaWeb.com*.

Kelly, Deirdre M. 1998. "Teacher Discourses About a Young Parents Program: The Many Meanings of 'Good Choices.'" *Education and Urban Society* 30.

Menconi, David. Oct. 21, 2005. "She's Still an Idol: Recent Controversy Doesn't Slow Fantasia." *Raleigh News and Observer*.

Porter, Connie. 2000. *Imani All Mine*. Mariner Books.

Taylor, Kate. March 6, 2013. "Posters on Teenage Pregnancy Draw Fire." *The New York Times*.

CHAPTER 4

Simone Shin

When Teachers Come Out: Introduction

BY JEFF SAPP

Jeff Sapp has been a teacher, writer, and activist for 36 years. He began his career as a middle and high school math and science teacher and is currently professor of education at California State University, Dominguez Hills. Jeff lives in Long Beach with his husband, Sino, and 6-year-old daughter, Helena. They spend their time gardening, renovating a 100-year-old bungalow house, and having lots of conversations about feminism.

The first game I remember playing as a child was peek-a-boo. I believed if I closed my eyes, my mom couldn't see me. Some years later, I graduated to my favorite childhood game—hide and seek. We ran wild, knowing we had only seconds to hide: "5, 10, 15, 20 . . . 90, 95, 100! Ready or not, here I come!" This game could be played either indoors or out. Outside, you hid in Grandma Rice's hedges. Inside, you ran for closets. I learned early where I'd feel safe.

By the time I hit adolescence and my hormones were attracted to boys instead of girls, I knew exactly what to do. I simply went into hiding. I lived in constant fear of being tagged a fag or a sissy.

It took me a long time to come out of the closet, but a lifetime of playing games finally wore me out. At 35 years of age, I chanted again my childhood mantra, slowly at first: "5, 10, 15. . ." Building volume and speed, I reached the end: "90, 95, 100." And then I screamed in full voice what I had known as a child but had somehow forgotten: "Ready or not, here I come!"

I officially came out on Oct. 3, 1993, and I remember the time, the place, and the first person I told. Coming out is a rite of passage for queer people. We stand on the shoulders of those who came out long before we did and marvel at their courage. We rejoice when we see children coming-out earlier and earlier, or not needing any kind of coming out experience at all, but just being.

Even though I first came out that warm California fall day more than 20 years ago, coming out isn't a one-time thing. We have to find the energy to do it over and over as teachers, parents, and allies committed to justice and equity. Coming out is never a finished experience.

Each semester there is the moment when I say to a new class of students at my university, "You know, I'm a big homo." This isn't the decision every LGBTQ teacher makes, can make, or should make, but for me it's relevant for many reasons. I teach multicultural education classes on anti-racism and anti-oppression, and coming out begins to situate me in movements toward justice. It helps open up conversations about marginalized identities, and creates a safer space for students to talk about their own lives and experiences. Each semester, students come up to me and tell me they're queer, too, and can we have a cup of coffee to speak about their fears about becoming a teacher?

Bringing LGBTQ content into the classroom is a form of coming out that's relevant for all teachers. For example, I teach a graduate course on children's and adolescent literature and have conversations with students about gender nonconforming characters in books like Tomie dePaola's *Oliver Button Is a Sissy*, Andrea U'Ren's *Pugdog*, Mary Pope Osborne's *Kate and the Beanstalk*, and Lesléa Newman's *The Boy Who Cried Fabulous*. In other classes I'll say "Yes, Eleanor Roosevelt had a lesbian relationship that was central to her life" or "How would you help students explore LGBTQ content of the Harlem Renaissance?" or "Did you know that King James of the King James Bible slept with men?"

As the parent of a young child, my perspective on coming out has grown recently. Our daughter finished preschool last year, and we had the best experience at her school. It took work to educate people about which one of us is Daddy and which one is Papa, but we've made some amazing parent friends. There were only a few parents who never met our gaze in two years. Then, just as we finally felt at home in our daughter's preschool, it was time for kindergarten at a new school and that meant, among other things, starting all over as "the gay dads," building bridges and coming out once again. We hope our daughter's teachers will always be welcoming and supportive.

This chapter of *Rethinking Sexism, Gender, and Sexuality* almost didn't exist. As editors, we were focused on curriculum, school culture, and organizing; we weren't sure a chapter on teachers coming out was necessary. Why not? Maybe because we have all been part of and heard so many stories about the difficulties of teaching in the closet and the anxieties of coming out—we succumbed to wishful thinking that we have moved beyond that point.

For LGBTQ educators, being out is about bringing the most authentic selves we can into the classroom.

But educators who submitted coming-out stories from around the country—including "progressive" big cities—begged to disagree with us, and emphasized their point by the sheer number of their submissions. The authors in this chapter highlight how important it is to recognize and talk about the impact of racism and other forms of oppression on the process. And how coming out as an educator now exists within the larger corporate attacks on teachers, schools, and education as liberation.

For LGBTQ educators, being out is about bringing the most authentic selves we can into the classroom. It's a central issue we grapple with in the first difficult years of teaching and afterward as well. An issue that requires thoughtful and strategic thinking about what is possible and what is safe. And one that our straight colleagues need to understand, too. Allies make all the difference.

In this chapter, we honor those stories and that process.

Katherine Streeter

"My Teacher Is a Lesbian"
Coming out at school

By JODY SOKOLOWER

Jody Sokolower is managing editor of Rethinking Schools.

A month into my first year of teaching 7th graders in Oakland, California, we were in the school library, using the big tables there to spread out as we outlined Africa on poster paper and added geographical features. My students chatted as they worked.

"Are you married, Ms. Sokolower?" one of them asked me. My stomach instantly tied in a knot. I was a brand-new teacher in what felt like an incredibly challenging teaching situation. But I knew I didn't want to teach from the closet. I started teaching at the middle school level partly because it is such a difficult time for kids struggling with their sexuality and there are so few role models. I just didn't know I would have to deal with this so soon.

"Well," I explained in what I hoped was a calm voice, "I have been with the same partner for a very long time, but we can't get married because we're lesbians. My partner's name is Karen and we have a daughter. She's 9."

Immediately, everyone had questions and comments. "Are you for real?" "How could you have a daughter?" "How do you know you're a lesbian?" "That's gross."

"Right now we're working on Africa," I said. "But I want to answer your questions. How about this? You think about appropriate questions and tomorrow we'll save some time to discuss this. I'll bring in pictures of my family to show you."

Twenty minutes later, as we walked back across the yard to our portable, my afternoon class came running toward me. "Is it true you're a lesbian? Will you talk to us, too?" I repeated my request that they think about appropriate questions and agreed.

That night I collected a few pictures of myself with my partner and daughter, cooking and hanging out at the playground, and one of our extended family. I also thought about how to explain this in a way that would be appropriate for middle schoolers.

I decided to say I knew I was different when I was in middle school and high school, but I didn't know what was wrong with me. When I was young, no one talked about being lesbian or gay—the whole subject was silenced. Later, I was lucky to be in college at the beginning of the women's movement and the gay liberation movement, so when I realized I was a lesbian I had lots of support. I met Karen when we were in our early 20s, and we have been together ever since. When I first told my parents I was a lesbian, they were really upset and that made me feel terrible. But eventually they realized that it is just part of who I am and that Karen is a wonderful person. I'm glad that now it is a little easier to come out than it was when I was young, but it still takes a lot of courage.

I also set clear parameters in my mind about what kind of questions I wouldn't answer: Nothing about sex and nothing that felt deliberately disrespectful. And I found wording in the social studies standards that I could use to back up my decision to do this.

The next morning, there was a note in my box to go see the vice principal. "I hear you're planning to tell your class about your sex life and show pictures," he said. "I forbid you to do that."

"I'm not talking about my sex life," I told him. "I'm talking with my students about what a lesbian family is. I promised them I would explain and answer their questions if they're appropriate, and I'm going to do that."

That day I spent about a half hour in each class telling my brief story, passing around the pictures, and answering questions. Several kids told me that their church says homosexuality is wrong; I simply acknowledged that I know many churches have that perspective. One of the kids asked a question about lesbian sex—not a disrespectful question, but a question. I said it was a good question for a sex education class, but that it wasn't something I could discuss. Everyone else had relevant and engaged questions or comments: "How does your daughter feel about having lesbian moms?" "How does your mother feel now? Are you still angry at her?" "How did you know you were a lesbian?" "My cousin is gay." "My aunt is a lesbian." "My dad says I'm lucky to have a teacher who will talk with us about so many important things." The next day, I received a letter from the principal, telling me that she was putting a formal complaint in my file. I also received emails from several teachers offering support and encouragement (including two from teachers who told me they were gay but asking me to keep their secret). There were no complaints from parents. I contacted my union representative, who sent a letter to the principal and to my file supporting me.

I felt only positive results in relation to the kids; I could see the progress over the year as the kids who thought homosexuality was a sin struggled with the dissonance between that belief and the reality of who I was and how I treated them. Two students told me in their journals that they thought they might be gay or lesbian. And I felt that my openness changed the class dynamic; the kids knew I trusted them with important, adult knowledge, and they responded accordingly.

In the spring, I received a notice that the district was not rehiring me. In response, the other teachers at the school raised such a clamor with the principal at a staff meeting that she told them it was a clerical error and renewed my contract.

Why am I telling this long story?

Even in the Bay Area, it's not easy to come out as a teacher, particularly at the middle school level. In my own case, after two years of battling homophobic administrations at two different middle schools, I opted to teach high school in a situation where I knew other teachers who were open with their students about being lesbian or gay. Each situation is different: each school, each district, each personal situation. In some places the risks are greater than the benefits, and I certainly don't want to push anyone who isn't ready to come out to their students. But I do want to talk about some of the reasons to come out, and to talk about ways to make it less risky.

To me, the overwhelming reason to come out is to make school a safer place for youth who know, think, or fear they are lesbian, gay, or bisexual. Adolescence is hard enough without positive role models for every aspect of who one is or is striving to become. One young lesbian told me I saved her from suicide; she was brought up in an abusive and homophobic family, and knowing that I had a family, a career, and a positive self-image made her life feel worth living.

In so many ways, silence is the enemy. Having it out in the open makes it easier for kids struggling with their own sexuality, but it also makes it easier for kids with lesbian/gay parents, siblings, cousins, aunts, and uncles. There are a lot of us, so there are a lot of kids affected one way or the other. It also is an important piece of education for students who are being raised in homophobic families or communities. There is nothing quite as strong as a living example to counteract stereotypes.

Coming out can protect lesbian or gay teachers, too, in many situations. Innuendo—the snide comments under kids' breath, the graffiti on the door—is an insidious opponent. Once it's out in the open, you can see where everyone stands and it's possible to engage the issues. When it's all rumor, nothing changes for the better.

Making It Work

I have the privilege of writing this from a section of the country where there is more support for lesbian/gay issues than in many other areas. For this, among other reasons, I can't say what will work for everyone. But here are a few ideas from my experience:

Don't come out to your students before you're ready. In particular, don't come out to your students until you've been "out" awhile in other areas of your life. In the beginning stages of coming out, it's almost inevitable to feel vulnerable and it's hard to have perspective. At the middle and high school level, students often react to teachers based on what's happening with a parent or elsewhere in their lives, and it's important not to take it personally. When you come out at school, you're deliberately creating a dissonance between who you are, as a teacher and human being, and the homophobia in the greater society and in some students' homes and churches. The process can be tumultuous as students wrestle with their feelings and thoughts, so you need lots of perspective and experience to ride it out.

Line up support ahead of time. Start with teachers who you know will be supportive. Find other LGBTQ teachers at your school or in your district. How have they dealt with it? Is there a Gay-Straight Alliance (GSA) at your school? If not, does it seem possible to start one? Is there a straight teacher who would be willing to co-sponsor it? (GSAs are not just for high schools; in some ways they're even more important at the middle school level.)

What about your union? Will they support you if problems arise?

On the other hand, I would think long and hard before talking with administrators. Unless you know that your principal is going to be supportive, you are probably better off coming out first. If they tell you not to do it or keep asking you to wait for some discussion or event that never happens, you're in a worse situation than if they have to decide whether to publicly defend or attack you afterward. But you know your own situation best.

When and How?

Over the years, I have sometimes decided to wait to come out to my students until a relevant situation arose, and other times decided to deliberately create a situation for coming out. For me, it works better to decide when and how to come out, and to do it very early in the year. That way, it's part of who I am from the beginning, not something that upsets the students' view of me later on. It also saves me the anxiety of constantly deciding when to do it, or whether a specific question from a student is the one I should respond to by coming out.

For example, one year early in my teaching career, a planned field trip to the Castro District of San Francisco sparked a deluge of homophobic comments throughout the 7th grade. I tried to organize a gradewide response, but the other teachers didn't want to confront the issue directly. I came out to my students that week; I didn't feel I could talk to them about the homophobia without being honest about my own relationship to it. But my disclosure created its own level of tumult and clouded the issues in a way that made me regret I hadn't come out earlier.

So I usually tell my students I'm a lesbian mom as part of modeling an introductory activity in the first couple of weeks of school. One way to do that is with an Identity Poster Project I use to push students to think about why larger social issues are relevant to their lives. As part of explaining the assignment, I show them my own identity poster. As I talk through the symbols I used, I tell them a number of things about my life—that I have asthma, that I'm a lesbian with a longtime partner and a daughter, that I love to read, that I cry easily. I mention that two people I love are in prison, and that this is a source of pain in my life. If questions arise about my lesbianism, I answer them, but mostly it's just part of who I am. I'm not making a big deal out of it, and I don't expect them to, either. I try to create an atmosphere where it's safe to be who we are, where we don't need to have secrets. At the same time, I emphasize that I am not pushing students to divulge information about themselves that they don't feel comfortable sharing.

Straight Allies

Teachers who identify as straight—and aren't vulnerable to homophobic attacks in the same way—can be really important sources of support. I had a striking personal example of this during my second year of teaching middle school, the year of the field trip to the Castro. The principal told me I should have known better than to come out because the students were too mean to trust with that kind of information. Then I was out sick for a week, and the adults at the school allowed homophobic graffiti to remain scrawled on my door for the entire time. But the students in my classes were supportive and open, our process was encouraging, and I thought I was coping well.

One day after school in the early spring, I noticed homophobic graffiti scrawled on a stairway wall. Dispirited, I walked into the room of the teacher next door to tell her about it. "Don't worry," she said. "Harris (a student working with her) and I will go clean it up. It's not just your problem." I burst into tears. Until that moment, I hadn't realized how isolated I had felt, or how important it is to have straight allies.

So if you're a straight ally, please take this on as your issue, too. Talk openly in class about lesbian/gay friends and family. Discuss homophobia when it comes up in class, in the halls, in the news, in literature. If your school doesn't have a GSA, think about starting one.

Integrate lesbian and gay issues into the curriculum—as protagonists in literature and activists in history. Science and math teachers may have a harder time with this. But if it's on your mind, you'll realize that word problems can include same-gender couples or parents. When teaching genetics, substitute male and female genes for mother and father. It might seem contrived, but every time we refer to genes as coming from a dad and a mom, we're reinforcing traditional families as the only norm.

Unexpected Side Benefits

Is coming out, particularly in a conservative school or district, worth the risk? Every situation is different and there is definitely a "can't put it back in the box" quality to this decision. On the other hand, taking this risk—to make it safer for teachers and students to be who we are—can lead to unexpected gifts. In my experience, it has played a significant role in establishing a kind of classroom community where students feel supported to be open about a whole range of issues, and to be able to talk about difficult topics—racism, sexism, sexual harassment—in ways that are thoughtful, deep, and respectful of each other.

Identity Poster

In this poster, we're exploring the relationship between who we are and how forces in the world affect us.

1. On a piece of lined paper, list the following categories that represent parts of your identity. After each category, leave two or three lines:
   - Personality
   - Background
   - Family
   - Physical appearance
   - Style
   - Likes
   - Dislikes
   - Fears
   - Ideas, beliefs, religion

2. Now think about the words or pictures that best express that part of your identity. For example, how would you describe or show your personality? Concentrate on how you see yourself, not how others see you. Feel free to add more categories.

3. On a large sheet of paper, draw an outline of yourself.

4. Inside the outline, use words and symbols to represent the items on your list. Put them where they make sense—for example, if you cry during sad movies, you might draw tears running down your cheeks. Let your imagination go—there are no right or wrong answers here. Don't worry if you aren't a great artist. This is history class, not art class.

5. The next part of the poster is about the forces in the world that have shaped your identity. Here are some examples:
   - Important events in your life that were positive
   - Important events in your life that were negative
   - Geographical issues—your neighborhood, moves you have made in your life
   - Important events in the world that affected you
   - Advantages or good things in your life
   - Obstacles or problems in your life
   - "Isms" such as racism or sexism if they have had an impact on who you are or how you live your life

6. Once you have decided on the specific events and issues for the forces in No. 5, write and draw those on your poster **outside the outline of your body**.

7. The point of this project is to explore your identity and what forces in the world have affected it. If you have another idea of how to show that, go ahead!

ca-e/Flickr

Two Men and an Imaginary Dog

By Shawn Chisty

Shawn Chisty's experiences as a gay teen and a first-generation immigrant inspired his lifelong dedication to education equity and improvement. He attended Vassar College, Columbia University, and the City University of New York. He is currently an educator at the Town School in New York City and the NYC site director of the Center for Talented Youth.

O n the second Monday of 2nd grade, I asked my students to draw a family. They could interpret that any way they wanted. Most of them drew their own families, some with wishful changes like a furry pet. I called them back to the rug to share. You were allowed to pass, but no one did. Their families were flat, but their explanations were florid. It was my first year as a teacher, so I took notes.

We listened, we laughed, we admired artistry . . . and then I posed this question: "Let's say I walk by this beautiful display of drawings that is soon to be in the hallway. How I will I know the people in the picture are a family?"

Luke: "I wrote *family*. See? F-a-m-i-l-y, family." It was one of our first word wall words, and he was proud to know it.

Sammy pointed out that her family lived under the brown triangle on crooked stilts, which had a curiously large flower sitting perfectly balanced on a crooked windowsill.

"Yes, but what makes a group of people a family no matter who they are?" They raised their hands instinctively and then retracted when they realized the question needed a deeper answer. My students looked to each other for support, and Sammy cleverly pointed to her heart. A chorus of answers followed, which unequivocally linked family to three words: love, care, and respect.

"Are there other kinds of families besides the ones we see on these pictures?" I asked; I had not noticed a significant variety.

Sammy: "Like with one parent?"

Jackie: "No, I have that in my picture." Others concurred.

I pressed further. I took out cardstock cutouts of blue adults and children and placed those down on the rug. They were all dressed in T-shirts and shorts, with "M" or "F" distinguishing the male and female natives of the blue race. Then I started the shuffle I had planned all along: "So here are two grandparents and a kid; are they are family?"

Lucy: "Yes, maybe their parents died."

A student sneered with an "eww," and I quietly internalized his hatred and perhaps fear of me.

We paused, we reflected, and concluded: As long as they have love, care, and respect, they are a family. I presented one parent and a child; children without adults; two adults, every example until I had spanned the range of family structures I had written out in my planning book: single parent, two parents, extended, nuclear . . . yes, yes, yes—as long as love, care, and respect were there.

I remember nothing more vividly from that first year than the moment that came after. I put M and M together, and F and F, each with a blue baby separating the two blue men and two blue women. "What about two dads and a kid—is that a family?"

I thought I was ready to field their confusion and had prepared a way to frame the conversation of queer families by centering it on that love, care, and respect. I had read the literature, pondered possible questions, and practiced the right language for my clever and politically progressive answers. As a fresh-out-of-college idealist, I had high hopes for that crisscross applesauce crowd. It was 2003, a year before gay marriage sailed into Massachusetts.

But I heard giggles from many of the children that day, particularly the boys. A student sneered with an "eww," and I quietly internalized his hatred and perhaps fear of me. Some did not react much, perhaps processing a novel idea or wandering back to any other event in their short lives that could help make sense of my statement.

I wondered if I had done the wrong thing by raising this issue. Would this fail and confuse the children more? In the moment, I rationalized that they laughed more from a lack of knowing, immaturity, or from translating what they had seen or heard outside the classroom walls. I thought about every word I uttered next even more cautiously. I explained that, yes, there are families where two moms or two dads raise the kids, that some girls or boys do grow up to love, care, and respect someone of their own gender. Although I felt satisfied with that explanation, I didn't receive the "aha" reactions I so desperately hoped for. Some continued to giggle, some sustained their blank looks, a few forged on with their disdaining expletives. It was not how I imagined it would go, but first tries hardly ever do.

"I don't have a wife. I do have this man in my picture, though."

I didn't come out to my kids that year. Was I selfish to press the agenda that far forward or to retreat when I did? Over the years, there's been even more reason to build a culture that shows acceptance for LGBTQ youth. When our children are brought to the brink of suicide, self-hatred, and misguided violence, we know there is a moral imperative. It stands as our duty and oath as educators to inspire a civility that is more informed than the one in which we were brought up.

That year I reflected, I wrote, I revised the lesson and kept it in a labeled folder on my desktop. I returned to it the year after, and the one after that. And I incorporated coming out to my students as part of our discussion. Although my students generally accepted the ideas, there was at least one child each year who laughed at the notion of gay families. Over the years, I shared my lessons with my colleagues as well, and other teachers brought the dialogue to their 2nd-grade classes. Only once did I hear of a parent complaint from a family dogmatically against this approach to family education. I was fortunate to work in a school that embraced an inclusive mission, where the administration fully supported the curriculum and lauded its value.

In 2007, and again in 2009, I had two students in my class from same-sex families. In the beginning of the year in 2009, a mother contacted me the day class lists were released to make an appointment to speak in person. At our meeting, she candidly explained that her son was being raised by two mothers and wanted to make sure I was aware. We even brainstormed the right words her son could use to communicate with his peers about his family. Our collaboration that year helped fuel my belief that queering elementary education was a timely and necessary movement to join. I asked permission of the parent to include her family as an example of families with same-sex parents. The parents were very supportive. I recall students still snickering during that year's conversation, but more students seemed to grasp the concept when an example included a family of their peers.

There have been only a couple of years when I did not come out to my students, when the demands of covering other curricular areas overtook our time. Sometimes I have used the video *It's Elementary* to lead into these conversations. Last year I returned to our family drawings lesson with a feeling of curiosity about how the world might have changed our classroom.

Notable differences. The children had drawn their pictures and were ready to share, but this year I had drawn one as well. They shared their pictures with infectious eagerness; nothing's changed about that in 10 years. Some passed, most didn't, and then it came to me.

Ashok: "What did you draw?

I had drawn myself, and I showed that. Next to me I drew my partner, another man, with a golden retriever between us both. The dog was a wishful addition.

Suraiya: "Where is your wife?"

Giggles.

A familiar feeling came about, the one that brings you right back in front of the mean kid at recess calling your ball toss a faggy throw. But I was going to push the envelope today: "Well, I don't have a wife. I do have this man in my picture, though. You see, when I grew up, most of the boys who grew up with me hoped to fall in love and have a family with another girl. But there were some of us, as it is today, who wanted to fall in love with another boy. That is called being gay. I am gay."

I had rehearsed that to sound thoughtful and clear but genuine. I don't know how it sounded to my students, but their reaction was phenomenal.

Well, first they were silent.

"So are you going to marry him?" one child asked, breaking the silence.

Ashok: "You can't marry a boy! Can you?"

Jay: "Yes you can. My aunt got married to her wife, and my mom said that boys can also marry boys."

"Yup, that's true," my co-teacher jumped in. I was still listening.

"Then get married already, Mr. Chisty!" they exclaimed with jovial smiles on several of their faces. I still hadn't spoken. It took a few extra breaths for it to sink in, and I couldn't help but beam. I had come out, and it didn't matter. It was the best reaction I had ever gotten, and I've been coming out on a regular basis for quite a while now. My co-teacher couldn't hold back her "aw," and she suggested we all go in on a group cheer, a tradition we summoned only during birthdays and special moments.

I sat down with my co-teacher that day to share our thoughts on the lesson. We both felt surprised and moved by the children's reactions. Although I have met children of friends and family members who at a similar age show acceptance and understanding of gay families, I was heartened by how many of the students in the class seemed so outwardly accepting. Their year began the summer after gay marriage was legalized in New York. Perhaps that had some influence; I was ready to take it as progress because it felt good to hear about gay marriage from someone who would inherit the world long after I retire my teacher totes. Till I do that, I aim to keep helping students redefine acceptance in schools.

Even this year, one of my students came to me to complain that someone called them gay. My colleagues and I addressed the situation immediately and later planned a class lesson, starting with a reading of *And Tango Makes Three*. I later realized that only addressing their lack of understanding after my students complained wasn't good enough. We as educators should read aloud books that highlight the diverseness of our global community and help cultivate a more tolerant and united future generation. We aren't there yet, but we might be taking some steps in the right direction. And, of course, by now, gay marriage is legal in all 50 states.

Children's days are filled with voices. Whose truths they understand and accept is impacted by how we frame conversations and where we have them. Schools are important places for discussions about global diversity because children can build understanding amongst their peers and with informed professionals (if time is spent on appropriate professional development and sharing of best practices amongst peers). My students will face a future where collaboration and understanding of people's diverse ways of life will empower their success in the world. The world they inherit may face more treacherous challenges in the future. If we can prevent them from adding useless hate for others and for themselves on top of all they will have to face in life, then shouldn't we?

Challenging Homophobia in the Classroom
Lessons from two students

By Lidia Gonzalez

Lidia Gonzalez is an assistant professor in the Department of Mathematics & Computer Science at York College. Her research focuses on the teaching of mathematics for social justice and issues of equity/diversity in mathematics education and teacher training. She has worked as a mathematics teacher in the New York City public school system and, with her partner, has taken on her most challenging "job," that of being a new mom.

This is the story of two very different students I taught in a 9th-grade mathematics class. One, the first openly gay student I ever had, gave me the push I needed to finally work actively at making my classroom a safe space for LGBTQ students. The other, a seemingly homophobic student who initially refused to work with one of her LGBTQ peers, showed me how teachers are uniquely positioned to help students understand difference and to foster acceptance. Both students reminded me that our role as teachers extends infinitely beyond the teaching of our particular disciplines.

As a math teacher in a large, comprehensive yet underperforming high school in New York City, I heard students make homophobic remarks much more often than I would have ever expected prior to becoming a teacher. Although I saw other teachers quickly and decisively challenge racist and sexist comments, I rarely saw homophobic language challenged in the same way. It troubles me to write this, but for years I failed to speak out against the homophobic statements made by students in my own classroom. Yet every time a student commented "This test is gay," it hurt me to hear it. Every time I heard a student insult another by calling their style of dress "too gay" it stung. Every time a student laughed or cringed at the mere thought of a same-sex couple, it hit me hard. As a lesbian, their comments felt as much aimed at me as at their classmates, even though they didn't know it. I was not out at work. Coming out to my family had been a slow, painful, and, at the time, incomplete process. I knew it was wrong for me to ignore the hateful comments that bounced around the walls of my classroom. I imagined there were students who also felt the sting of those words, but I was afraid. I feared that being too strong a voice against homophobia might lead others to question my sexuality. Being out at work was a terrifying prospect but not an excuse for failing my students through my silence.

A Student's Courage

A Gay-Straight alliance (GSA) was started at the school with the help of a community organization. In a school of more than 3,000 students, fewer than 10 attended regularly. One year, three members of the GSA were in my 9th-grade algebra class. They sat together whenever possible and often walked together from class to class. They were extremely supportive of one another but isolated from their peers. Emily was my first openly gay student. Her two best friends labeled themselves gay allies; neither referred to herself as gay. Emily did not challenge students who made homophobic remarks unless they were explicitly directed at her or her friends. Despite her tough exterior and forceful replies, I could sometimes see the hurt in her face or catch her rolling her eyes in frustration.

> I could not bring myself to lie to someone who, despite the difficulties she encountered at our school, proudly referred to herself as gay.

The minute Emily walked into my classroom it became impossible for me to remain silent about the homophobia I was witnessing. It was no longer about standing up for gay students in general—students I was sure were in my classes but whom I could not name. As of that moment, not actively challenging the homophobia meant failing Emily, so, despite my fears, I began to speak up.

I started tentatively with humor: "Really? This test is gay? Hmm, I didn't realize that this test is attracted to other multiple choice tests." Some students laughed but most looked at me as if I had lost it. Emily and her friends smiled and inside I knew I was finally doing the right thing. I made it a point to reply to each and every single homophobic remark that I heard. "Wow, he's got gay sneakers on. Tell me, how did you come to learn these sneakers are gay? Did they tell you their feelings?"

Within a few days the homophobic comments declined drastically, though not completely. With time and an increasing level of comfort, my replies became more forceful, more direct, and more clear about the fact that homophobic comments were not tolerated in our classroom. "I want you to think about what you say: Tests can't be gay, sneakers can't be gay. People are gay. People who deserve to be treated with respect, just like you want to be treated with respect. We will not disrespect each other in class." I know that my students were not all of a sudden more tolerant and accepting individuals, but they did become increasingly aware of what they were saying. Eventually these same students started challenging each other's disrespectful words. "Yo, you can't talk that way in here. Didn't you hear her?" Through the first few months of school, Emily and her friends spent more and more time with me. They came to voluntary tutoring after school, and often swung by my classroom during their lunch break to say hi and keep me up to speed on the GSA's latest events.

"Are You . . . You Know . . . Gay?"

I had made a deal with myself regarding my sexuality: avoiding the truth was acceptable but blatant lies were not. It made me feel less wrong about the lies I had told for years. I had never been asked outright if I was gay. People I knew who were less tolerant didn't really want to know or never saw it as a possibility. People who were accepting didn't ask, knowing that if I was gay, I would let them know when I was comfortable doing so. Teenagers, however, don't seem to follow the same social norms as adults.

One day after class Emily and her friends lingered, clearly in no hurry to rush to their next class.

"Hey, miss."

I turned to them. "What is it?"

Emily spoke softly, "Are you . . . you know . . ." and, after a long pause, "gay?"

I'm not sure how a minute gets to feel like an hour, but it did. Scenes of parents calling the school to complain about their child's lesbian teacher ran through my mind, as did thoughts of colleagues avoiding me on learning the news. Yet I could not bring myself to lie to someone who, despite the difficulties she encountered at our school because of it, proudly referred to herself as gay. "I am," I said, adding "but I'm not as comfortable as you seem to be." She smiled. "That's cool," and just like that, the three were gone.

It took very little time for the news to travel around school. I could swear students and teachers were talking about me behind my back as I walked the halls. Although this may have been partly true, my fear probably led me to believe it was more prevalent that it really was. Though they did not directly ask, some of my colleagues noticed I was struggling and offered support. Coming out to them, I learned that I had given my colleagues much less credit than I should have. They were incredibly supportive, and the community that I feared would be uncomfortable and unwelcoming felt just as much my home as it did prior. In many ways, I was quite fortunate.

I had a good relationship with the vast majority of my students. They knew how much I cared, not only about their academic development, but also for them as individuals. There were always students in my room during lunch or after school. On learning I was a lesbian, many of them became protective of me. When someone said something homophobic in class, another student yelled out, "You're talking about Miss G., too, you know, when you say that. It isn't right. You can't be like that to her!"

Emily and her friends had provided the push I needed to both actively challenge homophobia in my classroom and come out to some of my closest colleagues. I owe those young women a lot. My subsequent students owe them a lot, too, since the safer classrooms I work to build would not have become a reality without them.

Learning to Value Difference

It was after this that another student in that same class came to see me. Kianna had been openly homophobic at the beginning of the year, often making comments in class or laughing at the inappropriate comments of her peers. However, it became increasingly difficult for her to continue when she realized that she was insulting me as well. So, at least in my presence, she quickly stopped using homophobic language. Unfortunately, not long after, she refused to work with Emily on a math problem. When I pressed her on why, she was slow to explain but finally blurted out that she was uncomfortable working with a girl who "likes other girls." I spoke to her at length about how we are to treat our classmates with respect and how we often need to work with people who are different from us. It did not feel like a victory, but I was relieved when she finally sat down. However, even though Kianna begrudgingly followed my request, the two only worked with one another superficially.

Not long after this, Kianna hung around after class one day, waiting until the rest of the students had left. She had a habit of making sure she understood the work and asking me questions before leaving, so it did not surprise me that she stayed behind. What did surprise me was what she asked me.

> Her questions did not come from a place of hatred but from a lack of understanding.

"Miss, no offense or anything, but why would someone choose to be gay? I mean that's just so dis—I mean, I just don't get why."

I had not expected her question and fumbled through an answer. "Well, it isn't that one chooses to be gay. It's not a choice. It's ummm . . . people are born gay, just like you were born with blonde hair."

She took this in. "Yeah, but you don't have to go out with a girl. I mean, not just you but anyone, you pick who you go out with."

It amazed me how hard she worked to try not to offend me. "Kianna, if you dyed your hair black, it would look black but deep down it would still be blonde." She nodded. "A lesbian can technically go out on a date with a man and can act straight, but deep down they aren't straight." Kianna had been going out with a boy in another class and I wondered if I could use her experiences to help her understand. "Technically, you can go out with a girl." Her expression changed quickly, I wondered if I had made a mistake and feared she would stop engaging in the discussion.

"But I don't want to. It's . . . I . . . I wouldn't."

I smiled, thankful that she continued to talk to me. "It doesn't feel right to you to go out with a girl, does it? You'd rather go out with Kevin." She nodded. "It's the same for me. It doesn't feel right to go out with a guy. I can but I really don't want to." She nodded, smiled a bit, and turned to the door. "I think I get it, miss," she said as she walked out. "See you tomorrow." I waved goodbye and took a long, deep breath.

This would be the first of several such conversations with Kianna. On another occasion she dropped by after school. I was sitting at my desk in the empty room and asked her to pull a chair over.

How many of the students in our school had valentines they consistently wrote out of their stories?

"So," she began, "how does someone know they are gay? Like, if they don't decide, you know?" I asked her how straight people know they are straight. "What kind of a question is that?" she asked. "You just know!"

"Yeah, that's the same way gay people know. You just do."

This was not enough. She insisted that there must be something else, that it could not be that simple.

"What if this amazingly cute guy walked by a straight girl? What might she think or feel?" I asked.

"Is he like cute or is he like hot?" I did not respond. "I don't know, she might think he's hot or she might really want to go out with him, or want him to talk to her and, you know, stuff."

"So what you are saying is that she might be attracted to him." She nodded. "If that same cute guy walked by a gay man, that gay man might find him attractive in much the same way you described."

"What if the cute guy isn't gay?"

"Have you ever liked someone that didn't like you back?"

She started laughing as if she had the person's image in her mind. "Yeah. Same thing. Right, miss?"

I nodded.

I started to enjoy our conversations. Selfishly, I suppose, I valued the opportunity to talk to her because it made me more comfortable talking about these issues and, in turn, more comfortable fostering a "safer classroom" than I had in the past. But I was also impressed by her curiosity and eagerness to learn and grow. Her questions did not come from a place of hatred but from a lack of understanding. It gave me hope to see that the way in which she spoke of and to LGBTQ individuals was growing more accepting and caring with the passage of time. I clung to that hope, imagining that, if given the chance and the support, all of our students could grow to value difference.

When Valentine's Day came, Kianna asked me if I had a valentine, adding quickly, "It's OK if you don't, or don't want to tell me." She was holding a helium balloon and some flowers—from Kevin, I assumed.

"I do actually."

"Is your . . . ummm . . . is your valentine good to you? You . . . uhh . . . like each other a lot?" Kianna worked hard to avoid using a pronoun.

She began to put her things together. "You know miss, that's great. I'm glad you have a valentine."

"Me, too. Thanks."

"I hope you have a good Valentine's Day," she said, walking toward the door.

"You, too."

My partner, though I did not use that word when speaking to Kianna, and I had been together for more than seven years at that point and had recently begun living together. I didn't share the details with Kianna as she was my student and I feel that certain details of my personal life aren't student concerns. Yet talking to her in this vague way about my valentine reminded me that with my colleagues, I had not spoken about my partner in any way that implied we were partners. It had been difficult to consistently leave her out of my stories, or to alter who she was to me when I did include her. It made me wonder how many of the students in our school had valentines who they wrote out of their stories. It also made me wonder if knowing my valentine was a woman would make any of them more comfortable being honest about their valentine. I hoped it would.

The following year, though they were no longer in my class, Emily and Kianna still came by to talk to me. Emily had an aunt who agreed to take her to the Gay Pride Parade at the end of the school year. She continued to be a strong and outspoken advocate for herself and other LGBTQ students at the school. She was on a planning committee that organized our school's first Day of Silence, when students agree not to speak for an entire day in solidarity with the many LGBTQ people who feel silenced. Kianna, too, continued to grow and develop. Though not an outspoken ally, she quietly supported her LGBTQ peers. She asked me how my valentine was doing, and I saw in her questions genuine care and concern. I left the school at the end of that year to complete my graduate studies and later moved to university teaching, but I think of Emily and Kianna often, knowing that I am a better teacher because of them.

Katherine Streeter

Transsexuals Teaching Your Children

By Loren Krywanczyk

When he wrote this article, Loren Krywanczyk was in his fourth year as a 6th-grade English teacher at a public middle school in Brooklyn.

One of my 6th-grade students approached me during the independent reading segment of my English language arts class in our Brooklyn public school. He carried *Gender Blender*, a young adult novel about a high school girl who swaps bodies for a short period of time with a high school boy. When the student reached my desk, he scratched his head in confusion and held the book out for me to see.

"Mr. K., this book says that sex and gender are the same thing, but I thought they were different. Like, sex is what you're born as and gender is whether you're a boy or a girl when you grow up. Right?"

My impulse was to ask if he would teach a seminar to most of the adults I know—and some of the adults in our school—about the complexities of sex and gender. Instead, I commented, "That's an excellent observation. Does it seem like this book shows sex and gender in too simple a way?"

He nodded passionately. "Yes, because on the *Real World: Brooklyn* this season there's a girl who says she used to be a boy. Is that for real, Mr. K.?"

This 11-year-old had brought up transsexuality, completely unprovoked, at least three times during the school year up to that point. During one lesson a month before this conversation, I had defined homophobia to his class as "a hatred or intolerance of gay and lesbian people," and he had waved his hand wildly in the air to add "and transsexuals, too, Mr. K.!" It was clear to me that, for whatever reason, he had given the topic a great deal of thought, and that he had some kind of personal investment in it.

Since the end of class was nearing, I told him to stop and see me after I dismissed everyone else. When he came to my desk, I did something I had not yet done all year: I came out to him as a transgender man (a female-to-male transsexual). I explained that he seemed to care about trans issues (at which he smiled), and that I could attest to the fact that transgender people are very real. I explained that I don't talk much about my history, not because I am ashamed of it, but because it can be a distraction from lessons.

He thought very carefully for a moment and then asked, "So all the stories you told us about when you were in middle school . . . you were a girl then?"

I nodded.

"Wow!" he exclaimed.

After another moment, he said, "I'm going to write about this tonight. I may have some questions for you tomorrow. But don't worry, Mr. K., I won't tell anyone. Bye!" Then he ran out the door to catch up with his class.

Gender Matters in Public Schools

If only everyone handled transgender issues in public schools as smoothly and thoughtfully as this student.

Teachers have an unparalleled opportunity to foster this kind of awareness and critical thought about gender and sexuality. And the main point I hope to impart in this piece is how essential it is for educators to create an environment in our classrooms where we and our students are comfortable talking about issues of gender.

In order for this to happen, it is important to weave concepts of gender into our curricula instead of a tokenizing approach that isolates gender as a "one day" or "one week" topic. As individual educators, we must do whatever we can, regardless of our personal identities, although we also bear the responsibility of considering how our personal identities shape our pedagogy and our classroom environments. Role models are important—both those who are lesbian, gay, bisexual, transsexual, and/or questioning (LGBTQ), and also non-LGBTQ teachers who model that these issues matter to all of us.

> Middle school students are not only ready to examine complex issues of identity and power, but are forced to tackle them on their own.

It takes a lot of work for teachers to create spaces that are LGBTQ-friendly, physically and intellectually safe, and encouraging of dialogue about difficult topics. But fostering this kind of environment in our classrooms is sometimes a matter of life or death. Many horrific instances of homophobic or transphobic attacks in schools stand out as evidence of this. In February 2008, Lawrence King, a visibly gender nonconforming 8th-grade student of color, was shot to death by a fellow student in the computer lab of their California public middle school. King's school could be described as similar to the school where I have taught the past four years; King's identity and self-expression could be described as similar to that of several 6th-grade students I have taught in that time.

Lawrence King's death should remind everyone that middle school students are not only ready to examine complex issues of identity and power, but are already forced to tackle them on their own. Homophobia, gender policing, and queer bashing can be witnessed outside my classroom every day, and educators' ignorance of these realities of adolescent experience can be devastating. Unfortunately, many teachers maintain that middle school students are "too young" or "too immature" to handle discussions and readings about identity that go beyond tokenizing statements like "We're all really the same inside" or "Gay is OK!"

We cannot simply rely on anti-bullying projects to address this immense, deep-rooted problem. Anti-bullying, as crucial as it is, is limited in scope. Anti-bullying emphasizes "You should be nice to everybody" and "Don't pick on people," but it does not build or encourage an understanding of other ("different") people and their experiences. Anti-bullying is behavior-based as opposed to understanding-based, which means that an overemphasis on anti-bullying can actually deflect students from deeper thinking and understanding. Educators must navigate between confronting problems directly using anti-bullying methods and simultaneously opening discourse about gender and sexuality in our classrooms to proactively provide support for LGBTQ youth.

From what I have seen, educators are reluctant to delve into complicated dialogue about LGBTQ issues with students for several reasons: trouble with classroom management ("If I go there, who knows what will happen?"), fears of reprimand that often depend upon an unfounded projection of feelings onto an imagined third party ("I would talk about the problems with stigma around HIV and AIDS, but my students' parents would be angry"), or internalized bias.

These fears sometimes prompt administrators to criticize teachers who try to engage students in critical analysis about identity. Last year, I shared a news article about Lawrence King's murder with my students. In doing so, I posed questions about the decision to try 13-year-old shooter Brandon McInerney as an adult, and about the politics of hate crime legislation. Before doing so, I shared copies of the news article with the staff at my school, explaining in an accompanying memo that I thought they, also, might want to discuss the news with their students. I received admonishments from administrators and some colleagues, who claimed that I should "be careful" because the material was "awfully mature for 6th graders!" Only two colleagues approached me to express appreciation for my decision to share with my students the events taking place at other schools across the nation.

Weaving Gender and Sexuality into the Curriculum

Any educator can bring a critical examination of gender and sexuality into their classroom and curriculum. I've found it to be particularly easy to do as an English teacher. Last year I read aloud to my classes Jacqueline Woodson's *From the Notebooks of Melanin Sun*, a phenomenal novel about a 14-year-old biracial boy whose mother comes out to him not only as "queer" (her term of choice) but as in love with a white woman. This text practically creates lessons about identity for teachers.

Throughout *Melanin Sun*, readers are exposed to LGBTQ experiences that include but also extend beyond simplistic portrayals of bullying, teasing, and homophobia. Kristin, the partner of Melanin's mother, explains to Melanin that "family" came to mean "a chosen family" for her after her birth family disowned her when she came out as queer (again, her self-identification). This example is particularly poignant because many LGBTQ youth face the very real prospect of being disowned by their birth families because of their identities.

This book encourages students to think about who "owns" language and terms that relate to identity. Woodson tosses out daunting terminology to refer to sexuality: "queer," "fag," and "dyke." The words "lesbian," "gay," or even "homo-sexual" are rarely seen in the book. Some of the issues students brainstormed as we went along were questions: What does "queer" mean, and why do Melanin's mother and Kristin use it? What does it mean for them to identify as queer? How can Melanin's mom be a lesbian if she has a kid? Did she choose to be queer? We had full class debates about when, if ever, the words "fag," "dyke," and "queer" should be used, and by whom. Instead of brushing off words like "gay" or "faggot" with hasty or offhand reprimands of "Don't say that word!" I try to walk the fine line of preventing name-calling while encouraging analysis of the varying meanings of words—literally, historically, and colloquially—just as I would in studies of other words students stumble across in texts.

To make my classroom an open and safe space for LGBTQ people and allies, I try to open, and never close, dialogue. This includes incorporating conversation about identity and authorship into my lesson plans. For example, during our poetry unit last spring, I shared several Langston Hughes poems with my students. We read "Dream Deferred," "Theme for English B," and the following short "Poem":

I loved my friend.
He went away from me.
There's nothing more to say.
The poem ends,
Soft as it began,—
I loved my friend.

I encouraged students to break down the poems and read between the lines, to try to decipher meaning and make as many inferences as possible about what the poet is trying to say. They had a great time doing this and seemed to love the thrill of approaching poems like mysteries or riddles that they could solve.

At the end of the week, I shared a biography about Langston Hughes' life with students, and we dived into his investment in civil rights, and in racial and economic justice.

"Oh, and one more thing," I added at the end. "I find it interesting that this biography doesn't mention this fact about Langston Hughes: He was romantically involved with men."

Students went completely silent, deep in thought. Finally, one boy raised his hand.

"Wait, so he was GAY?"

"I'm not sure if he called himself gay, but he dated men," I responded.

Students seemed shocked by this information, and even more shocked that I would so comfortably bring it up. Instead of focusing exclusively on Hughes' sexuality, I brought our conversation back to the main purpose of the lesson.

"Now that you've learned so much about Langston Hughes' life and views, do you see his poems any differently? Or are they the same to you? Let's take them out and re-read them, thinking about this."

Some students said their opinions and interpretations did not change because Hughes' identity wasn't relevant to his art. Some students chose to re-read "Poem" as (potentially) a tribute to a past lover. Many students re-examined "Dream Deferred" and expressed more awareness of how politically poignant and incisive Hughes' poems could be. The exercise provided an excellent opportunity to debate the relationship between author identity and written pieces. I don't think I had seen my students so excited about a week of lessons all year.

My Shifting Identity

Any educator can incorporate this kind of curriculum into their teaching in a way that is geared toward his or her own identity, personality, and rapport with students. However, I must admit that the exercise with Langston Hughes was made tremendously easier because my students perceived me as a white, straight, cisgender (born with that gender) man.

My transition, from being Ms. Krywanczyk my first two years at my school to being Mr. Krywanczyk last year, was illuminating. Faculty members and older students at my school were aware that I used to be female-identified, but most of my 6th graders last year remained unaware of my transition. I can't explain why this was the case. Perhaps the older students had an implicit understanding of discretion, or perhaps 6th graders, as the youngest in the school, just "didn't get the memo." When I was Ms. K. and identified as a butch dyke, my gender non-normativity stood out and seemed to beg questions from curious students: Why did I look like a boy? What happened to my tits? How long had I known I liked girls? My visible masculinity—short hair, wardrobe of button-down shirts and khakis, and butch mannerisms—in combination with my femaleness made it difficult at times to stop conversations about LGBTQ issues. Eventually I implemented a drop box for students to leave any questions they had that were unrelated to the lesson. Every Friday I would set aside five minutes to go through the drop box with my classes and answer a few appropriate questions. I would discuss what my parents thought about my queerness (which is the term I used to describe myself), how old I was when I knew, if I would have chosen to be straight if I could have. My presence and outness as a lesbian in my classroom explicitly helped me make connections with some students and open dialogue.

> All aspects of teaching are definitely
> easier when one is perceived as
> straight, cisgender, and male.

Last year, my first year as Mr. K., was very different. The more normatively male I appeared over time (as hormone therapy took effect), the more authority I seemed to have in my classroom and the less my 6th-grade students asked about me personally. The power automatically granted me by my students astounded me. All aspects of teaching are definitely easier when one is perceived as straight, cisgender, and male.

It was my first experience being a rare model of a straight, (assumed) cisgender man who comfortably and proactively discussed LGBTQ affairs. Over the course of the school year I came to realize that there are plenty of opportunities for a teacher in my position (straight and male) to be radical, progressive, and

LGBTQ-friendly in my teaching practices. If anything, LGBTQ movements sorely lack straight male allies, and I was more than happy to play that role in my classroom. In fact, though it's frustrating to observe, my students were more open, honest, and comfortable in their engagement with LGBTQ issues with Mr. Krywanczyk than they had been in the past when they suspected Ms. Krywanczyk of dictatorially imposing a gay agenda on them.

My personal identity and history is significant only with regard to how I can best incorporate it into my mission to create a welcoming and supportive atmosphere for all students, regardless of their gender or sexuality. I do not need to be transgender, or out as transgender, to do this. At the same time, exuding confidence as a transsexual in front of students who know my history is important to me, and, in certain situations, coming out to students who do not know has been effective, and even necessary. It is important for every educator in a school to take on these issues, regardless of their personal experiences, but it is also important for students to have role models.

Hence the reason why I came out to the student mentioned at the very beginning of this piece. The day after I came out to him as a transgender man, the student placed a sticky note on my desk with three questions on it: "What did it feel like to change and was it hard?" "Do you feel better now that you know yourself?" and "Do you ever think 'Why did this happen to me?'" I wrote the student a pass to visit me during lunch that day, and I took a few minutes to address his questions.

I hope our discussion made him feel supported about his own emerging identity. After all, there are students of all shapes, sizes, backgrounds, and experiences in every single public school across the nation who can identify in some way with Lawrence King. As educators, we must each determine the best way to individually and proactively demonstrate our openness and support for LGBTQ people in our schools.

Resources

Hughes, Langston. 1996. *The Dream Keeper and Other Poems*. Knopf.

Woodson, Jacqueline. 1995. *From the Notebooks of Melanin Sun*. Scholastic.

Steve Skjold

"She's for Real"
An 8th-grade teacher comes out

By Tracy Wagner

Tracy Wagner is the director of teaching and learning for Ipswich Public Schools and an expository writing teacher for the Crimson Summer Academy at Harvard University, both in Massachusetts.

On Monday, March 26, 2001, I took a deep breath and told my 8th graders the truth. Ebony twisted her braids around her index finger, a sleepy smile on her face. Shawn and Pao whacked each other on the shoulders, saying, "She for real? No, she for real?" as if it were all a strange teacher trick.

What my students didn't know was that as an almost-graduated student in the University of Wisconsin's Teacher Education program, I had struggled for two years with what could and could not be said in the classroom. And, finally, at this, a charter school with a majority of lower-income, African American students, I felt comfortable—even bound—to let these students who respected me know that I was a lesbian.

Every day for months, something a colleague, a student, or a novel said would reference my world outside of school. I quietly held my secret in, a tightly wound fist right there—below my chin, beside my heart.

During my first semester of student teaching, a small group of girls had caught on to this absence of information during a unit that I had prepared on the writings of Gertrude Stein, a well-known lesbian essayist. One afternoon, two of these students called me over. "Ms. Wagner," one of them asked, "have you seen *If These Walls Could Talk 2*" (an HBO movie with a focus on lesbian couples)? I smiled and nodded. She nudged her friend in the stomach with her elbow. "*Better Than Chocolate?*" When I nodded again, both girls grinned, two glittery eye-shadowed Cheshire cats beaming within the confines of the library. After this day, a hesitant but increasing manifesto of poetry and short stories from these girls graced my Creative Writing "in" assignment box, always featuring the heartache of love in a world where no one knows.

Luckily, Lori Nelson, my cooperating teacher in my final student teaching semester, shines as an old-school *Ms. Magazine* feminist. She's an inspiring teacher, always connecting what she teaches her 8th graders in the context of an impending high school world that too often shelves lower-income African American kids in the back of the room.

Lori encouraged me to come out. She'd lean against the custodian's closet during passing time, telling the kids stories about her partner (a man), her grandson, her cats. I wanted to be like that—standing with arms crossed in front of the lockers as the kids bang doors shut. I wanted to reciprocate the trust, the caring, that the kids showered upon me. I wanted to tell them the truth about my life. Every time I heard one of them say "That's so gay" or occasionally scream "Fag!" down the hall, my sense of closeness took 10 steps back.

Coming Out

Then the opportunity presented itself. As part of a three-week unit on "Healthy Students, Healthy Schools," a friend who works at a local group for students dealing with sexual orientation and I developed a one-day lesson on tolerance. The timing felt right. I knew I was legally protected by the anti-discrimination policies of the state of Wisconsin, the school district, and my teacher education program. And I also had the encouragement of an amazing cooperating teacher.

So, based on activities suggested in the resource *Tackling Gay Issues in Schools*, my friend and I led the students through an assortment of activities. I remember standing in front of a sheet of paper tacked to the wall with a line drawn down the middle. On one side, students had described a gay man as, among other things, wearing earrings, having a "certain look," and having a preference for brightly colored shirts. There was much debate on whether or not gay high school boys usually joined the drill team. On the other side of the sheet, students defined a lesbian as "looking like a man," having hairy legs, and not wearing makeup. That morning before school, I had put my finger on this line in our lesson plan—right there, between listing the stereotypes and actually calling them such—as the place where I would tell my students the truth.

> # I felt comfortable—even bound—to let these students who respected me know that I was a lesbian.

"Really?" I asked, turning to motion to the words, "This is what gay and lesbian people look like." The students nodded emphatically, and I took a deep breath. "Because I'm gay, and I don't look like this." I turned to the sheet and, as planned, contradicted each factor one by one. "I like to wear makeup. I usually shave my legs. I definitely don't want to be a boy." I told them how it felt to be standing in the hall and hear someone say "That's so gay." I told them that they could never know who around them might be gay or lesbian, bisexual or transgender. I watched the students giggle, whisper, and shake their heads. And, then, amazingly, some of them shared, too. "My auntie's a lesbian, so I hate it when kids make fun of gay people," one said. Another said, "My dad was gay. He died of AIDS." A third remarked, "I thought so—was that your girlfriend at the dance?"

The following day, students in fifth-hour Language Arts wanted to talk and rapidly fired questions at me: "How did you know you were a lesbian?" "What did your parents say?" And, most amazingly, "Why didn't you tell us before?" I remember that moment, my legs shaking underneath the table, as each of the students verbally fell over each other to share their conversations with their families the night before. "My mom said that you were very brave to tell us," said one. "My dad said that we can't be prejudiced against anyone," said another. After the bell rang and the students rose to leave, Lori and I walked toward each other and hugged. Everything had changed.

The Aftermath

Thinking back, I have to admit that I told the students about my sexual orientation for my own emotional well-being, to live up to my beliefs of what it meant to be a teacher. What I found out was that this disclosure resonated profoundly in our classroom. I could feel it in small ways, each and every day—the way students more eagerly shared their poetry, the way they chose the more private of two journal entries to read. Things weren't perfect—a student's parents complained to the principal, wishing that their child had been given a "permission slip" for the tolerance lesson. Some students talked about their religious beliefs, and how their parents had said it was OK for other people to be gay—but not for anyone in their family. I feared being known as the "lesbian teacher."

This year, I am at a new school in my first year of "real" teaching, at a high school. Disclosure to my colleagues has consistently brought the advice "You have to be careful—you don't want students to think that this is your issue only because you're gay."

I have not told my current group of students, although the issue runs through every lesson plan like a bad voice-over. What if someone asks about the picture of my partner on my desk? What if someone asks about the "Safe Space" sticker on my pushcart? What happens when they ask if I'm married? Through the walls, I hear other teachers framing lessons with stories about their wives/husbands/children, and I wonder when I will be able to contextualize lessons in that way, too. Seating charts and penciling names into my gradebook pass by as I wait for the right time to stop explaining why saying "That's so gay" is unacceptable in merely an ethical sense.

And, always, I remember my 8th graders, and how maybe not this year, but someday, one of them will think of me and stop their friend from teasing someone because they "look" gay. I think how my coming out might stop one of them from letting questions about their own sexual orientation place them in the staggering statistics of gay, lesbian, or transgender students dealing with depression, substance abuse, homelessness, or thoughts of suicide. I remember how maybe when a parent, friend, or family member comes out to them in the years to come, the memory of what happened in that 8th-grade classroom might stop them from walking away.

Resource:

Tackling Gay Issues in Schools. 1999. Published by the Gay, Lesbian & Straight Education Network of Connecticut.

A Xican@ Teacher's Journey

By Marisa Castro

Marisa Castro was born and raised in the Bay Area and currently teaches high school in San Francisco.

I am a high school teacher because I want to be the teacher I never had. How would my childhood have been different if I'd had a genderqueer teacher in elementary school? A teacher named Mx Castro who used gender-neutral pronouns and explained to the class that some boys like to wear girl clothes and some girls like to wear boy clothes. How would it have been different if there had been a place at school where it was OK for me to be myself and get to know other people who were part of the queer and trans community? What if there had been a curriculum that spoke to my needs?

I am no longer afraid, but I spent more than 20 years afraid of being my true, authentic self. Now I wonder how I can transform our schools so other marginalized groups do not have to exchange their safety or happiness for a seat in the classroom. This is what I work on in my teaching.

Lessons in Survival

When I was a child, I hid all of my hair under a baseball cap so people would believe I was a boy. I wore my brother's jeans and T-shirts. Back in those days, my family would tease me, take off my baseball cap, and call me a tomboy.

In elementary school, I learned quickly that if I continued to be who I was, I'd be very unpopular. The popular girls wore pink clothes and never hid their hair under baseball caps. I was lost during recess because I wanted to play with my brother and his friends out in the field, but I also wanted to be friends with the girls.

One day I came home and asked my mom to take me shopping for a dress. She was in the kitchen, washing dishes. Her face lit up with excitement; she was proud of me. I returned to recess and joined the rest of the girls.

By the time I was in middle school, my inner tomboy sometimes came out. I would experiment, walking outside our apartment complex wearing a bandanna on my head or baggy clothes like my brother. On the rare days I took that risk, my peers or family would tease me. I was gender policed, constantly pushed back into my "girl" gender box. I finally caved in and stopped trying to be different. I always felt happier wearing masculine clothes, but I compromised my happiness to fit in.

Looking to Resist

When I was in the 7th grade, I joined a walkout in solidarity with my undocumented classmates. The California electorate had just passed Proposition 187, which eliminated access to social services for undocumented students statewide. [Editor's note: Proposition 187, which was approved by 59 percent of California voters in 1994, was later ruled unconstitutional by a federal court.] With a father who immigrated from Mexico and grandparents who never learned English, I saw how the system makes distinctions based on country of origin. There was very little difference between those students who were no longer eligible for public education and myself.

Like most of the people in my neighborhood, I grew up in a low-income, transient household. At school, I did not learn anything that would help me understand why my family was not like a "normal" family, which I grew up believing lived in a big house with a picket fence. My family was nothing like that white, middle-class, nuclear family. When my parents struggled, we only ate flour tortillas smothered in butter. I am proud to say that—even when my parents were barely making it, my mother always found a way to feed us.

My father had bloodshot eyes and carried a Budweiser can in his hand. He abused all of us. My mother finally left the man, choosing to raise three children on her own. She taught me life lessons about survival and how to fight for my freedom.

> On the days I did go to school, I was invisible; none of my teachers noticed I had been gone.

Graffiti was another way I expressed my resistance to oppression during middle school. I decided to "get up to get fame." A few writers asked me to join their crew and I kicked it with them for a minute, but by the time I started high school I needed more walls, so I picked up a journal and left my streaks and cans at home.

Writing in my journal saved my life in high school. There was so much I did not understand. I had so much pain and I did not know how to release it. I was closeted, passing as hetero. I shut down any feelings of love and numbed out with alcohol and drugs; I hardly went to school. On the days I had enough energy to go to school, I was invisible; none of my teachers noticed I had been gone. None of them asked why I was unmotivated and high all the time. I was the student who used every opportunity to flee from their presence. Junior year I was placed in a continuation high school with the other kids who weren't making it. We were shunted to the periphery of the campus.

No one—not a teacher, not my family, not a counselor—had ever mentioned I could go to college. I thought that was another universe. Then one day I went to a workshop where financial aid counselors explained that it was possible for me to go to college, that I could get financial help. I was stunned. Even though my time at school had been so hard, I decided to pursue college. The irony was that I was trapped in vocational courses, so by then my only option was to start at community college. I did that, eventually transferring to San Francisco State University.

Beyond Ethnic Studies

The ethnic studies classes I took in college finally helped me understand my family's lineage. I found a new sense of pride when taking those classes; I also became angry because I realized that I had been denied my own history for most of my life. I began to question why I never had access to classes that highlighted the history of people of color.

However, the ethnic studies frameworks I encountered in college rarely found a place for gender and sexuality. For example, I had a teacher who talked about the high rate of homicides in Oakland, saying, "Our communities are in a crisis, we need to respond to what's happening." But he never opened up a dialogue with us about who the perpetrators of violence are, or the relationship between violence and patriarchy.

When I was a first-year teacher, the kids would ask me: "Are you a man or a woman?" How do you respond to that as a teachable moment?

That's where ethnic studies fails. Ethnic studies changes education so that it's no longer Eurocentric. It teaches communities of color about race, ethnicity, and oppression; but that's not enough. We need language and curriculum that confronts the intersections of race, heteropatriarchy, sexuality, and gender identity.

Bringing it back into the classroom, we need to think about how our young men are socialized to be nonemotional; we need to challenge the perspectives on what manhood and masculinity mean. We need to bring gender and sexuality into the conversation about addressing violence in communities.

Life as a First-Year Teacher

I went through a lot of struggle and a lot of healing to be able to understand and forgive my own family. I had so much anger and so much resentment toward them. Once I learned about oppression and once I was able to think critically about why things happened—why my mom was never home, how my father had his own struggles as an immigrant—I could start making sense out of everything. If I'd had a teacher who talked about those things in the classroom, and at the same time maintained high expectations and pushed me, my life would have been a lot easier. That's what I wanted to bring to my students.

So 12 years after I left high school, I became a teacher. Not much had changed. The passing-as-hetero students were still in the closet, and the straights claimed nearly every space at school, policing those who stepped out of their assigned gender roles. Queer and trans people did not exist in the curriculum, hallways, school dances, classrooms, yearbooks, or bathrooms—but "faggots" and "homos" were everywhere, and "so gay" was the new "fuck you."

My first year I taught 9th-grade African American History, 10th-grade Modern World History, and 10th-grade AP Modern World History. It was a lot of preps for a first-year teacher. It set me up for failure. At the same time, many of my students used homophobic and transphobic language. The kids would ask me: "Are you a man or are you a woman, which one?" How do you respond to that as a teachable moment? What do you do when you hear "faggot" in the classroom? There were so many fires; which one should I put out first?

As a first-year, gender nonconforming teacher, I realized that the honorific "Ms." erased half of my gender identity. I decided to ask students and staff to refer to me by what I use as my first name, Castro. When I encountered a transphobic backlash from students, parents, and fellow colleagues, the administration did not provide any support in addressing it. I had a teaching coach who told me: "We need to talk about your name. There's been community response and a lot of talk about your career, your professionalism, and your job here." That was the moment when I cracked. It was a toxic environment. I was doing everything I could, trying to do my best and survive, and it came back to my name. That's when I drew the line. If the administration couldn't have a dialogue with me and the coach who was supposed to be supporting me with curriculum development was focused on my name, I had to resign. When I met with the administration for the last time, they said they did not know how to "legally" support me.

Claiming Allies/Reclaiming Education

The next year, I started to teach at the school where I had completed my student teaching, and I continue to work there to this day. My relationships with the administration, teachers, and students are totally different. No school is perfect, but when incidents happen I have support. I realize the necessity of supportive colleagues' voices in staff meetings when issues of homophobia and transphobia come up—of colleagues who are allies of the LGBTQ community. I need people I can go to and say, "This is what happened, what do you think?" And they help me resolve whatever problems arise. I don't have to convince anyone that I'm experiencing homophobia. For instance, I had a colleague who told me: "Oh no, that student has been homophobic, that's their worldview. I've known this student since freshman year, and this is one of your challenges." Or another colleague who said: "I'm teaching queer and trans history and authors so that when they get to your grade, they will have already worked through their discomfort with me as an ally." At this school site, I have realized how affirming it is to have colleagues who validate my experiences—colleagues who support me and other LGBTQ staff and students, and who help build a safer school climate for everyone.

Last year I was the LGBTQ liaison at my school. We started an LGBTQ and allies group called Just Fierce Alliance (JFA). We had meetings during lunch once a week. The first year, we had more staff than students as participants. I know that means we still need more education about LGBTQ issues, especially in 9th grade. Many students might not yet feel safe enough to join.

But even with our relatively small membership, we accomplished a lot. Our school has a social justice pathway (similar to a major) that collaborates with LYRIC, a community-based LGBTQ youth organization here in San Francisco. LYRIC and JFA worked together to research problems that transgender youth face and to propose an all-gender restroom. We presented our ideas to the school's leadership team, which agreed to set up one or two all-gender restrooms by the fall of 2015.

JFA students performed in four different assemblies and sponsored a few schoolwide events. One student wanted to call attention to the Black Lives Matter movement. Representing JFA, he and his boyfriend sang Beyonce's song "Halo" during the school's Universal Human Rights assembly in front of 1,400 students and staff. That same student gave a speech and did a belly dance at another assembly to call attention to our all-gender restroom campaign. Staff came up to me afterward, crying. "We thought we were going to lose him," they said. "Look at him now." Before this year, he was definitely a victim of homophobia and, as a result, dealt with a lot of self-hatred. Even his family would call him derogatory names in Tagalog. JFA, and the positive relationships he formed with teachers, made an enormous difference in his life.

We need to ask ourselves, how can we pave a new path for our LGBTQ youth? As teachers in an often homophobic and transphobic institution, how can we be better allies to students who are questioning their sexuality and gender? How can we model acceptance for heterosexual students who have not yet learned to treat their LGBTQ peers with respect? These are questions that, as educators, we have to consistently ask ourselves to ensure that we continue to create a safer learning community for all students.

CHAPTER 5

David McLimans

Beyond the Classroom: Introduction

By Rachel L. S. Harper

Rachel L. S. Harper is an artist, educator, and activist in Chicago. She leads the Teacher Institute at the Museum of Contemporary Art and teaches pre-service teachers at DePaul University. She is a founding member of ChiQueer, a teacher collective for LGBTQ issues in education, and her current artist project, Seen + Heard, advocates for cultural works of people 0–12 in a variety of settings.

Like many kids who grow up to become teachers, I liked school from day one. I loved Mondays. I had an unexplainable affinity for the smooth feel of my little wood-colored desk, the cheerful bulletin boards, and the itchy smell of my freshly sharpened pencils all carefully lined up, ready. I admired my teachers, felt pretty safe in the miniature universe of the self-contained elementary classroom, and I liked the feeling of learning through being taught. Yet, when I reflect on my school days, I know that the lessons that most transformed me happened in spaces beyond the classroom: the playground, the school bus, the bathrooms, the unsanctioned spaces where kids come together to play and explore, and the secret places I tucked myself away in to be alone with my thoughts. These were places where I experienced education through deeper kinds of confusion and wilder discoveries.

By the time I was in middle school, I rode the train to school with 100 other kids.

"Hi. Can I ask you a question?" Vanessa sat down near Logan, on the edge of the seat behind me.

"A question?" Logan took out her little spiral-topped reporter's notebook and a silver-colored ink pen. "OK, go ahead."

"Are you a boy or a girl?"

Vanessa's question cut right through the conversation I was having with other 7th graders nearby, and we spun around to see Logan's reaction.

Logan nodded and wrote in her notebook while repeating back "Are you a boy or a girl?" She looked up. "Did I get that right?"

"Go away, Vanessa," said Jennie from the seat next to Logan.

"No, it's OK," Logan offered. "It's a really good question. A boy or a girl. . ."

Logan and Vanessa sat in a long silence, looking at each other.

"Thanks for asking," said Logan. Vanessa nodded and then she left.

I turned back around in my seat and looked out the window. Why didn't Logan answer the question? Or had she answered? Why was Vanessa confused enough by tomboyish basketball shorts to have to ask, when it was totally obvious? Logan was a girl. Or was she?

This moment, like a million similar moments every day, had no resolution, and yet lessons about gender were taught and learned. In many schools today, investigation of gender and sexuality are not incorporated into the taught curriculum, but every student has a gender and a sexuality to understand. So it is in conversations outside the classroom, or in solitary contemplation, where students grapple constantly with these important issues. What happens when the school community becomes a supportive space for this kind of work? Who gets to say what is worth knowing about gender and sexuality, and about queer issues at school? How do safe school spaces go further and become liberatory spaces where students and teachers get to be themselves, and where they get to try thinking new and better ideas together?

Many North American high schools have feminist clubs—perhaps a chapter of the National Organization for Women (NOW) or a Gay-Straight Alliance (GSA). These student-led groups offer space to share personal stories, get support, and build community. Whether they are isolated safe spaces or propellants toward something bigger depends largely on teachers' and administrators' interest in students contributing meaningfully to the curriculum and the school culture.

In many cities, there are also independent youth-led initiatives like Seattle's Reteaching Gender and Sexuality and Chicago's Gender JUST, which counter heteronormativity, homophobia, and sexism through activism focused on the intersectionalities of gender, sexuality, race, class, and ability. These initiatives are often markedly different from the LGBTQ organizations that dominate popular culture, such as the Human Rights Campaign (HRC), the It Gets Better Project, and GLSEN (Gay, Lesbian & Straight Education Network). Instead of didactic narratives on the "facts" of LGBTQ issues, rights, and experience, these youth ask radical questions. They see gender and sexuality as concepts that are constantly in flux and must be redefined relative to evolving social contexts. For example, queer youth from Make It Better assert that they should not have to suffer homophobia while waiting for things to "get better" at some indeterminate later date.

The lessons that most transformed me happened in spaces beyond the classroom.

When I first began organizing with Chicago's Teachers for Social Justice, I joined a work group now called ChiQueer, which was organized to research queer issues in our schools, develop curriculum for students and teacher development, and advocate for LGBTQ rights. After a few months together, we were practically wearing matching rainbow tracksuits, reveling in the joys of reaching beyond the confines of our solitary classrooms to form a community of educators from schools across the district, happily implementing new educational programs for hundreds of our colleagues.

But I've often wondered why our first meetings were such a peculiar kind of difficult. We greeted each other jovially, goofily joking about the daily grind and sharing vegan pot stickers. But as we began to talk deeply—discussing articles, speculating about queer issues in education, sharing our experiences as queer and allied teachers at school—we grew serious, quieter and quieter, and spoke with greater and greater pauses, until we often sat in long silences of thinking together. In those times, I often experienced a loss for words about issues I never imagined myself to be unsure about, and I surprised myself more than once by bursting into tears on the drive home. These were work sessions, not therapy sessions, so why were we so fraught?

Over the weeks, the rhythm of our discussions picked up, and we never looked back on the early days. So what had been happening there?

I think that the issues we were trying to discuss mattered more deeply than we could comprehend. Gender and sexuality are knitted into the most essential reaches of individuality, identity, intimacy, pleasure, humanity, and love. At the same time, sexism, heteronormativity, and homophobia are thoroughly institutionalized in most social constructs, maybe especially in schools. This turns the water we swim in into a corrosive substance that's at odds with all the swimmers, not just the queer ones. This is why we are called to queer the curriculum, and to create safer and more liberatory spaces at schools, not just in individual classrooms, but beyond.

That's the challenge the authors in this chapter have taken on: creating liberatory spaces that reach past the classroom. Some of them, including Maiya Jackson, Adriana Murphy, and T. Elijah Hawkes, are administrators working on schoolwide change. Candice Valenzuela addresses the specific needs of Black girls. Shannon Panszi reaches out to other parents of transgender children. Jacqueline Woodson talks about writing the books our children need to read. Patrick McLinden is a student working on districtwide policy change. We hope all of the articles in this section inspire you to take change beyond the classroom.

Ask Me Who I Am

BY SAM STIEGLER

Sam Stiegler is a doctoral candidate in the Department of Curriculum & Pedagogy at the University of British Columbia, where his research focuses on the educational experiences of queer and trans youth both in and out of school. He has worked for and with queer and trans youth in educational settings for more than 15 years.

Sahara had a bright personality and booming voice; you knew she was coming down the hall before she walked into a room. She was a long-time member of the LGBTQ youth services agency where I had recently started working. From the moment of our introduction, I knew her spirited energy would positively impact the summer program I was facilitating.

The morning before the first session, I accessed the agency's client database to create our sign-in sheet. It showed that Sahara's legal name was not Sahara. But since that was the name I knew her by, I typed "Sahara" on the sign-in sheet and hit "print" without giving it another thought.

That afternoon, Sahara was the first to arrive, greeting me with a bellowing "Hi, Sam!" Well accustomed to the agency's sign-in process, she dutifully walked over to sign her name.

After quickly scanning the paper, she looked back across the room at me. "Sam, my name's not on here!"

I assured her that it was. She looked back down and then slowly lifted her head with an expression on her face I could not interpret.

"Sahara, are you OK?" I asked.

"I've never seen it written down before," she said, her finger still touching the place where her name was typed.

I've never seen it written down before.

In school records, government documents, and even our LGBTQ youth-serving agency, Sahara had never seen her name affirmed in writing. Instead, she had received questioning glances and doubting requests for documentation anytime she uttered her name. The impact of this repeated delegitimization weighed on her, as evidenced by the visceral response I witnessed that day.

What would it take for people to simply accept Sahara instead of questioning her identity? How might our schools be different if students were allowed to take the lead in their own gendering? What if there were space for students to say "I identify as. . ." or "I use _____ pronouns"? What if teachers and adults listened to students instead of making judgments based on their own assumptions about a student's gender? What if a student's preferred name was allowed to trump the name written on their legal documents?

I do not mean to imply that any one teacher could stop the process of gendering all alone. But I believe these questions can begin to crack away at some of the gender constraints at work in our schools and society—and give Sahara and others a little more room to carve out their own gendered spaces and identities.

During more than a decade of working alongside LGBTQ youth, I have met many students whose gender identities, expressions, and presentations diverge from what is expected of them based on their bodies and other people's perceptions of their bodies: Young people who could not use either gendered restroom at school (due to policy or fear) and whose attendance dropped as a result. Students who got thrown out of gym class for refusing to participate because they feared talking to the teacher about wearing a binder over their breasts or a gaff to hold their penis and testicles between their legs. Young men who were told repeatedly—and sometimes violently—not to wear nail polish or makeup. Students who felt uncomfortable checking either of the gender boxes.

All of these youth, in various ways, complicate the idea that there are two types of bodies—male and female—and that there are clear and distinct expectations for those bodies: clothing, hairstyles, names, pronouns, mannerisms, professions, and societal roles. Their experiences highlight the pressures—and often emotional, psychological, and physical dangers—inherent when a person presents a gender that deviates from society's expectations. How can we create school environments where one's gender identity need not be verified by anyone other than oneself?

This question is especially important in light of the significant number of trans-friendly school policies that have been enacted in recent years across the United States, including a statewide law in California and districtwide policies in places ranging from New York City (with its more than a million students) to rural Elkhorn, Wisconsin (which serves slightly more than 3,000 students). These landmark laws and policies take bold steps to protect students' rights to access gendered school facilities and programs according to their gender identity—locker rooms, restrooms, and sports teams—and to protect trans and gender nonconforming students from discrimination and harassment.

The pushback against these trans-inclusive policies has capitalized on the misconception that one's gender identity must be authenticated by an outside observer (see, for example, Privacy for All Students, the group that formed to fight the California law mentioned above).

Microaggressions

Scholars have long argued that schools are sites where gender and sexual norms are enforced and reproduced. Overtly violent expressions of gender control—a student is called a derogatory name or thrown up against locker—are easier for teachers and administrators to notice and respond to. Although many schools now have nondiscrimination policies and anti-bullying mandates, the cumulative emotional and psychological harm Sahara experienced when she said her name out loud could not have been prevented with policies alone.

Covert microaggressions—subtle slights and insults directed at various pieces of one's identity—need to be addressed as well. Damage is done when someone asks a transgender student "No, but what's your *real* name?" Reprimanding a student for calling another student "fag" and then asking, "Can I get a few strong boys to move this table?" or suggesting that "boys do this" and "girls do that" is limiting for all children.

How might our schools be different if students were allowed to take the lead in their own gendering?

School traditions, norms, and structures can also be problematic. Proms are often yearly scenes of microaggression based on "appropriate" dress. The emotional and physical well-being of a young person shifting their gender expression—or one who doesn't feel comfortable with either side of the gender binary—is at stake as they navigate the rigidly gendered structures of schools—locker rooms, bathrooms, dress codes, sports teams, and so on. Having to constantly claim a gender throughout the school day affects students for whom making that statement is no simple declaration (see "When the Gender Boxes Don't Fit," p. 97).

Expanding the fight against harassment and discrimination in schools—beyond overt acts of aggression to include the everyday regulation of gender and sexualities—frees us all, no matter what our age or identification.

What We Can Do

I ran a GED preparation program for LGBTQ youth for four years. Transgender and gender nonconforming youth consistently comprised at least half, if not more, of the enrollees. And, in fact, a study on the experiences of transgender youth in the United States by the National LGBTQ Task Force shows that transgender and gender nonconforming youth are more likely to leave school before graduating. I did not need statistics to show me that the classroom was a space of historical trauma for many of my students. Unfortunately, the LGBTQ-friendly space we fostered was not enough to counteract the stigmas associated with schooling. I witnessed deeply ingrained hurts and fears about curriculum, test-taking, and general class procedures.

I do not know exactly why my students left high school before graduation, and I'm not implying that their reasoning was based solely on their experiences of gender. But I do wonder how their schooling experiences might have been different if there had been discussions about the impact of microaggressions on them. Given my experience, I offer the following suggestions to educators—ones I continually reflect on myself as a cisgender educator who works with transgender and gender nonconforming youth—as tools to help rethink gender in schools:

- Be conscious of commonplace comments (from adults and students) that police gender expression, for instance: "Boys will be boys," "Act like a lady," "Man up," "Boys/girls aren't supposed to do that."
- Begin class with students and staff stating their preferred gendered pronouns and talk about what to do when someone uses an incorrect pronoun. Asking all students to be explicit about their pronouns lessens the pressure on trans and gender nonconforming students.
- If you are not sure of a student's gender pronouns, ask: "Which pronouns do you prefer?"
- When a student's stated name is incongruent with the name "in the system," default to the student rather than the computer. Work with the school administration to include students' preferred names in school record-keeping systems. Students will often be aware of the limitations (e.g., having to put their given name on government documents—like a state-mandated graduation test—until it is changed legally), but schools can support them in-house.
- Rethink structures like gendered dress codes and school uniforms, prom king and queen, and separate sports teams for boys and girls.
- Ungender any single-stall, lockable restrooms in the school building and start a conversation about how to make multi-stall restrooms both gender neutral and safe for all.

> Damage is done when someone asks a transgender student "No, but what's your *real* name?"

I know some of these suggestions are not easily implemented. But we need to start somewhere. Some schools allow trans students to use a private restroom in the nurse's or principal's office. More recently, some districts and schools have created one multi-stall restroom in each school building to support trans and gender nonconforming students, because allowing students access to a single staff restroom can be isolating and logistically impossible during busy passing periods. Another possibility is a bathroom with multiple locking stalls and a common sink area.

By opening discussions about ungendering school structures, we illuminate the gendering that upholds and reproduces misogyny, homophobia, transphobia, and heteronormativity. These difficult yet important conversations need to be happening at every school, not just those with an out trans student. The policing of gender identity and expression impacts and limits everyone. We never know what feelings students are just coming to terms with, or how many parents, staff, siblings, and others in the school community will be supported by less rigid policies.

A note from the author: Since I first wrote this piece, Sahara has passed on. The moment I described is but one of many I will cherish and remember. Sahara's bright, endless smile will forever warm my heart and soul. And she will continue to inspire me to advocate for spaces where students' names can be penned across any page without a skeptical glance or quizzical request for "proof."

Reference

Grant, Jaime, Lisa Mottet, and Justin Tanis. 2011. "Injustice at Every Turn: A Report of the National Transgender Discrimination Survey." National LGBTQ Task Force. Available at thetaskforce.org.

Alaura Seidl

We Begin to Know Each Other

By Maiya Jackson

Maiya Jackson began teaching as a 16-year-old in the Summerbridge program and now is the upper school director at Manhattan Country School. She chaired the 2015 Progressive Education Network national conference, "Access, Equity, and Activism: Teaching the Possible."

I first heard about Laura when she applied for 8th grade at Manhattan Country School, where I am upper school director. Laura was being pressured to leave her school because someone from her previous school was transferring in. At her current school, everyone knew Laura as a girl, but in her previous school, everyone knew her as a boy, the gender she was assigned at birth. Not ready to deal with the questions that would arise from Laura's secret being out in the open, the school had asked Laura to leave. When our admissions director told me about Laura's situation, I was appalled.

Manhattan Country School (MCS) is a pre-K–8 progressive school in New York City with a social justice mission. Our student body has no racial majority, and we have a sliding-scale tuition system that supports socio-economic diversity. We had talked about gender equity, but mostly through the lens of how we teach boys and girls.

Our admissions team wanted to trust that our school would be a safe, welcoming place for Laura. But we weren't sure if the staff—or the wider school community—would be receptive to talking about transgender identity. We spent a lot of time thinking about how other students might react and what questions they would have. We also considered our school farm, where students spend three weeks out of the school year. Would families feel comfortable with transgender students on overnight trips? Would Laura sleep in a boys' room or a girls' room?

We wanted MCS to be a place where Laura could be her complete self for a year before moving on to high school. Even though we had questions about the path ahead, we made a commitment to welcome and support Laura in our community.

Welcoming Laura

With her warm, easygoing manner, Laura was a remarkably straightforward and self-aware 8th grader. She loved softball, was a good friend and math student, wasn't sure about her study skills, and was thrilled to be going to a new school. She knew a little about MCS because of Cometfire, a citywide group for LGBTQ middle school students and their allies. Sophia, a rising 8th grader at MCS who had been out as a lesbian since the 5th grade, went regularly to Cometfire, often bringing other MCS students for support.

Laura was relieved to finally be in a place where she could be honest about her identity. She talked about being ready to be out as a transgender student for the first time, and she knew it would not be easy.

What about crushes and dating?

The admissions team met with the school psychologist to talk about Laura's adjustment and how we could support her and the MCS community as we learned about transgender identity. Laura was entering a class with three gay families; Sophia had already blazed a path to talk about gender and sexuality. The class's 6th-grade activism project had been lobbying for marriage equality at a state senator's office; their 7th-grade project was leading a campaign to stop bullying of LGBTQ students. We knew this class was ready to welcome Laura.

But we also knew there would be inevitable challenges—uncomfortable questions and occasional teasing. When I talked with Laura before school started, I was careful to communicate that there would be teachers who would be her unwavering supporters, and that any time students were being rude, cruel, or offensive, Laura should come to me right away.

Taking Our Lead from SJ

Just as we were getting ready to begin the school year, I received an email from Janet, Sophia's mother. She wrote that Sophia had gone to a camp for gender nonconforming kids that summer. "At camp Sophia made a transition to being called by her initials, SJ, and tried on living in a masculine spectrum (camp words). This was very meaningful and important, and SJ would like to continue in this transition identity this year at school."

SJ had expressed questions about his gender identity before. In the 1st grade, he asked to be called Patrick, which his teacher and classmates honored. This situation was different. SJ was entering 8th grade, and we knew there would be lots of questions. Again, we wondered about the farm. Would he play on the boys' basketball team?

Laura would be coming to our school having already made her transition. SJ was someone we knew, and we would all have to get used to his new self. Janet offered the following: "SJ knows that it takes time for people to adapt, and that people forget, especially those of us who have known Sophia for so long. In fact, SJ has chosen these initials as the transition identity so people don't have to adapt to a more masculine name that is completely different." Taking our lead from SJ, we prepared for the year ahead.

The 7th- and 8th-grade teachers spent a lot of time talking about bathrooms. All the bathrooms in the school were unisex until the 7th and 8th grades. There are two bathrooms on their floor, each one a small room with a stall that locks and a sink. They were labeled with roughly hewn "boys" and "girls" signs made during a shop class. We wanted to remove the signs and take this daily choice out of the equation, but that would mean that students would need to lock the door to protect their privacy. It made us nervous to think of middle schoolers being able to lock the outer doors. We finally settled on a solution of creating laminated "*Ocupado*" (Occupied) signs that students would hang outside the door. The system was flawed; the signs were frequently forgotten and often went missing or had to be repaired. (This year, we just have big signs that say "Please knock before entering," but students still have trouble protecting their privacy.)

Talking with Staff

In preparation for the opening staff meetings, I met with the director and the school psychologist to talk about how we would discuss gender variance and transgender identity. The psychologist suggested that this could be a challenging topic for many staff members and to go slowly without making assumptions that everyone would be immediately accepting. The lower school director, whose daughter was in the 7th grade, shared some of the chatter that was already happening among students on Facebook; so far it mostly reflected excitement and curiosity. The admissions director and I spoke about Laura's family and their process in supporting Laura's decision, one that had included several bumps along the way.

There were other, more informal conversations. We kept coming back to how young SJ and Laura were; they were making such life-changing decisions at an age when we remembered being barely aware of who we were. After listening to everyone's feedback and reading all the articles I could find, I developed a workshop using elements of the Seeking Educational Equity and Diversity (SEED) model that was already familiar to our staff.

The first staff development session about gender identity opened with a writing exercise: Write about the first time you were aware of your gender. Small groups talked animatedly, but few wanted to share with the larger group.

The rest of the session was mostly informative. I read the email about SJ's transition and told the story about why Laura sought out MCS. Questions were about bathrooms, when we would tell the other children, and how we would tell families. Some people expressed nervousness about students' reactions. Teachers told stories about other students they had known dealing with gender variance—including a boy in pre-kindergarten who came to school in a red velvet dress. The school psychologist had coached me to communicate that we were open to different reactions among the staff as well as students, and to acknowledge that people would need time to process and ask questions.

I was relieved at the end of the meeting; no one resisted the idea of having transgender students at our school, though there were lingering questions. I gathered the articles I had read into a binder of readings for staff.

> "When people say that I am technically a boy it's not true at all. I am a female from head to toe."

The 7th- and 8th-grade team prepared to help students support SJ and Laura. We decided the 5th- and 6th-grade teachers would also tell their students, and then we would wait and see if there were questions from the lower school students.

Coming Out to Classmates

On the first day of school, as all of the 7th and 8th graders sat in a circle, I made my opening remarks for the school year. I talked about the importance of community. Then I introduced SJ: "We have a member of our community who has asked me to share something for him. Over the summer, Sophia made a decision to live as a boy. He would like to be called SJ and he prefers male pronouns. I'm sure some of you have questions, and that's OK. We will be talking about this more in advisement on Friday."

The room was quiet for a beat. Some students already knew this was happening and nodded. Others looked a little confused. Some just looked bored.

We moved on to an icebreaker—everyone said their name with an action after repeating all previous names and actions. When it was SJ's turn, he did all the other moves that came before him, then made an energetic lunge with his hand in a fist and blurted out: "Sophia! I mean . . . SJ!" We all laughed together, and felt a little more at ease. If SJ himself was still getting used to his new name, it was OK if we occasionally made mistakes, too.

A few days later, Laura told her story to her advisement while the rest of us told our groups. We explained what transgender meant and that Laura, like SJ, identified as transgender. In my group, it took a couple of tries for everyone to understand what I was saying, since there was nothing about Laura that would have made anyone question her gender. Students had questions about the farm first: How would it work? We talked about the privacy rules that we already had in place.

Students had lots of questions about changing gender: How did they pick their new names? Were they going to have surgery? Were they taking medication? What if they change their minds? And what about the boys who thought Laura was cute?

Some students were confused or wanted to know more about Laura, including her name when she was a boy. We explained that respecting Laura meant accepting her new identity, that she would just be Laura to us. For the most part, students accepted the news with a fairly matter-of-fact attitude, and we moved on to the business of school.

Laura and SJ were individuals, with all the complexities that go beyond one facet of identity.

When a teacher saw Laura later that day, the teacher asked her how it went in her group. "Amazing!" Laura exclaimed with a huge smile and a high five.

Teachers Share Reactions, Stories, Questions

The second teacher workshop opened with a prompt asking us to share reactions, stories, and questions. We discussed articles and watched a film about parents raising transgender children. I shared a little about how things were going for SJ and Laura, and then we opened up the discussion.

Some asked questions about medication and what it meant to transition at such a young age. Another shared a story about an alumnus who transitioned in adulthood and wondered if he knew during his time at MCS. We also talked about the importance of integrating identity into the curriculum as a way to support children.

The people who shared aloud were feeling positive about our school taking on this issue. But not everyone wanted to share, and I left with the lingering feeling that people still had questions they weren't asking. In their reflections, there was a range of responses:

> I admire Laura and SJ for their bravery to be so open and honest to share their experiences as transgender youth with the community. SJ is being incredibly patient and open with friends. I am honored that they are part of MCS and have created discussion on this topic.

> I have questions about adolescents taking medication that will change their bodies. This is such a volatile time for kids, when they are trying on lots of identities. Why would their parents let them make a choice that can't be undone? It's fine for them to live as a boy or a girl, but what if this is just a phase?

> My biggest questions are about the kid world, the layer beneath what we—the adults—see. How do [the students] negotiate Laura and SJ's gender identity expressions in the time of crushes and dating and the development of sexual identity? Do other students figuring out their own sexual identities feel somehow left out of this current conversation?

> This has been a welcome reminder for me, as an educator and a parent, how much we have to learn, as adults, from children and how resilient and open and mature they can be.

Ongoing Discussions with Students

Although students were accepting in the beginning, over time other reactions emerged. It became clear that students would need workshops as well.

A couple of students who had strong Christian beliefs had serious questions about changing the body that was given by God; they weren't sure if the acceptance we were asking for contradicted their religious beliefs.

In other cases, being transgender became an easy target for insults when kids were upset. When a student didn't like Laura or SJ, was it because they were transgender or because it was annoying when one of them talked too often in class?

Teachers rarely heard open confrontations or insults, but occasionally students would share what was being said beyond our earshot. Some students felt Laura had an unfair athletic advantage as a girl. SJ was pressured to play on the girls' basketball team because the girls thought they needed him to win, even though he told us before school started that he wanted to play with the boys. And there were uncomfortable jokes about crushes and dating. The 8th-grade girls kept asking a 7th-grade girl why she wasn't interested in dating SJ, who had a crush on her. "But he's a boy now," they kept saying, implying that she was being a bad friend by not choosing to go out with him.

We had several meetings throughout the year, starting with written questions from the students:

- How do you know if you are transgender?
- What happens when a transgender girl gets turned on?
- Does it bother transgender people when people they knew before call them the wrong gender?
- Did Laura get made fun of at her old school for being transgender?

We spent a lot of time defining terms. The "New Diagram of Sex and Gender" (see Resources) was a helpful framework, but it seemed almost impossible to get some students to understand that biological sex, gender identity, gender expression, and sexual orientation could all be different things. We read an account of being transgender from curriculum developed by the Gay, Lesbian & Straight Network and the Anti-Defamation League. Some students left the room during the sessions because they were uncomfortable, which was both better than saying something disrespectful and a statement of silent protest.

After the first session, we separated the 7th and 8th grades, since the 8th grade had done so much more work on these issues and was able to have more nuanced discussions. The 7th graders were stuck on questions about bodies, surgeries, medication, and the meaning of choice. We tried to answer all of their questions without sharing specifics about Laura's and SJ's experiences, in hopes that it would quell their curiosity. Instead, it seemed to push them to ask questions that became offensive. We backpedaled, focusing on language and respect instead. It was the only diversity issue in my time at MCS when we asked for tolerance rather than acceptance.

Part of me knew that being in a diverse community meant respecting other points of view. Another part of me was sure we could convince students that being transgender was OK. I stubbornly left definitions and charts hanging on the wall, so students would know that this topic was important and that we would keep struggling with it. Still, we had to find ways to make room for all of our students. We also had to remember that our students were in middle school, a challenging enough time to think about identity without upending a category most of them had taken for granted. Our group was young to be taking on these topics. They needed time, and we had to be patient.

The one group we did not have as many discussions with was parents. I told parents during a meeting in the opening weeks of school that we had two transgender students in the 8th grade and that we would be talking about gender identity throughout the year. There were a few questions but not many. We tried to put together a parent forum to talk about gender issues, but it never got off the ground. One parent emailed me when his daughter was becoming close friends with Laura. He was fine with their friendship, but he wanted to know more about transgender identity. And he had some doubts about slumber parties. We talked and I sent articles. Sometimes, the lack of questions and conflict made us wonder if it was too easy. It was hard to know if we were pushing the community as much as we should be.

Laura's Talk

Toward the end of the year, I asked Laura if she wanted a chance to talk to the 7th and 8th grades about being transgender. She had expressed a desire to talk to the whole group before school started, but we had thought that would be complicated before we had done the work of exploring gender identity with students. By this point, we had reached a shared understanding, but there were lingering points of discomfort among the students. The teachers and I hoped that hearing Laura's story might be a helpful step. Rather than sharing the stories of others, this would be the story of a friend, which engenders a different kind of empathy.

Laura jumped at the chance. She came to school the next day with a four-page speech. As Laura read to the group, it was obvious that she spoke from the heart, and that she had a depth of courage, strength, and grace that was hard to fathom in a 14-year-old.

> Many people think that being transgender defines a person, but it really does not. I am a girl. I never thought of myself as a boy. There are many struggles that I have gone through to accept myself as the female I am today. . . . Now I feel as if I have finally found my place. I understand many of you do not feel comfortable with the idea of a person being transgender, but really we are no different than any boy or girl in your class. When people say that I am technically a boy it's not true at all. I am a female from head to toe.
>
> I want all of you to close your eyes and imagine seeing yourself in the mirror, but instead of seeing yourself as your biological sex, imagine you are the opposite sex. If you are a boy, imagine yourself as a girl. If you are a girl, imagine yourself as a boy. Now open your eyes. Some may have liked the image they saw and some may have not. If you did not like the image you saw, imagine what it would be like to live 11 years of your life as that image. Would you want to be unhappy as your biological sex or would you come out and say "Wait, I am actually a boy or a girl!"

I understand that feeling comfortable and accepting a transgender person does not happen overnight or right after a person writes a speech about being transgender. But I ask that you treat me and anyone that you meet who is transgender with respect and not treat them differently just because they were born a different sex.

When Laura finished speaking, everyone clapped. There were questions, but they were thoughtful, sensitive questions about her life experiences. It was a moment of enormous pride, not just for Laura and SJ, but also for the whole community. It had been a year of tough conversations, and this process of exploring transgender identity had pushed us out of our comfort zone in valuable ways.

In the months that followed, we reflected more on the intersection of race and class with gender. How was the experience of SJ, a student of color, different from Laura's, who was white? Was it more difficult for SJ to be accepted by boys than it was for Laura to be accepted by girls? Were we too quick to decide that students of color who had trouble accepting the concept of gender identity were transphobic? As a person of color, I found that I was wary of the students of color being pigeonholed by an assumption that Black and Latina/o people were more likely to be homophobic or transphobic, even as I wanted them to change their points of view. We are still unpacking the events of that year, and the conversations about gender identity are ongoing.

When we first started talking about Laura and SJ being transgender, it was an idea, a concept to wrap your mind around. By the time Laura read her speech, she and SJ were individuals, with all the complexities that go beyond one facet of identity. Their stories underscore what happens in school when we live our lives together, so that we begin to know each other.

Resources

Anti-Defamation League, GLSEN, & StoryCorps. 2011. "Unheard Voices: Stories of LGBT History." glsen.org/unheardvoices.html.

Bryan, Jennifer and Sebastian Mitchell Barr. 2011. "New Diagram of Sex and Gender." nysais.org/uploaded/diversity/new_diagram_copyright.pdf.

Lee, Susan. "When It Counts: Talking about Transgender Identity and Gender Fluidity in Elementary School." genderspectrum.org/images/stories/Teaching_About_Gender_Identity_and_Fluidity_in_Elementary_School.pdf.

R. Gregory Christie

Space for Young Black Women
An interview with Candice Valenzuela

By Jody Sokolower

Jody Sokolower is a political activist, teacher, writer, and editor. She is the managing editor at Rethinking Schools.

A few years ago, Candice Valenzuela created and facilitated a group for young Black women at Castlemont High School in Oakland, California. She shaped the group around the students' needs, grounding her work in womanist, Black feminist, and critical pedagogy, as well as her own lived experience as a Black multi-ethnic woman of working-class origins and a history of trauma. Valenzuela currently coaches early career teachers in culturally relevant teaching, critically conscious pedagogy, holistic wellness, and earth-based spiritual healing.

A Focus on Young Black Women

Jody Sokolower: How did you end up running a group for African American girls?

Candice Valenzuela: I was teaching English at Castlemont High School. The school was transitioning to a focus on social justice, equity, and social change, and it was our pilot year. We noticed certain populations were struggling. And the group that stood out most was African American girls—they were the ones most out of class, the ones their teachers found to be the most challenging, and the ones who had the most complaints about school. We decided to form a class to support them specifically. At the time I was in grad school, so it wasn't my first choice to be running such an intense group, but the principal convinced me to take it on.

JS: There is so much focus on the crisis among African American boys. Very few people—and most of those seem to be African American women—are talking about African American girls. It's interesting that at Castlemont, Black girls were identified as the group that was really struggling. Do you think there's a connection between the focus on Black boys and how much crisis these girls were in?

CV: I do think it's connected. I want to preface by saying, based on my years of working with students in Oakland, almost all students feel unseen. Period. Across lines of color and gender. Ageism is real, and youth in our society suffer from a lack of voice, and a lack of adults seeing them as full human beings with rights and capacities.

And then, too many of our young people experience added layering to that invisibility. With young Black women, it's extreme.

The research does indicate that African American males are being targeted as far as suspension rates, policing in schools, incarceration. There is a historical racialized fear of Black males that plays into those overt and covert strategies to marginalize them.

But there's also a gendered way research happens. At least in Oakland, I don't think that Black girls are doing substantially better than Black boys when it comes to academics. And what happens if you bring truancy into the picture? Are Black girls actively pushed out or are they just not showing up? We're not looking at rates and impact of sexual harassment on academic achievement and social development; we're not looking at rates of sexual trauma. If you look at that stuff, you're going to get a whole other picture. Black girls specifically, and then queer Black youth additionally, are facing marginalization and attack throughout society.

We have to be aware of whether we are allowing Black girls to be visible in our classrooms. They don't benefit from us letting them off the hook. How are we holding them accountable for their own liberation?

I boil inside because there's such a high need with the girls. It's not to say that Black males don't need to have their own holding space. What I have issue with is when we promote that as the priority above all others, instead of finding ways to serve all young people, even if that means creating targeted campaigns for various subgroups.

JS: What is the impact on Black girls?

CV: One student said: "I feel invisible." I can't find a better way to say it. Even when a Black male is harmed, he has a mother, he has sisters, all these women who care for him are harmed when he's harmed. You are putting these girls in between a rock and a hard place. Obviously they love their brothers and their cousins, and they want the best for them. But why is it always at the expense of Black girls?

So that narrative has to be reframed. Yes, you're trying to help a certain population, but the perspective is too narrow-minded and you're again privileging males. And whenever you privilege a certain group, it's at the expense of others.

Black girls specifically, and then queer Black youth additionally, are facing marginalization and attack.

JS: How did you decide who would be in the class?

CV: Initially the administrators wanted to choose the girls they saw as having the most issues. I pushed against that. I feel that we benefit the most with diversity, when we can all learn from one another. Young people don't all struggle in the same ways, so we often see the ones who are loud, not in class, and making a big noise. But the children who are yelling still have their voices. There's something inherently healthy about openly resisting a system that's not built for you. Sometimes it's the quiet ones, who might even be making straight A's, who are struggling in different ways or directing their hatred inward. We miss them when we only focus on the loud ones.

So I reached out to teachers and asked them to recommend Black girls who they thought might benefit from community, who might need support to develop as leaders or to come into their voices, those who might be able to help guide others, who might benefit from added support and be open to receiving it. I wanted to create a core group in the midrange of students who might get passed over.

JS: How was the class defined?

CV: It was originally listed as advisory. I fought that because it looks like nothing on a high school transcript when students apply to college. We listed it as women's studies so they could get social studies credit.

I took a holistic approach because that's who I am, and I think that's what women need, especially in that age group. It wasn't text-heavy. I wanted to give them exposure to different concepts and theories, but that was a small percentage of what we ended up doing. It was more of a support group. I focused on being present for whatever need was showing up in that moment.

"I'm Not Black"

JS: How did you get started?

CV: The young women in the group were under such constant trauma and triggering of past traumas—in school and in the rest of their lives—that creating a safe space to talk and help each other was a huge challenge.

To build community, instead of having rules, we had a code. We called it the Sisters' Code. I created it before school started. If I were to teach this class again, I would have that be one of our first projects—to co-create our code—but I was trying to establish some foundations. We discussed it, memorized it, performed it as a class, and revisited it throughout the year. We had T-shirts made.

The girls' initial reactions were mixed. They felt happy to have that space, but then they often tested and challenged it. We know that happens in the classroom, but this was a little different. I felt there was deep fear or uncertainty about what it meant to have a space that was only young Black women. That wasn't something they had been in, not intentionally so—amongst their friends maybe, but not like this class, which was just for them.

In the beginning, it was hard for them to sit with that and figure out what it meant. It brought up a lot of their internalized self-hatred, their internalized sense of not being worthy. They weren't sure why it mattered for them to develop their own race and gender consciousness.

So some of them would come to my class late, or come in and be silly. There was a lot of passive resistance.

A lot of the initial work was helping them uncover for themselves: Why do we need to do this work? Why do I need it? What do I think? I had them talk and talk and talk. I brought in media, readings, and poems—anything I could think of to prompt them to do their own discovery around what it means to be a young Black woman.

JS: And what did they say?

CV: In the beginning, a lot of the girls said "I'm not Black." They didn't like the term. That was hard for me. I had to hold back because I feel very strongly about Black liberation. But they had experienced it as a label of harm. So they'd say, "I'm not Black, I'm brown." And what that said to me was they didn't feel seen.

I asked them: "What are all the negative things that are associated with Blackness?" We did a huge brainstorm that I left on the wall. It was painful, but I wanted them to remember and ask themselves: Is this who we are or is this a misrepresentation that we don't agree with? Externalizing those reflections was helpful because they had internalized it so much.

Now, it's true that race has no scientific validity. By the end of the year they understood that it's a social construct, but also that we have a great history of building solidarity around our experience within that construct. What we live and breathe every day as racialized beings is real.

Then, once those initial walls were down, when I would touch something deeper, they often tried to avoid what was painful by making fun of someone else in the class. The infighting and backbiting were fierce. Even on a good day, they would often throw verbal jabs at each other.

How can I show up for you and your struggle when I can't even see my own?

I would call their awareness to the way those jabs accumulate over time and tear at our self-esteem. We have to treat each other better than that if we want to be treated better ourselves. We know we're worth it. It took a long time to get to that place. A lot of it was returning over and over and over to the conversation. And then modeling something different for them—being conscious of how I engaged with them and how I talked to them, always coming from a place of love and respect so that they knew that was the standard.

What was most difficult for me were the emotions they brought in—the deep pain or sense of hopelessness, their sense of not being worthy, of not being seen. The need for social emotional support was so high; even those receiving therapy needed more. That created a whole different challenge for me than being a general ed teacher. I talked to my own therapist about it. She told me that the teacher holds the hope and the therapist holds the hopelessness. Being in a space where people can actually show you their despair is not as rewarding in a day-to-day way. As a teacher, I always engaged in a hopeful way and brought that out in young people, but in this group, I wasn't the one who got to witness most of their transformation.

Their teachers would say to me: "What's going on in that class? Are you drugging them? They're doing so much better. They're being so helpful to the other students. They're acting as leaders." Over and over again, I heard rave reviews from their teachers. Although the girls often resisted me and each other during class, they couldn't stop talking about the class to folks outside of it. But that wasn't what I saw. When we were together, what I often saw was the pain. I had to hold hope myself.

Confronting Conflict

JS: Did you have a curriculum for the class?

CV: I decided that the most meaningful thing I could give them was a space that was unapologetically different from everything else they were doing—a space that was completely different from school as they knew it.

We had reflective writing and journaling when they came into class. And then an open share; we would gather in a circle and use a talking piece. Sometimes, as long as it was respectful, I would let them keep talking and talking. Then I might guide the conversation with another question to more critically investigate whatever was coming up. And then we'd send the talking piece around again.

Of course, that meant the teacher inside me was often screaming, "But we're not reading anything!" That was my own internalized voice saying that reading and writing are the most important ways of learning. But that's not always true.

The first content area that I pulled out was looking at conflict: How are we dealing with conflict now and does that approach serve us? We spent two solid weeks on it and then kept coming back to it. The reflective writing assignments included: What is conflict? What kinds of conflict have you been in? Describe a conflict that you thought went well. Describe a conflict that you thought ended horribly. What was the impact of each? Who do you tend to get into conflict with the most? Why do you think that is?

They had so much to say, so much to discuss. As they talked, I would listen and write. I have three notebooks full of the girls' words.

When I got home, I'd sit with what had been shared and I'd think. Where do we go from here? What's the need they're expressing? Is there some area where they can be pushed to learn something new or to see themselves in a more holistic and more humanizing way? The girls' words were my text.

The girls were very clear that what they needed and what they wanted was the social emotional support. Whenever I came too close to my teacher role, they said, "No, we don't want you as a teacher, we want you as a mentor, we want you as a counselor, and we want you as a mom." Since I had been clear in the beginning that the purpose was to support them, I took their feedback seriously.

JS: Did you do work with conflict resolution or transformative justice?

CV: We were fortunate that another teacher was able to bring a conflict mediator to the school. Haneefa Olufemi, an amazing conflict mediator, built a great rapport with the young people. Sometimes she would come to our class and we would have a healing circle or do conflict mediation. That's where a lot of growth happened.

JS: What other topics were important to the group?

CV: We talked about friends and the way they treated each other. Sometimes their friendships included a lot of talking behind each other's backs, making fun of each other, betraying one another, lying to each other. So I asked them: "What does it mean to be a friend? What does that word mean to you?" We had to keep coming back to that. Some were able to say, "I'm going to try and act a little differently." Others realized that every time they hung out with a particular friend, they got in trouble or there was drama. Often it boiled down to repressed hurt and anger. Each time we came around to the same topics, we peeled back more layers.

Every week we had free art days when the students created collages or paintings about different areas of their lives—looking at family, love, relationships, culture, the media. Two days a week we did movement: African dance, yoga, Tae Bo. I was blessed to have a volunteer, Kihana Ross, who was doing research for her PhD on strategies for African American wellness. She helped me bring in guest speakers and co-led different activities. We both fundraised so the girls could have food every day, so they'd focus and feel cared for.

JS: It sounds like the beginning was difficult. How did you know that the group was starting to have a positive impact?

CV: About two months in, the younger students started running to my class. They knew exactly when my car pulled into the parking lot. I started getting text messages throughout the day, letting me know what was going on in the community or what they were doing. Then I knew that things had shifted and they had accepted me as being on their side, being in their corner.

One girl often found herself in a lot of conflict. When she reached out to me before going up to someone and challenging them, I knew that was an important shift. She was seeking counsel. And she had opened herself up to growing and changing. It wasn't perfect, but she grew throughout that year in how she addressed conflict. It was incremental.

Other girls in the school started coming up to me and saying, "I want to have a Polynesian girls group," "I want to have a Native American girls group." That's when I knew they were talking about it with their friends and other girls were seeing the need in themselves to speak out and claim a space that was just for them.

One of the young women who had said "I'm not Black, I'm not Black" in the beginning focused her final junior English project on Black women's empowerment. Now here she was, saying, "I am proud to be a Black woman. I am proud of who we are."

All of them at the end of the year said unequivocally they were so thankful for the space, and they believed that every Black girl should have that space.

The girls' words were my text.

What Does It Take?

JS: This was a great thing you were able to do for these girls. But wasn't it an exceptional situation? You got to say how many kids you wanted, you had extra people coming in. There was money for food. What are the implications for teachers at schools that don't have those options?

CV: Our situation was in *no* way ideal. We were in East Oakland, in a school that had three principals in three years, in a hostile environment and an extremely traumatized neighborhood, where Black girls were last on the list for services.

I would say the No. 1 thing is to not be afraid to advocate for what you know the students need, and to do so in a way that's creative, collective, and forward thinking. I wasn't going to the principal and saying, "Give me this, please, please." If you're always putting yourself at the beck and call of those in power, then you're never going to have anything.

The resources we had weren't coming from the school, they were things I advocated and fought for, alongside other allies at the school site. The money we raised was through crowdsourcing. Other folks who want to do this kind of work could also reach out to local universities or folks doing similar work.

My advice to teachers is to always push back against the isolation. They set us up in these situations where we feel isolated and overwhelmed. I make an effort to know each person at the site and have a personal relationship.

I think it's important to figure out who are your comrades, who are your allies, and who is politically opposed to what you're doing. I navigate each group differently. Then it's the same advice I give to students. You don't have to like everyone, but it's important to ask: "How can we work together? How do we leverage the resources we have amongst ourselves to work toward a common goal, even in the face of differences?" I believe any teacher can do that by learning to read the lay of the land at their school site, and asking: "How do I move these pieces strategically on this chessboard, so to speak, in the interests of my students and what they need?"

JS: Then the district changed the school's direction again, and you didn't get to do a second year. What was that like?

CV: That year was so hard because I started at zero. It was all about building trust and community amongst the girls. In the second year we could have done some of the revolutionary projects that I envisioned. I know I would have seen them step up as leaders and begin to show up more in the community, not just in our circle.

I wish we could've had another year. And I wish that folks could have taken on working with the other groups of girls so we could build solidarity. How can I show up for you and your struggle when I can't even see my own? It would be great to build different groups up strong and then bring them together to dialogue and build a deeper unity across all of the cultures. I would love to see that. That's one of the major problems with how much churn there is in schools these days—we rarely get to build on the foundations we've laid.

This course was a labor of love for me. I often felt personally, emotionally, and physically challenged by the group in ways that were uncomfortable. The group landed in a place that was far from where I ultimately wanted to go, but the end result reflected both my and the girls' authentic growth and needs. The experience taught me to honor where people are at, starting with myself.

SISTERS Code

Sisters in Solidarity, Transforming, Encouraging, Resisting, and Succeeding!

 We respect, love, and care for each other as sisters would. We keep our conversations confidential and don't spread gossip from this class. We listen to each other when we speak.

 We understand that our struggles are connected, but our people are divided. We do our best to resolve conflict and come together. We stand in solidarity, making connections to sisters of other races and backgrounds.

 We are growing and changing all the time, inside and out. We make the commitment to change for the better. We understand that when we transform, our families and communities transform too.

 We take the time out to focus on the positive and encourage one another through our struggles.

 We don't quietly accept our oppression. We stand up for ourselves and for each other. We challenge ourselves, and those around us, to resist all the things that hold us down.

 We put our education first and do our best. We know that no one can save us but ourselves. We look for jobs, we work hard in school, we prepare for college and we NEVER GIVE UP on our path to succeeding!

Katherine Streeter

"Save the Muslim Girl!"

By Özlem Sensoy and Elizabeth Marshall

Özlem Sensoy is an associate professor in the Faculty of Education at Simon Fraser University in Vancouver, Canada. She teaches courses on social justice education, critical media literacy and popular culture, and multicultural education. She is co-author of *Is Everyone Really Equal? An Introduction to Key Concepts in Social Justice Education* and co-editor of *Rethinking Popular Culture and Media*.

Elizabeth Marshall teaches in the Faculty of Education at Simon Fraser University Vancouver, where she researches children's and young adult literature and popular culture. She is a former public elementary school teacher and co-editor of *Rethinking Popular Culture and Media*.

Young adult titles that focus on the lives of Muslim girls in the Middle East, written predominantly by white women, have appeared in increasing numbers since Sept. 11, 2001. A short list includes Deborah Ellis' trilogy *The Breadwinner*, *Parvana's Journey*, and *Mud City*; Suzanne Fisher Staples' *Under the Persimmon Tree*; and, more recently, Kim

Antieau's *Broken Moon*. These titles received high praise and starred reviews from publications like *Horn Book* and *Publishers Weekly*. Each features a young heroine trapped in a violent Middle East from which she must escape or save herself, her family, and other innocents in the region. Authors portray Muslim girls overwhelmingly as characters haunted by a sad past, on the cusp of a (usually arranged) marriage, or impoverished and wishing for the freedoms that are often assigned to the West, such as education, safety, and prosperity.

Young adult literature about the Middle East cannot be separated from the post-9/11 context in which these books are marketed and increasingly published. *The Breadwinner*, for instance, was originally published in 2000, but Groundwood publishers rushed to re-release a paperback reprint of it in the United States after 9/11. By 2003 it had been translated into 17 languages and had become an international bestseller (Atkinson, 2003); in 2004 it was selling an estimated 15,000 copies a month in the United States (Baker & Atkinson, 2004). "Save the Muslim girl" stories emerge alongside a preoccupation with Islam in mainstream news media and a surge in U.S. and Canadian military, political, and economic activities in the Middle East and West Asia. The texts are framed and packaged to sell in a marketplace at a particular moment when military interventions are centered on predominantly Muslim organizations and countries.

As many teachers have found, these stories offer an enticing way for students to engage with current events, language arts, and social studies curricula. However, given that these books are written for and marketed primarily to a Western audience, what ideas do they teach young adult readers about Muslim girls, Islam, and the Middle East? In what follows, we detail three lessons that dominate the "save the Muslim girl" stories.

Our interest here is not to defend any particular doctrine (fundamentalist Christian or Islamic). Rather, in this article we identify how these books reproduce—and offer opportunities to challenge—long-standing ideas commonly associated with Islam: backwardness, oppression, and cultural decay. We believe that these novels can best be used to teach about the common Western stereotypes that are universalized in these books rather than to teach about Afghanistan, Pakistan, or Islamic cultures.

Learning a Stereotype Lesson #1: Muslim Girls Are Veiled, Nameless, and Silent

Young adult books about the Muslim girl usually feature a veiled adolescent on the cover. Her face is cropped and concealed, usually by her own hands or her veil. Much of her face is covered, including, most significantly, her mouth. Images serve as a shorthand vocabulary. Consider how iconic images—a white or black cowboy hat, a scientist wearing a white lab coat, a princess—set up a stock plot. The repeated images of veiled girls reinforce familiar, mainstream ideas about the confined existence of Muslim women and girls. This is the Muslim girl story we expect to read.

These kinds of images have a long history in the West. Steve McCurry's famous 1985 photo of 13-year-old Sharbat Gula on the cover of *National Geographic* provides the most well-known example. When we show the photo of the famous green-eyed Afghani girl in our education courses and ask students to write what they know about her, every student recognizes her image, yet few if any know her name, where she comes from, or that her photograph was "captured" in a refugee camp by a white U.S. journalist. Interestingly, the 2004 Oxford edition of Deborah Ellis' *Mud City* reproduces a photo of Gula on its front cover, taken from the same series of photographs McCurry captured in the mid-1980s. The cover of Antieau's *Broken Moon* has a virtually identical image: a close shot of a young girl with a veil covering her mouth, and her hands cupping her lower face. What ideas about Muslim or Middle Eastern girls—specifically Afghani girls—are we as audience invited to imagine?

> The way the girls' mouths are covered reinforces existing ideas about their silence and suggests that we in the West need to help unveil and "give" them voice.

Just about every book in this genre features such an image on its cover. These are familiar metaphors for how the Muslim girl's life will be presented within the novel. The way the girls' mouths are covered reinforces existing ideas about their silence and suggests that we in the West (conceptualized as "free" and "liberated") need to help unveil and "give" them voice. The images also invite ideas about girlhood innocence and vulnerability, and invite Western readers to protect, save, and speak for these oppressed girls.

But, is it not true that Muslim girls are oppressed and voiceless? We would argue that all women experience gender discrimination in different ways and with different consequences. The experiences of a U.S. woman (for example) will vary greatly if she is heterosexual or a lesbian, living in an urban center or a rural area.

Imagine this rural lesbian is Black, or Black and Muslim, or Black, Muslim, and a non-native English speaker. In this way, her experiences are determined not simply by her gender, but also by her racial, ethnic, and sexual identity. What strikes us about the books that we review here is that they are written by white Western women who author, organize, and interpret stories about Middle Eastern girlhoods for Western consumption. This raises questions about the politics of storytelling. For instance, how do (white) Western women decide for "global" women what their issues and oppressions are? Who tells whose story and in what ways?

Richard Dyer reminds us that while we may believe that stereotypes are derived from a limited truth about particular people, we actually get our ideas about people from stereotypic images. So it isn't the kernel of truth that results in stereotypes. Stereotypes are created and reinforced by the repeated appearance of particular images and the exclusion of others. Thus, the repeated circulation of the image of the veiled, sad Muslim girl reinforces the stereotype that all Muslim girls are oppressed.

Stereotypes are particularly powerful in the case of groups with which one has little or no personal relationship. Thus, for young people who get most of their ideas about "others" from textbooks or from media, we need to ask what ideas are learned when they "see" a very limited image of Muslim girls.

Learning a Stereotype Lesson #2: Veiled = Oppressed

Gendered violence in Middle Eastern countries, or the threat of it, organizes many of the books' plots. With few exceptions, the "good" civilized men in the girl's family are taken from her. In *Under the Persimmon Tree*, a brother and father are forced to join the Taliban as fighters, while in *The Breadwinner*, the Taliban places the father in jail because he was educated in England. *Parvana's Journey* opens with the father's funeral, and a deceased dad also figures in *Broken Moon*. This absence leaves the heroine vulnerable to the roving, indiscriminate, uncivilized "bad" men who will beat her for going out without a male escort (*The Breadwinner* and *Broken Moon*), confine her to the house (*The Breadwinner*), or beat her to preserve the honor of the community (*Broken Moon*).

In this context of an absent/immobilized parent, the girl is placed at the center of the plot, further emphasizing the danger and vulnerability of her existence. Parvana in *The Breadwinner* and *Parvana's Journey*, Nadira in *Broken Moon*, and Najmah in *Under the Persimmon Tree* each cut their hair and disguise themselves as boys. This cross-dressing draws heavily on Western ideas that girls should be unfettered by the requirement to cover themselves, and authors present this type of transformation as the only humane alternative to wearing a burqa and the only way to travel safely outside the domestic sphere.

The veil or burqa, which has exclusively functioned as the shorthand marker of women's oppression, is a much more complicated thing. To give you a sense of the range of meaning of the veil, consider for instance that in Turkey—a predominantly Muslim country—the veil (or "religious dress") is outlawed in public spaces as a means to underline the government's commitments to Kemalism, a "modern," secularist stance. In response and as a sign of resistance, some women, especially young university students and those in urban areas, consider the veil to be a marker of protest against government regulation of their bodies and the artificial division of "modern" versus "faithful." Similar acts of resistance are taken up by feminists in Egypt who wear the veil as a conscious act of resistance against Western imperialism. As another example, before 9/11, the Revolutionary Association of the Women of Afghanistan (RAWA) documented the Taliban's crimes against girls and women by hiding video cameras under their burqas and transformed the burqa from simply a marker of oppression to a tool of resistance.

It is problematic to wholly and simplistically equate women's oppression with the burqa, just as it would be problematic to claim that once Western women stop using makeup to cover their faces, it will mean an end to domestic violence in the United States and Canada. While veiling has different meanings in different contexts, it exclusively carries a negative connotation in the "save the Muslim girl" texts. For example, in *The Breadwinner*, the reader is educated about the burqa through the main character, Parvana:

"How do women in burqas manage to walk along the streets?" Parvana asked her father. "How do they see where they are going?"

"They fall down a lot," her father replied.

Nusrat, the American aid worker in Staples' *Under the Persimmon Tree*, describes the burqa similarly: "In the cool autumn air, Nusrat forgets how suffocating the folds of the burqa's synthetic fabric can be in hot weather, and how peering through the crocheted latticework eye piece can feel like looking through the bars of a prison."

In contrast to these confined women, the heroines of these novels, like "free" girls in the West, wear pants and experience freedom of movement. The freedoms associated with Western women are further emphasized in these texts by the addition of non-Muslim characters. The French nurse in *Parvana's Journey* (who works in Pakistan for a relief agency) and the American Nusrat in *Under the Persimmon Tree* (who establishes and runs a school for refugees) each choose to come to the Middle East to help. A white woman veterinarian who "wore the clothes of a Westerner" tends to the camels in *Broken Moon*. These "choices" that enable non-Muslim women to move and to work are placed in contrast to the experiences of the girls/women in the story who are at the mercy of violent events and settings in which their mobility (not to mention their way of dress) is strictly regulated and supervised.

There is a compelling character in *The Breadwinner* who offers the potential to represent Afghani women's liberation in more complex ways. This is Mrs. Weera, who leads a women's resistance group. She also convinces Parvana's mother to join her in running a covert school for girls. It is regrettable that Mrs. Weera does not occupy a more central place in the story since, unlike any other adult woman in the "save the Muslim girl" literature, she offers a transformative representation of activism among Muslim women in Afghanistan.

Again, we want to reiterate that we are not arguing that women and girls in the Middle East or predominantly Islamic societies do not experience domestic violence. In fact, we believe that domestic violence is a global epidemic that most countries, including predominantly Christian countries such as Canada and the United States, have neglected to face head on. Rather, we are arguing that the victim narrative that is so often a part of these young adult novels about Middle Eastern women reinforces the idea that the region is inherently violent and that women must be protected by outside forces. These young adult novels serve as de facto legitimization for the U.S.-led incursions in the region as a project of women's emancipation. As Laura Bush argued in her radio address on Nov. 17, 2001: "The brutal oppression of women is a central goal of the terrorists." In this way, the complexities of Afghanistan's history, as well as U.S. interest in the region and ties to violence, escape attention.

How do (white) Western women decide for "global" women what their issues and oppressions are?

That girls in the Middle East are consistently at risk of gendered violence implicitly suggests that girls in the "civilized" West are immune to such threats. The education students with whom we work are very familiar and comfortable with the stereotype that the lives of Muslim women are *inherently* scary, that they cannot work or vote or walk around without the threat of violence. Of course there are Muslim women who live in oppressive or patriarchal regimes (in the Middle East and elsewhere). What we contend is that young adult novels written by white women and marketed and consumed in the West consistently reinforce the idea that Muslim women are *inherently* oppressed, that they are oppressed in ways that Western women are not, and that this oppression is a function of Islam. By positioning "Eastern" women as the women who are truly oppressed, those in the West pass up a rich opportunity to engage in complex questions about oppression, patriarchy, war, families, displacement, and the role of values (imperialist or faith-based) in these relations.

While some might argue that an author's literary imagination is her own, we suggest that these representations of Muslim girls do not—and cannot—exist independent of a social context. That these "save the Muslim girl" stories continue to be marketed by major publishers, reviewed favorably by literary and educational gatekeepers, and/or achieve bestseller status like *The Breadwinner* suggests an intimate connection to the current ideological climate within which these stories are told, marketed, and consumed.

Learning a Stereotype Lesson #3: Muslim Girls and Women Want to Be Saved by the West

For many in the West, the plight of Afghanistan is framed exclusively within a post-9/11, U.S.-led "war on terror." Although radical women's organizations like RAWA have condemned brutality against women in Afghanistan for decades, their voices were absent, and are now muted, in a landscape of storytelling that is dominated by white Western women representing them. In an open letter to *Ms.* magazine, for instance, a U.S.-based supporter of RAWA notes that U.S.-centric women's organizations such as the Feminist Majority fail to give "credit to the independent Afghan women who stayed in Afghanistan and Pakistan throughout the 23-year (and counting) crisis in Afghanistan and provided relief, education, resistance and hope to the women and men of their country." Novels like *Broken Moon* play on popular scripts in which the West saves the people of the "East." These stories cannot be seen as simply works of fiction. They ultimately influence real-world experiences of girls in the Middle East and (most relevant to us) of Muslim and non-Muslim girls in our schools in the West.

> "This isn't the first time the welfare of women has been trotted out as a pretext for imperialist military aggression."

Deborah Ellis and Suzanne Fisher Staples gain legitimacy as authors because they have visited, lived, and/or spoken to real girls and women in the Middle East. The *Breadwinner* trilogy and *Under the Persimmon Tree* each include a map and an author's note that touches on the "tumultuous" history of Afghanistan and a glossary. The history offered in the end matter and in the texts themselves glosses over the history of colonization in the region. The authors dilute what is an extremely complex history that has led up to the current violence in the Middle East, particularly the role of U.S. foreign policy and military interventions that contributed to the rise of the Taliban.

The authors fail to capture the complexities of U.S. involvement and intervention in favor of stereotypical lessons about educating and saving Muslim girls. As Sonali Kolhatkar, vice president of the Afghan Women's Mission, and Mariam Rawi, a member of RAWA, argue: "Feminists and other humanitarians should learn from history. This isn't the first time the welfare of women has been trotted out as a pretext for imperialist military aggression" (2009). On one level these texts are part of a larger public pedagogy in which the United States and its allies are framed as fighting a good fight in Afghanistan and other regions of the Middle East. Readers are encouraged to continue to empathize with the lead character and the ideas that are associated with her: saving wounded children rather than critiquing U.S. policy, "pulling oneself up by one's bootstraps" rather than organizing together, fighting against all odds—ideas firmly rooted in mainstream U.S. ideals of exceptionalism and Western values of individuality.

Teaching a More Complicated Truth

We support teachers using books like *The Breadwinner* with the pedagogical goals of critical examination. We are not advocating for the one "right" Muslim girl story, nor do we suggest that teachers avoid using these books in classrooms (for we recognize that in many cases, decisions about what books teachers have access to are made by economic constraints at the school and district levels). We would, however, like to offer suggestions for the kinds of questions teachers could ask in order to use these resources in ways that are critically minded:

- How are Muslim girls visually depicted on the cover? You might ask students to generate a list of adjectives that describe the girl. The curriculum *Scarves of Many Colors* is a terrific resource for exploring the relationship between graphics and students' ideas about people. Consider questions of accuracy, context, and motivation. For example: How accurate are the details in the image? When and how will this image be "made sense of"? Who produced this image and why?

- Which parts of the novel are you absolutely certain are true? How do you know? Where did you learn this information? Students can try to pinpoint the resources they rely upon to get their "facts."

- Who is the author of this story? How do they legitimize themselves as an expert? What might be their motivations? Who are they speaking to and for?

- How is the book marketed and what does it intend to teach Western readers? Students might examine the description on the back of the book, the author's note, the map, the glossary, and book reviews to make observations about what kinds of readers are being targeted.

- How does Afghanistan (or Pakistan) fit into the region? In the author's note, Deborah Ellis points out that Afghanistan has been at war for decades. Often we study one country at a time. A more critical approach would investigate the relationships among countries. Students could explore the historical and current relationships (economic, political, cultural) between Afghanistan and other nation-states such as the former Soviet Union, Pakistan, Iran, and China.

- Whose story is missing? Students can create visual representations of the social locations (e.g., the race, class, gender, education) of each of the characters. Given these details, whose story is this? Whose stories are not here, and where might we go to learn about their stories?

While these examples of young adult fictions do not offer much in the way of transformative education about the Middle East, they do offer the potential to educate us about our own assumptions and our pedagogical purposes when we teach the "oppressed Muslim girl" stories. It is in this capacity that we hope educators will take up these novels.

References

Antieau, Kim. 2007. *Broken Moon*. Margaret K. McElderry Books.

Atkinson, Nathalie. 2003. "A Timely Trilogy." *Publishers Weekly*. November 17. publishersweekly.com/pw/print/20031117/22797-a-timely-trilogy.html. Accessed February 2009.

Baker, John, and Nathalie Atkinson. 2004. "The World Needs More Canada." *Publishers Weekly*. publishersweekly.com/pw/print/20040517/33215-the-world-needs-more-canada.html. Accessed November 2008.

Bigelow, Bill, Sandra Childs, Norm Diamond, Diana Dickerson, and Jan Haaken. 2000. *Scarves of Many Colors: Muslim Women and the Veil*. Teaching for Change.

Dyer, Richard. 1993. *The Matter of Images: Essays on Representation*. Routledge.

Ellis, Deborah. 2000. *The Breadwinner*. Groundwood Books.

Ellis, Deborah. 2002. *Parvana's Journey*. Groundwood Books.

Ellis, Deborah. 2003. *Mud City*. Groundwood Books.

Kolhatkar, Sonali, and Miriam Rawi. "Why Is a Leading Feminist Organization Lending Its Name to Support Escalation in Afghanistan?" July 8, 2009. alternet.org/world/141165.

Miller, Elizabeth. 2002. "An Open Letter to the Editors of *Ms. Magazine*." *Off Our Backs*, September/March: 59–61.

Sensoy, Özlem. 2009. "Ickity Ackity Open Sesame: Learning About the Middle East in Images." *Rethinking Curricular Knowledge on Global Societies*. Ed. Binaya Subedi. Information Age Publishing: 39–55.

Staples, Suzanne Fisher. 2005. *Under the Persimmon Tree*. Simon & Schuster.

Those Who Carry Bias

By T. Elijah Hawkes

T. Elijah Hawkes is co-principal at Randolph Union Middle/High School in Randolph, Vermont. He was founding principal of the James Baldwin School in New York City. His writings about adolescence, schooling, and democracy have appeared in the *Huffington Post, Ed Week, Phi Delta Kappan, Schools: Studies in Education*, and in Rethinking Schools' *New Teacher Book*.

Many of them, indeed, know better, but, as you will discover, people find it very difficult to act on what they know. To act is to be committed, and to be committed is to be in danger.

—*James Baldwin*

I f James Baldwin is right, engines of injustice keep running, but not because people are unaware. In their hearts, many people know that something is wrong. But they don't act on what they know because such commitments are risky.

Whether our communities are confronting racism or homophobia or another brand of bias, Baldwin's insight applies: There is danger for everybody. The target of bias or hate is in obvious danger. Bystanders face the self-negation of cowardice and silence, or the risk of social marginalization from speaking out. And agents of bias perpetrate the erosion of their own humanity.

With all of these different dangers at play—for everyone—how can we help a community become a safer place—for everyone?

Members of the queer community and their allies were asking this question at our school. Several years ago, courageous students formed a Queer-Straight Alliance (QSA) and began having regular meetings. Attendance was modest though consistent.

As efforts to make the school a safe place for queer youth became public, there were some reactionary responses. QSA meeting signs were torn down occasionally. We heard slurs in the hallway and saw scrawls on the bathroom walls.

Randolph Union is a 7th- to 12th-grade school serving the towns of Randolph, Brookfield, and Braintree, as well as several rural hamlets where what defines the center may be only a general store, a few old tombstones, or a long-closed, one-room schoolhouse. Some might think it's no big deal to start a QSA club in a central Vermont high school. Vermont is known nationally for being among the bluest of liberal states, and the place where civil unions first became legal. But it's also rural. The smells of mud, manure, and chainsaw oil walk in on boots every day, and many students live an hour away on winding dirt roads. Gun laws are permissive, hunting camo is fashionable in any season, and Confederate flags wave from belt buckles. It's no small thing to be openly gay.

Indeed, most Vermonters are a mix of both conservative and liberal values. This comes from living in small, connected communities where people make their decisions based on what's good for themselves and their neighbors, voting their consciences, and caring for each other without rigid regard for political brand.

Still, a humane, small-town community-mindedness, wherever you are, can come with provincialism: a lack of exposure, understanding, and respect for difference. I grew up here, and this was true of me. I used the words "Jew" and "gay" as insults toward my buddies all the time.

Breaking Silences

Vermont's 2011 Youth Risk Behavior Survey (YRBS) pinpointed several of the problems we faced at Randolph. Nearly all of our students in grades 9–12 took the survey, so it was a reliable sample. Of these hundreds of students, not enough responded to the question about being "gay or lesbian" for there to be any reportable data on that question. (Seven percent of females did identify as "bisexual.")

I began to have conversations with school counselors and others. Why the silence at our school, even on this anonymous survey? And what could we do about it? I taped a small rainbow flag outside my office door. And I gave one to Dave, my co-principal, who likewise posted the symbol—a sign to whoever might pass that inside the office sits an ally.

> Why the silence, even on this anonymous survey?

The culture change we sought involved work of many different types: from repairing signs and erasing graffiti to posting rainbow flags; from private conversations with those who expressed bias to schoolwide programs and performances; from staff trainings to following the lead of the queer students and their allies who were determined to make the school a safer place.

As co-principal, I spent time with kids outside the alliance, those who may, as Baldwin says, have known better in their hearts. But that didn't mean they wanted to face the risks of revising their outward habits and beliefs.

One student, Alan, was taken to a Fairness hearing that November for using "Jew" as an insult. Fairness is a restorative justice body that responds to violations of the school's core values. The committee is ad hoc, shaped around specific needs and circumstances. It includes the person brought to Fairness, a facilitator, and a panel of two students and one teacher.

Alan's meeting went well. He was engaged, if not talkative. One-word comments were typical of him at that age. At one point I asked him if he knew what the Holocaust was.

"No."

We asked if he would read a text and discuss it with his humanities teacher.

"Whatever." For him this actually was "yes." He agreed to the consequences we collectively determined, including meeting regularly with his teacher to read about and discuss how even casual expressions of bias can become the building blocks of persecution.

My work with Alan continued through the year: We had meetings, both disciplinary and informal, that centered on other instances of his sometimes mean or narrow thinking. After a school dance and a young woman in tears, we discussed his casual disdain for overweight women; on other occasions, we discussed his homophobia and his assertion—made privately to me—that he hated Black people.

These were two-way conversations. I shared my own journey with him. I told him that just up the road where I grew up, I used to speak some of the same hurtful words. I later realized that I was dear friends with people hurt by those words. My ability to love expanded as I discovered the true diversity of my own circle of family and friends.

Some days Alan would be withdrawn or impatient. "Are we done? Can I leave now?" Other days he would listen, reflect, and share his own stories. Alan justified his racist remarks with what he saw as negative experiences at an elementary school where he was one of a few white people in a largely Black school community. I listened and then tried to make a distinction: For him to talk over his memories in my office was one thing, but saying racist things in public was another. "In public, if you use those words, you offend lots of people and sometimes deeply hurt them." I told him the same is true of homophobic language.

Alan could be curt and dismissive. "I don't care what they think." Or "It's how I feel, so I say what I feel. You don't want me to lie, do you?"

"What about you? How do you want people to talk about you?" I asked. "Do you want to be known as a bigot?"

"What's that?"

"A bigot uses hateful words that hurt people."

Alan's journey was a difficult one. He experimented with cutting himself, using pain as an anesthetic. He sometimes talked wildly about punching teachers. And so I spent a lot of time with him—as did our guidance staff and his advisor. We disciplined and reprimanded, met with his family, and sought therapeutic support. But we also listened to Alan and asked him questions. We were trying to build trust—to value the thoughts, history, and humanity of this young man— in order to build capacity for changing his thinking before he walked out our doors. In the words of Frederick Douglass: "It's easier to build strong children than to repair broken men."

Alan to Fairness, Again

By April, Alan had made some progress, expressing less anger and bias, voluntarily walking into my office more often than being sent for misbehavior. And so, when a teacher came to tell me she heard Wade teasing a friend in the hall with the word *fag*, I thought of Fairness, and of Alan.

We set up a meeting with Wade and I asked Alan to participate, explaining it as an opportunity to apply lessons he'd learned about the impact of being public with your bias. We ask kids who have participated in Fairness to serve on the committee at someone else's hearing. It allows them to come full circle, to play a different role, to feel some redemption.

> The activism and courage of queer youth and their allies help us become a stronger community.

Alan agreed. We also asked Sarah, one of Wade's female peers. After introductions and framing the process, my colleague shared her recollection of what happened in the hallway. Then Wade shared his. "I was just joking with my friend. He knew I was joking. He says it to me, too."

We discussed how a word can be harmful no matter the speaker's intent. I asked which of our community values they thought had been violated in this incident. Wade suggested citizenship, one of our Habits of Heart.

Sarah agreed: "Even if your friend knew it was a joke, it could have offended others."

I asked Alan which value he thought had been violated. "Respect for others," he said. We ultimately decided on both.

Next we determined how to repair the damage. We open each of our whole school assemblies with a space for "appreciations and apologies." My colleague suggested that perhaps this could be a place for Wade to make a public apology. We all agreed that, since the action occurred in a public space, a private apology was less appropriate than a more general and public gesture. But Wade seemed hesitant about addressing the whole school, and I was worried that he might not be able to approach the task with the right seriousness. I suggested that a more symbolic gesture could also be restorative, mentioned the flag outside my office, and said a student had come in recently to appreciate it. Ultimately, the committee decided that everyone around the table, not just Wade, would put a color copy of a rainbow flag up in some visible place in the school. Wade's jobs included getting the images laminated in the library and to each of us.

Wade required several reminders to get his jobs done. Then, without any prompting, Alan borrowed tape during lunch one day and put up his flag next to the window of the school store. Soon there were rainbow flags in conspicuous locations around the school.

Acting on What We Know

By the following year, our QSA had taken on a new name, GLOW: Gay, Lesbian, or Whatever. One of their first initiatives was the distribution of GLSEN (Gay, Lesbian, & Straight Education Network) stickers to every teacher. The stickers say "Safe Space" against a rainbow background. GLOW asked teachers to post the sticker if they were willing to make their classrooms safe for everyone and to intervene to stop bias. They also brought a facilitator from Outright Vermont to meet with students in 9th-grade humanities classes and with our faculty for an inservice training.

Three years later, our school continues to make progress. Posters stay up on hall walls and GLOW openly sponsors whole school events and learning opportunities. On the 2013 YRBS survey, 6 percent of males at our school identified as "gay, lesbian, bisexual, or unsure." A student in our filmmaking class created a documentary about coming out in our community, and there were public showings in our town. Other signs of progress include the courage of two trans students who have publicly adopted new gender identities. Last spring, GLOW offered a teach-in for faculty featuring testimonial from one of these students. The student noted some bumps in the road, but affirmed that the transition was met with acceptance and kindness.

The change we seek is sometimes about being consistent with the values we declare and acting on the knowledge we carry in our hearts. Posted on the walls of our school and in our classrooms are those values we discussed with Alan at Fairness: integrity, respect for others, respect for self, adaptability, citizenship. These public declarations proclaim that we know better.

Although there is more work to do, the activism and courage of queer youth and their allies continue to help us act on what we know in our hearts and become a stronger community.

Excerpt from *A Is for Activist* by Innosanto Nagara

T is for Trans.
For Trains, Tiaras,
Tulips, Tractors
And Tigers too!

Trust in the True
The he she they that is you!

Dear Parents of Transgender Children

By Shannon Panszi

Shannon Panszi is a proud parent of three sons, one of whom is transgender. With a background in obstetrics and gynecology, she has been a fierce advocate for transgender rights through her work with the medical community. Currently she is the daytime caregiver for her children, works with the national transgender advocacy group FORGE, helps to organize a local parents support group, and gives lectures around the country on transgender healthcare.

D ear parents of transgender children,
        You are not alone.
        My husband and I have discovered that talking about the peaks and valleys we have encountered—with our family, within our cir-

cle of friends, and in our school—became easier after we connected with other parents who have had similar experiences and felt similar emotions. In our day-to-day interactions with neighbors and on the school playground, we sometimes find ourselves being judged. But when we're with other families in our support group, we have no fear that they are making assumptions about the validity of our child's gender identity—or questioning his (or our) sanity.

Our Story

The summer our eldest child, Sam, was 7, I learned about Coy Mathis, a 6-year-old transgender girl who won the right to use the school bathroom designated for the gender with which she identified. I felt a shock of recognition. Sam had been assigned female at birth, but had a long history of telling people he was a boy, only wanting to play with other boys, drawing and dressing himself as a boy (including male-identified superhero costumes). But we hadn't considered that our child could be transgender.

In college, I had learned about what was then called "gender identity disorder." I was taught that people who identify as transgender were mentally ill or had been traumatized in some way. The media reinforced my misconceptions, and like most people I know, I had never met a transgender person. Even as an OB/GYN doctor who had been accustomed to declaring "It's a boy" or "It's a girl" based on genitals, I hadn't learned about gender identity development.

I had been telling my child for years that he was a girl because he had a vulva. The night I saw the Coy Mathis story, I suddenly realized that I'd been wrong. After the children went to bed, I searched the internet. I found many articles that described my child. My husband was on a plane halfway across the country; I left urgent text messages for him to call me.

My husband and I agreed that we didn't want to put words in our child's mouth, but we did want to let him know that he could tell us who he was without fear of being corrected. And so began our journey.

> Sam's best friend seemed happy to see him—until his mom and brother joined us.

With a new name, new pronouns, Star Wars underwear, and a new haircut, our child started his 2nd-grade year as Sam the boy. Some people in our community quickly became inhospitable. Sam's best friend from the previous school year seemed happy to see him—until his mom and brother joined us. Then he became visibly uncomfortable and silent. Moms who had always returned my calls became suddenly too busy and couldn't find time to let the children play together.

On the other hand, other parents began seeking out play dates. I got the impression that those parents were trying to guide their children to nurture inclusive friendships. Even though I was grateful for those well-intentioned parents, the journey still felt pretty lonely. We didn't know any other parents who were on this path.

Parent Support Group

I desperately looked for support, and was able to receive some through a transgender adult support group and a national listserv. It was the first time in a month that I felt that I could breathe.

At one of the adult meetings we watched *A Self-Made Man.* The movie showed a parent support group; I longed to have a place like that. When I shared my wish with the director of the adult group, he asked me to help him start our own parents' group.

Our parent support group is still small. We are still learning how to reach the people who need us—and avoid people who may wish us harm. The support we receive from some in our community is not the same as being able to share with parents who are negotiating some of the same things we are. We listen, empathize, and give guidance based on our own experiences. We are able to share books and news about quickly changing laws, and media about people advocating for more understanding for our children.

The parent support group is a place where we celebrate each other's victories. We cheered when one of our families was able to get "gender identity" and "gender expression" included in their school's nondiscrimination policy. We also empathize with each other's fears for our children's safety or the rejection they and we may experience from family and friends.

If you are the parent of a transgender child, I hope that you will find—or create—a place to go where you will know that you are not alone. I hope you will meet others navigating a similar trail, gain knowledge from others' success in overcoming obstacles, and most importantly, have a place to let down your guard and be able to talk, laugh, or cry freely in a room full of people who will smile and pass the tissues.

Resource

A Self-Made Man. Dir. Lori Petchers. 2013. 5Efilms. DVD. "PFLAG." community. pflag.org/transgender.

Ariel Schrag

Rethinking the Day of Silence

By Adriana Murphy

Adriana Murphy is the middle school head at Friends Community School in College Park, Maryland, where she is an 8th-grade ethics and leadership teacher and a 5th- and 6th-grade advisor. She is a member of the Association of Independent Maryland Schools' Gender and Sexuality Diversity Committee and presents nationally on LGBTQ topics in education and the workplace.

B
ack in 2006, 7th and 8th graders at Green Acres, the K–8 indepen- dent school where I taught in suburban Maryland, participated in the Day of Silence. The Day of Silence is a national event: Students across the country take a one-day pledge of silence to show that they

want to make schools safe for all students, regardless of their sexual orientation and gender identity/expression. The idea is for students to better understand—and to express solidarity with—people who feel they must remain silent about who they are. In theory, the event is a good one—after all, who doesn't want students to develop empathy and understanding? But in practice, we found that the Day of Silence presented two fundamental challenges:

1. Middle schoolers are not very good at being silent.
2. Students wanted to know how their silence actually helped people who felt they weren't free to be themselves.

Several students gave their best effort to remain silent for the day, but for the majority, an hour was the maximum. If the purpose of the day is to teach students how hard it is to be unable to fully express oneself, it did not take students more than an hour to figure that out. Telling middle schoolers that they are not allowed to speak is akin to telling teachers they can't teach—it just goes against their essence. In that first year, we figured that perhaps we just didn't enforce the "no talking" rule well enough, so we tried it again, but year two yielded the same results. When it came to LGBTQ topics, the students did not want to be silent—they wanted to talk.

At the end of our second Day of Silence, the director of diversity, the school counselor, and I debriefed the event with students. We wanted to know what, if anything, students gleaned from participating in the event and how we could make it better. We asked: How has the Day of Silence impacted your thinking about the freedom to be yourself? What changes would you recommend to the Day of Silence organizers? As we listened to students, it became clear that nobody wanted to name names, but that students were concerned about one of their classmates:

"I think the Day of Silence is a good start, but I want to know how to help. What if there was a student who was out at our school, but couldn't come out at home? We might be the only safe place for that person."

"We need to do something besides be silent all day. The Day of Silence should really be a Day of Action where we have different workshops and learn how to be allies."

"Yeah! How does my silence help someone who doesn't feel safe?"

There was a collective pause in the room. Among the student body, there was at least one student for whom the Day of Silence was every day and everyone knew it. The student felt safe at school, but not at home. For this student's peers, understanding what it was like to be silent wasn't the issue, figuring out what to do about it was. How could we, as a community, support this student? Surely, there were more students like this one. What could we do to ensure that our school was as safe and informed as it could be?

"What would be helpful?" I asked.

"First of all, let us talk! And then, rather than just hearing from each other and our teachers, let's invite different speakers who we could talk to. Teenagers would be good. I want to know how to be an ally or what it's like to be gay from a teen's perspective," pleaded a student.

Some students wanted to hear positive stories about LGBTQ teens instead of always hearing tragic stories of bullying and suicide. Many students wanted to know more about what it was like to come out, and how they could support their friends in the process. Students wanted practical tools to support their classmates and to make the school a safe place for all.

A Day of Action

The format of the Day of Silence needed to change. Students renamed the Day of Silence the Day of Action because they wanted to focus on actions they could take to support their LGBTQ peers and to stand up against bullying and discrimination. I met with the head of the middle school, the director of diversity, and the 5th-/6th-grade dean to discuss the changes that students were seeking. We agreed on a workshop format that would allow students to choose which sessions they wanted to attend.

> When it came to LGBTQ topics, the students did not want to be silent— they wanted to talk.

So the day went from a struggle to be quiet to students participating in an array of workshops offered by community members, high school students, and Green Acres teachers, staff, parents, alumni, and trustees. Our speakers were recommended by and connected to Green Acres teachers and staff; I had sent an email asking for family members, friends, and/or alumni who would be willing to share their stories of being LGBTQ or of supporting someone who is LGBTQ.

We knew that one of the risks of inviting guest speakers to offer workshops was that we had less control over what they might say, but we also knew that authenticity had to be a pillar of the program for it to be successful. The trick, of course, was balancing honesty with how much middle school kids were ready to hear—in other words, being attuned to what was developmentally appropriate. When preparing the speakers for the event, we told them to share a story or an event—a coming out story, a story about bullying, a story about being supported—and to focus on the emotions. We knew that not everyone in the audience could relate to their stories, but everyone could relate to being scared, nervous, rejected, hopeful, or loved. We wanted to show students that even amidst seemingly different experiences, there are human emotions that connect us all.

At our first Day of Action, we offered eight 35-minute workshops; students could attend two. After discussing the purpose of the Day of Action and reviewing workshop descriptions during advisory period, students made their selections on a Google form that asked them to rank their top four choices. The form automatically downloaded onto a spreadsheet that made it easy for organizers to place students in workshops by preference. Workshops included:

- Being an Ally
- How Words Can Hurt and What You Can Do About It
- Discrimination in the Workplace
- Coming Out: Teen Issues
- Being a Bisexual Mom
- Coming Out, Being a Gay Dad
- Marriage Equality in the News
- Supporting a Lesbian Daughter

When arranging the workshops, we had to balance student interest and need, available speakers, diversity of topics, and budget (speakers were unpaid, but we gave them a $20 gift card).

The day of the event, we found that the speakers were incredibly nervous, despite many of them having spoken in public before. The nervousness made the presenters unexpectedly more appealing to the students because it made them real. In one workshop, a speaker began to tear up as she talked about how hard it is to hear that kids tease her daughter for having a lesbian parent. A student in the audience spoke up and said: "That's so mean. That's why we have a Day of Action. I wish she could come to our school."

In another session, students role-played what to say and what not to say when friends come out or share that they are questioning their sexual orientation or gender identity. In the session with local teens, one said: "This is actually a great place to be a gay teen. Montgomery County is one of the most accepting places in the country. It's not perfect, of course, but there are a lot of accepting and supportive kids here." At this point, I caught the eye of the Green Acres student who was open about his sexuality at school, but not yet at home. He gave me a nod.

After the two 35-minute sessions, we all came together to debrief the morning. When asked if they preferred this format to the Day of Silence, every student raised a hand. Some students said they learned how to respond to "That's so gay." Others offered insights on the impact of teasing and bullying; hearing it from the people who are affected made them realize just how awful it really is. A few students appreciated learning more about the (now successful) fight for marriage equality in Maryland. By far, the greatest hit of the day was the session offered by the teens. Even after we wrapped up the event, Green Acres students continued talking to them and asking questions. Lesson learned: If you want to capture the attention of middle schoolers, bring in a group of high school students to talk to them.

Parents Need Education, Too

Although the Day of Action was an overall success, it did not go off without a hitch. The new format raised concerns for some parents. Some believed that the topics were not developmentally appropriate for middle school students and responded by keeping their children home for the day. Others argued that the topic wasn't "relevant" or questioned why we were focusing "so heavily" on this minority group.

For an inclusive school like ours, these comments were unusual and unexpected. We realized that, unlike other topics of diversity, sexuality and gender expression force adults to confront religious and political beliefs that are sometimes far more complicated than the messages of understanding, respect, and safety that we saw the Day of Action as promoting. We saw the students addressing moral and ethical issues—how to treat others with respect, how to support peers who may be LGBTQ, how to use inclusive language, and how to stand up against bullying and/or discrimination—but the adults who were most concerned feared that we would focus on the physical aspects of sexuality, namely sex. Of course, nothing was further from the truth, nor would it have been appropriate.

"How does my silence help someone who doesn't feel safe?"

In retrospect, we should have informed parents earlier and given them an opportunity to learn more about the program's goals. Instead, we assumed we had communicated with parents clearly and that they would treat the Day of Action as any other school day. We assumed that because our school had a history of equality (we were the first racially integrated school in Montgomery County and on the forefront of publicly welcoming same-sex families to our school), our community would fully support making school a safe and welcoming place for *all* people, regardless of their sexuality or gender identity. What we learned was that sending letters out about the event was not enough. We had to offer parents the same opportunity we gave students to listen to stories about why a Day of Action was needed. We had underestimated the anxiety that some parents have about this topic.

To address parental concerns, the next year the school partnered with Family Diversity Projects, a nonprofit organization based in Amherst, Massachusetts, that specializes in anti-bias education and professional development using traveling photo exhibits. We hosted the *Love Makes a Family* photo-text exhibit, which fights homophobia by telling the stories of ordinary people and by helping students to affirm and appreciate diverse family compositions. We invited parents to visit the display during an Evening of Action parent information session. Peggy Gillespie, the co-founder and executive director of Family Diversity Projects, was the keynote speaker for the Evening of Action and facilitated a panel discussion.

With the exhibit as a backdrop, speakers discussed some of the same topics that students would explore at the Day of Action a week later. One of the parents who had kept her child home a year earlier came that evening to learn more about the day and its goals. Among the panelists were a local psychiatrist, an adopted gay teenage boy, and the straight son of two lesbian mothers.

A parent on the panel shared her regret at not replying to her gay colleague's email the night before he committed suicide. "Education is our only hope," she said, fighting to hold back her tears. "I wish every school had a Day of Action so that kids could actually listen to the stories of people they think are so different from them. Once you listen to someone's story, it's hard to hate."

"I understand now. Thank you for sharing these powerful stories," said the parent who had kept her child home. A week later, when the students' Day of Action took place, her daughter was in attendance.

As for the student who was open at school but not at home, I spoke with him after he graduated. He confided: "I remember the teens who talked to us at the Day of Action. It was the first time I heard that I was lucky to be gay. From that moment on, I realized that being gay wasn't a curse and that I would be OK."

He is OK. And he has promised to return as a speaker for Green Acres Day of Action.

Gay-Straight Alliances Align with Restorative Justice
An interview with Geoffrey Winder

By Annika Butler-Wall

Annika Butler-Wall is an editor of *Rethinking Sexism, Gender, and Sexuality* and an editorial intern at Rethinking Schools.

F aced with daunting statistics—eight out of 10 LGBTQ youth are verbally harassed about their sexual orientation, six out of 10 feel unsafe at school—and devastating reports of harassment-related suicides, many schools have targeted bullying as a priority.

Unfortunately, given the prevalence of zero-tolerance discipline policies that rely on suspension, expulsion, and police involvement, advocating for "stricter" anti-bullying policies often means sending students straight into the school-to-prison pipeline.

How can we simultaneously work to eradicate bullying, keep students out of the criminal justice system, and create safer schools for all? The GSA Network, a national organization that connects student-run Gay-Straight Alliances across the country, is collaborating with organizations fighting the school-to-prison pipeline to find answers to this question. GSAs have long been a much-needed safe space in schools for LGBTQ students, and now the network is defining GSA goals within the broader movement for education justice. Geoffrey Winder, formerly senior manager for racial and economic justice programs for GSA Network and now co-executive director, spoke with Annika Butler-Wall about those efforts.

Beyond Zero Tolerance

Annika Butler-Wall: How long have you been working for the GSA Network? What is your work focused on?

Geoffrey Winder: Back in 2001, one of my first jobs after graduating from high school was as GSA Network anti-racism initiative coordinator for a summer-long project. I came back as a staff member in 2008. My work now is focused on the organization's current national priorities: school discipline reform; immigration reform and providing resources to undocumented queer students; and nontraditional education settings for GSAs, including alternative schools and continuation schools. We're also considering charters as nontraditional spaces because, unlike for public schools, there isn't a federal law that mandates that they host a GSA.

How can we eradicate bullying, keep students out of the criminal justice system, and create safer schools for all?

ABW: The GSA Network has a campaign, #GSAs4Justice, looking at the intersections between GSAs and restorative justice. How did the campaign come about?

GW: Historically, we worked on passing anti-bullying laws that relied on the discipline structures that schools already had in place. But we realized there were students who started the school year in a GSA but weren't in school at all by the end of the year. We tried to figure out what was going on, why students weren't finishing. It's cool that they have a GSA, but it doesn't do them any good if they're not in school to go to it.

So we started partnering with groups that were looking at other types of school transformations—school discipline reform and restorative justice. When we started the work, there was a lot of media attention around bullying suicides, and there was a mandate from the federal government that all school districts needed to have an anti-bullying policy in place. But there were no guidelines. We felt it was critical to shift the narrative away from zero tolerance.

ABW: What is zero tolerance?

GW: Zero tolerance means no questions asked, this offense equals this punishment. There's no leeway if a student was getting harassed all year and this was the one time they fought back, or if a student got kicked out of their home the night before and is having trouble being present in school.

The way we were seeing the zero-tolerance anti-bullying policies being implemented was that both students involved would get suspended or expelled at the same rate. Or the student's LGBTQ identity had been seen as the problem throughout the year, and this was the chance to take care of that problem for good. The LGBTQ student would get expelled and the other student would come back.

We are trying to get school districts to eliminate zero-tolerance policies. That means we need to tell them what we think they should be doing instead. Restorative justice as an option for LGBTQ issues is fairly new. What we have heard from places like Oakland, where they have restorative justice programs, is that it allows for a more holistic accounting of what happened.

ABW: What do you mean by restorative justice?

GW: We use the terms *restorative justice* and *restorative practices* interchangeably. We don't have an organizational position on a certain type of restorative justice circle or program. We support solutions that try to restore balance or harmony, or at least encourage dialogue versus shutting down the dialogue and excluding students from education. It doesn't have to be a restorative justice circle; it could be additional resources, counseling, and support services. We're looking at a whole host of things that we consider as restorative for the students, and enable them to be present and safe in the school.

ABW: How do punitive discipline policies affect LGBTQ youth?

GW: The challenge with the data is that we don't really know what is happening to LGBTQ youth. We've been working with the California Department of Education on how to track the outcome of bullying cases and whether both students get the support they need to stay in school. We're trying to figure out if we want them to track it when the student identifies as LGBTQ, because then that information is part of the official school record. Nationally there's a law that schools can't "out" students, so that's a factor. And if students aren't out at home, that raises other liability and ethical issues. Tracking trans students is easier when they are officially transgender on paper.

We have done our own small research study of gender nonconforming students and school discipline. We found that queer youth of color who are female-identified, masculine of center, are being disciplined in similar ways as young men of color. Gender nonconforming students' identities and appearance are often considered "willful defiance."

And we can see where LGBTQ students are ending up: 20-40 percent of homeless youth are LGBTQ; we can pretty much imagine those students are having a hard time going to school. Among youth in foster care, 20-40 percent are LGBTQ, and youth in foster care are three times more likely to not finish school. And almost 15 percent of those in the juvenile justice system identify as LGBTQ. So if we just look at where they're ending up, even if we don't know what's happening in schools, we can see that something is really going wrong.

Far too many LGBTQ youth are marginalized and aren't getting access to education.

Another focus of my work in the Racial and Economic Justice Program is looking at the school-to-prison pipeline as one of the primary ways queer youth of color are targeted and taken out of the school system, especially through involuntary transfers to alternative and continuation schools. Schools are basically saying, "You would be much safer at this other school, they will be able to give you more individualized support." Then there is no support. Rarely are there GSA clubs at alternative or continuation schools. This has become core to our mission of school transformation in general.

Building a Chorus

ABW: How are you working with other social justice groups on these issues?

GW: Our collaboration with the Advancement Project and Alliance for Educational Justice grew out of a 2011 grouping of folks who said, "OK, all of our students are in similar neighborhoods, we're working in public schools, and these are the conditions that all of our students are facing." The folks who are doing restorative justice as a way to reduce racial disparities definitely are on board with seeing how we can reduce bias-based disparity in general.

A big part of our coalition building with education and youth justice groups has been creating mechanisms to support queer students in the spaces that they're already in—organizing in the educational justice groups and making them more queer friendly. There are LGBTQ students who are participating and leading in those groups, they just haven't been talking about being LGBTQ. But we don't want queer youth to feel like they either have to go start a different group or stay and feel alienated from the group that they're in. So, for example, at Sistas & Brothas United in the Bronx, they started a community GSA to meet the needs of their LGBTQ members who did not go to or have traditional GSAs. In Wisconsin, GSAFE, the GSA organization there, organizes a class called Foundations of Leadership, a gifted and talented class for LGBTQ youth of color who may or may not be in traditional schools with GSAs.

ABW: What has been happening with the campaign?

GW: In the aftermath of Michael Brown's murder in Ferguson, we joined the #BlackLivesMatter movement and we started a #BlackFutureLegends month to highlight the connections between Black history and queer history, build community and solidarity amongst Black LGBTQ youth, and to look toward the future.

Our 2014 national conference was in Minneapolis, which passed the first statewide restorative justice anti-bullying law. We're trying to build on that momentum. In addition to our work with juvenile justice activists, we're working with the AFT [American Federation of Teachers] and the NEA [National Education Association] to show that it's not just LGBTQ youth who are saying this—youth of color are saying it and the teachers are saying it. We're trying to build a chorus around the need for restorative justice.

Several GSA networks around the country have been funded to do educational justice work or are working in collaboration with education justice organizations. In Wisconsin, their GSA network organized a broad, statewide education justice coalition. Milwaukee passed an anti-bullying law that cites restorative justice as the solution. In Colorado, Denver passed the first memorandum of understanding (MOU) between the local police force and the schools about when it is OK for the police to intervene and when it is not. That's another model we're trying to push throughout the country—establishing MOUs with school resource officers and police about how and when to interact with an LGBTQ student. For example, what is the minimum level of training they need to engage with LGBTQ students? How is engaging with an LGBTQ student who is homeless or dealing with family rejection different from dealing with another student? You can't just call their parent.

ABW: What's ahead?

GW: We've rooted the notion that zero-tolerance and anti-bullying aren't a good combination, so now we're looking at the policies local districts and states are adopting as alternatives. For example, California has passed an addendum to their anti-bullying policy that says there are 14 other corrective methods you need to try before you get to suspension or expulsion—including talk to the student, have them see a counselor. We're encouraging other states and districts to do something similar.

The GSA movement is a little late to the game with the school discipline stuff, which I think has been part and parcel with larger parts of the LGBTQ movement, which has too often been single-issue in the way they have approached things. In the past, folks haven't looked at GSAs as able to push social justice agendas in the way we are imagining. I think that going forward there will be a lot of energy and exciting initiatives coming from GSA clubs.

Resource:

"Restorative Practices: Fostering Healthy Relationships and Promoting Positive Discipline in Schools." 2014. otlcampaign.org/sites/default/files/restorative-practices-guide.pdf.

San Francisco Unified School District & Design Action Collective

Policy Change: A Student Perspective

BY PATRICK MCLINDEN

Patrick McLinden is a student at the University of Michigan, pursuing a joint degree in immunology and Spanish with hopes of becoming a doctor. He harbors a passion for social justice and will continue to pursue writing as a hobby.

A few years ago, my high school elected a transgender student as prom king. One reason this was possible was because the school's Gay-Straight Alliance (GSA) advisor was also the student council advisor. His relationship to both organizations meant that he saw an opportunity for a transgender student to see that success. But what if he had not been the advisor? What if a transgender youth wanted to become prom king at a different school? What needs to be in place to ensure that transgender and gender nonconforming students can seek the same opportunities as other kids?

Wisconsin's pupil nondiscrimination law (state statute 118.13) protects students from discrimination based on "sex, race, religion, ancestry, creed, pregnancy, parental status, marital status, physical disability, mental disability, emotional disability, or sexual orientation." Although it provides coverage for almost every possible identifying tag, the statute has forgotten about the *T* in LGBTQ.

Title IX, the federal law, covers transgender students, but that fact is not widely known. A decade ago, there were no nondiscrimination policies for transgender and gender nonconforming students in Wisconsin school districts, according to Brian Juchems, senior director of education and policy at GSAFE Wisconsin (Gay-Straight Alliance for Safe Schools). But Brian J., as everyone calls him, has been working with districts around the state, and today there are more than 10 districts with nondiscrimination policies. That number is climbing.

I am a Milwaukee Public Schools (MPS) high school student. When word got out that Brian J. was pushing for a policy change to protect transgender and gender nonconforming students in Milwaukee, I jumped at the opportunity to help. Along the way, I learned a lot about creating nondiscrimination policy change in a school district. I want to share the lessons we learned.

Why Trans Students Need Nondiscrimination Policies

Nondiscrimination policies help schools implement clear and explicit expectations about how transgender and gender nonconforming youth should be treated and included—inside and outside the classroom. When trans students enter new classrooms each year, they are presented with many physically and emotionally uncomfortable situations. Nondiscrimination policies, coupled with targeted professional development, can ensure that teachers know their students' preferred names and pronouns and how to introduce transgender and gender nonconforming students to others.

The policies also lay the basis for the creation of inclusive bathrooms and locker rooms. For example, gym students and athletic team participants are often forced to change their clothing and shower in gendered locker rooms. This can be uncomfortable for many students, but for transgender and genderqueer kids, the locker room can be a dangerous place. These students are often subjected to questions, teasing, or outright abuse by fellow classmates.

"Research shows," Brian J. explains, "that when students know they are protected around a particular identity, they report feeling safer and more included at school."

A Recipe for Change

The fight to implement trans supportive policies can be a tough one. Brian J. follows the example set by his mentor, Marilyn Levin, creator of a community-based LGBTQ youth program in La Crosse, Wisconsin. She taught him the importance of educating the community as a way to bring about positive change. She urged him to "treat people as the allies you want them to become."

Brian J. remembers well what can happen when you are not prepared. In one district, word got out to students' families that there would be a proposal to add transgender and gender nonconforming youth to the nondiscrimination policy. At the school board meeting, things took a turn for the worse. Brian J. recalls: "I attended the next policy committee meeting and it was pretty ugly. There were about 70 or 80 people in the room, all of whom I would characterize as angry and very upset white Christians. Many of them, including three pastors of local churches, spoke in opposition to the policy changes. I was the only person who spoke in support of transgender students."

"Treat people as the allies you want them to become."

This illustrates why preliminary meetings, proper education, and support are key. Alone, Brian J. stood no chance. It's important not to make hasty decisions or alert possibly unsympathetic administrators or superintendents too early. Building community and leadership support first are critical. When there is a group of well-educated and principled supporters, school board meetings with strong opposition in attendance can still be productive.

Here is how Brian J. approaches building this important work and how that looked in Milwaukee:

1. Establish an "on-the-ground" team. First, Brian J. seeks out advocates in the communities served by the school district by asking his networks of educators, parents, and students. Advisors of school GSAs are some of the first to be contacted. This was the case in Milwaukee, where my GSA advisor received an email from Brian J., asking for his help with the policy campaign and asking him to extend that invitation to any students who might want to participate. I was one of the students he approached. Brian J. also reached out to the organizers of Milwaukee's Educators' Network for Social Justice, who host an annual conference focused on anti-bias teaching. The year before, Brian J. gave a workshop at the conference and made several connections, including one with an elementary teacher who was concerned about a gender nonconforming student. In Milwaukee, our team began with two students, a handful of teachers, a University of Wisconsin–Milwaukee professor, the mother of a transgender

MPS elementary school student, and a young woman from the South Milwaukee school district.

We had preliminary meetings at the local LGBTQ community center about once every three weeks. First we got to know one another and talked about how each participant was willing to contribute. We also learned about the nondiscrimination policy, talking points on gender issues, student demographics, and the inner workings of how district policies get changed.

2. Develop a strategy. One critical discussion concerns the identification of a school board member who will act as a "champion." When Brian J. says "champion" he isn't talking about Rocky Balboa, but rather a school board member who will agree to sponsor the proposed changes to the district's nondiscrimination policy. In Milwaukee, a school board member first introduces a proposed policy change at a subcommittee meeting. If the subcommittee supports the change, they recommend that it move on to the full school board for a vote.

Finding the right person to work with us required some strategizing. At first, the choice appeared clear. There is one school board member who is well known for proposing progressive policies and changes. When we approached him, however, he was concerned that if he introduced the policy change, we might encounter more opposition than if another, less outspoken, board member introduced it. Our changes were so reasonable, he said, this was an opportunity for another school board member to take a stand.

So we considered two other possibilities. Both were known as progressive and were well respected by their colleagues on the board. The board member we decided to ask was the chair of the Parent and Community Engagement Committee, and some members of our team had a history of positive interactions with her. The other board member we considered was the chair of the Accountability, Finance, and Personnel Committee. One motivation for adopting trans antidiscrimination policies is the desire to create facilities like single, nongendered bathrooms and inclusive locker rooms. This takes money, so the finance committee was a logical home for our proposal. But the chair of that committee didn't seem to be sympathetic to our cause.

So, after many weeks of meetings, preparation, and planning, a member of our group contacted the chair of the Parent and Community Engagement Committee and asked if she would introduce an addition to the nondiscrimination policy to protect transgender and gender nonconforming students. After some discussion and education, she agreed.

3. Anticipate questions. Taking the time to organize a diverse group of people to support the policy change is instrumental to its success. When facing what is likely to be "a small but loud minority," Brian J. says, "smart talking points, piercing data, and appealing to a general sense of humanity" is the best course of action. You need a strategy to combat opposition and address difficult questions while supporting the policy. This includes engagement with those "on the ground"—insiders in the district—to make sure they are well educated and well versed in responding to questions of all kinds.

Here are some of the questions we prepared to answer:

- What's the difference between sex and gender?
- What would stop boys from going into the girls' bathrooms or vice versa?
- How do you know someone is trans?
- What does cisgender mean?
- What does transgender mean?
- How do we know our district even has transgender students?
- Why does this matter when we have so many other problems to deal with?

For example, if someone asks whether this policy would mean boys could enter the girls' bathrooms, one response is to describe how the nondiscrimination policy promotes inclusive facilities (such as single, nongendered bathrooms or a nongendered group bathroom with locking stalls and a common sink area). This ensures that no one has to worry about being told they are in the "wrong" bathroom.

People sometimes pose questions in ways that are agitated and aggressive. Brian J. emphasized to us that a key part of preparing for meetings is ensuring that everyone is ready to respond in a calm, collected, and smart manner. Responding with anger or equal aggression can result in an even more polarized debate, rather than understanding and resolution. Practicing is essential!

Follow-through ensures that, after the policy is changed, it doesn't just sit there on paper.

4. Introduce the policy with care and patience. Policy change is not an expeditious process. Brian J. says: "On an individual district level, it hasn't been hard as much as it's taken longer than expected to move the request for change forward. In some districts, it's because there is another pressing issue that the board is dealing with, and either they don't have the time to take this up, or we decide it isn't strategic to move it forward [right then]. In other districts, it takes time to find a champion among district leadership who will move the request forward."

In our case, the meeting at which our champion intended to introduce the policy was overloaded with other pressing issues, so we chose to wait to introduce it until a time when it could be given more attention.

Have you ever been in the midst of cooking when you turned your back for two seconds, only to return to the stove to a burning dinner? Then, managing to avert a culinary crisis, you salvage most of it? Well, this is exactly what happened in Milwaukee. After the delay, our group was not informed when the policy was finally introduced. The proposal was to add it to the bullying and anti-harassment/anti-bullying staff policies but not to the nondiscrimination policy. That was a problem because the bullying policies are largely reactive rather than setting guidelines for inclusion. The district's bullying policy was moved through the committee and on to the full school board, and the measure passed. However, probably through a misunderstanding rather than malice or strategy, the district nondiscrimination policy was not changed. This mistake could have been avoided if we had given the school board a copy of the original district policy and a copy with our proposed changes. Absent that, the board assumed we were talking about the bullying policy.

> With almost every discussion about LGBTQ issues focusing on marriage equality, it can be easy to neglect the *T*.

So this was a partial victory. The school board added "gender identity, gender expression, [and] gender nonconformity" to two important policies. This was a victory, but there is more work to be done to change the nondiscrimination policy. We also discovered an additional section of MPS' administrative policies that needs gender expression clauses—the equal employment opportunity policy.

Our group met once again and discussed reintroducing the policy changes in the same committee. This time we decided to ask a different school board member to sponsor the changes, reasoning that if more than one board member was raising the issue of gender expression, it might gain more traction. This time, we would be prepared with the clear intention of adding gender expression clauses to the nondiscrimination policy and the equal employment opportunity sections.

5. Follow-through. Policy change without implementation is wasted effort. Follow-through ensures that, after the policy is changed, it doesn't just sit there on paper. Once a policy is successfully ratified, the next step is to present the school district with an outline for how to enforce and effectively oversee policy use.

Brian J. says: "Ideally, we would be able to work with districts to develop implementation guidelines for their new policy, which means coming up with clear, districtwide strategies for addressing concerns. Policy is just one piece of the puzzle. . . . This coming year we'll be working on developing a model for working with school districts on best practices." We need to make sure that school districts are walking the walk, not just talking the talk.

One of the greatest challenges for Brian J. and others who do similar organizing is keeping the momentum going. Brian J.'s goal for Wisconsin is to eventually add transgender protections into the state statute. However, that process will be difficult as long as the state legislature harbors its current conservative composition. In the meantime, ensuring that districts are following the regulations set forth by revised policies and continuing to work on new policy changes is of primary importance.

With almost every discussion about LGBTQ issues focusing on marriage equality these days, it can be easy to neglect the *T*. But the challenges faced by transgender and gender nonconforming students continue. Brian J., GSAFE, and their many volunteers and supporters still have a lot of work left to do. With more than 400 school districts in the state of Wisconsin, total equality seems far away. Yet hope remains and victories continue to be won. As long as the good people of GSAFE and each of us advocates for fair policy with regard to sexism, gender, and sexuality, there is hope that all schools will eventually protect everyone's rights.

David Flores

Renée Watson (left) and Jacqueline Woodson

Mirrors and Windows
Conversations with Jacqueline Woodson

BY RENÉE WATSON

Renée Watson is an author, performer, and educator. She lives in New York City.

I t is March 2015. America is reeling from the killings of Michael Brown, Eric Garner, John Crawford, and Ezell Ford. As the hashtag #BlackLives-Matter is trending, images of unarmed Black women killed by white shooters begin streaming on Twitter feeds: Aiyana Jones, Renisha Mc-Bride, Shereese Francis, Rekia Boyd. Gay marriage is debated; violence against transgendered youth persists.

There was a lot to talk about.

I was honored to be in conversation with Jacqueline Woodson at the Schomburg Center in Harlem to celebrate her award-winning new novel, *Brown Girl Dreaming*, and mine, *This Side of Home*.

There was no way we could talk only about our lives as writers. Talking about why we write meant talking about our history as Black women—Black women who have little ones we worry about because they, too, might one day fit the description, be at the right place at the wrong time. I knew Jacqueline wouldn't want to ignore the backdrop of our conversation. Her stories are filled with characters who don't fit into neat, predictable boxes about what it means to be a girl, or Black, or gay, or white, or a teen. There is no shying away from difficult, painful topics. Light and dark are always present, side by side. Her books mirror reality.

Jacqueline's love for writing started when she was a child: "Sometimes, when I'm sitting at my desk for long hours and nothing's coming to me, I remember my 5th-grade teacher, the way her eyes lit up when she said, 'This is really good.' The way, I—the skinny girl in the back of the classroom who was always getting into trouble for talking or missed homework assignments—sat up a little straighter, folded my hands on the desk, smiled, and began to believe in me."

That is who Jacqueline is writing for. The child in the back of the classroom, the one buried in a book, creating paragraphs in a hidden journal. She is writing mirror books for young Black children who need to see themselves in the pages of a story. She is writing window books for readers to strengthen the muscle of empathy and look into someone else's world.

A few weeks after our Schomburg conversation, and after Jacqueline had been named Young People's Poet Laureate by the Poetry Foundation, she answered questions for Rethinking Schools readers:

Renée Watson: Many of your books deal with the intersection of race, sexism, gender, and sexuality. Why do you weave these together in your stories?

Jacqueline Woodson: I think it's important to respect the genre of realistic fiction by keeping it real. I also am concerned with making sure the stories of people who have been historically missing from our body of literature are on the page. I try to mirror their experiences in the real world. My hope is that my work reflects a broad range of identities and experiences.

RW: Your books are so rich in terms of character development, dialogue, and taking on social justice issues—how do you balance all of these elements without being dogmatic?

JW: I have a deep respect for my audience. I know that young people read to experience a good story, another world. They read for the same reasons that I read. And I never write to teach—I write to learn. I write because I have questions, not answers.

For example, *If You Come Softly*, which I wrote long ago, is a retelling of *Romeo and Juliet*. I remember there were (and sadly, it hasn't changed) so many cases of police brutality against Black men going on. I thought: If people could see my character as human and truly love him, what would that mean? What would that look like? Who would he be? Would that make people want to change the world?

RW: One of my favorite moments in *Brown Girl Dreaming* is when your big sister guides your hand with hers and teaches you how to write your name. Throughout the book we see a strong sisterhood between women of the older generation and the younger. How will mentoring younger generations be a part of your role as the Young People's Poet Laureate?

JW: I've had mentors without knowing that's what they were—teachers, parents, neighbors, friends, books, authors, newspapers—the list goes on. Every piece of something or someone who inspired me became a mentor. And this is what I hope to bring to my role: I want young people to see poetry everywhere, to understand that we can live lives as poets just by showing up, being present, bearing witness to the world we live in. I want young people to understand they have stories to tell and poems to write.

RW: *Brown Girl Dreaming* opens with a poem about the day you were born:
. . . I am born as the South explodes
too many people too many years
enslaved, then emancipated
but not free, the people
who look like me
keep fighting
and marching
and getting killed
so that today—
February 12, 1963
and every day from this moment on,
brown children like me can grow up
free. Can grow up
learning and voting and walking and riding
wherever we want . . .

This could very well be about the times we are currently living in. How can parents and educators encourage young children—especially brown children— to hold onto their dreams and self-worth as movements like Black Lives Matter remain necessary?

JW: Love them up. Let them know they're loved. Let them know that you're behind them. Teach them how to walk safely through the world. Teach them how powerful their brown bodies are. Read *Between the World and Me*, by Ta-Nehisi Coates. Impart the knowledge he's passing on.

RW: Many educators shy away from discussing race, sexism, gender, and sexuality. How do you hope teachers use your work in the classroom?

JW: First and foremost, I think we should be careful not to bring our own fears and discomforts to the classroom. My books aren't about race, sexism, gender, etc.—they're about people in the world and they're stories that, hopefully, will keep young people entertained as they reflect on a greater good. So the first thing to do is introduce them this way—not via the vehicle of our own prejudices.

I've heard people say *From the Notebooks of Melanin Sun* is a book about a mom who is coming out. And to the adult, maybe that's the first story they see because they're looking at it through their own lens. But to the young person, it's the story of a boy trying to figure out who he is in a changing world and he's embarrassed by his mom—what young person doesn't know that story? So, my hope is that teachers are presenting my books through the young person's lens.

RW: Often, when students learn about Langston Hughes and Lorraine Hansberry, their sexual orientation is not included. Many people don't realize until they are adults that these writers were gay. Do you think it's important for young readers to know the sexual orientation of the author they are reading?

JW: I think it's tricky because it comes back to the lens: How is this writer being presented? How is their sexuality being introduced? Is this the first time sexuality is being discussed in the classroom? We don't want students to fixate on sexuality and not see the beauty of the work. It's complicated, and I'd rather a teacher who is uncomfortable with discussing sexuality just talk about the work. Once the student falls in love with the writer, they will follow them anywhere—and eventually want to know more about them.

RW: Do you call yourself an activist? Do you ever fear that being outspoken about social justice issues will affect your career in a negative way? What advice can you give teachers who struggle with that dilemma?

JW: I am an activist and, as an activist, I can't walk through the world afraid. I think my fearlessness has allowed me to do some of my best writing. My biggest fear would be to be dishonest to myself, to live a half-life, to not tell the stories I was put here to tell.

Resources

Coates, Ta-Nehisi. 2015. *Between the World and Me*. Spielel & Grau.

Watson, Renée. 2015. *This Side of Home*. Bloomsbury USA.

Woodson, Jacqueline. 2014. *Brown Girl Dreaming*. Penguin.

Woodson, Jacqueline. 1998. *If You Come Softly*. Speak.

Woodson, Jacqueline. 1995. *From the Notebooks of Melanin Sun*. Puffin Books.

CHAPTER 6

Kim Cosier

Anastasia Pellecchia

smarter
self educating

NOT A TOM BOY

different
and proud

Break
stereotypes
of gender
role + attire

Teacher Education, Continuing Education: Introduction

By Kim Cosier

Kim Cosier is associate dean of the Peck School of the Arts, professor of art education at the University of Wisconsin–Milwaukee, and founding faculty member of a Master of Arts in Teaching program at the Vermont College of Fine Arts. Her research and teaching interests focus on art and education for social justice, particularly related to intersecting cultural and social factors including gender, race, sexuality, and class. She is founder of the Milwaukee Visionaries Project, an award-winning media production/literacy program for urban youth. She lives in Milwaukee with her wife, Josie, and dogs, Evie Mae and Roger, and has fun making trouble with her friends in the Educators' Network for Social Justice.

Not too long ago my wife, Josie, and I were catching up with friends at our neighborhood book club. We all began talking about some old family photographs hanging on the wall. Someone mentioned that her grandfather had worked as an engineer, although he never went to college. "He would never be able to do that now," she said.

Then she turned to the case of a mutual friend who, she said, "would be a *great* teacher, but she just doesn't have that piece of paper—it's a shame." Apparently not realizing that she had just declared my life's work a sham, she described her own undergraduate experience as more about partying than anything else and moved on to another topic.

I keep thinking about that conversation as I write this introduction. The popular storyline—that time spent pursuing teacher education is wasted—is now being perpetuated by folks of all political stripes. It has been repeated earnestly for well over a decade, first by the right, which sees teacher educators as dangerous leftist ideologues and, more recently, by the neoliberal corporate reformers, who see teacher education as an unnecessary barrier to more efficient, competitive, and profitable pathways to the nation's classrooms. This story has been told so often that it has reached the level of Common Sense.

But that "piece of paper," or at least the education it represents, does matter: First, content knowledge is not value neutral, and what passes for knowledge in textbooks and other commercially available teaching tools is rife with biases that perpetuate the status quo. Engaging in a critical dialogue about the politics of content knowledge is part and parcel of a good teacher education program (which is, of course, why it is seen as dangerous).

Second, what we teach is only part of what we need to know to be good teachers. The interconnected web of how, why, where, and who we teach is incredibly complex and not at all self-evident. Future teachers almost always lack a deep understanding of the ways society is constructed to keep those with power firmly in power, and how teaching fits into this system of oppression and privilege. Teacher education programs worth their salt engage students in praxis that enables them to enter the profession armed with a full understanding of the politics of teaching.

I am an art teacher educator, and the student who comes to our program well versed in contemporary art practices is rare; rarer still is the student who intuitively understands how to turn culturally relevant content knowledge into empowering pedagogical experiences for children and youth.

An activist stance is the key to success in teaching about sexism, gender, and sexuality.

Each year, when I get a new group of students, a similar scenario plays out. My classes are full of female-identified students who are averse to the "f" word (of course I mean feminism). When I ask them to engage in exercises meant to jump-start an investigation into the social and cultural formation of identity, they consistently cite only family, friends, and (for a significant number) their faith as the influences that have shaped them. They almost never include sexism, gender, or sexuality as having an impact. Neither do they include popular culture—advertisements, movies, television, YouTube videos, music—even though a recent comprehensive study by the Kaiser Family Foundation found that the average young person today devotes an average of seven hours and 38 minutes each day to "using entertainment media."

The dominant narratives, with their consistently narrow view of identity, are incredibly effective tools of manipulation, being nearly invisible as pedagogy. Commercially produced educational materials also teach us how to be and how to perceive others—usually in service to the institutionalized racism and patriarchy that prop up our unjust and unequal society. Finally, the innumerable dramas that play out in school hallways, locker rooms, playgrounds, and social media sites teach powerful lessons about who we are and what we are allowed to do with our bodies and minds.

It takes work on my part to get my students to recognize that who they are—and who they think their students are—has been formed within a system that perpetuates violence and inequality.

Most of my students are aware of the risks LGBTQ kids face. The high rate of suicide among students who identify as, or are perceived to be, LGBTQ is now widely known, largely because of the popularity of the It Gets Better campaign begun by sex columnist Dan Savage and media coverage of cases of young people dying as a result of peer bullying. But most preservice teachers are unaware of other ways that LGBTQ students, and others who do not fit into the rigid social norms of schools, may show signs of distress.

Teachers who are prepared to connect content to enduring ideas about the human condition are much better teachers than those who just "know their stuff."

Neither are they aware of the ways school communities engage in practices that work against the well-being of those students. Partly as a result of the narrow focus on bullying that has been the general response to these incidents, they see the problem as one of badly behaved individuals rather than a symptom of a culture that perpetuates violence and oppression. They need to be guided by teacher educators who have spent time thinking long and hard about such matters, and who can guide them in developing a critique of a culture that sees girls as objects of male desire, and children who do not fit into a false gender binary as the source of the problem. They also need to learn how to queer the curriculum so that it works for positive change, and how to access resources that can help with all this.

Obviously, guiding students to become change agents is not high on the list of the corporate reformers, who would like to see teacher education programs either hobbled by regulations or put out of business altogether. The issue of values in relation to content gains greater import as more and more of what is taught in schools is drawn from teaching materials devised by corporations that are firmly entrenched in the business of perpetuating the status quo.

Research has shown that teachers can have an enormous influence on student success. However, as it stands, the current federal mandate for "highly qualified teachers" only narrowly conceives of what high qualifications and success mean. Teaching that is grounded in an ethic of social justice means that we are not just preparing teachers to teach chemistry or reading, we are preparing teachers to teach children about the world, regardless of discipline. Teachers who are prepared to connect the content of their discipline to enduring ideas about the human condition are much better teachers than those who just "know their stuff," so to speak.

An activist stance, in which a teacher sees herself as a change maker, is the key to success in teaching about sexism, gender, and sexuality. New and veteran teachers alike need time and support to develop the reflective praxis necessary to become effective educational activists. Social justice can fall by the wayside as educators struggle to keep their heads above water without proper support. The authors in this section know this. But they believe it is possible to help pre-service and inservice teachers jump through the many bureaucratic hoops set before them, while still tending a passion for the larger purposes of education.

Teacher education, at its best, is so much more than a piece of paper.

Resource

Henry J. Kaiser Foundation. Jan. 20, 2010. "Generation M2: Media in the Lives of 8- to 18-Year-Olds." kff.org/other/event/generation-m2-media-in-the-lives-of.

"Let's Put Our Bias Goggles On"

Reading representations of Black girl identity through critical lenses

BY KIM COSIER

Kim Cosier is associate dean of the Peck School of the Arts, professor of art education at the University of Wisconsin–Milwaukee, and founding faculty member of a Master of Arts in Teaching program at the Vermont College of Fine Arts. Her research and teaching interests focus on art and education for social justice, particularly related to intersecting cultural and social factors including gender, race, sexuality, and class. She is founder of the Milwaukee Visionaries Project, an award-winning media production/literacy program for urban youth. She lives in Milwaukee with her wife, Josie, and dogs, Evie Mae and Roger, and has fun making trouble with her friends in the Educators' Network for Social Justice.

I came up with the silly metaphor "bias goggles" one day in my art education methods class when we were discussing social constructions of identity and their bearing on teaching. We were getting ready to watch a scene from Disney's *The Lion King* as a way to look closely at how identity is constructed for young children. I jokingly said, "Let's put our bias goggles on and watch a scene together." That simple trick helped students feel ready to watch with open minds, and to detect hidden messages that prop up the status quo and work against equality for all. Using lenses that filter texts through feminist, queer, critical race, and disability theories, bias goggles can facilitate deep thinking and new insights.

I am a teacher educator in an art education program with an urban focus and a social justice mission. Because of this, one of my fundamental teaching objectives is to help students understand themselves in relation to the complexities of identity. Most of my students are white women from working- and middle-class backgrounds. Most come to our program with a sincere desire to "help" urban students, but little understanding of how complex that desire is within an unequal system that is meant to maintain power for those who already have it and block access to those who don't. Because teaching and learning about institutional systems of oppression and power can be difficult, we use humor and story as much as possible.

We want students to be conscious of the many factors that influence identity

THE BIAS GOGGLES

"Construction of Childhood Innocence"

The character that most kids will gravitate towards to is probably Simba. Throughout the movie, Simba is never seen preying on other animals. He's the hero, and the Herd only eats insects that tastes like chicken!

So when Timon is the one telling Simba we have to eat, I didn't get it until I got hungry myself.

This is misleading, especially for me when I first saw it. It wasn't after watching a pack of lions hunt, did I realize that my concept of a lion is off. Go animal planet!

One thing that bothered me was that eventhough Scar and Mufasa were brothers, Scar, the villain is dark skinned.

!?

Xai Thao

as they develop their teaching philosophies and form the expectations they will hold for their students. For many of them, engaging in inquiry about identity is a new and challenging process. They have thought little about how their own identities have been formed or how they have come to perceive gender, race, class, sexuality, and other markers of identity in others. They take for granted that their life experiences are "normal" and, most often, do not recognize that their worldviews have been shaped by stories passed down from family, teachers, community members, and through media and popular culture.

It takes sustained work on their parts to understand that the forces that seek to maintain power limit the stories they have been told all their lives. As Judith Butler teaches us in *Undoing Gender*, a steady barrage of limited story lines in mainstream narratives have become so normalized that people most often don't even notice them. Lessons about what are acceptable and desirable beliefs and behaviors are taught through narratives that conceal socially binding rules. These stories are part of the support structure for institutionalized sexism, racism, classism, and heterosexism—the legacies of colonialism, Puritanism, and slavery that have persisted since the beginning in the United States.

"When the monkey priest holds Simba up to the sky for the other animals to see, we are supposed to feel it is a glorious thing. But now I have this feeling—everything is not OK."

The following is a story of how my students and I engaged in viewing, reading, and writing about film-based narratives with a focus on relationships between power and position in the social construction of identity. In classroom dialogues, journal entries, and research assignments, we paid particular attention to sexism, gender, sexuality, and race. This experience gave my students entry points to understand the complex nature of identity—and to begin to answer the question posed by Parker Palmer in *The Courage to Teach*: "Who is the self that teaches?"

Understanding Power and Position

Our day began with a class discussion of readings I had assigned, including art educator Elizabeth Garber's article "Teaching About Gender Issues in the Art

Education Classroom" and an excerpt from *Undoing Gender*. I asked students to consider Butler's main premise—that all gender is performance—in relation to Garber's equation of power and position. I had given them the following questions to consider while reading:

- If gender is performed, how do we account for inequality?
- How are lessons about identity taught?
- How do individuals and groups comply with, or resist, the order of things?
- Who benefits from these dynamics?

We began by looking at images of the work of two African American artists. Carrie Mae Weems' photographic, performance, and video work investigates "family relationships, gender roles, and the histories of racism, sexism, class, and various political systems" (see Resources for all references); Kehinde Wiley is a queer artist who is best known for very large-scale paintings of African American men situated within appropriations of historical paintings. The discussion was lively, but it lacked a connection to students' personal stories. To facilitate a deeper and more personal dialogue, I followed our preliminary discussion by showing the "Circle of Life" clip from *The Lion King*.

Encounters with a Blond Boy King

Here's my take on the scene: The light-furred, male lion cub, Simba, is scooped from the bosom of his heteronormative parents' loving arms and presented by a colorful, primate shaman to an adoring throng of all the less regal animals of Africa. They all bow down before the babe as their natural king while a shaft of light shines down on them, implying a big "thumbs up" from The Man Upstairs. A rousing, orchestrated musical score, with a dash of African voices thrown in for authenticity, sweeps us off our feet and seals the deal on the message that what we are witnessing is perfectly fitting and natural. I kept this reading of the clip to myself, however, until after my students made their own discoveries.

Before we watched the clip, I joked that students should put their bias goggles on. Afterward, I gave them five minutes to discuss it in small groups at their tables. While they talked, I handed out sets of cutouts of characters from the movie, along with a picture of the sun. I asked each group to arrange the characters in relation to the sun, which I said represented power. I was happy to hear them actively thinking aloud about power and position as they engaged in the activity. After about five more minutes, I asked them to report out what they had learned.

Within a beloved film from their youth, students were astonished and dismayed to suddenly see hidden (and not so hidden) messages about gender roles, race, and colonialism. The discussion took off like wildfire, with students shaking their heads and furrowing their brows. Lucy said what others seemed to be thinking: "How did I not see this before?"

"I know! Right?" another student blurted out. "It's depressing to think that I watched this as a kid and soaked it all in without knowing . . . without my mom knowing it!"

Lucy continued: "When that monkey priest holds Simba up to the sky for the other animals to see, we are supposed to feel like it is a glorious thing. But now I have this feeling—the old way of seeing it is being pushed out by a sinking feeling—everything is not OK."

"Yeah," said Natalie, "when the sunlight came out of heaven, it hit me: This movie is telling us that white people are *supposed to be* the leaders."

Most student comments aligned with Lucy and Natalie's take. Not surprisingly, however, a few argued that we were making too much of the symbolism of the film. "I think you can turn anything into an evil plot if you want to," said Sarah, who often resisted participation in discussions.

"Yep, if you try hard enough, you always find what you are looking for," said Joel. One or two others nodded their heads in agreement.

I try to remain faithful to the tenets of feminist pedagogy, so I resisted an urge to drive the discussion. I was thankful that Lindsey, a class leader, challenged the incredulous ones: "But if they made it obvious, it wouldn't work, would it? Just like in the Judith Butler reading, these lessons are made to seem natural, so we don't even know we are learning them." Students debated for some time, with the Disney defenders sad but mostly swayed by points made by their classmates in the end.

Wrapping up the discussion, I asked students to make entries in their visual journals about what they had taken away from this experience. Visual journals are an important component of coursework throughout our program, as a place for students to wrestle with ideas through imagery and words.

Two Stories About Black Girls

I ended the morning's class by mentioning two very different films that I thought would be interesting to watch with our bias goggles on: *The Princess and the Frog* and *Precious*, both recently released stories about young Black girls.

I had to leave right after class to go to a meeting. When I returned, I discovered that my students had all stayed in our classroom and illegally downloaded both movies! I re-entered the darkened classroom to find the difficult story of *Precious* unfolding on the interactive whiteboard. Although I was squeamish about the way they had seen the movies, I could not ignore this opportunity to engage in an important lesson. The room was nearly silent when the movie ended. I acknowledged that it is a tough one to watch and takes time to digest. I asked them to reflect on the movies, do some online research about critical responses to them, post questions on our online discussion board, and come back to class prepared to talk.

What struck students the most about *The Princess and the Frog* was the irony that Disney's first African American animated heroine spends most of her time in the story as a "reptile of color." That said, most students agreed that the movie did not harbor as many negative messages about race and gender as *The Lion King* and other Disney films.

To be honest, I expected *The Princess and the Frog* to be more problematic than it is. I was pleasantly surprised to see that it even gives a nod to institutionalized racism and sexism in a scene in which two sleazy, white realtors tell Tiana, the lead character, that they have sold her beloved restaurant out from under her, and that it is probably for the best given her "background."

We decided that, instead of siding with whiteness and maleness, which is the implied position of the audience of *The Lion King*, in this film we are meant to identify with a young Black woman and to be outraged at the discrimination she faces—a pretty big leap for Disney!

To further examine power and privilege, we made a list of other Disney princesses, including Cinderella, Belle (*Beauty and the Beast*), Ariel (*The Little Mermaid*), Jasmine (*Aladdin*), and Mulan. We asked:

- What are one or more strong attributes of the princess?
- On a scale of 1 to 10, how helpless/self-reliant is this princess?
- What is/are her goal(s)?

The students devised a scoring system, and we used printed images of the characters to create a Princess Power Chart to visually represent how each fared by our measures. My students decided that, stacked against the other princesses, Tiana is a much better role model. She is beautiful in stereotypical ways, but has other important qualities: a strong work ethic, determination, and the ability to dream of a better future. Tiana is more self-reliant; instead of just wanting to marry a prince, like so many others, Tiana works hard to own her own business. Of course, it is to please another man (her father), but you can't have everything.

Through online research, a number of students found positive commentary from Black film critics. For example, Gretchen wrote in her visual journal: "In her review of *The Princess and the Frog*, Demetria Lucas wrote, 'We all know Black folk have a murky history with our stories being told by non-Blacks; too often our culture seems to get lost in translation from one side of Du Bois' veil to the other. But not this time. Disney's much-anticipated *The Princess and the Frog* is finally here, and our Black princess doesn't disappoint—in fact, she exceeds expectation.'" Gretchen agreed with this point of view, for the most part, but was still bothered by the fact that Tiana is a frog for most of the movie.

Some students discovered, however, that not all critics were so in love with Tiana. Film critic Armond White saw much to criticize in the movie. Jessica read a quote: "Hyped as offering the Walt Disney Corporation's first African American animated heroine, *The Princess and the Frog* actually refrains from expanding our social imagination. Based on the venerable *The Frog Prince*, it uses that fairy tale's moral about seeking inner value and personal worth to exploit 'post-racial' complaisance."

In *The Princess and the Frog,* Disney's first African American animated heroine spends most of her time as a "reptile of color."

White not only slams the film's portrayal of racial identity but also points out its issues with gender representation. As Jessica explained: "Armond White doesn't think that Disney really allowed Tiana to be one of the princesses. By turning her into a frog for most of the movie, Disney 'does not confer a modicum of idealized beauty or grace on a Black girl's countenance.' So Tiana, being a frog for most of the movie, is not allowed to be on the same level as Cinderella, or Belle, or even Ariel, who started out as part fish!"

Through our discussion of White's analysis, students recognized an implied reinforcement of the notion that class and race are naturally linked within the bootstrap narrative: Hard work lifts the poor Black girl into a better life. This contrasts revealingly with Lottie, Tiana's rich, white friend, who can expect to have her every whim granted by virtue of her birth into wealth and whiteness.

Finally, Joe, a gay male student, pointed out that both girls in *The Princess and the Frog* are indoctrinated into heteronormative, race-specific gender and sex roles in the movie. I agreed and added that the villain, Doctor Facilier, carries on the Disney tradition of making bad guys sound effeminate. Overall, students felt that Disney did a better job than they expected, but still had a long way to go if it truly wanted to tell a story about Black girlhood that does not reinforce stereotypes and limit little girls' imaginations about the possibilities of identity.

Precious

Next we turned our attention to *Precious*. Our discussion raised numerous thought-provoking aspects of the film. Lindsey talked about the powerful performances by women, including surprising roles for singer Mariah Carey as the social worker and for comedian Mo'Nique, who transformed herself into the horrifying character of Precious' mother.

Carrie noticed the near absence of male characters in the movie. Jenni added that the one male character with a speaking part, a nurse played by Lenny Kravitz, is a caretaker, a role usually filled by women. Students puzzled over this. Someone wondered if the absence of men was meant to reflect the high rate of incarceration of African American men.

Joe steered us in another direction when he asked, with obvious irritation, "Did you notice that all of the helpful characters in the movie are light-skinned and the evil ones are dark?" Many admitted they had not noticed, but realized that it was true once Joe pointed it out. They linked it to *The Lion King* and marveled at the way these details—often unrecognized by viewers—reinforce racist stereotypes.

Tera said: "But this movie was made by a Black guy! Why would a Black director do that, make the good guys light and the bad ones dark?" Troubled by this, we decided that it was a good question to pursue more deeply.

I asked students, once again, to do some research. I suggested they consider the historical context of the story—Harlem circa 1987—and urged them to think about ways context impacted the meanings we could make out of the movie. To complete the assignment, they were to write responses to one or both of the movies on our online discussion board and in their journals as preparation to engage in a deeper discussion when we came back to class.

"Did you notice that all of the helpful characters in *Precious* are light-skinned and the evil ones are dark?"

Some online digging revealed that Lee Daniels, the director of the film, admitted to being prejudiced against people with dark skin when he started the movie. Several students found a *New York Times Magazine* profile by Lynn Hirschberg in which she quotes Daniels: "Precious is so not PC [politically correct]. What I learned from doing the film is that even though I am Black, I'm prejudiced. I'm prejudiced against people who are darker than me. When I was young, I went to a church where the lighter-skinned you were, the closer you sat to the altar."

In our online forum, and again in our next class, we discussed this quote in relation to the film, which was widely touted as transcending race. My students were dismayed that Daniels claimed to have learned that he is prejudiced, yet that knowledge seemed to have no bearing on his analysis of the final product or on his decisions to cast actors in ways that reinforce stereotypes.

Hirschberg quotes Daniels as also saying: "Anybody that's heavy like Precious—I thought they were dirty and not very smart. Making this movie changed my heart. I'll never look at a fat girl walking down the street the same way again." When a student read that aloud in class, I was astounded. I shared with the class that those were the same words that I had heard from numerous wealthy, white people who had seen the film and been swept away by their first experience of identifying with a poor African American girl. These superficially empathetic statements belie a new stereotype that overweight Black girls in the United States now have to carry: They will be patronizingly assumed to have the capacity to overcome being poor, illiterate, abused in every way imaginable, and HIV positive—given the care of the perfect teacher.

This is a problematic narrative of universality. Daniels was asked in another interview if his identification with the story "meant that he was Precious, too." He said yes. "And so are you. . . . That's what I learned. I didn't know it would affect people the way it has. I thought maybe my family, neighbors, and people I went to school with [would relate to the film]. I didn't know it would have a universal appeal."

As art students, my class was familiar with postmodern arguments against universality in relation to multicultural art—it was a pretty easy leap to make connections from there to the film. Like Daniels, many viewers and mainstream critics suddenly felt compassion for a person with whom they thought they had nothing in common. But, because of the structure of the movie, they were able to exempt themselves from being implicated in the circumstances of Precious' oppression.

I asked students what they had discovered about the historical context. Maikue noted that the date of the story was featured only briefly in text at the beginning of the movie, with little else about the film indicating the historical period. Joe remarked that the hopeful ending of the film glosses over the fact that in 1987 an HIV diagnosis "would have probably been a death sentence for Precious, because our government had turned its back on the AIDS epidemic." The students agreed that the date and its significance could easily be overlooked by viewers, who would unwittingly place the narrative in a contemporary framework.

Emily explored the welfare narrative, which provides another example of how the context of *Precious* matters. Welfare emerges as an evil presence in the film, set against the foil of the American Dream/bootstrap narrative. Emily wrote in her journal and shared with the class: "Coming from a very Republican family, I always heard about the 'welfare leeches' who are 'too lazy' to find a job. Sadly, the movie really reinforced this." In fact, in Wisconsin, where my students will most likely be teaching, welfare disappeared when they were small children. The vast majority of my students were unaware of this. Ronald Reagan's narrative of the "welfare queen" persists even though welfare is a thing of the past in this state. Putting this together with the bootstrap narrative, we came to understand that when white viewers identify with Precious, they are really identifying with her ability to break free from her perceived pack, to rise above what Black girls are assumed to be.

The notion of universal appeal—"We are all Precious"—was marketed by not only Daniels and Lionsgate, but also by nearly every movie critic we uncovered in our research. A notable exception was, once again, Armond White, who criticized the film as a "con job": "The hype for *Precious* indicates a culturewide willingness to accept particular ethnic stereotypes as a way of maintaining status quo film values. . . . Excellent recent films with Black themes . . . have been ignored by the mainstream media and serious film culture, while this carnival of Black degradation gets celebrated." He called the fanfare around *Precious* "a strange combination of liberal guilt and condescension." Our investigation into the film and its social/cultural implications led my students and me to agree with him.

Reflecting on Our Experience with Stories

Constructing and deconstructing stories is a powerful pedagogical tool that can help students understand the complex nature of identity without hitting them over the head with dogma. "Reading" stories through our bias goggles was fruitful, particularly as we began to focus on relationships between power and position. With protracted focus on both movies, but especially on *Precious*, we deepened our understandings of the stories that make us who we are, as well as the stories we make of the lives of others. Students shared in discussions and in their journals that, as a result of our sustained engagement with these stories, they now had a much more complex and complicated view of race, gender, identity, and power, a view that will make them stronger teachers. This was reflected in their teaching philosophies and other work throughout the year.

As I explained to my students, bias goggles can come in handy in the K–12 classroom as well, helping children and young people read the world with an eye toward justice. This past semester, one of my students made an actual pair of goggles for her kindergarten students to wear while they looked closely at the children's book *The Rabbits*, written by John Marsden and illustrated by Shaun Tan. The class responded with eager attention and sharp eyes to her lesson, which dealt with colonialism in a way that was accessible to young children.

Engaging students with story is a priority as we encourage teacher education students to answer Palmer's question, "Who is the self that teaches?" With our metaphorical bias goggles, we can help them understand their own relationship to how gender, race, class, sexuality, and other markers of identity are represented and inextricably linked.

Resources

Butler, Judith. 2004. *Undoing Gender*. Routledge.

Garber, Elizabeth. 2003. "Teaching About Gender Issues in the Art Education Classroom." *Studies in Art Education* 45.1:56–72.

Hirschberg, Lynn. Oct. 21, 2009. "The Audacity of *Precious*." *New York Times Magazine*. nytimes.com/2009/10/25/magazine/25precious-t.html?pagewanted=all.

The Lion King. Dir. Roger Allers and Rob Minkoff. 1994. Disney.

Lucas, Demetria. Nov. 25, 2009. "It Ain't Easy Being Green: 'Princess and the Frog.'" Essence.com. essence.com/2009/11/25/it-aint-easy-being-green-princess-and-th/.

Palmer, Parker. 2007. *The Courage to Teach: Exploring the Inner Landscape of a Teacher's Life.* Jossey-Bass.

Precious. 2009 . Dir. Lee Daniels. Lionsgate.

The Princess and the Frog. 2009. Dir. Ron Clements and John Musker. Disney.

Weems, Carrie Mae. carriemaeweems.net/bio.html.

White, Armond. Nov. 4, 2009. "Pride & Precious." *New York Press.*

White, Armond. Dec. 3, 2009. "Warts and All." *New York Press.* nypress.com/warts-and-all/.

Wiley, Kehinde. kehindewiley.com.

Roxanna Bikadoroff

Still Miles of Sexist Aisles
Helping students investigate toy stores

By Sudie Hofmann

Sudie Hofmann is a professor in the Department of Human Relations and Multicultural Education at St. Cloud State University. She is an activist and writer on education and equity issues.

Ten years ago I conducted research on children's toys and gender bias for a *Rethinking Schools* article, "Miles of Aisles of Sexism." After completing my original investigation in 2004, I designed a project for my students in a university human relations course that asks them to explore a local toy store and report back to the class. Ever since, they've continued to see overwhelming, persistent sexism in every aisle.

I recently returned to the same toy stores that I visited in my original investigation. There are some changes from visits 10 years ago. I now have to constantly put on and take off my reading glasses. Some toy packaging gives a nod to racial diversity—there might be one girl or boy of color among three or four white children. Disney now markets Dottie (Doc) McStuffins, a 6-year-old

African American female aspiring to be a doctor. And manufacturers of science, technology, engineering, and math (STEM) toys might include a girl on a boxed item if there are several other versions of the toy that only include boys.

But, for the most part, girls continue to primp and clean their way to some bizarre approximation of success while boys wage war on imaginary countries, people, animals, and, in the case of some video games, women.

Corporations say they are just giving consumers what they want by providing products that will put smiles on kids' faces. Yes, trendy toys and gadgets reflect societal values, habits, and the quest for stimulation. But let's look at the long-term messages that are sent to kids. What roles do toys encourage boys and girls to take on during play? Are toys providing innocent fun, or are children being socialized in ways that could ultimately influence career and life choices?

What I found in 2004 and again in 2014, was that most toy companies—and the big-box stores the toys are sold in—conduct their marketing practices in a way that is calculated, unconscionable, and highly profitable.

Violence, Science, and Power Tools

When I returned to take a look around Walmart, Kmart, Target, Creative Kidstuff, Toys R Us, and many online catalogs, I found that the boys' section continues to be dominated by weaponry and the unabashed glorification of war. The colors commonly used on the packaging are black, red, and deep yellow—providing images of flames. Jagged letters suggest lightning, the icon for speed and power. Boxing gloves, punching bags, action figures, swords, hand grenades, guns, rifles, and a variety of other "lethal" toys abound in aisles that were predominately blue 10 years ago but now use black pegboard and endcaps.

Language on packaging ostensibly encourages the use of force or violence in the name of being a "peacekeeper," completing a "mission," or being a "superior defender." Toys are promoted with violent language: "bashing," "kicking," "deadly," "assault."

Some toys perpetuate ethnic and racial stereotypes. With short beards and dark complexions, the NECA's Assassin's Creed Brotherhood and Revelations action figures are clearly supposed to be Middle Eastern men.

In addition to war toys, the male area offers word games, chess, and other challenging board games. Boys—and their dads, presumably—are prominently featured on the boxes. Planetariums, globes, interactive world maps, and atlases fill the shelves. EduScience offers Introduction to Chemistry, Science of Magnetism, Tyrannosaurus Rex Dino Dig, and microscopes. The adult scientist pictured on every box is male.

Toys by John Deere, Black and Decker, Tonka, and Home Depot fill up an aisle in the boys' section at Toys R Us, but I could not find a single female on any of the packaging. The Home Depot area had a 42-inch sign: "I Can Do It Like Dad." Apparently females do not use power tools, drive trucks, own work benches, or work in the agricultural industry.

Popularity, Consumerism, and Cleaning

Glitter, pastels, and Pepto-Bismol pink reign in the girls' section. The edges of the letters are smooth and sometimes dotted or crossed with a heart or star. Packaging includes words such as "kitten," "princess," "fairy," "precious," "wish," "dream," and "wonder."

The focus of many toys in the girls' area—or fantasyland—is being popular with boys. Packages offer tips about how to be trendy and get noticed. Vanity mirrors, combs, brushes, nail kits, makeup, crowns, tiaras, and polyester hair extensions abound. Girls can pamper themselves with spa kits. The Barbie Digital Makeover Mirror encourages girls to use an app to apply virtual makeup to their faces. Even "science" kits marketed to girls focus on beauty: Lovely Lip Balm Kit, Perfume Science, and Luxury Soap Science.

> Are toys providing innocent fun, or are children being socialized in ways that could ultimately influence career and life choices?

The girls' section is short on board games that stimulate creative thinking or higher-order reasoning. Games include the Disney Princess Cupcake Party, Barbie Hair Challenge, and My Quinceañera Countdown. Sticker books, coloring books, and simplistic crafts are readily available.

After getting the guy by playing spa or beauty salon, the girls get the ironing board. Housekeeping toys include the Mini Dirt Devil vacuum, Mighty Tidy Sweep Set, and My Cleaning Trolley. Strollers, cribs, diapers, and baby dolls are plentiful. Walmart had half an aisle of kitchens in the girls' section. Boys are noticeably absent from any of the advertisements, promotions, store posters, or packaging for toy household cleaning products, kitchen items, or childcare toys.

More than 90 percent of U.S. women—and about 70 percent of moms—work during their lifetime. But it's hard to get even a glimpse of that reality. Even the much-respected Melissa and Doug products—carried by both big-box and independent toy stores—have missed the lesson on gender equality when it comes to careers. Their occupation puzzle includes a baker, construction worker, police officer, doctor, and firefighter—all appear to be male; the physician is of ambiguous gender. The other puzzle for this age group, Dress-Up, includes five females: a ballerina, mermaid, princess, bride, and a girl with a crown of flowers and wings. I am not sure what a mermaid is being paid right now. Would she have benefits or would she be a contract worker?

Action Research for Students

In most of my classes I favor projects that send students out into the real world; these assignments frequently direct the students to retail stores. In the fall, I send my students to seasonal stores to determine which Halloween costumes perpetuate racism. In the spring, I ask students to analyze the colors, fabric weights, and appliqués on children's jackets and outerwear.

We begin the action research project on toys by reviewing class material on gender socialization. To explore gender role expectations we read Lois Gould's classic *X: A Fabulous Child's Story*. I then place students in groups of five to answer the following question: At what age are sex role expectations placed on most children?

The first answers usually range from 2 to 5 years. As I push students to think more deeply, someone eventually blurts out the correct answer: before birth, if parents know the sex of the child.

Then I ask the students to formulate a list of things that parents commonly do to reinforce their sex role expectations. I ask them to think about clothing, nursery lamp bases, toys, and wallpaper borders. I have them make two columns on newsprint, one for males and one for females.

After we define sexism as an issue of power that is both personal and institutional, we begin to explore definitions of masculinity in U.S. culture by watching *Tough Guise: Violence, Media, and the Crisis in Masculinity*. We also use a variety of resources to explore gender pay gaps, gender bias in the schools and media, body monitoring, self-esteem, eating disorders, self-injury, and the increase in plastic surgery. We read Michael Salzhauer's *My Beautiful Mommy*—written to help children understand mom's latest plastic surgery procedure, and watch

Nour Tohmé

Miss Representation, America the Beautiful, and/or *Killing Us Softly 4*.

Before heading to the stores, my students and I generate a list of things to look for. Typical questions include: How do you know where the boys' and girls' sections are? What types of toys are in each section? What type of lettering is used? What do the toys promote? What careers are associated with the toys?

The assignment includes a written and oral report to the class summarizing findings. Some students ask to give their report as a group; these presentations are often lively and interactive. One group somehow came up with the funds to buy many of the toys they researched. They provided the class with an array of war toys, Barbies, Bratz, and action figures. The men in the group were the most vociferous in their critique of the messages sent to children, particularly boys who play with war toys. One of the students had been in the military and said he felt angry about the socialization he had absorbed from toys, such as assumptions that men make war, war is exciting, and new weapons are fun to use.

A student wrote: "Toys represent males in power in all aspects of women's lives. They are the leaders and controllers, and boys are taught that this is their destiny. It really made me angry to stand in a toy store and realize this on a new level."

Socialization

When young boys engage in dress up, pile on the necklaces, enjoy painting their nails, or select other "girl" toys, cultural norms or homophobia often correct the behavior. In fact, in toy lab studies, when staff members observed children behind one-way glass, they found that boys played with "girl" toys if they thought they were in a safe environment to do so.

My students frequently offer supporting evidence from their part-time jobs at after-school programs about boys crossing gender lines. They believe that young boys relish the chance to get their nails painted and have their hair styled with product when girls are doing it as a special activity. One student said: "I think boys just like the closeness of being with a staff member, being touched while we paint their nails, and talking with us."

In the video *Tough Guise*, Jackson Katz explores the ways boys are taught to be tough, and how they're encouraged to define manhood in ways that hurt themselves and others. Katz points out that toy action figures have increased in size over the decades, mirroring the ratcheting up of violence in popular films. According to Katz, boys are socialized to be solitary, independent, and often violent through toys, video games, and Hollywood movies. The cultural message is that emotional connections and vulnerability are for sissies.

Even the STEM-based toys are solitary, don't present opportunities for verbal or social development, and often encourage violence. Packaging hints at being the best, or creating and building superior models or designs, and some toys encourage boys to create things that they can later destroy. Crayola's Create

2 Destroy series invites boys to "Build it. Launch it. Smash it."

While boys are encouraged to be tough and solitary, girls are taught to compete with each other for male validation. Girls' toys often promote unattainable physical perfection and convey cultural messages of inferiority and second-class status that continue to affect girls' self-image, physical ability in sports, and academic performance.

The sexualization of girls can be observed in almost every toy aisle. Girls who look coy or flirtatious are in evidence everywhere, even in products for very young girls.

As toy manufacturers reduce girls to objects of desire to be controlled by various beauty and diet industries, girls receive the implicit and explicit message: It has always been this way and it will continue to be this way.

While they are being sexualized for the male gaze at the toy store, according to the U.S. Department of Justice, 1 in 6 females in the United States has experienced an attempted or completed rape. This reality is standard fare for video games. The video games in Toys R Us and Target are found adjacent to the boys' section and display an array of images of women that could rival some covers in an "adult" bookstore. Grand Theft Auto V (GTA V), which made $1 billion in the three days following its 2013 release, is the fastest selling entertainment product in history. The *Los Angeles Times* reports that a man in GTA V states: "I don't care if you're 12, I'll still rape you." A player can crush the sternum of a woman during sex and one can hear a voice claiming: "Women love that."

Forces for Change

There's some hope that things might be beginning to change. In many communities, independent toy stores think about gender and other forms of equity when they stock their shelves.

Some toy manufacturers are promoting change. Hearts for Hearts Girls—featuring female dolls with a story and a message about global issues and human rights, offers "stories, games, and great ideas on how you can be a girl who changes the world." GoldieBlox, founded by Stanford engineering graduate Debra Sterling, sells engineering toys for girls that are creative, ingenious, and fun.

Organizations are advocating for change, too. Through a petition on change. org, U.K.-based Let Toys Be Toys pressured 12 retailers in the U.K.—including Toys R Us, Harrods, Tesco, Sainsbury's Boots, and T. J. Maxx—to change their marketing policies and practices in the areas of signage and gender segregation. Stores in Ireland, Sweden, and Australia have also addressed sexism in their company policies.

After getting the guy by playing spa or beauty salon, the girls get the ironing board.

I contacted Toys R Us and inquired as to whether the company has plans to desegregate the U.S. stores (by gender). The vice president of corporate communication wrote: "There are no gender-specific toy sections in our U.S. stores. Toys are merchandised by product category, so customers can easily see the breadth of assortment." I went to their website and clicked on "shop by." The first two lines state: "Boys' toys," "Girls' toys."

As I left Toys R Us on my last research trip on a cold dark night, I stared up at the yellow giraffe on the outside of the building for a few moments. I wondered how people in the toy industry—as well as the adults who purchase the toys—could demean boys to this extent. But what is even more distressing is the complete demoralization of girls. I don't think the bar could be set any lower. It is with highest hopes that I look to advocacy groups and progressive toy companies to prevail as agents of change.

Postscript

The *Rethinking Schools* editors asked me to do a bit of additional research for this article. They wanted to know if McDonald's and Burger King still asked customers if they wanted a boy or a girl toy when ordering a children's meal. To make my research as reliable as possible, I drove to several McDonald's and Burger King drive-through windows and briefly interviewed the crew members at the windows.

Workers at all the restaurants told me the same thing: They ask if the child is male or female. A McDonald's employee explained that they have three buttons for toys: truck for boys, doll for girls, and under age 3. He even offered to photograph the keypad with his camera phone. I told him thanks, but it wasn't necessary. Given what I know about kids' toys, I didn't have any trouble believing him.

Laura Trafí-Prats

Fisher

BY PATTI SIMMONS

Patti Simmons lives with her husband and two children in Columbus, Ohio. A homeschooling mom and a lifelong learner, she spends time exploring different subject areas, trying out new hobbies, and helping her children pursue their interests with gusto. She loves the outdoors, spending time with friends, and hearing people's stories.

My son was just shy of his 11th birthday when he was inspired by a music video to take dance classes. As we talked about what type of class he would take and whether or not there would be any boys in the class, he began sobbing and ran up to his bedroom. Perplexed, I sat on the edge of the bed and asked him what was wrong.

"I don't want to be a boy anymore!" he said.

Oh.

This didn't catch me entirely by surprise. Fisher has never been a particularly masculine boy. From a young age, he enjoyed dressing up in his friends' princess dresses and pretending to be female video game characters. And he occasionally expressed his feminine side in a number of small ways, such as choosing pink socks with cupcakes on them for crazy sock day at school. I'd always loved that he didn't feel constrained by gender expectations, although I did occasionally suspect that he was holding himself back a little bit. For several years, he wanted to be a female character for Halloween, only to change his mind at the last minute—not wanting to deal with uncomfortable questions or comments at school.

We were edging toward something that I didn't completely understand.

During his 3rd-grade year, Fisher began to experience some school-related anxiety; the underlying cause was not entirely clear. Despite the fact that he had almost always been a rule-follower, he seemed to be fearful of getting caught breaking rules. He also began refusing to use the restroom at school. He told me it was because he didn't like using public restrooms, but I wondered if it was something more. For these and many other reasons, we decided to try homeschooling for a year.

After leaving the school environment, Fisher's anxieties disappeared. I was no longer called into his bedroom at night to remind him of anxiety management techniques we'd learned from the book *What to Do When You Worry Too Much*. We found an inclusive and welcoming homeschool group. And for the first time Fisher felt comfortable dressing up as a girl for Halloween—albeit a very gross zombie girl.

As the year went on, I saw a stronger feminine side beginning to emerge. Fisher bought some leggings with cats on them from the girls' department at Target. He used his own money to buy a couple of dresses for dress-up from a resale shop. And he chose a pair of pink-laced black and rainbow running shoes from the girls' area.

I was happy that Fisher was feeling comfortable being himself. Yet I felt like we were edging close to something that I didn't completely understand. I remembered joking when he was 5 that I was raising a future drag queen, but at 11 years old it seemed less like a joke.

If this sounds confusing and difficult, it is. We will sometimes go for days or weeks without the subject coming up, and I feel like we are coasting. Then something happens that triggers an emotion for Fisher, and we spend a few days talking through his feelings. For example, he recently had someone ask about his gender in a room full of people and someone else answered for him. This made him uncomfortable because he does not want people to speak for him, and also because he was not entirely sure how to answer for himself. I am grateful for his openness, but these conversations can be confusing and leave me anxiously pondering what the future will look like for Fisher. This ambiguity is the most difficult part of having a child who is "in the middle." I cannot focus on the man he will become, because that end cannot be guaranteed. It takes a great mental shift to focus on simply helping my child on a path of self-discovery— wherever that may lead.

Many questions remain unanswered. I think Fisher is beginning to understand that it is going to take some time for him to figure out exactly who he is. For kids like Fisher who do not feel certain about their gender identity, puberty can be a clarifying time. And although we have learned that gender and sexuality are unrelated, it is possible that Fisher's gender nonconformity is related more to his emerging sexuality than his gender identity. But as there is absolutely no way to know this, we are working to give him the acceptance, time, and freedom he needs to figure out who he will become.

An Open Letter to My Son's Teacher

By Shannon Panszi

Shannon Panszi is a proud parent of three sons, one of whom is transgender. With a background in obstetrics and gynecology, she has been a fierce advocate for transgender rights through her work with the medical community. Currently she is the daytime caregiver for her children, works with the national transgender advocacy group FORGE, helps to organize a local parents support group, and gives lectures around the country on transgender healthcare.

My son Sam is going to be in your class this year. Like most parents, I am entrusting you with the education of my child. I am hoping that, with us, you will help him continue to grow into a self-confident person who loves learning, feels confident to speak his mind, and is sure of himself in social situations. Unlike most parents, I worry that my son's gender identity will become an issue in your classroom or other places in the school, like the bathroom and the playground. Until this year, you see, the school community has known my child as a girl, but this summer Sam had the courage to transition to be his true self.

Sam is a boy. He's been telling other children on the playground that he is a boy since he was 3. I used to "correct" him, but now I know I was wrong. It has taken our family a little time to understand and catch up to Sam's wisdom.

Everything changed when I heard the story of Coy Mathis, a 6-year-old transgender girl who won the right to use the school bathroom designated for the gender with which she identified. My child was a year older, and I had not thought it was possible to have a developed gender identity at his age. I started searching the internet for any information I could find on children's gender identity. It was then that I learned that gender identity is sometimes developed by the age of 4. I learned that gender is determined by the brain and how a person feels in their heart, not by their anatomy. Four years ago when I insisted Sam tell the "truth" on the playground, I was really telling him to lie.

Since his transition, Sam has become more confident and happy. We are learning as we go, and recognize that you and the rest of the school community will have to learn as well. People asked us if we would change schools to make the transition smoother. We considered switching schools to give Sam and his brother a fresh start, but we were unable to find a school that we thought would be a better fit. We've been happy with the education our son has received here; with your help, we hope he can continue to thrive. We've met with the principal and feel confident that our family will be supported here.

We have some suggestions for things to consider:

Roll call. Make sure you and substitute teachers use Sam's new name.

Gender separation. If there has to be separation by gender (in lines, the bathroom, and so on), let Sam be on the boys' side.

Safety—particularly in the bathroom and on the playground. Please make use of the buddy system so that he is never alone.

Learn as much as you can. Arm yourself with knowledge. We can help.

Be an alert advocate. Be vigilant and prepared to intervene when intentional harassment or unintentional hurtful comments and actions occur.

There may be times when my son uses the word transgender. This summer he was talking to friends about boycotting Jelly Belly because the company's chairman donated funds to anti-transgender groups. My husband and I often wonder how teachers and children will react when Sam shares such a story during class. Even though Sam is aware that most children won't understand such a complex issue, he still feels the need to inspire change. We are proud of him for his convictions and bravery.

I didn't set out to be an activist. We've always raised our children to be open-minded individuals and prided ourselves on being mindful about gender roles and sexual orientation, among many other factors that can come into play over the course of a child's development. We hadn't considered the possibility that one of our kids was going to take us along on this journey. But now we find ourselves here and hope that you will be our partner this year.

We know that this letter is just the beginning of our work together to make Sam's educational experience positive. We believe our work will help all children and adults feel safer at school and happier to be themselves. We've asked the principal to share our expectations and goals with all teachers in your school. We hope we can count on you to partner with us, as well, to make this school year successful for all your students.

Thank you, in advance, for your support.

Framing Identity
Using photographs to rethink sexism, gender, and sexuality

By Kim Cosier

Kim Cosier is associate dean of the Peck School of the Arts, professor of art education at the University of Wisconsin–Milwaukee, and founding faculty member of a Master of Arts in Teaching program at the Vermont College of Fine Arts. Her research and teaching interests focus on art and education for social justice, particularly related to intersecting cultural and social factors including gender, race, sexuality, and class. She is founder of the Milwaukee Visionaries Project, an award-winning media production/literacy program for urban youth. She lives in Milwaukee with her wife, Josie, and dogs, Evie Mae and Roger, and has fun making trouble with her friends in the Educators' Network for Social Justice.

When I talk to people about art in schools, they often see it as a way for students to "express themselves" and "be creative." More and more, I hear "We need art because it is a release for kids who take too many standardized tests!" And it's true: Making art is incredibly important, especially in times when the imagination is being starved to death by standardization, and the curriculum is being anaesthetized.

But making—devoid of making meaning—is not enough. Art is also a way of inquiring about the world. The true power of education through art has as much to do with looking, talking, reading, and research as it does with making. I do believe that making art can have therapeutic, healing power, but the power of art is truly harnessed in pedagogical spaces where students go beyond just expressing themselves. Teachers can use the power of art to engage students in thinking deeply about big ideas and addressing questions about the nature of our existence.

You don't have to be an art teacher to harness this power. Teachers regularly use images to activate discussions in their classrooms. Using images that are created to cause viewers to think—rather than simply instruct, as more didactic visual materials do—is what bringing art into the classroom is all about. Using works of art to engage students in dialogue about ideas can be a potent tool in any teacher's toolbox. In

Lois Bielefeld

CHAPTER 6: TEACHER EDUCATION, CONTINUING EDUCATION   397

terms of the themes of this book, discussions about sexism, gender, and sexuality can be expanded and deepened through classroom experiences that take advantage of looking and talking about the work of contemporary artists. With its power to literally frame identity, photography can create pedagogical spaces in which teachers and their students engage in careful looking and deep discussion about identity, representation, and diversity.

There are numerous photographers whose work can help students rethink sexism, gender, and sexuality, including Cindy Sherman, Claude Cahun, Shirin Neshat, Catherine Opie, Yasumasa Morimura, Debbie Grossman, and others (see Resources). Jess T. Dugan and Lois Bielefeld, two artists who focus on gender identity, have given us permission to share their photographs with you. In this article, I discuss their work and ideas, as well as offer questions and activities you could use with their photographs in the classroom.

Jess T. Dugan: *Every Breath We Drew*, *Transcendence*, and *To Survive on This Shore*

Dugan's work deals with a wide spectrum of gender identities. She treats her subjects, who represent a range of queer identifications, with respect and care. They are shot in natural light at close range, often looking directly at the camera, which brings us, the viewers, into a relationship with them. Dugan's photographs have a power to engender empathy. The photographs in all three of these series would be powerful tools in classroom dialogues about gender diversity.

According to Dugan, the series *Every Breath We Drew* "explores the power of identity, desire, and connection through portraits of myself and others." People who identify across a range of possible genders, including transgender, male, masculine female, genderqueer, and more, are represented. A few photographs show scars after chest reconstruction surgery; however, many are less overtly focused on the mechanics of transgender identity and would be "safe" for classroom use.

The series *Transcendence I* was shot in black and white. (See Resources.) One good jumping-off point for classroom discussion might be excerpts from Dugan's statement about the series:

> In our society, it is assumed that there are only two genders, both of which come with very specific expectations and roles. I aim to challenge that assumption by portraying people whose identity falls outside of these preconceived notions. *Transcendence* is a collection of portraits within the transgender and gender-variant community. These photographs show that there are an endless number of gender identities, specific to each person, while illustrating that gender identity and biological sex are two distinct constructs. More broadly, they call into question societal expectations about gender roles and how these expectations affect everyone, including those who are not

Tasha's story (excerpted):

When I was growing up, I knew that something about me was different. I knew that I liked the guys. And from Day One, I've always felt like a woman born in a man's body. That's the way I live. I didn't get to the place of where I'm so all right with this until later in life—at a young age I would've had a sex change. But today, I'm so all right with me, it doesn't even cross my mind.

I have never been a clear-cut case of being in the closet. I've always been wide open. And back in that time of the Civil Rights Movement, I still didn't have any problem. I was still wide open. I participated in the marches and stuff. I was arrested, wet up with the hoses, all that stuff. Whether you say, "Yes, ma'am" or "Yes, sir," I'm all right. I'm all right. I don't let nothing like that bother me.

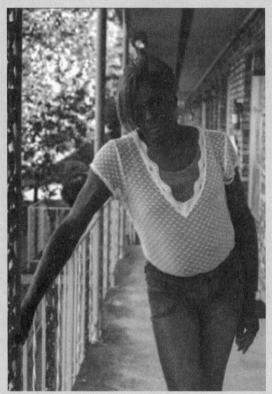

At times it was kinda rough growing up when you had to hear guys call you all kinda names, such as freaking fag and all this kinda stuff. It used to hurt and make me angry. But as I got into the church and started letting the verse of John 3:16 register in me, a whole lot of stuff changed. It said, "For God so loved the world that whoso-ever will, let them come." And after that, I felt like I was one of the "whosoevers." I stopped getting mad. I stopped fighting and just be who I am—and just be me.

Now I am real respected in my neighborhood as Tasha because a lot of people don't even know my real name. I'm Tasha to everybody. And most of the children say "Miss Tasha." But when I come upon situations where children are curious and ask, "Are you a man or a lady?" I don't lie to them. I just tell them I'm a man that lives as a woman. And then I have no problems with them.

All in all, I feel that I done had a good life. I'm just happy with me today, real happy.

Jess T. Dugan/Vanessa Fabbre

a part of the transgender community.

Through sharing individual experiences, this work honestly and openly portrays a community that is often overlooked, fetishized, or misrepresented.

I was excited to learn about Dugan's most recent project, portraits that are part of a series she is creating with her partner, social work researcher Vanessa Fabbre. Called *To Survive on This Shore*, the project focuses on transgender and gender-variant older adults from across the country. Fabbre interviews people and Dugan makes photographic portraits to accompany the stories. The addition of the portraits brings Fabbre's qualitative research to life. As Dugan and Fabbre explain: "Photographs and words are both powerful narrative tools. Especially in combination, they have the power to tell meaningful stories, elicit empathy, and promote social change."

Lois Bielefeld: *Androgyny*

Lois Bielefeld is a Milwaukee-based photographer. By day she shoots fashion photography and, on her own time, what she calls "conceptual portraits." Her series *Androgyny*, *The Bedroom*, and *Weeknight Dinners* all contain images that could be used to create learning experiences guiding students toward more complex understandings of gender, sexuality, family, and identity (see Resources). The *Androgyny* series, in particular, is a fantastic resource for engaging students in dialogue about gender identity and expression.

Androgyny is an especially important concept at this particular time in our history. We find ourselves in an age of rapid expansion of human rights for certain LGBTQ people, while others are left behind to fend for themselves. The great legal, cultural, and social shifts that are taking place around marriage equality and transgender rights actually prop up a social system that privileges a particular kind of relationship and a binary system of gender. Queer people who do not want to marry or do not want to transition from one gender to another continue to be marginalized, even as human rights are expanded for those whose identities allow them to more easily assimilate into the mainstream. Bielefeld's work can be a fantastic resource for exploring this contradiction.

Androgyny, with characteristics that are both traditionally male and female, offsets the more mainstream forms of lesbian, gay, and transgender identity. Every school has its androgynous community members, but teaching about diverse gender identities remains out of the norm. Bielefeld's work gives us a way to approach the topic.

As with Dugan's work, the great thing about the photographs in *Androgyny* is that you really get the sense that the subjects are looking you in the eye. And, in this case, photographs of gender-variant children and youth are a distinctive part of the *Androgyny* project, which sets Bielefeld's work apart from Dugan's and makes it more easily relatable for students. The website also includes audio and video. One video in particular, *Boy, Girl, Both*, documents the journey of Alexis and Allie, who co-developed and led a lesson on gender identity for 2nd graders after being disrespected for not conforming to rigid gender roles. (See Dale Weiss' article, "Believe Me the First Time," Chapter 2).

Workshopping Photographic Pedagogies

One approach to using these photographs is to broaden discussions of bias past the anti-bullying language that is common in schools today. At the 2015 annual convention of the National Art Education Association in New Orleans, co-editor Rachel Harper and I led a curriculum workshop called "Beyond Bullying: New Approaches to Queering Art + Design Education." Following that, I led a similar workshop for teachers of all subjects at the annual conference of the Educators' Network for Social Justice in Franklin, Wisconsin. Both workshops used images and processes drawn from art to create a space for teachers and students to engage deeply in discussions and to generate questions for teaching about sexism, gender, and sexuality.

We began by noting that anti-bullying programs have become widespread in schools, but violence and harassment persist. We briefly discussed the genesis of this book and gave an overview of Lyn Mikel Brown's article "10 Ways to Move Beyond Bully-Prevention (and Why We Should)" (see Chapter 2). Then we worked with participants to craft new possibilities for education that go beyond anti-bullying to liberatory, affirming teaching practices. We began with the following objectives:

The activities we brainstorm today will help students:
- Acquire relevant vocabulary to talk about gender identity and stereotypes.
- Grapple with the notion of realness as it relates to gender.
- Look at images of Dugan's and Bielefeld's work and relate them to the big idea of identity.
- Understand how stereotypes can result in unfair or even harmful situations.
- Devise a plan for art-based projects that expand our understanding of gender.

With those objectives in mind, we embarked on a brainstorming activity based on Dugan's and Bielefeld's images. First, we developed potential discussion questions for students viewing Dugan's and Bielefeld's work:
- What do you see in this picture? (Always a good place to start.)
- Who do you think this person is?
- Tell me a story about the person/people you see in this photograph.
- What is gender?
- How can we know a person's gender identity?
- What makes someone be a girl? A boy? Can someone be a little of both?
- What are some ideas about how people of different genders "should" be or act?

 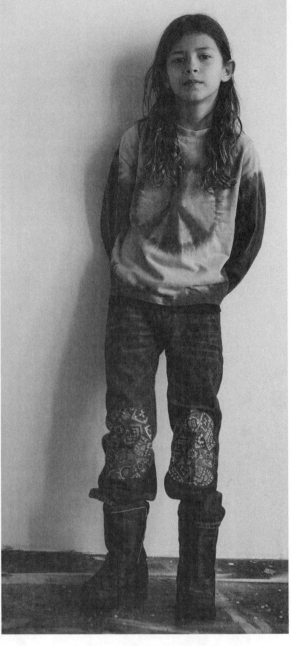

- Have you ever heard someone say "real men/real women do ____?" Let's talk about that.
- Have you heard the word *transgender*? What do you think it means? Do any of these pictures give you more understanding?
- Let's talk about what *gender variant* means.
- What is a stereotype? How do stereotypes affect people as they grow and live their lives?
- What are ways you can think of to make our community and school welcoming to someone who does not fit rigid gender expectations?
- Did the work of artist Jess Dugan and/or Lois Bielefeld make you think differently about gender and stereotypes? Let's talk about that.

Then, we moved on to brainstorming possible art-making projects that could extend student learning:
- A photography project in which students are challenged to show complexity in their own and others' identities.
- Visual journaling activities about ways a student's own identity is being formed.
- A project using the methods of *To Survive on This Shore*, which combines social science with photography. Conduct interviews and create a photographic series of portraits that say something new to you about gender.
- Design badges or trophies for aspects of gender that are not typically celebrated in schools.
- A social practice art project like the *Bathroom* installation (see Bielefeld's website): Develop questions you might ask community members, recording their responses. Propose an installation plan to accompany the audio.
- A public service announcement video that addresses an aspect of gender people should know more about.
- An exhibition that visually compares and contrasts representations of gender. For example, juxtapose images from advertising to some made of real people in your school.
- Comics of superheroes that bend gender rules to make the world a safer, more inclusive space for all.

Resources

Lois Bielefeld
loisbielefeld.com

Claude Cahun
courses.washington.edu/femart/final_project/wordpress/claude-cahun
Cahun is the only artist on my list who is no longer living. Her work is so important to the work that followed, I could not resist including her. Cahun was

part of the Surrealist art movement in Europe and a creative queer pioneer. She combined writing and image making to expand ideas about gender and identity. Toward the end of her life she became an antiwar activist and a target of the Nazis. Her story is fascinating and should not be lost from history.

Jess T. Dugan
jessdugan.com

Jess T. Dugan and Vanessa Fabbre
To Survive on This Shore
tosurviveonthisshore.com
For additional information, see Bernstein, Jacob. March 6, 2015. "For Some in Transgender Community, It's Never Too Late to Make a Change." *New York Times*. nytimes.com/2015/03/08/fashion/for-some-in-transgender-community-its-never-too-late-to-make-a-change.html.

Debbie Grossman
My Pie Town
debbiegrossman.com/index.php?/projects/my-pie-town
According to the artist: "*My Pie Town* reworks and reimagines a body of images originally photographed by Russell Lee for the U.S. Farm Security Administration in 1940. Using Photoshop to modify Lee's pictures, I have created an imaginary, parallel world—a Pie Town populated exclusively by women."

Yasumasa Morimura
saatchigallery.com/artists/yasumasa_morimura.htm
Morimura is best known for a series of self-portraits in which he transforms himself into famous film stars such as Audrey Hepburn and female subjects in art such as the Mona Lisa.

Shirin Neshat
gladstonegallery.com/artist/shirin-neshat/work#&panel1-2
Neshat grew up in pre-revolutionary Iran. She came to the United States in the 1970s as a student and became an internationally recognized artist, with exhibitions around the world. But, she says: "I had an incredible urge to reconnect to Iran. So art in a way became an excuse to reconnect to my home, my family, and the country. . . . I feel, as a woman, as an Iranian, completely conflicted by who I am in nature, someone . . . very healthy and strong, but also extremely fragile; [there is] also my identity as a Muslim, as a person, as a Westerner, as an Easterner. So my work is exactly that expression of that sense of duality that I feel is the core of who I am."

Catherine Opie
Domestic
regenprojects.com/exhibitions/catherine-opie3

Opie photographs diverse families in domestic settings.

Portraits
regenprojects.com/exhibitions/catherine-opie
The work for which Opie first became well known, photographing queer subjects using lush colors that seduce the viewer into looking closely at individuals who some might never see. One of my favorites is "Oliver in a Tutu": regenprojects.com/artists/catherine-opie#31.
At the Guggenheim: web.guggenheim.org/exhibitions/opie/exhibition.html.

Cindy Sherman

cindysherman.com
According to the Museum of Modern Art in New York City, Sherman is "widely recognized as one of the most important and influential artists in contemporary art. Throughout her career, she has presented a sustained, eloquent, and provocative exploration of the construction of contemporary identity and the nature of representation, drawn from the unlimited supply of images from movies, TV, magazines, the internet, and art history."

Photographs Do Not Bend

photographsdonotbend.co.uk/gender-identity-the-other
This website includes a collection of short articles about photographers whose work engages ideas about gender identity and expression.

Sergio's Voice
Fostering writing lives

By Lilia E. Sarmiento

Lilia Sarmiento teaches in the College of Education at California State University Dominguez Hills in Carson, California, where she works in the preparation of bilingual teachers, in local districts, and researching biliteracy, English language development, and writing. She is a former bilingual educator and administrator, and collaborates with teachers from Central America and the Dominican Republic.

After listening in on the Family History Writing Project conference presentation, Sergio walked up to me, grinned, and put his arms around me in a warm embrace.

"It's good to hear you sharing the importance of developing writer's voice at this bilingual conference," he said. "It would be great if others had the chance to write the way that you inspired us to do. I came to tell you that I have continued to write. I started another notebook. I have to have a place to write down what I am feeling. I need that."

As we continued to catch up on the months that had passed since Sergio had been a preservice teacher candidate in my reading methods course, I asked about the hardbound book of his writing he had created. "Have you had a chance to share your book with anyone?"

Sergio shook his head. "If you mean my family—no. I'm not ready to have them read my book."

The reading methods course I teach is designed for students preparing to become elementary Spanish bilingual teachers. During the first nine weeks of the class, I work to develop knowledge about teaching strategies by giving preservice teachers opportunities to write. Sergio had used this writing space to share his family heritage, explore his identity as a gay male, and begin to make his voice public.

When I originally designed the writing component of the course, my goal was to create a positive and collaborative classroom writing culture that supported the learning and teaching of writing. What I didn't realize was how much I would learn. Sergio's writings taught me how important it is to create spaces for future teachers to share stories and struggles that are often silenced; his writing offered insight into the struggles many LGBTQ young adults face—ongoing degrading comments and fear of revealing their true selves.

As they write and share personal issues, I hope that the bilingual students I work with teach each other awareness, tolerance, and empathy that they'll apply in their own teaching practice.

Family History Writing Project

Writing teachers need to see themselves as writers and understand the intricacies of the writing process firsthand. I created the family history writing project to give my students a chance to write for themselves and their families—and not for academics—as part of that process.

The project requires students to write a minimum of six family stories in different genres: autobiographical or biographical narratives, family legends, letters, recipes, descriptive pieces, historical accounts, and poems. I encourage students to write in Spanish—to develop their Spanish skills, to express themselves in a language with which they might have a stronger emotional connection, and to make their writing accessible to their Spanish-speaking family members.

Sharing writing creates opportunities to develop empathy and understanding.

Sharing writing—with partners, small groups, or the whole class—creates opportunities to develop empathy and understanding. Students have written about deeply personal experiences and issues—the joys and challenges of their lives. They have shared personal accounts of how families were torn apart, the terror of running across the border and hiding with helicopter blades whirring overhead, the effects of the Vietnam war on grandparents, the death of a baby, homelessness, and terminal illness.

On a weekly basis, students bring writing drafts to share with others for feedback. At the end of the nine-week writing unit, I send students' final drafts, photographs, and drawings to be published into a hardbound book at no cost to them. I hope that students take the lessons they learn—from their own writing experiences and from hearing classmates' stories—into their future classrooms.

Creating a Classroom Writing Culture

As an instructor of writing I continue to seek opportunities for professional and personal writing development. My involvement with the UCLA Writing Project and attendance at a weeklong institute led by Natalie Goldberg, author of *Writing Down the Bones*, sparked my own desire to write. In my university courses, I model what I have learned about writing—and about myself as a writer—as an example for my students.

To support students as writers, I set up rituals and routines. Reading is just as important as writing. Students read works by authors such as Sandra Cisneros, Helena Viramontes, and Isabel Allende. I usually begin with a short story or an excerpt from a story or a book, which serves as a mentor text—an exemplary piece of writing that includes a specific writing craft that I want to highlight and that might serve as a model for the students' own writing. I want students to study the strategies that professional writers use and ask how those writers produce texts.

Students read each text twice: first, solely for enjoyment; second, slowly, deliberately pausing at interesting parts. Adapting Katie Wood Ray's "read like a writer" strategy from her book *Wondrous Words*, I ask students to *notice* something about the craft, develop a *theory* as to why the author wrote that way, *name* the craft, and then *envision* that craft in their own writing.

After sharing our insights about a mentor text, I write a short personal piece, talking aloud to make my thinking visible. I want to show students some of the many decisions I make when writing—how I select a precise word to enhance an image or a feeling, how to provide a bird's-eye view of a scene, or how I decide when to zoom in and insert more details. After seeing and hearing me write, students write for 10 minutes, and then share their writing with a partner.

Taking Risks

Critical to this work is the sharing of my own personal stories. I take risks just as I expect students to take risks in writing about themselves and their families. I write about my dad's harsh life working in the copper mines of Sonora, as a fisherman sailing from the port of San Pedro, and the problems that alcoholism can bring upon a family. I reveal the challenges and joys of raising a child with a learning disability and share stories of his adaptation, rejection, and loneliness.

I am explicit about my own thinking processes. On a document camera, I draw a floor plan of the house where I grew up in south Los Angeles. I label each room and jot down ideas as I reminisce about my family and memories of mischief, scheming, disaster, and love. I then ask students to draw their own floor plans of places that were significant to them growing up.

Students remember people and places that are important to them during this assignment. For example, Sergio flashed back to his youth in Ensenada. He sketched the floor plan of his grandparents' two-bedroom house, including a pathway to the warehouse where he had spent time with his grandfather conversing and watching him make boxes for sea urchins, which were then exported to Japan.

After sharing the floor plan with a classmate, students make lists of memories the house elicited and the people connected to the house. Sergio shared: "I was like my grandfather; we had similar personalities. In fact, I look like him when he was younger. . . . He had a strong bond with my mother, his favorite daughter. That bond carried over to me."

Then students choose one of their ideas and write for 10 minutes. Sergio's pen flowed across the page: *"El señor de la casa era el señor de mi mundo infantil. . . . Durante mi niñez siempre fui el reflejo de sus ojos brillantes en una noche oscura. ¿Quién puede reemplazar esa generosidad que ha brindado a tanta gente?"* (The man of the house was the man of my childhood. . . . During my childhood I was the reflection of his brilliant eyes in a dark night. . . . Who can replace the great generosity that he so willingly gave?)

Sergio later shared that this floor plan triggered memories that led him to write a letter in which he came out to his grandfather. They had shared so much while his grandfather was alive, but Sergio's secret had been left untold.

Writer's Notebook

In addition to the writing we do in class, I also ask students to write for at least 10 minutes, no less than three times a week, for nine weeks. Adapting Natalie Goldberg's writing practice, I suggest five guidelines: 1) keep your hand moving, 2) lose control, 3) be specific, 4) don't worry about punctuation, spelling, grammar, and 5) don't censor. The intent is to free the students from roadblocks and give them permission to write wherever their writing minds lead them. They can fold over a page or pages if they don't want me to read something when they turn in their notebooks.

For example, freewriting in his writer's notebook gave Sergio the option to tap into the reservoir of the heart. Frustration, exhaustion, and pain flowed through many of his entries. Examples included: "I feel like shit," "I am frustrated, irritated, and annoyed. . . . This workload that is stressing me out will be pointless when I actually start teaching. . . . Everything I do is not good enough."

"It is difficult to live in silence."

Other entries were filled with love and hope. *"La alegría es la motivación para vivir día a día."* (Happiness motivates me to live each day.) "Unconditional love can never be bought or sold." "I love my 4th graders . . . the future leaders of this country. . . . I have developed self-sufficient learners who believe in themselves." The writing in Sergio's notebook reflected his daily ups and downs as well as the realities and conflicts of his personal and professional life.

Sergio's Letter to His Grandfather

Another way I cultivate a safe writing climate in the classroom is by encouraging students to send me their drafts. This gives me the opportunity to get to know them on a more personal level and give them one-on-one feedback.

I often personally connect with students' thoughts and experiences, but other times I am unprepared for their revelations. That was the case the evening I received Sergio's first writing piece via email, which I've translated:

> *Querido y Amado Tata* (Beloved grandpa),
>
> I am writing to you from my usual corner where I drink my iced coffee. . . . On days like this, rivers of dry tears flow from my crying eyes. But I shouldn't feel weak. I am at a point in my life in which I am most blessed. My *amá* and *apá* continue to share their blessings that give me strength.
>
> Tata, I am full of life and energy. I still have faith and hope that I will reach my goal of being a primary school teacher and buy my own house to raise my own family. . . . I miss you so much, Tata. Although you left this world 10 years ago, I still feel your presence and unconditional support.
>
> But Tata, I want to tell you that it is difficult to live in silence. My parents still don't know that I am *el otro, el gay, el joto, el homosexual,* or *el puto*, words that fall out of their mouths in a mocking and hurtful manner. How can I confront my parents if they still refer to being gay as something revolting or a joke in the Mexican tradition?
>
> I'm gay but I'm still the same person. . . . I know that you, Tata, have always been at my side, guiding me. . .
>
> Chetito

I was taken aback by the very personal nature of the letter. Sergio later reflected: "I felt like I was having a conversation. What I was saying in my head I was typing. My fingers were my mouth. This was my chance to tell my grandfather who I was. . . . I felt a sense of relief."

Sharing Writing and Receiving Feedback

One way I try to support students' writing and sharing is by embedding talk into the teaching of writing. Students rehearse their story ideas and share their writing with classmates.

At the beginning, students share from their notebooks. Later they share typed drafts for their books. Through sharing, students gain access to each others' familial and educational histories—and, together, we create a writers' community within our classroom.

Both peer feedback and my feedback served a role in Sergio's writing process. Although he viewed his writing as personal, he formed his own writing community with one other student whom he trusted to read his writing. Her comments sometimes made him take another look at his writing to make sure it expressed exactly what he wanted to say, to make sure his intended audience would understand it. But Sergio wasn't looking for someone to tell him how to improve his writing; he knew the words that he wanted to say and the emotions that he wanted to convey.

When Sergio emailed me the letter to his grandfather, I spent a lot of time thinking about how to respond. I wanted to encourage Sergio to continue to write. Instead of commenting on the content, I asked questions for elaboration: "Tell me more about. . . ," "What were you feeling at the time. . . ," "Clarify what you mean by. . . ."

Since I also wanted to support my bilingual teacher candidates in the mechanics of writing, I made editing marks focused on paragraphing, spelling, and correct accentuation of words in Spanish.

Later in the semester Sergio commented:

> I was hesitant [for you to see my writing] because it was personal; I didn't consider it academic. I had never let a professor read that side of me or get to know me outside of my student life. . . . I was afraid of you judging [my writing] because I didn't want to alter it. Your feedback surprised me because you said it was really good. That motivated me to keep writing. . . . I appreciated that you took the time to review my writing and provide constructive feedback.

Empowerment Through the Heritage Language

Another way I support students' writing is by inviting them to write in their home languages. Spanish was Sergio's language from birth, his home language, and the one he had used to build close ties with his grandfather. Sergio wrote all of his final drafts in Spanish.

Peter Elbow reminds us why writing in home languages is so important: "Unless we write in the language that is in touch with our unconscious, we lose half our mental strength" (Sumaryono and Ortiz, 2004). Although Sergio is proficient in both English and Spanish, he drew upon the power of his heritage language for the strength to find his authentic voice and tell his story—including the parts he had left unsaid for so many years.

Sergio's writing spoke of empowerment but also screamed of anger, hurt, and regrets. I hoped the initial steps of writing and sharing his writing with classmates would lead toward healing. And I knew that Sergio's reflections were helping me—and hopefully his classmates—understand the power of creating classroom spaces for students to share their lives.

Making His Voice Public

Over the course of the nine weeks, Sergio composed six different narratives celebrating his cultural and queer identity. He included an autobiographical narrative describing his birth and how he was named after his father, with the expectation that he would carry the family name. Sergio wrote two coming out letters: one to his grandfather, the other intended for his mother and father.

Unfortunately, throughout his life, in particular within his family, he has battled and continues to battle with homophobia. Sergio has felt that he has to align himself with the expectations of a heterosexual lifestyle to maintain harmony. Now, at least written within the pages of his book, that is not the case. Sergio's book *Mi voz, mi vida, mi alma* (*My Voice, My Life, My Soul*) conveyed his desire to be open and accepted.

After Sergio turned in the final assignment, I wondered if sharing his story might help other LGBTQ students. I sought out a gay faculty member for his perspective. Then I approached Sergio and began a series of conversations that led to the writing of this piece.

As he says:

> It took me years to accept the fact that I am gay, a *joto de primera* (first-class gay). My biggest challenge during the writing process was to fully acknowledge my deepest desires on paper without having critics' eyes. In the writing process I was becoming an individual with a voice embarking on a journey of hopes and desires. . . . The journey allowed me to unexpectedly shape the queerness to my writing and proclaim my identity as an educated gay Latino man.

Conclusion

Getting to know Sergio has made me reflect on the importance of creating a positive, caring, and collaborative classroom writing culture that supports the learning of writing. I constantly look for ways to maximize thinking, writing, and sharing time in class. I try to provide more time for small group discussions centered on peer feedback, what students have learned from other writers, and what they have learned about themselves as writers. I realize I don't need to be afraid to give concrete feedback on writing that deals with strong, emotional issues.

As college instructors, it is critical that we orient our literacy courses and instruction to promote teachers as writers. The more teachers practice writing, the more able they become to support and provide concrete suggestions for developing writers.

Teacher credential students need spaces to write—to explore and voice their own identities—and share the stories of their lives that have been silenced. We can help make meaningful changes in the lives of our teacher practitioners and, in turn, they can make a difference in their own students' lives.

Sergio has continued to write. He drives around with his writer's notebook and his bound book in the trunk of his car. They have become his support system, his counselors. He often retreats to the comfort of his book to give him strength for what lies ahead.

After we met again at the conference presentation, Sergio came out to one of his cousins and to his mother. Both shared that they already knew that he was gay. They assured him that nothing would ever be different because they loved him.

Resources

Goldberg, Natalie. 2005. *Writing Down the Bones: Freeing the Writer Within.* Shambhala Publications.

Sumaryono, Karen, and Floris Wilma Ortiz. 2004. "Preserving the Cultural Identity of the English Language Learner." *Voices from the Middle* 11.4:16–19.

"It's Not Appropriate!"
Sexual orientation in teacher preparation curriculum

BY NANCY NIEMI

Nancy Niemi taught middle school English and social studies in Horseheads, New York, where she also spent nine years as an elected school board member. She is currently a professor of education in New Haven, Connecticut, where she researches equity and stirs up trouble by asking her students to cause a constructive ruckus as they teach!

From Dr. Spock on, there has been a procession of child development experts to whom parents have turned for advice. Though they talk about topics ranging from sleep patterns to tantrums, child development experts rarely address issues of gender or sexual orientation. Preservice teacher educators can make this same mistake: We are highly trained in children's development and, for the most part, speak very little about children's gender identity and/or sexual orientation. We too often ignore the role that these issues play in children's school and home lives and, most urgently, we forget the positive impact teachers can have when we choose to end that pedagogical silence.

As experts in teaching children, we know that students who do not conform to traditional gender norms are more likely than other students to say they are called names, made fun of, or bullied at school. We know that the suicide rate for LGBTQ adolescents is at least two to three times higher than the average rate for straight adolescents. We also know that making schools safer and more accepting for all children makes schools better for everyone. And yet, teacher preparation programs frequently leave gender expression and sexual orientation out of curriculum and clinical practice.

When we do include it in our curriculum, it is most often in human development or foundations class discussions about the great variations in people. We often leave the discussion out of strategies courses, where new teachers would discuss how to apply this information to their practice. Even when teacher preparation programs undergo reform, it is easy to include gender and sexual orientation issues as a one-day, stand-alone activity, dutifully checking it off the list of requirements.

There are many aspects to working with teacher candidates on issues of gender identity and sexuality at different levels of child development. In this article, I will focus on sexual orientation.

There are many reasons why teacher educators tread lightly on issues of sexual orientation. We speak softly because teachers often work in politically conservative school climates despite national progress toward a more supportive view of LGBTQ issues. We know teachers may face pushback from parents, administrators, and boards of education that may argue that sexual orientation should not be addressed in school curriculum. But most of all, we are afraid: We are afraid of being accused of pushing a "pro-gay agenda," of being asked questions when we don't know the answers, of being fired for straying from approved curriculum and, ultimately, of confronting our own biases.

"It's not a matter of *bringing* sexual orientation into the classroom. It's *there*."

In the education department at the University of New Haven, we are working through our fears in order to change this. We feel ethically bound to include curriculum and discussion about sexual orientation and its role in all children's lives.

Creating Space in the Curriculum

Creating space for socially progressive curriculum in an already packed elementary teacher preparation program means choosing what curriculum to take out, or getting smarter about how we infuse it into existing, required curriculum. My colleagues are dedicated teacher educators who have spent the last 15 years creating a comprehensive, theoretically sound program with more than 1,000 hours of clinical experience for each student. As U.S. culture has changed, so has our department. As sexual orientation equity issues have become increasingly prominent in the media, our discussions about their inclusion in the program have, too. Some of us felt sexual orientation was most appropriate for our required human development course; others felt it belonged as part of a 7th through 12th grade social studies strategies course.

It was when it came to making space for discussions of sexual orientation as a standard part of the elementary curriculum, however, that our faculty began to wrestle with "appropriateness." We know our preservice teachers will likely be challenged with the argument "It's not appropriate" when they bring sexual orientation in the elementary classroom. So, we try to protect them and ourselves from potential discomfort or conflict, even when we know that we cannot and should not.

To help ease us into discussions about infusing sexual orientation into our curriculum, I bought lots of curricular materials for our department's library. Books like Barbara Regenspan's *Parallel Practices* (2002) and Joan Wink's *Crit-*

ical Pedagogy (2011) helped us have discussions in which sexual orientation was a part of, but not the whole conversation. I bought children's books that featured families of all kinds, and asked my colleagues to suggest titles. I sent articles about a variety of social equity topics to department members.

I also stepped back from my role as department chair and thought about how I might help students see different points of view. This humbled and reminded me to listen and offer spaces for students to think aloud with each other; I needed to let my colleagues do that, too.

Following the advice I give to new teachers, I found ways to integrate sexual orientation into the material I already teach, carefully researched what I wanted to include, connected the new material to state and national standards, and created what I hoped were pedagogically sound lesson plans. Then I found a place in my classroom calendar and I taught.

Speaking Out

I decided to start by addressing sexual orientation in my Elementary Social Studies Methods course. I began with a pre-discussion activity early in the trimester. In this activity, I had students identify the characteristics of diversity they were most afraid of addressing from a list in *Social Studies in Elementary Education* (Parker, 2011):

- Ethnicity
- Social class
- Race
- Culture
- Religion
- Language and dialect
- Gender
- Sexual orientation
- Giftedness, disability
- Multiple intelligences

When I asked students which of these characteristics they feared addressing most, hands shot up around the classroom.

"Sexual orientation," said one student.

I looked at the others whose hands were up and asked how many of them were going to say the same thing. All of them. I told them that we would be addressing this issue specifically in the coming weeks.

"Oh, good," said the student I had called on, "because I don't know how to bring that into the classroom."

"It's not a matter of *bringing* it into the classroom. It's *there*. What we need to discuss is how you'll address it." I did not say "*if* you'll address it" though I know some may not. If I don't use the language of option, I hope that some students will hear that it isn't one.

"If most of you agree that teaching about sexual orientation is the right thing to do, what are your fears?"

To introduce this idea, I began with the Berenstain Bears, a common and popular children's book series. I put a picture of the Bear family on the classroom screen—Mama, Papa, Sister, and Brother Bear. The picture led us to discuss how heterosexuality is the norm in children's literature.

I then displayed the text of Martin Niemöller's "First They Came." Lines such as "First they came for the communists, and I didn't speak out because I wasn't a communist" helped us reflect on the ways our own identities affect our willingness to speak out against injustice. I asked a student to read Niemöeller's poem aloud. Then we read a modern rewording of it called "Regaining Unconsciousness" from the band NOFX:

> First they put away the dealers,
> keep our kids safe and off the street.
> Then they put away the prostitutes,
> keep married men cloistered at home.
> Then they shooed away the bums,
> then they beat and bashed the queers,
> turned away asylum-seekers,
> fed us suspicions and fears.
> We didn't raise our voice,
> we didn't make a fuss.
> It's funny there was no one left to notice
> when they came for us.

I asked students to compare the two poems. Doing this allowed students to connect past and current political contexts—to note that the issues Niemöller raised are just as relevant now as they were a half century ago.

"But this doesn't happen now," said one of my students.

"Even though there has been a lot of progress around same-sex marriage, homophobia is alive and well," I responded. "Public schools, and elementary classrooms in particular, still aren't places where people expect sexual orientation to be discussed." Students mentioned the reality that many of the schools they work in would not be very welcoming of this discussion. I shared that when I taught middle school in upstate New York, it was still legal for the district to use homosexuality as a reason for not hiring or firing someone.

It was surprising to students to learn that an estimated 6 to 11 percent of all schoolchildren have gay or lesbian parents or siblings (Groundspark) and 10 percent of youth are LGBTQ (National Coalition for the Homeless, 2009). My students' faces blanched as they began to think about the power of their inactions in classrooms.

We then discussed language. I asked my students how many of them remembered using homophobic language as children. This led to a robust discussion of what they had heard their own students say in their clinical practice work. We discussed how negative language about gay and lesbian people is common on the playground, in hallways, and in teachers' lounges—and that many children and school personnel are adversely affected.

One of the teacher candidates pushed back: "But it's just language. Everyone knows that people are just kidding."

"Sure. Sometimes kids are just teasing each other. But think about when Harry Potter and his friends don't use the name Voldemort. Instead of calling him by his name they say, 'He who shall not be named.' Doesn't that carry power?" Students came up with other examples where words have tremendous power to hurt, connecting name-calling to their own lives.

"What Are Your Fears?"

Brainstorming answers to the question, "Why address sexual orientation in the elementary classroom?" brought us to the heart of the discussion. Students' answers came slowly at first, then accelerated:

"Because it's right."

"Their parents won't do it."

"So they can learn."

"Students will see things on the internet or television."

"Because other teachers might not."

"So," I said, "if most of you are agreeing that teaching about sexual orientation is the right thing to do, what are your fears? What do you think parents or your principals will say?" It's then that the conversation really started warming up.

"Isn't it more appropriate to wait until they're in middle or high school?" one student asked. We discussed how students are already aware of sexual orientation at young ages, and the media and cultural norms students are already exposed to.

"Yeah," said another student. "You should see what my 7-year-old brother watches."

"What if parents' religions say that being gay or lesbian is wrong?" asked another student.

A student responded: "Kids don't have to agree with their friends. When we were talking about having no school on Good Friday, I had to tell some students what it was. I don't think any parent would think I was trying to convert her child to Catholicism just because I answered that." Heads nodded.

Another student asked, "What if parents don't want their kids discussing gay sex?"

"I don't think that anyone is advocating you discuss any kind of sex in your classroom," I said. "We're talking about—"

"—love," interjected one student. I couldn't have said it better.

We need to prepare preservice teachers to confidently address sexual orientation with their own students.

It's Elementary

To honor voices of elementary students in our discussion, we watched *It's Elementary*, a documentary that addresses teaching about sexual orientation in schools. It's a wonderful resource for many reasons, but especially because children of various ages (5 to 14 years) and teachers from different schools around the country talk about issues of sexual orientation. The film does not present teaching about sexual orientation as easy or uniform; the filmmakers are careful to feature some students who voice their parents' opposition to the subject and others who voice their own stereotypes and prejudices. They also include principals' commentaries about how they tackle sexual orientation issues with parents.

I planned a lot of time after the film for my students to discuss what they saw. I posted the following questions on the board:
- Did anything in the film surprise you? What moved you and why?
- Has your thinking changed on the topic since you saw it?
- What questions do you still have? What concerns?

During the discussion, I incorporated students' reactions to a now older but still controversial article, "The Democratic Sieve in Teacher Education: Confronting Heterosexism." In the article, John Petrovic argues that new teachers' demonstrated ability to address issues of sexual orientation should be the single litmus test for whether one is qualified to be a teacher. This is an extreme view and always provokes heated conversation, providing another context in which to analyze the film and my students' responses to it. It was particularly interesting to hear students' comments in light of what just moments prior was an easy conversation: "You can't use someone's personal opinions to judge whether or not they can be a teacher!"

"Why not?"

"Just because they believe something doesn't mean that they would use that on kids."

Another student chimed in, "But how do you know whether their beliefs would come through anyway?"

"If we start making a rule about teachers' beliefs about homosexuality, couldn't we make a rule about teachers having a certain religion?"

"Do teachers only create space for discussion so that they can convince others of their own beliefs? What's different, if anything, about teachers being public employees?" I asked. "Does that change the question?"

"I know we're supposed to teach everyone. But I don't think that testing me is appropriate."

"Is there anything that all teachers should be?" I asked.

"They should love all children," was the consensus of our class. After the discussion came to a close—and I had to stop it because students had a lot to say—I gave students Debra Chasnoff's "Five Ways to Address Gay Issues in the Classroom" so would have something concrete when they get to their own classrooms and need somewhere to begin.

"You know," said one of my students after the discussion, "at first I thought that discussing sexual orientation was just inappropriate for little kids. I think I'm afraid, but I have to try."

Worthwhile Work

I hope that all my preservice teachers find ways to incorporate sexual orientation in their curricula. As teacher educators working with preservice teachers, it is essential that we do the same. Preservice training is often the only place in their education that future teachers are exposed to issues of sexism and homophobia that are critical to their teaching. In the same way that we work with preservice teachers on issues of race, we need to prepare them to confidently address sexual orientation with their own students.

I hope that as we grow, our department will find more ways to incorporate issues of sexual orientation—and other social equity issues—into our already packed curriculum. If we as teacher educators believe that school is a place where the development of a democratic society might flourish, we have to work through our discomfort and tackle oppression wherever we find it.

Resources

Groundspark. "Why Address Gay Issues with Children." groundspark.org/latest-news/presskits/elementary_kit/ie_kit_whygay.

It's Elementary: *Talking About Gay Issues in School*. Debra Chasnoff. 2007. New Day Films. DVD. Available from groundspark.org/our-films-and-campaigns.

National Coalition for the Homeless. 2009. "LGBT Homeless." nationalhomeless.org/factsheets/lgbtq.html.

Niemöller, Martin. 1955. "First They Came." *They Thought They Were Free: The Germans, 1933-45*. University of Chicago Press.

NOFX. 2003. "War on Errorism." Fat Wreck Chords.

Parker, Walter. 2011. *Social Studies in Elementary Education*. Pearson.

Petrovic, John. 1998. "The Democratic Sieve in Teacher Education: Confronting Heterosexism." *Educational Foundations* 12.1:43–56.

Regenspan, Barbara. 2002. *Parallel Practices. Social Justice-Focused Teacher Education and the Elementary School Curriculum*. Peter Lang.

Wink, Joan. 2011. *Critical Pedagogy: Notes from the Real World, 4th Edition*. Pearson.

"Are You a Girl or a Boy?"
Reading *10,000 Dresses* with college students

By Robert Bittner

Robert Bittner is a doctoral candidate in gender, sexuality, and women's studies at Simon Fraser University in Vancouver, B.C. He specializes in young adult and children's literature with LGBTQ themes.

Every night Bailey dreamed about dresses. A long staircase led to a red Valentine castle. On each stair was a brand-new dress, just waiting to be tried on! 10,000 dresses in all, and each one different!

So begins Marcus Ewert and Rex Ray's richly nuanced and whimsically illustrated picture book *10,000 Dresses*, the story of a young child named Bailey who lives as a girl within her dreams and as a boy to her family. When Bailey tells her family about her dreams, her hopes of having a beautiful dress in her real life are crushed. After meeting repeated disappointments trying to explain herself to her mother, father, and brother, Bailey meets Laurel, a girl who lives at the end of the block and is the only one willing to let Bailey be herself.

What makes this book particularly significant within children's literature is its approach to gender pronouns. Although her family is insistent that Bailey is a boy, the author respects her wish to be accepted as a girl and refers to Bailey as "she." This creates a complex and discussion-provoking story.

Recently I read *10,000 Dresses* to 35 undergraduate students enrolled in an introduction to children's literature class. I began with a brief survey of children's literature in English with LGBTQ content, including gender nonconformity. I started with *X: A Fabulous Child's Story*, by Lois Gould, and *Heather Has Two Mommies*, by Lesléa Newman, and continued through to *10,000 Dresses*.

Then I asked students to take out a sheet of paper and get ready to respond to some questions as I read *10,000 Dresses* aloud and projected images of the pages at the front of the classroom.

"Looking at the cover," I began, "what assumptions do you make about the main character?"

"The boy is wearing a dress," one student responded, "possibly gay—although not necessarily—because of what he is wearing."

"I assume the main character is either gay or transgender or gender confused."

"A boy who identifies as a girl, perhaps a gay boy, intersex?"

"Boys shouldn't wear dresses. He will most likely be homosexual when he grows up."

Bailey's short "boy's" haircut is associated with maleness and masculinity, but the addition of the dress, an image associated with femaleness and femininity, confuses a simple reading of the image. This led my students to make assumptions about not only gender, but also about sexual orientation, even though there is nothing on the cover (or in the book) to indicate the character's sexual interests. At this point, though, I simply collected their first reactions and began to read the book.

In the first few pages, Bailey tells her mother about a dream she had of a dress made of crystals. Then she says:

"And I was wondering if you would buy me a dress like that?"

"Bailey, what are you talking about? You're a boy. Boys don't wear dresses!"

"But . . . I don't feel like a boy," Bailey said.

"Well, you are one, Bailey, and that's that!"

I posed a second question: "After the dream sequence and the conversation with Bailey's mom, what, if anything, has changed about your assumptions?"

One student noted that she was "unsure of whether the character is a boy or a girl (sense of ambiguity?) *HE or SHE?!*"

Another student "assumed the character could be gay [and] reading [the] book confirmed these assumptions."

One more student noted that the "main character doesn't seem so happy after all— disappointed in family? My assumptions didn't change, but I was interested in the changes in pronouns."

Conflating Gender and Sexuality

My students' responses mirror positions on gender in society on a larger scale. The first of these is the strong social need to know a person's gender. If gender is not easily placed, people often feel frustrated. This is obvious in the anxious comment

Story by **MARCUS EWERT** • Illustrations by **REX RAY**

"HE or SHE?!" The second position is the conflation of gender and sexual identity, grounded in the assumption that femininity in men is equal to a gay sexual identity. The students' responses also reflect how much we tend to place emphasis on clothing, speech patterns, makeup, and accessories to "determine" a person's sexual orientation as well as their gender identity.

I continued reading the story. At the end, Bailey meets Laurel, who knows how to sew but doesn't have any good ideas for dresses. They decide to collaborate and create a pair of dresses covered in mirrors that, in Bailey's words, "show us OURSELVES." Laurel tells Bailey: "You're the coolest girl I've ever met."

After we finished the last page, I asked students a third question: "In what ways does this book challenge adult ideas of childhood innocence (innocence when it comes to gender)?"

One student wrote that *10,000 Dresses* "challenges assumptions of sexuality/gender identity in children prior to adolescence" and another that "adults try to protect children from sexuality/gender difference because they think it will corrupt them." Yet another student wrote that "adults often don't take time to listen and understand unconventional gender expression in children." The students' responses show the versatility of this text as one that elicits different interpretations, but can, in the end, provide a deeper understanding of gender and gendered behavior/expression as seen from the perspective of children, their families, and their friends.

One student wrote: "All the people (except for the last girl) disagreed with the main character and expected him to act like a boy. Maybe the child is just enjoying themself rather than thinking about the things they're doing as 'girl' or 'boy' things." This is an exceptionally pertinent comment, especially in this sociopolitical climate of extremely gendered toys and activities. In her blog *Raising My Boychick: Parenting, Privilege, and Rethinking the Norm*, Arwyn notes: "[Many] girls enjoy 'girly' things, such as dresses, but I am always concerned when such desires are presented as absolutes: that Bailey wants to wear a dress *because* she is a girl, and she is a girl *because* she wants to wear dresses." Although Bailey's gender is a source of education and consideration throughout the book, the binary association of dresses with female gender identity is indeed problematic. This is the perfect place for a parent or teacher to ask: "What do you think? Should dresses be just for girls? Do boys sometimes like to wear dresses, too?"

After we finished reading the book, I gave students more information on the differences between gender and sexuality, using a combination of discussion and visual aids (see Resources for "The Genderbread Person"). I explained the terms *gender identity, gender expression, biological sex,* and *sexual orientation.* We discussed some of the reasons why gender identity and sexuality are so often conflated. We also talked about the possibilities for using the text in classroom discussions with children. Much of the discussion focused on whether the book would reinforce stereotypes about boy activities and girl activities, or girls' clothes and boys' clothes. Students were concerned that children might be confused, but ultimately came to the conclusion that a rich discussion of the book would be beneficial to young readers.

> # *10,000 Dresses* warmly and respectfully speaks up for children's right to define their own identity at every point in their development.

After the class, I brought home student responses and analyzed them for patterns or common sources of confusion or misunderstanding. As with many large classroom situations, it is not possible to know for sure what impact my teaching had on all of my students. Later in the semester, however, I did notice a number of final papers focused on gender, sexuality, and related complexities.

Conclusions

10,000 Dresses warmly and respectfully speaks up for children's right to define their own identity at every point in their development. Bailey is still a young child and therefore in a category not often recognized as having the ability to make decisions regarding lived identity. LGBTQ books for children are usually about adult characters. *10,000 Dresses* raises a new set of questions because it assumes that a young child may have a solid sense of identity, even if that identity is at odds with family and societal expectations. Cheryl Kilodavis' *My Princess Boy* and David Walliams' *The Boy in the Dress* address similar themes.

I hope we will continue to see more and better representation of gender-related themes within the expanding body of children's literature. As with any new movement, it takes time, dedication, and a lot of trial and error on the part of authors, publishers, parents, and educators.

I taught *10,000 Dresses* in a university classroom and wrote about it here to underscore how important it is that parents and teachers take the time to understand gender and sexuality in order to help children and youth in the development of positive identities. We want children to develop and evolve into who they are in caring and knowledgeable surroundings in order to avoid confusion, frustration, or tragedy. Literature can be incredibly helpful in this journey, preparing all young people for a more diverse, accepting future, rather than one based on fear, difference, and misunderstanding.

Picture books, when looked at critically, explore an incredibly diverse range of themes and lessons for parents and teachers, as well as children. And often it is adults rather than children who need the greatest amount of education when it comes to gender expression and identity. Books like *10,000 Dresses* are much needed additions to current conversations.

Bibliography

Arwyn. 2010. "The Boychick's Bookshelf: *10,000 Dresses*." *Raising My Boychick*. Retrieved from raisingmyboychick.com/2010/04/the-boychicks-bookshelf-10000-dresses.

Ewert, Marcus. 2008. *10,000 Dresses*. Seven Stories.

Gould, Lois. 1978. *X: A Fabulous Child's Story*. Daughters Publishing Company.

Killermann, Sam. "The Genderbread Person." *It's Pronounced Metrosexual*. Retrieved from itspronouncedmetrosexual.com/2012/01/the-genderbread-person.

Kilodavis, Cheryl. 2010. *My Princess Boy*. Aladdin.

Newman, Lesléa. 2000. *Heather Has Two Mommies: 10th Anniversary Edition*. Alyson.

Walliams, David. 2010. *The Boy in the Dress*. Harper.

Teaching and Learning About Sexism
3 conceptual challenges

By Leigh-Anne Ingram

Leigh-Anne Ingram is a researcher, English language teacher, and teacher at the University of Western Ontario. When not attached to her computer or teaching, she loves to dance salsa, travel, and get out into green spaces to connect with people, dogs, and trees.

On Oct. 11, 2012, I celebrated the first International Day of the Girl with four young women activists from the Toronto area and hundreds of students and teachers at an all-girls school in Western Canada. The teen activists I traveled with had been invited to share the work they were doing to raise awareness about girls' rights in the developing world.

When asked what she liked about being a girl, one primary school student said: "I feel great to be a girl because I get to wear stuff in my hair. I might not feel good to be a girl in Africanistan because they aren't allowed to go to school." Her comment—conflating Afghanistan with all of Africa, and assuming that girls "over there" suffer from a universal level of misogyny entirely missing from our wonderful post-sexism life here in the "West"—jarred me into a deeper consideration of the contradictions of the event we were celebrating.

Over the past several years, I have worked with a group of high school activists in the Greater Toronto Area —the four who attended the celebration and three others—to explore their perspectives on gender, citizenship, and schooling, and learn about the complex web of messages they are receiving about being young women in Canada. They are part of a group organized by an NGO doing international work on girls' rights. Together we embarked on Project Citizen-Girl, in which the young women took photographs to illustrate their lives and ideas.

I have spent countless Saturdays eating pizza, looking at photographs, and having animated conversations with these young women about their lives, media, feminism, gay rights, and social justice movements. They are informed young people from diverse backgrounds involved in exploring the arts and social justice activism in their schools and communities.

Since my own grandmothers immigrated to Canada from Sweden and Poland, significant progress has been made to address gender inequality around the globe. There are now more girls in schools, more women in policy and decision-making positions, and new legislation being introduced that addresses a variety of violent, patriarchal practices. Books and movies—including the PBS book and series *Half the Sky* and the film *Girl Rising*—are stimulating public debate.

Yet "women's work" remains outside most debates in government, the media, and school curricula. Ideas of leadership, wealth, and power continue to be associated with men and masculine characteristics. Approximately 70 percent of the world's extreme poor are girls and women, and less than 18 percent of the world's legislators are women. Canada, despite its reputation for gender equality, ranks among the lowest in terms of the political participation of women among G20 countries. Even as local school boards and provincial mandates in Canada have brought greater attention to equity and representation in education, our federal government has dismantled programs promoting greater inclusion of women, people of color, and working people.

Are we equally outraged at the patriarchy, racism, and homophobia in our own communities?

As I reflected on the International Day of the Girl celebration and my conversations with the young women in our group, I wondered: As we focus on girls around the globe, are we ignoring gender equity issues within our own borders and within our own schools? Is this increased global focus on girls and girls' education addressing the underlying causes of gender discrimination and patriarchal relations, or is it an example of market forces co-opting feminism to distract us from systemic injustice?

In my work exploring gender equity as a classroom teacher, teacher educator, and researcher, I have found three common conceptual patterns—or challenges—that limit our thinking about gender equity: over there, in the past, and girls versus boys. Because my discussions with the teen activists have helped me understand these issues, I have woven their comments through this piece.

Over There

The first conceptual trap is thinking that gender equity issues are problems of other cultures in other places. Yasmin Jiwani describes how North Americans and Europeans often express outrage at the poor treatment of women in the developing world while ignoring the ways patriarchy, colonialism, and domination continue to affect their own societies and shape global systems.

The "over there" conceptual trap pervades Western media. A few days before we arrived for the event in Western Canada, 15-year-old Malala Yousafzai was shot by religious extremists for speaking publicly about the need to support girls' education in Pakistan. When we arrived in British Columbia, many of the girls at the school wanted to discuss the shooting and share their indignation.

Their outrage, which I shared, was framed by the mainstream media's colonial views about girls and women in the Global South.

Although there is no doubt that the shooting was horrific and that Malala, who won the Nobel Peace Prize in 2014, is very brave, it is troubling that Western media primarily focused on religious extremism in Pakistan and the terrible treatment of girls and women in rural areas. Rarely did the coverage link Malala's story to larger issues of gender inequality and gender-based violence that exist around the globe. Rarer still was any discussion of the historic relationships between Pakistan and the countries and organizations that helped to create the very complexities they now criticize. We tend to separate ourselves and our societies from Malala's context instead of working to identify the intersections of sexism, racism, and colonial legacies that connect us to Malala.

Özlem Sensoy and Elizabeth Marshall describe how popular novels about "the plight of the Muslim girl"—*Three Cups of Tea, The Breadwinner*—convey messages that poor, downtrodden girls in the Global South "must harness Western girl power to survive." According to Sensoy and Marshall, the portrayal of mostly dark-skinned girls in the Global South as victims needing to be rescued by the West ignores the vast complexity within the Muslim world and the Global South—as well as the continued existence of gender-based discrimination and violence in North America and Europe. If not taken up critically by educators, these narratives reinforce paternalistic, racist attitudes and a sense of smug satisfaction.

These contradictions were particularly heavy for the young women in my group who were immigrants. They struggled to put positive life changes resulting from moving to Canada into a larger political context. For example, Mihika shared a photograph she took while walking to school in suburban Toronto. The image, shot from the perspective of a person looking down while walking, shows Mihika's right foot taking a step alongside the foot of her friend. Mihika described the photo:

> This is a picture of my friend and me walking home from school. It reminded me that when I was in Sri Lanka, the girls weren't allowed to walk alone. They would go and come back to school with their parents. Whatever they did, they had to have someone with them. Here, we are allowed to do things by ourselves. We have the opportunity to go to school. It's really important to be thankful for where you are. My parents are Sri Lankan and if I were still there, I wouldn't have half the opportunities I do here, like education, opportunities to volunteer, classes, like being here now!

Macy, a 15-year-old of Chinese and Polish heritage, said she was proud to be Canadian because her neighborhood was free of crime. As she described her semi-urban community outside of Toronto as "safe," the other young women challenged her, questioning whether that description was true of their communities, reminding us that we can't generalize about communities, even within one city. When pushed, Macy explained that "compared to other countries, I'm glad to be in Canada and not the Congo, where they treat women very poorly."

Andrea, a 17-year-old Chinese Canadian whose parents moved to Canada when she was young, described how her schooling promoted the idea of gender as a problem elsewhere:

> We talked about gender issues in the context of other countries, which left people to kind of make their own conclusions about Canada. We just talked about sexual slavery and human trafficking—all those issues that prevail in other parts of the world, things outside of Canada. I did my project on sexual slavery and it opened my eyes to prostitution in Canada and the United States.

It is important for educators to provide spaces for young people to analyze these powerful dominant narratives. To avoid falling into the trap of thinking that sexism is only a problem "over there," we must tie these individual stories to larger discussions of power based on gender, race, and colonialism. We also need to connect them to the impact of sexism, racism, and colonialism in our own communities. What are we doing to address the thousands of murdered and missing First Nations women in Canada? How does this connect to Canada's colonial history? What are we doing to address the wage discrepancies between men and women in Canada, which haven't improved since 1970?

In the Past

A second conceptual challenge is the notion that gender inequality is a problem in North America's distant past—that sexism is a historical relic, not something that affects our lives today.

In one of our discussions, the young women reflected on how rarely women and gender came up as issues in their education. Andrea said:

> In class you see the past that women have had, but you don't see the present of women—the things that they are doing right now to move society forward. Because I was interested, I was able to make inferences, search things out, and find out more about Canadian society. Most people just go around living their lives, because Canada—for people who really don't want to look hard—seems like a pretty ideal society.

Mihika said:

> Every time we learn about scientists, poets, artists, whoever, they are always male—because they are recognized more. So for art, it's the

obvious Andy Warhol, Leonardo da Vinci. I never hear about female painters and artists. It's sad. We know that females are capable of being amazing scientists, artists, and poets, but we just don't recognize them. And the more we don't recognize them, the more they are disregarded.

The young women agreed that they wanted more examples of men and women throughout history who defied the dominant assumptions about gender. As Australian scholar Victoria Foster suggests, we cannot just "add women and stir," and expect young people to come away with a deep understanding of how gender continues to shape our society. We cannot portray gender inequality as a problem in the distant past or in distant lands. We must go beyond a list of token female "firsts" so students can critically examine the role gender plays in their lives today.

Girls Versus Boys

The third conceptual trap is pitting boys against girls. One aspect of this relates to gender stereotypes, and this is something that the young women in my group recognized and resisted. For example, Jane brought a picture of a canoe portage at camp to one of our gatherings:

> This is all of us in the middle of a portage at camp. I've always been like the boys, the ones roughing it outside. The stereotype is that girls are prissy and can't break a nail or get dirt on their outfit, and that they don't want to go outside and get their hands dirty. I've always been the kid who likes to run around and hike and swim and dance in the rain. Even though there's less of a divide between boys and girls today, I think the reason some women wouldn't have done it is the pressure to always look perfect and be put together; if you're letting loose you're breaking some big taboo.

But another aspect is the focus on "boys in trouble," as if addressing sexism is what puts young men at risk. In one of my teacher education classes, I described how the young women in my study demonstrated the complex ways in which they continue to be socialized into traditionally feminine roles. A female teacher candidate stood up and said, "You know, honestly, with all this focus on girls, it really makes me worry about the boys."

In the past few decades, educators and researchers have been preoccupied with the perception that boys are "falling behind." *Failing Boys*, a 2010 Canadian report conducted by the popular newspaper, the Globe and Mail, found that, as a group, boys rank behind girls in nearly every measure of scholastic achievement. They earn "lower grades overall in elementary and middle schools. They trail in reading and writing, and 30 percent land in the bottom grades of standardized tests." There are similar reports in the United States and across Europe. In contrast, girls are frequently described as the academic success story of the past decade.

> We must go beyond a list of token female "firsts" so students can critically examine the role gender plays in their lives today.

Although it is important to examine the different ways that girls and boys are being socialized, we need to go beyond simple oppositions. When we focus just on girls' or boys' achievement, we fail to see the role of race, sexuality, culture, and socio-economic status. Instead, we must examine *which* girls are succeeding and *which* boys are falling behind—and why.

The young women note that most of the young people in their advocacy and volunteer work are girls. This raises questions about the messages boys receive about masculinity and their responsibilities as citizens. We need to provide opportunities for young people to unpack hegemonic ideas of masculinity and femininity, so girls can see themselves as powerful—as equals and as leaders—and boys can see themselves as caring and nurturing citizens.

Conclusion

The International Day of the Girl is a day to celebrate, but also a day to critically reflect on what still needs to be done to rid *all* societies from gender-based violence, colonial attitudes, and deep-seated patriarchal ideas. As educators, we must not only consider what we are choosing to raise with our students, but also how we choose to discuss these issues, what we are not discussing, and why. We must, as Peggy McIntosh put it, continuously unpack our invisible knapsacks and examine our own assumptions and expectations.

The stakes are high because we're educating the next generation of activists. As Mihika explained:

> We actually have power over the things that surround us. Whether it's our family or friends, or things in our school, we can make a difference. I learned this as we spoke of our pictures and problems in

our society. Gender inequality still exists and is terrible, but the girls and I were still able to think of ways of solving the issues we noticed. We are girls of many ethnicities and values, but we all believe in a better day, a day of no injustice and hate."

References

Abraham, Carolyn. Oct. 15, 2010. "Part 1: Failing Boys and the Powder Keg of Sexual Politics." *Globe and Mail*.

Foster, Victoria. April 1996. "Gender Equity, Citizenship Education and Inclusive Curriculum: Another Case of 'Add Women and Stir?'" Paper presented at the Annual Conference of the American Educational Research Association, New York.

Jiwani, Yasmin. 2006. "Racialized Violence Girls and Young Women of Color." *Girlhood: Redefining the Limits*. Black Rose Books.

McIntosh, Peggy. 1989. "White Privilege: Unpacking the Invisible Knapsack." *Peace and Freedom*. July-August.

Sensoy, Özlem. and Elizabeth Marshall. 2010. "Missionary Girl Power: Saving the 'Third World' One Girl at a Time." *Gender and Education*: 1–17.

Gayvangelical: Teaching at the Intersection of Religious and Queer

By Jeff Sapp

Jeff Sapp (jeffsapp.com) has been a teacher, writer, and activist for 36 years. He began his career as a middle and high school math and science teacher and is currently professor of education at California State University, Dominguez Hills. Jeff lives in Long Beach with his husband, Sino, and 5-year-old daughter, Helena. They spend their time gardening, renovating a 100-year-old bungalow house, and having lots of conversations about feminism.

A preservice teacher asked to see me after our children's and adolescent literature class one evening. We walked outside to a bench and sat down. She said: "I don't think you should adopt this child. And I don't think you should be with this man. I think you should marry a woman, as God wants you to, and have a child that looks just like you. This is what I am praying for you."

I was shocked. As our class had discussed children's books that portray different ways families are made, I had mentioned that my partner and I had been attending adoption classes. Hearing this student tell me that my partner and I should not open up our hearts and lives to a child was immensely disturbing.

But, by this time in my career, I'd been through experiences like this many times. I consider myself a "gayvangelical." I'm a queer whose early life was shaped by religious fundamentalism. I grew up in evangelicalism and, right out of high school, I went to Jerry Falwell's Liberty Baptist College. It is because of my gayvangelical background that I have found myself regularly in the role of a cultural translator for colleagues who have difficulty negotiating students' religious identities in queer-affirming multicultural education courses.

What happens when some Christians experience an affirming queer curriculum—a curriculum their religious belief system wholeheartedly rejects? How do critical multicultural educators negotiate conflicts around some Christian interpretations of scripture and homosexuality?

I am careful to use the term "some" Christians and not "all" Christians. Like all terms in identity politics, the term "Christian" is politically charged. Not all Christians are homophobic. Some churches are queer-affirming. Some queer people are dedicated to their communities of faith. Yet there are anti-gay communities of faith that use the Bible as their foundation for anti-gay rhetoric. Although similar issues arise in relation to other religions, this article specifically addresses Christians who use their faith and scripture as weapons of homophobia.

The Clobber Passages

One evening, Alison asked if she could speak with me at break. "I'm really uncomfortable with what you just shared."

"What exactly were you uncomfortable with?"

"Well, I'm a Christian and what you just taught us about what the Bible says about homosexuality is different from anything I've ever heard before in my church."

"What was different about it?"

"I've always been taught that homosexuality was a sin. Don't get me wrong. I have lots of gay friends. My best friend is gay. It's just that I've never heard anyone interpret scripture like you just did in class, saying that the Sodom and Gomorrah story isn't about the sin of homosexuality, that it's about the sin of how Christians were inhospitable to others. I don't think that's right."

"Thank you for having the courage to speak with me about your discomfort, Alison. I want to make sure that your discomfort was about the content—a different read of scripture—and that it wasn't about feeling like you needed to convert to my way of seeing things."

"No, no, no, I didn't feel like I had to believe what you were saying . . . and I don't, by the way. But it did make me uncomfortable because I don't remember a professor talking about religion so openly in class before."

"We began this class by acknowledging that talking about race, class, gender, sexual orientation, and other identity issues might invite many of us into places of discomfort. So I'm going to ask that you sit with your discomfort and not try to move beyond it quickly. I think it's OK to be uncomfortable."

Alison wasn't the only Christian in my class experiencing disequilibrium about our discussion. Don asked to speak with me after class that same night.

"Dr. Sapp, that was really interesting to me. I'm a Christian and, well, I don't agree with what you said about Sodom and Gomorrah."

"Thanks for being frank, Don. Remember, I wasn't trying to convert you to my interpretation but only demonstrating how some queer people—myself included—interpret scripture differently."

"Well, I've been told my entire life that Sodom and Gomorrah was about the sin of homosexuality, that the Sodomites of the city wanted to rape the angels that God had sent to see whether or not there were any righteous people left in those two cities."

"I understand, Don, and what I want to mirror back to you is that what you've been told your entire life is a certain interpretation of scripture. I'm asking whether or not you've looked into it yourself or if you've just taken someone else's point of view as your own. What I showed you in class had to do with the original Hebrew, not someone's interpretation. When the Bible says that the 'men' wanted 'to know' the angels, some people have mistranslated that to mean men wanted 'to lie down with' the angels sexually. I've shown you that 'men' more accurately translates as 'all the people' of the city and that 'to know' actually means 'to be acquainted.' There isn't anything sexual about Genesis chapter 19. This mob of people wanted to attack and murder the visitors; it's about the townspeople being inhospitable to the visitors."

"Sorry, Dr. Sapp, but that is *not* how I interpret that scripture. No way. Jesus is condemning homosexuality in Genesis 19."

"I started tonight's class with the speech by Chimamanda Ngozi Adichie on the danger of a single story because that's the main point I wanted to make, that there are different ways to interpret scripture. This is about opening up respectful dialogue, not about converting anyone to a different path."

There are eight passages of scripture that supposedly address homosexuality: Genesis 19:1-5; Leviticus 18:22 and 20:13; Deuteronomy 23:17; I Corinthians 6:9-10; I Timothy 1:9-10; Romans 1:26-27; and Jude 1:6-7. Many in the queer community refer to these eight passages as the "clobber passages" because queer people have been beaten up with them for so long.

At protests for equal rights for queer people, we often see an iconic protest sign that says: "Here is what God says about homosexuality in the Bible: " ." There is nothing in the eight clobber passages that condemns homosexuality. That is the biblical truth. So what's the problem then? I think part of the answer lies in hearing a single narrative about these verses over and over again. If it is all I have heard forever, then it must be true. Also, it is rare to actually study the original Hebrew and Greek of these eight clobber passages. Instead, people usually rely on a preacher to study and interpret scripture for them. Preachers often study commentaries, a single author's series of comments, explanations, and annotations about a text. And if it is a single author's interpretation of scripture, then it comes with that author's bias. And if the author's bias is that "God hates fags," then that is what will be in the commentary.

Affirming Communities of Faith

But it isn't the purpose of this article to look at queer interpretations of these clobber passages. Instead, I'll focus on how teacher educators can respond to those who use these eight clobber passages as weapons of homophobia. The following ideas are strategies I've used over the years to bridge the gap between queer affirmation and people committed to their communities of faith.

Many students are dedicated to their communities of faith. Faith communities are where they have their friends and find comfort, peace, and motivation to live their lives. Even though students who have strong ties to faith communities are a part of our classroom communities, some critical multicultural educators are uncomfortable with religion.

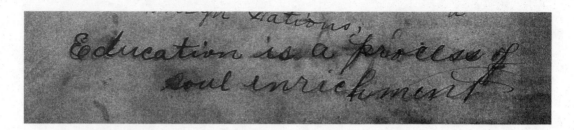

Why would critical multicultural educators *not* want to affirm such rich diversity and bring it into classroom dialogue? How can we include communities of faith as a vibrant part of our multicultural curriculum? As poet Adrienne Rich says: "When someone with the authority of a teacher . . . describes the world and you are not in it, there is a moment of psychic disequilibrium, as if you looked into a mirror and saw nothing."

One way I affirm communities of faith is by drawing on my evangelical Baptist past. I recently spoke to 80 beginning educators in our teaching credential program about the power of reflective practice. I had a colleague count the number of references I made to the spiritual life and communities of faith. She noted that I made more than 20 references to faith, beginning with a question I asked while explaining Howard Gardner's theory of multiple intelligences: "How many of you—like myself—have been drawn to things of the spirit since you were a young child?"

Later in the talk I showed the preservice teachers my grandmother's teacher training materials from 100 years ago, inviting them to mine their own family histories to see what they might discover about the history of our profession. A century ago, my grandmother penned this in her class notebook: "Education is a process of soul enrichment." I mentioned that I still believe that education should be about "soul enrichment"; many students nodded in agreement.

As I walked through school documents from my own childhood, I shared the purple ditto copy of an Easter poem I wrote in 6th grade on the death and resurrection of Jesus. Then I showed a picture of myself as a teenager at summer church camp and mentioned that it was in my community of faith that I first felt that educational settings could be transformational. Many students again nodded in agreement.

And when I introduced the power of metaphor as a tool of teacher reflection I joked: "I already told you that I grew up in the Baptist church so I wasn't allowed to dance as a child, but somehow dance has become the dominant metaphor through which I reflect on my teaching practice. As teachers we are choreographers in the classroom, choreographing the flow of learning that occurs." These types of spiritual and faith references demonstrate that I am faith-friendly and welcome this core piece of students' identities.

Another way I affirm both faith and queerness in multicultural education courses is to introduce students to the websites of LGBTQ people committed to the same community of faith they attend. These websites abound on the internet. Examples, among many, are Gay Christian Network (gaychristian. net), Imaan: LGBTQ Muslim Support Group (imaan.org.uk), Dignity for LGBT Catholics (dignityusa.org), Affirmation for Mormons (affirmation.org), and Jewish LGBT Network (jewishlgbtnetwork.com).

When we discuss philosophies of education, I include holistic education, which asserts that everything is connected; everything is in relationship. Holistic education seeks to educate the body, mind, *and* spirit. I often fold knowledge of this philosophy into coursework as a logical way to include diverse spiritual communities.

Respectful Dialogue

I have a colleague who teaches a required multicultural education credential course who says that he "lashes out in a stern way" at Christians in his class who use the Bible to underpin their homophobia. I believe that anger is not an appropriate response to injustice. I also know—from experience—that heated discussions attempting to convert someone to my point of view are futile. Why would I want to convert you to my thinking regarding the eight clobber passages of scripture? If that were my goal, would I be any different from the Christian who seeks to convert me from my sexual orientation? Conversion battles can become about winning the convert instead of bridging understanding. For me, the goal is respectful dialogue.

For example, in an elementary methods course, I address how to guide elementary students into respectful dialogue. I encourage preservice teachers to try to avoid using the word "but" as it negates others' statements. Instead, we use the word "and" to acknowledge others and add our point of view. Knowing that this is difficult for many students, I have made up a poster of prompts students can use to avoid saying "but:"

- "You're right and this is how I feel/think. . ."
- "That's OK and. . ."
- "That's true for you and what's true for me is something else. . ."
- "That's a really good point and I feel/think differently. . ."

I tell students that because I've had a history of people telling me that I'm going to hell because I'm gay, I often rely on the third statement: "That's true for you and what's true for me is something different."

Another poster I hang in the classroom suggests prompts for probing questions that help suspend judgment:

- "I was curious about what you thought when you said. . ."
- "I was wondering what you thought/felt when you said. . ."
- "Can you tell me more about what you meant when you said. . ."

I also try to model respectful dialogue in meaningful ways. After our discussion at break, I asked Alison if she would be comfortable having the same conversation in front of the class as a model of how we can disagree with grace. She quickly agreed. It was a powerful experience. The majority of my class belonged to communities of faith and I think they appreciated our open-mindedness and courage in dialoguing about difficult topics. I think it's important to show pre-service teachers how we can discuss controversial topics with each other without coming to agreement.

For me, the goal is respectful dialogue.

In addition to practicing dialogue with each other, I invite speakers who are both queer and spiritual and let them speak for themselves. One of my former students speaks as an ordained minister and heterosexual ally. I also invite a person who is Navajo, who speaks about "two-spirit" people. Other religious leaders round out the panel, some affirming of queer people and others who believe homosexuality is a sin but choose love rather than judgment. Students hear how people of faith—even those who disagree with homosexuality—engage in respectful dialogue. The documentary *Fish Out of Water*, which explores homosexuality and the Bible, also provides useful dialogue models.

Great pieces of literature can also open reflection and dialogue. One of my favorite quotes is from Rainer Maria Rilke:

> I want to ask you, as clearly as I can, to bear with patience all that is
> unresolved in your heart, and try to love the questions themselves,
> as if they were rooms yet to enter or books written in a foreign
> language. Don't dig for answers that can't be given you yet—because
> you would not be able to live them now. For everything must be
> lived. Live the questions now; perhaps then, someday, you will gradually, without noticing, live into the answer.

I emailed this piece to Alison the day after she spoke to me of her discomfort.

Teachable Moments

A principal in Tennessee made national headlines after she told her high school student body that if they were gay they were going to hell and if they were pregnant their lives were over. Unfortunately, there are always plenty of horrible examples to bring to students to discuss. What would they do if this hate happened on their campus? What are ways they can peacefully respond to hate? Do our elementary and high school students know their rights and what actions they can take if they hear hate speech from the adults in their school and community?

During discussions on classroom management, beginning teachers often bring up stories about students' inappropriate language. I've developed a "Stand Up!" assignment that asks teachers to anticipate inappropriate student speech and come up with a plan to address it. Students often admit they hadn't thought of speaking up for children who are called names or bullied. This assignment helps preservice teachers respond to the teachable moments that arise in their own classrooms.

For example, one preservice teacher decided to work with the inappropriate statement "Shut up, faggot!" and listed these possible responses:

- Discuss the meaning of homophobic words. Sometimes younger students have no idea what they mean.
- Talk about the welcoming and safe classroom community we are trying to create.
- Give students a response to being called a "faggot" when they are walking with a friend of the same sex: "We like each other and for your information, we're not gay."
- Analyze and discuss song lyrics (e.g., the music of Holly Near).
- Invite guest speakers.
- Discuss gender expectations.

Another way I work to harness teachable moments is to acknowledge aspects of identities that are often silenced or erased. A wonderful classroom poster says: "Unfortunately, history has set the record a little too straight." It shows the photographs of 10 famous men and women throughout history who were gay or lesbian. So many people in the history and English canons were queer—James Baldwin, Willa Cather, Eleanor Roosevelt, Walt Whitman, Virginia Woolf.

Our Responsibilities

As teacher educators—and specifically as critical multicultural educators—we promote and model teachers as reflectors. In *The Courage to Teach*, Parker J. Palmer says:

> The question we most commonly ask is the 'what' question—'What subjects shall we teach?' When the conversation goes a bit deeper, we ask the 'how' question—What methods and techniques are required to teach well?' Occasionally, when it goes deeper still, we ask the 'why' question—'For what purpose and to what ends do we teach?' But seldom, if ever, do we ask the 'who' question—'Who is the self that teaches? How does the quality of my selfhood form—or deform—the way I relate to my students, my subject, my colleagues, my world?'

We all carry bias within us and becoming a serious student of ourselves—confronting our often hidden bias—is a cornerstone of great teaching; we need to model and remind students of this.

I find a common ground: love.

Another way I bring up our responsibilities as educators is by discussing legislation. Some states, like California, have laws that mandate educators to make schools safe for all children. AB 537, the California Student Safety and Violence Prevention Act of 2000, changed California's Education Code by adding actual or perceived sexual orientation and gender identity to the existing nondiscrimination policy. This provides an opportunity to discuss bias with educators who resist affirming queer children in their classes because it expands the conversation to "actual or perceived sexual orientation." The discussion reminds us that heterosexuals who don't fit narrow definitions of gender expression can also be targets of homophobia and that ending homophobia and discrimination is crucial for *all* people.

And I try to model responsibility by holding students accountable for the things they say. One of the most irritating things I hear from students who tell me I am doomed to hell because I am gay is "It isn't *me* saying this, it's God." I respond: "No way! You are the one speaking and delivering this violence to me and I am holding you 100 percent responsible. I invite you to consider if this is really what you want to communicate to me."

Finding Common Ground

In my gayvengelical role as translator between religious fundamentalism and critical multicultural education, I find a common ground: love. Christians are usually familiar with the biblical passage: "And now these three things remain: faith, hope, and love. But the greatest of these is love" (I Corinthians 13:13). Love as a fundamental principle also resonates with students who practice other faiths.

As Freire states: "Dialogue cannot exist . . . in the absence of a profound love for the world and for people. The naming of the world, which is an act of creation and re-creation, is not possible if it is not infused with love. Love is at the same time the foundation of dialogue and dialogue itself." Love demands that we honor people whose points of view are different from our own. It demands equity, justice, and respect.

GLOSSARY

By Annika Butler-Wall

Annika Butler-Wall is an editor of *Rethinking Sexism, Gender, and Sexuality* and an editorial intern at Rethinking Schools.

"When we become acutely, disturbingly aware of the language we are using and that is using us, we begin to grasp a material resource that women have never before collectively attempted to repossess."

—*Adrienne Rich*

Introduction

I t is hardly shocking that, as editors, we believe language is important. What is shocking, however, is how quickly accusations of "political correctness" or "word policing" can shut down discussions about what language means and why and how we use it. How many of us as children were told to soothe our hurts with the adage "sticks and stones may break my bones, but words will never hurt me"? Words can hurt, but words can also heal, empower, and fight back.

As socially just educators, we need to counter the anti-PC backlash by opening up conversations about how language functions and why we should care about it. Words do matter, especially in periods of perceived tolerance. Celebrities like Beyoncé have introduced the concept of feminism to millions of fans; we need to push the conversation toward intersectionality. What does feminism mean if African American women still make 68.1 cents to every white male dollar and Latinas make 61.2, while white women make 78? Caitlyn Jenner put the T of LGBTQ on the cover of *Vanity Fair*, but we need to ask why 72 percent of all LGBTQ homicide victims are trans women, and 67 percent are trans women of color. The Marriage Equality Act has legalized the partnerships of same-sex couples across the country, but we need to look at other, less visible people in the LGBTQ community who are facing workplace discrimination, challenges accessing healthcare, and disproportionately high rates of incarceration, police harassment, and homelessness. Understanding the specificity of different terms helps de-homogenize the LGBTQ movement and make visible how structures of oppression function differently based on factors like age, race, class, and ability.

Language is constantly changing. We recognize that many of our readers may contest our definitions or see others that are missing. Many of the terms listed could be (and surely are) the subjects of doctoral theses. Our goal, however, is to provide a resource to help guide readers unfamiliar with some of the language used by the authors in *Rethinking Sexism, Gender, and Sexuality*. Think of this glossary as an invitation to dialogue rather than a definitive guide.

Most importantly, many people have strong personal and political reasons for using or not using certain terms to describe themselves. Their right to self-determination should always be respected.

Looking back at the history of the term "queer" from its historically derogatory use to its reclaimed position at the front of a political movement, it is hard not to see the power of language to change the world we live in. Adrienne Rich, writing in the heart of the second-wave feminist movement, described how "the commonest words are having to be sifted through, rejected, laid aside for a long time, or turned to the light for new colors and flashes of meaning: *power, love, control, violence, political, personal, private, friendship, community, sexual, work, pain, pleasure, self, integrity.*" That was 1977. Today, these words have evolved and others have been added to the mix. The constantly changing nature of language can cause anxiety. Faced with a new word, we struggle with when to use it, how to use it, and fear that we may use it incorrectly. Let's embrace our discomfort. You never know which words might start a revolution.

AGENDER: People who are agender don't identify as female or male. They see themselves as outside the gender binary.

CISGENDER: A person whose gender identity, gender expression, and biological sex all align with what they were assigned at birth (e.g., man, masculine, and male). Most cisgender people do not have to worry about being mistaken for a gender they do not identify with and benefit from cisgender privilege. One example of cisgender privilege is using public restrooms without fear of harassment.

FEMINISM: According to bell hooks in *Feminist Theory: From Margin to Center*: "Feminism is not simply a struggle to end male chauvinism or a movement to ensure that women will have equal rights with men; it is a commitment to eradicating the ideology of domination that permeates Western culture on various levels—sex, race, and class, to name a few—and a commitment to reorganizing society . . . so that the self-development of people can take precedence over imperialism, expansion, and material desires." (See the introduction in Chapter 1 for more on the definition of feminism.)

GAY: Most often used to describe men who are attracted to other men, gay can also refer to women who are attracted to other women or as an umbrella term for all same-sex relationships.

GENDER: The complex interrelationship between an individual's sex; internal sense of self as male, female, both, or neither; and outward presentation and behavior. Gender is also a social construct that categorizes people, assigns characteristics to those categories, and places values on those characteristics. Like other social constructs (e.g., race), gender is reinforced by society in many ways. Practically everything in society is assigned a gender—toys, colors, clothes, and acceptable behavior are some of the more obvious examples.

GENDER BINARY: The idea that there are only two distinct genders: female and male, woman and man, girl and boy. Often these are treated as opposites.

GENDER CONTINUUM/SPECTRUM: The idea that gender is not binary and that individuals may fall anywhere on a feminine/androgynous/masculine spectrum.

GENDER EXPRESSION: How we communicate our gender to others—through clothes, hairstyle, mannerisms, speech patterns, body language, social interactions, choice of activities, etc. Gender expression is usually the basis for the assumptions we make about the gender of others.

GENDER FLUID/GENDER EXPANSIVE/GENDER CREATIVE: Umbrella terms for individuals who broaden commonly held definitions of gender. Some individuals do not identify as either male or female; others identify as a blend of both. Still others identify with a gender, but express their gender in ways that differ from stereotypical presentations.

GENDER IDENTITY: One's internal, deeply felt sense of being girl/woman, boy/man, both, somewhere in between, or outside these categories.

GENDER INDEPENDENT/GENDER NONCONFORMING: A person with gender characteristics and/or behaviors that do not conform to traditional or societal expectations of their biological sex. Gender independent/nonconforming people may or may not identify as transgender, lesbian, gay, or queer. Gender nonconformity does not determine sexual orientation.

GENDERQUEER: People who identify outside of the male-female binary.

GENDER ROLES: Socially constructed and culturally specific behaviors—including educational expectations, access to political power, clothing and hairstyles, communication styles, careers, and family roles—imposed on people based on their biological sex assigned at birth. Gender interpretations and expectations vary widely among cultures and often change over time.

GENDER TRANSITION: The journey from living as one gender to living and identifying as another. To affirm their gender identity, people may go through different types of transitions. Social transition can include changes in name, pronouns, and clothing. Medical transition includes hormone replacement therapy. Surgical transition modifies the body to remove or add gender-related physical traits. It is a very individual process.

HETERONORMATIVE: The expectation that all individuals are heterosexuals, that heterosexuality is the "norm," and that all children will grow up to be "straight." For example, a permission form that asks for the signature of the mother and father is based on a heteronormative concept of family.

INTERSECTIONALITY: This term, developed by Kimberlé Crenshaw, acknowledges that it is not possible to tease apart the oppressions that people experience. Racism for women of color cannot be separated from the oppression they face as women. A trans person with a disability cannot choose which part of their identity is most in need of liberation. Intersectionality is a framework for social justice work. (excerpted from Uwujaren and Utt).

INTERSEX: People who are born with chromosomes, hormones, genitalia, and/or other sex characteristics that are not exclusively male or female.

LESBIAN: A woman or female-identified person who is attracted to other women or female-identified persons.

LGBTQ: Acronym for lesbian, gay, bisexual, transsexual, and queer.

MISOGYNY: The belief that maleness and masculinity are superior to female-ness and femininity; fear or hatred of women.

PATRIARCHY: A social system organized around male power.

QUEER: An umbrella term for people who do not conform to heterosexual and/or gender binary norms. Originally a derogatory slur, queer is a word that has been reclaimed.

SEX: The external genitalia, sex chromosomes, hormones, and internal reproductive structures that are used to assign an infant as male or female at birth. Also referred to as biological sex, anatomical sex, or assigned birth sex. Traditionally, gender is thought of as the social component of biological sex—in a binary system, those with anatomical, chromosomal, and hormonal male indicators are men and those with female indicators are women. Even with a more expansive definition, biological sex is often seen as the fixed component with which one's gender might or might not align. However, researchers are realizing that biological sex is not necessarily a binary or clear cut.

SEXUAL ORIENTATION: Who an individual is attracted to—physically, romantically, or emotionally. The continuum ranges from people who are only attracted to those of another gender (heterosexual or straight), to both or all genders (bisexual), to others regardless of their gender identity or biological sex (pansexual or omnisexual), and to only the same gender (lesbian or gay).

STRAIGHT: Slang word for heterosexual.

TRANSGENDER: Describes a wide range of people whose gender identity and/or expression differs from conventional expectations based on their assigned biological birth sex. Susan Stryker defines transgender in the introduction to the *Transgender Studies Reader*: "What began as a buzzword of the early 1990s has established itself as a term of choice, in both popular parlance and a variety of specialist discourses, for a wide range of phenomena that call attention to the fact that 'gender,' as it is lived, embodied, experienced, performed, and encountered, is more complex and varied than can be accounted for by the currently dominant binary sex/gender ideology of Eurocentric modernity."

TRANSSEXUAL: A person who seeks to live in a gender different from the one assigned at birth.

TRANS MAN/TRANS BOY/AFFIRMED MALE: A person who was assigned female at birth but who has a male gender identity. (Note: trans man, not transman.) This is considered more accurate and respectful than female-to-male or FTM.

TRANS WOMAN/TRANS GIRL/ AFFIRMED FEMALE: A person who was assigned male at birth but has a female gender identity. (Note: trans woman, not transwoman.) This is considered more accurate and respectful than male-to-female or MTF.

Sources

Gender Spectrum. "Understanding Gender." genderspectrum.org/quick-links/ understanding-gender.

hooks, bell. 1984. *Feminist Theory: From Margin to Center*. South End Press.

Qmunity. 2013. "Queer Terminology from A to Q." qmunity.ca/wp-content/ uploads/2015/03/Queer_Terminology_Web_Version__Sept_2013__Cover_and_pages_.pdf.

Serano, Julia. 2007. *Whipping Girl: A Transsexual Woman on Sexism and the Scapegoating of Femininity*. Seal Press.

Stryker, Susan, and Stephen Whittle. 2006. *The Transgender Studies Reader*. Routledge.

TransActive Gender Center. "Transgender Spectrum-Related Vocabulary, Slang, and Terminology." transactiveonline.org/resources/guides/terminology.php.

Uwujaren, Jarune, and Jamie Utt. 2015. "Why Our Feminism Must Be Intersectional." everydayfeminism.com.

Welcoming Schools. "A Few Definitions for Educators and Parents/Guardians." welcomingschools.org/pages/a-few-definitions-for-educators-and-parents-guardians.

ADDITIONAL RESOURCES

COMPILED BY JEFF SAPP

W e asked our authors and editors to recommend a few resources—texts that have shaped our thinking on sexism, gender, and sexuality. This list isn't comprehensive by any means, but we hope it provides ideas for broadening perspectives and exciting reading for students of all ages. At the end, we've included additional resources from librarians.

Curtis Acosta recommends:

Chang, Jeff. 2006. *Total Chaos: The Art and Aesthetics of Hip-Hop.* Basic Civitas Books.

Robert Bittner recommends:

Butler, Judith. 1990. *Gender Trouble: Feminism and the Subversion of Identity.* Routledge.

Naidoo, Jamie Campbell. 2012. *Rainbow Family Collections: Selecting and Using Children's Books with Lesbian, Gay, Bisexual, Transgender, and Queer Content.* Libraries Unlimited.

Savin-Williams, Ritch C. 2006. *The New Gay Teenager.* Harvard University Press.

Teich, Nicholas M. 2012. *Transgender 101: A Simple Guide to a Complex Issue.* Columbia University Press.

Annika Butler-Wall recommends:

Anzaldúa, Gloria. 1987. *Borderlands/La Frontera: The New Mestiza.* Aunt Lute Books.

Foucault, Michel. 1978. *History of Sexuality Vol. 1: An Introduction.* Vintage Books.

Puar, Jasbir. 2007. *Terrorist Assemblages: Homonationalism in Queer Times*. Duke University Press Books.

Rubin, Gayle. 2011. *Deviations: A Gayle Rubin Reader*. Duke University Press Books.

Somerville, Siobhan B. 2000. *Queering the Color Line: Race and the Invention of Homosexuality in American Culture*. Duke University Press.

Warner, Michael. 1993. *Fear of a Queer Planet: Queer Politics and Social Theory*. University of Minnesota Press.

Kim Cosier recommends:

Bornstein, Kate. 1994. *Gender Outlaw: On Men, Women, and the Rest of Us*. Routledge.

Butler, Judith. 2004. *Undoing Gender*. Routledge.

Faderman, Lillian. 1991. *Odd Girls and Twilight Lovers: A History of Lesbian Life in 20th-Century America*. Penguin Books.

Feinberg, Leslie. 1993. *Stone Butch Blues*. Firebrand Books

Halberstam, Judith. 1998. *Female Masculinity*. Duke University Press

Smith, Rachelle Lee. 2014. *Speaking OUT: Queer Youth in Focus*. PM Press.

Kimberley Gilles recommends:

Kaufman, Moises. 1998. *Gross Indecency: The Three Trials of Oscar Wilde*. Vintage.

Levithan, David. 2005. *Boy Meets Boy*. Alfred A. Knopf.

T. Elijah Hawkes recommends:

Hardy, Kenneth V., and Tracey A. Laszloffy. 2006. *Teens Who Hurt: Clinical Interventions to Break the Cycle of Adolescent Violence*. The Guilford Press.

Kay, Philip, Andrea Estepa, and Al Desetta, eds. 1998. *Things Get Hectic: Teens Write About the Violence that Surrounds Them*. Youth Communications.

Sudie Hofmann recommends:

Bloom, Lisa. 2013. *Swagger: 10 Urgent Rules for Raising Boys in an Era of Failing Schools, Mass Joblessness, and Thug Culture.* CreateSpace Publishing.

Brown, Christia Spears. 2014. *Parenting Beyond Pink and Blue: How to Raise Your Kids Free of Gender Stereotypes.* Ten Speed Press.

Geena Davis Institute on Gender in Media. seejane.org.

GoldieBlox. goldieblox.com.

Let Toys Be Toys. lettoysbetoys.org.uk.

Levin, Diane, and Jean Kilbourne. 2008. *So Sexy So Soon: The New Sexualized Childhood and What Parents Can Do to Protect Their Kids.* Ballantine.

Powered By Girl: The Online Magazine for Girls by Girls. poweredbygirl.org.

Princess Free Zone. princessfreezone.com.

The Representation Project. therepresentationproject.org.

Strauss, Susan L. 2011. *Sexual Harassment and Bullying: A Guide to Keeping Kids Safe and Holding Schools Accountable.* Rowman & Littlefield Publishers.

Wardy, Melissa Atkins. 2014. *Redefining Girly: How Parents Can Fight the Stereotyping and Sexualizing of Girlhood, from Birth to Tween.* Chicago Review Press.

Maiya Jackson recommends:

Gender Spectrum. genderspectrum.org.

GLSEN Transgender Awareness Week Resources. glsen.org/tdor.

The Youth and Gender Media Project. youthandgendermediaproject.org.

A. J. Jennings recommends:

Brill, Stephanie, and Rachel Pepper. 2008. *The Transgender Child: A Handbook for Families and Professionals.* Cleis Press.

Chrisman, Kent, and Donna Couchenour. 2002. *Healthy Sexuality Development: A Guide for Early Childhood Educators and Families.* National Association for the Education of Young Children.

Ehrensaft, Diane. 2011. *Gender Born, Gender Made: Raising Healthy Gender-Nonconforming Children.* The Experiment Publishing.

Evans, Kate. 2002. *Negotiating the Self: Identity, Sexuality, and Emotion in Learning to Teach.* Routledge.

Abby Kindelsperger recommends:

Christensen, Linda. 2000. *Reading, Writing, and Rising Up: Teaching About Social Justice and the Power of the Written Word.* Rethinking Schools.

Michie, Gregory. 1999. *Holler if You Hear Me: The Education of a Teacher and His Students.* Teachers College Press.

Weinstein, Susan. 2009. *Feel These Words: Writing in the Lives of Urban Youth.* State University of New York Press.

Kathleen Melville recommends:

Bulllied. 2010. Southern Poverty Law Center.

No Dumb Questions. 2001. Dir. Melissa Regan. New Day Films.

Nancy Niemi recommends:

It's Elementary: Talking About Gay Issues in Schools. 1999. Dir. Debra Chasnoff and Helena Cohen. Groundspark.

It's Still Elementary. 2008. Dir. Debra Chasnoff and Johnny Symons. Groundspark.

Meyer, Elizabeth. 2009. *Gender, Bullying, and Harassment: Strategies to End Sexism and Homophobia in Schools.* Teachers College Press.

Margot Pepper recommends:

Clarke, Jess, ed. *Race, Poverty and the Environment*. reimaginerpe.org.

Jody Polleck recommends:

Bass, Ellen, and Kate Kaufman. 1996. *Free Your Mind: The Book for Gay, Lesbian, and Bisexual Youth and Their Allies*. Harper Perennial.

"GayYA: LGBTQIA+ Characters in Young Adult Literature." gayya.org.

Jeff Sapp recommends:

Day, Frances Ann. 2000. *Lesbian and Gay Voices: An Annotated Bibliography and Guide to Literature for Children and Young Adults*. Greenwood Press.

hooks, bell. 2004. *The Will to Change: Men, Masculinity, and Love*. Atria Books.

Pharr, Suzanne. 1988. *Homophobia: A Weapon of Sexism*. Chardon Press.

Rofes, Eric. 2005. *A Radical Rethinking of Sexuality and Schooling: Status Quo or Status Queer?* Rowman & Littlefield Publishers.

Vaccaro, Annemarie, Gerri August, and Megan S. Kennedy. 2011. *Safe Spaces: Making Schools and Communities Welcoming to LGBT Youth*. Praeger.

Straightlaced: How Gender's Got Us All Tied Up. 2009. Dir. Debra Chasnoff. Groundspark.

Stephanie Anne Shelton recommends:

Blackburn, Mollie V. 2011. *Interrupting Hate: Homophobia in Schools and What Literacy Can Do About It*. Teachers College Press.

Mayo, Cris. 2013. *LGBTQ Youth and Education: Policies and Practices*. Teachers College Press.

Jody Sokolower recommends:

Coville, Bruce. 1995. "Am I Blue?" in Bauer, Marion Dane. *Am I Blue?: Coming Out from the Silence*. Harper Teen.

Giddings, Paula. 2007. *When and Where I Enter: The Impact of Black Women on Race and Sex in America*. William Morrow Paperbacks.

hooks, bell. 1994. *Teaching to Transgress: Education as the Practice of Freedom*. Routledge.

hooks, bell. 1984. *Feminist Theory: From Margin to Center*. South End Press.

Marshall, Paule. 1959. *Brown Girl, Brownstones*. Random House.

Moraga, Cherríe, and Gloria Anzaldúa, eds. 1981. *This Bridge Called My Back: Writings by Radical Women of Color*. Persephone Press.

Randall, Margaret. 1999. *Gathering Rage: The Failure of 20th Century Revolutions to Develop a Feminist Agenda*. Monthly Review Press.

Serano, Julia. 2007. *Whipping Girl: A Transsexual Woman on Sexism and the Scapegoating of Femininity*. Seal Press.

Walker, Alice. 1982. *The Color Purple*. Harcourt Brace Jovanovich.

Woodson, Jacqueline. 2014. *Brown Girl Dreaming*. Penguin Group.

Woodson, Jacqueline. 1995. *From the Notebooks of Melanin Sun*. Puffin.

Sam C. Stiegler recommends:

Bornstein, Kate. 1997. *My Gender Workbook: How to Become a Real Man, a Real Woman, the Real You, or Something Else Entirely*. Routledge.

Melissa Bollow Tempel recommends:

Bollinger, Michele. 2012. *101 Changemakers: Rebels and Radicals Who Changed U.S. History*. Haymarket Books.

Creighton, Allan, and Paul Kivel. 2011. *Helping Teens Stop Violence, Build Community, and Stand for Justice*. Hunter House.

de Haan, Linda, and Stern Nijland. 2003. *King and King*. Tricycle Press.

dePaola, Tomie. 1979. *Oliver Button Is a Sissy*. HMH Books for Young Readers.

Howe, James. *Pinky and Rex Series*. Simon Spotlight.

Kuklin, Susan. 2015. *Beyond Magenta: Transgender Teens Speak Out*. Candlewick.

Newman, Lesléa. 2007. *The Boy Who Cried Fabulous*. Tricycle Press.

New Moon Girls Magazine. newmoon.com.

Polacco, Patricia. 2009. *In Our Mothers' House*. Philomel Books.

Willhoite, Michael. 1990. *Daddy's Roommate*. Alyson Books.

Willhoite, Michael. 2000. *Daddy's Wedding*. Alyson Books.

Yulo, Michele. 2011. *Super Tool Lula: The Bully-fighting Super Hero*. BookLogix Publishing Services.

Zolotow, Charlotte. 1985. *William's Doll*. Harper & Row.

Tracy Wagner recommends:

Colombo, Gary, Robert Cullen, and Bonnie Lisle. 2007. *Rereading America: Cultural Contexts for Critical Thinking and Writing*. Bedford-St. Martin's.

Helms, Janet E. 1992. *A Race Is a Nice Thing to Have: A Guide to Being a White Person or Understanding the White Persons in your Life*. Content Communications.

Jay Weber recommends:

Gould, Lois. 1978. *The Story of X*. Daughters Publishing Company.

Hannigan, Katherine. 2011. *True (. . . Sort of)*. Greenwillow Books.

Don't Forget to Ask Your Librarian

We can't possibly provide you with all of the resources that are available when it comes to sexism, gender, and sexuality. We did, though, ask Andrea Cosier, head of youth services at Manistee County Library in Michigan, which books she and her colleagues would recommend. You might consider asking your librarian the same thing. Book recommendations are what librarians live for, and they'll be excited to show you a great selection of books. Also, asking them about books on sexism, gender, and sexuality will focus their eyes on current and new resources so that your school library will be better equipped to answer the many questions that students have about these important topics.

Picture Books

Morris Micklewhite and the Tangerine Dress by Christine Baldacchino
Ruby's Wish by Shirin Yim Bridges
Meet Polkadot by Talcott Broadhead
Do Princesses Wear Hiking Boots? by Carmela LaVigna Coyle
Jacob's New Dress by Sarah and Ian Hoffman
I Am Jazz by Jessica Herthel and Jazz Jennings
My Princess Boy by Cheryl Kilodavis
A Girl Named Dan by Dandi Daley Mackall
Sleeping Bobby by Mary Pope Osborne and Will Osborne
William's Doll by Charlotte Zolotow

Juvenile

The Accidental Adventure of India McAllister by Charlotte Agell
No Castles Here by A. C. E. Bauer
Better Nate than Ever by Tim Federle
My Mixed-Up Berry Blue Summer by Jennifer Gennari
Princess Academy by Shannon Hale
The Misfits and *Totally Joe* by James Howe
The Evolution of Calpurnia Tate by Jacqueline Kelly
The Misadventures of the Family Fletcher by Dana Alison Levy
Gracefully Grayson by Ami Polonsky

Teen

I Am J by Cris Beam
Beauty Queens by Libba Bray
Someday This Pain Will Be Useful to You by Peter Cameron
Beautiful Music for Ugly Children by Kirstin Cronn-Mills
The Miseducation of Cameron Post by Emily M. Danforth
If You Could Be Mine by Sara Farizan
Sister Mischief by Laura Goode
Will Grayson, Will Grayson by John Green and David Levithan
Two Boys Kissing by David Levithan
Ash by Malinda Lo
Huntress by Malinda Lo
Hidden by Donna Jo Napoli
Tomboy: A Graphic Memoir by Liz Prince
Aristotle and Dante Discover the Secrets of the Universe by Benjamin Alire Saenz

Award Winners

Amelia Bloomer Project: ameliabloomer.wordpress.com
The Rainbow List: glbtrt.ala.org/rainbowbooks/rainbow-books-lists
Stonewall Book Awards: ala.org/glbtrt/award

Resource Sites

A Mighty Girl: amightygirl.com/books
Rad Books for Rad Kids: radbooksradkids.wordpress.com

INDEX

Note: Page numbers in italics indicate illustrations.

C

Empire of Illusion (Hedges), 171–172

"Encoding/Decoding" (Hall), 171

entertainment media, 370

equality, 27–36. *See also* marriage equality
   building coalition/community/conversation, 31–33
   gender inequality, 429–433
   leaving no one behind, 33–34
   and liberation, 30–31
   pioneers of, 28–29
   progress narratives about, 27–28
   "queer," use of, 29–30
   rising up, 34–36
   trans/gay resistance to being criminalized, 29
   for women/girls, progress on, 429–430

Erikson, Erik, 151

Espelage, Dorothy, 47

Espinosa, Lisa, 82–90

Ethical Culture Fieldston (New York City), 212

ethnic studies, 297–298

evangelicalism, 436

Every Breath We Drew (Dugan), 398

Everything You Always Wanted to Know About Sex (Allen), 152

Ewert, Marcus: *10,000 Dresses*, 137, *137*, 139, 424–428, *425*

F

Fabbre, Vanessa, *400*, 401

Failing Boys, 433

Fair, Molly, *32*

The Fairer Sex, 87

Fairness, 338–341

faith communities, affirming, 438–440

Falwell, Jerry, 436

Families (Kuklin), 41–42, 128–129

Family Diversity Projects, 349–350

family history writing project, 409

Farley, Olive, *22*, *123*

fears, exploited, 186–187

feminism, 445
   critiques of, 69
   defined, 13–14, 446
   early, 200 (*see also* Women's Rights Convention)
   feminist clubs in high schools, 303
   on history, 20
   perceptions of feminists, 84

Feminism Is for Everybody (hooks), 86

Feminist Majority, 334

Feminist Theory: From Margin to Center (hooks), 13, 446

feminized literature, 69

figure–ground reversal, 222

The First Part Last (Johnson), 259, 261

"First They Came" (Niemöller), 419

Fish Out of Water, 441

"Five Ways to Address Gay Issues in the Classroom" (Chasnoff), 422

Fleischman, Karl, 22, 24

Fleischman, Sasha, 22, 26

Flores, David, *363*

fluidity vs. binary thinking, 15–16, 98, 447

Fluke, Sandra, 17

Ford, Ezell, 363

Foresta, Carol Michaels, 92–96

Foster, Victoria, 433

Foundations of Leadership, 354

Fox News, 260

Francis, Shereese, 363

Freire, Paulo, 83, 255, 443

From the Notebooks of Melanin Sun (Woodson), 287–289, 366

The Front Runner (Warren), 122

Fruitvale Station (Coogler), 168–169

"Fuck You Lucy" (Atmosphere), 179–180

G

Game of Thrones, 27

Gao, Deanna, 119–120

Garber, Elizabeth: "Teaching About Gender Issues in the Art Education Classroom," 374–375

García, Ramón: "La Llorona: Our Lady of Deformities," 178

Gardner, Howard, 439

Garner, Eric, 363

gay, defined, 446

Gay, Lesbian & Straight Education Network. *See* GLSEN

Gay, Lesbian, or Whatever (GLOW), 341

Gay Christian Network, 440

Gay Community News, 30

Gay Liberation Front, 35

gay liberation movement, 267

gay rights in the military, 14, 31

Gay-Straight Alliance (GSA), 33, 48, 99, 188, 269, 271, 279–280, 303, 351–355

Gay Sunshine: A Newspaper of Gay Liberation, 30–31

"gay" used as an insult, 40, 278, 293, 298, 338

gender. *See also* sexism; transgender people
    bias in early elementary literature, 66–67
    collaborating with a student on a teaching unit, 73–80
    defined, 15, 446
    double standards in families, 82–83
    expression of, 447
    feminized literature, 69
    fluid approach to, 15
    gender binary, 15–16, 446–447
    gender boxes that don't fit, 97–101
    gender fluid/gender expansive/gender creative, 447
    gender independence/gender nonconformity, 447
    gender inequality, 429–433
    gender-neutral pronouns, 42
    genderqueer, 447
    gender transition, 447
    gender independence, defined, 59
    gender-independent children, bias against, 101
    gender-independent children, supporting, 56–62, 101–102
    getting comfortable teaching about, 132–133, 135
    lesbian mom and teacher's perspective, 100–102
    media images of girls/women, 87
    New Diagram of Sex and Gender, 212–213, 316
    as performance, 374–375
    photographs used to rethink, *397,* 397–407, *399–400, 403–404*
    primary-school training on, 58–59
    and race/media, intersections of, 168–174
    resources for studying, 86–87
    roles, 447
    self-identifying, 303, 305–309
    and sexuality, in a 5th-grade curriculum, 130–135
    vs. sexuality, 151, 215, 285, 426–427
    Shakespeare used to teach gender diversity, 211–216
    stereotypes, 42, 58–59, 63–65, 80, 84–86, 136, 194 (*see also* sexism)
    women's portrayal in literature, 146
    woven into the curriculum, 287–289

Gender Blender, 284–285

gender identity disorder, 343. *See also* transgender people

Gender JUST, 303

generative themes, 255

Gerber, Henry, 30

Gesuden, Liza, 168–174

Gibbs, Brian C., 185–191

Gilles, Kimberley, *217,* 217–224, 452

Gillespie, Peggy, 350

Gilmore, Ruth Wilson, 17

Ginsberg, Allen, 34

"Girl" (Kincaid), 86

Girl Rising, 430

girls. *See* Muslim girls; women/girls

GLOW (Gay, Lesbian, or Whatever), 341

GLSEN (Gay, Lesbian & Straight Education Network), 48, 101, 303, 316, 341

Godner, Deborah, 192–196

Goldberg, Natalie, 409, 411

GoldieBlox, 388

Goldman, Emma, 186–189

Gonzalez, Jose, 179

Gonzalez, Lidia, 278–283

Gould, Lois
    "The Story of X," 63
    X: A Fabulous Child's Story, 386, 424

graduation preparation, 237

graffiti, 271, 297, 338

Grant, Joanne, 20

Grant, Oscar, 168–169

grassroots movements, 48

Grauert, Christiane, *126, 211*

The Great Big Book of Families (Hoffman), 41

Great Books Foundation, 66, 68–69

Green Acres school (Maryland), 345–350

Greene, Maxine, 124, 218

Grimké, Sarah and Angelina, 205

Groundwood Books, 329

Growing Up: Teaching Sexual Health, 133

GSA. *See* Gay-Straight Alliance

GSAFE (Wisconsin), 354, 357, 362

#GSAs4Justice, 352

Guadalupe Hidalgo, Treaty of, 206

Gula, Sharbat, 330

as dropouts, 353
in foster care, 353
gym class/locker room issues for, 306, 357
harassment of, 351
homeless, 353
isolation of, 12
in the juvenile justice system, 353
outing by schools, laws against, 353
police engagement with, 355
schools as unsafe for, 23
Southern attitudes toward gay people, 111–112
suicide by, 351, 370, 416
support for, 116–117
violence against, 217–224, 286

liberation and equality, 30–31

Liberty Baptist College, 436

life stages, 151

Limbaugh, Rush, 17

"Lindo y Querido" (Muñoz), 178

The Lion King, 372, 375–377, 379

Locked Up & Out (Ware), 238

A Long Way Gone, 142–143

Lorde, Audre, 30, 35

Loredo, Jeydon, 26

Los Angeles Times, 388

Los Angeles Unified School District (LAUSD), 123

love, 443

"Love and Appreciate" (Murs), 179–180

love and marriage, 50–55

Lucas, Demetria, 377

Ludwig, Trudy
    Sorry!, 127
    TroubleTalk, 127

LYRIC, 300

M

Macklemore, 170

Madison High School (Portland), 142–143

Make Lemonade (Wolff), 259

Making History: The Struggle for Gay and Lesbian Equal Rights (Marcus), 122

male- and white-centric Western tradition, 69

Manhattan Country School (MCS; New York City), 310–316

March on Washington (1963), 35

Marcus, Eric: *Making History: The Struggle for Gay and Lesbian Equal Rights*, 122

marginalization, 142–148, 219, 320

marriage, 50–55. *See also* marriage equality

marriage equality, 311, 362, 401, 445
    4-year-olds discuss love and marriage, 50–55
    marriage vs. civil union, 51
    and patriarchy, 12
    same-sex marriage, legalization of, 22, 27, 276–277
    same-sex marriage, parents' attitudes toward, 53–54

Marsden, John: *The Rabbits*, 381

Marshall, Elizabeth, 328–336, 431

Marshall High School (Portland), 142–143

MAS (Mexican American Studies; Tucson), 175–176, 179, 182

Mathis, Coy, 343, 393–394

Mattachine Society, 35

Matthes, Colin, *226*

Ma Vie en Rose, 171

McBride, Renisha, 363

McCormick, Willow, 126–129

McCurry, Steve, 330

McInerney, Brandon, 287

McIntosh, Peggy, 434

McKinney, Aaron, 217–218, 220, 222–223

McLimans, David, *301*

McLinden, Patrick, 304, 356–362

MCS (Manhattan Country School; New York City), 310–316

media
    analyzing, 89–90
    and gender/race, intersections of, 168–174
    images of girls/women by, 87
    literacy about, 170–173

Meet Polkadot (Broadhead), 74

Meiners, Erica R., 27–36

Mejia, Maria Teresa, 178, 181–184

Melville, Kathleen, 226–234, 454

Men Can Stop Rape (website), 87

The Merchant of Venice (Shakespeare), 113–114

Mexican American Studies (MAS; Tucson), 175–176, 179, 182

Resources from RETHINKING SCHOOLS

"Whenever teachers ask me for resources, I refer them to the work of Rethinking Schools."

HOWARD ZINN (1922–2010)
Author of *A People's History of the United States*

Subscribe to the leading social justice education magazine.

Every issue of *Rethinking Schools* overflows with creative teaching ideas, compelling narratives, and hands-on examples of how you can promote values of community, racial justice, and equality in your classroom — while building academic skills. Plus: news and analysis by and for education activists.

"As a teacher and researcher, I rely on Rethinking Schools *for information, insight, and inspiration. It has become an indispensable part of my reading regimen."*

SONIA NIETO
Professor Emerita, University
of Massachusetts Amherst

Use code RSBK19 to get 10% off your 1, 2, or 3 year subscription.

ORDER ONLINE: www.rethinkingschools.org
CALL TOLL-FREE: 800-669-4192

The New Teacher Book THIRD EDITION
Finding purpose, balance, and hope during your first years in the classroom

Edited by Linda Christensen, Stan Karp, Bob Peterson, and Moé Yonamine

Teaching is a lifelong challenge, but the first few years in the classroom are typically the hardest. This expanded third edition of *The New Teacher Book* grew out of Rethinking Schools workshops with early-career teachers. It offers practical guidance on how to flourish in schools and classrooms and connect in meaningful ways with students and families from all cultures and backgrounds.

Paperback • 352 pages • 978-0-942961-03-4 **Print $24.95***

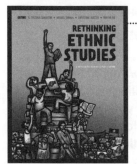

Rethinking Ethnic Studies
Edited by R. Tolteka Cuauhtin, Miguel Zavala, Christine Sleeter, and Wayne Au

Built around core themes of indigeneity, colonization, anti-racism, and activism, *Rethinking Ethnic Studies* offers vital resources for educators committed to the ongoing struggle for racial justice in our schools.

Paperback • 368 • 978-0-942961-02-7 **Print $24.95***

Teaching for Black Lives
Edited by Dyan Watson, Jesse Hagopian, Wayne Au

Teaching for Black Lives grows directly out of the movement for Black lives, recognizing the impact of anti-Black racism. Throughout this book, we provide resources and demonstrate how teachers can connect curriculum to young people's lives and root their concerns and experiences in what is taught and how classrooms are set up. We also highlight the hope and beauty of student activism and collective action.

Paperback • 368 pages • 978-0-942961-04-1 **Print $29.95***

A People's Curriculum for the Earth
Teaching Climate Change and the Environmental Crisis
Edited by Bill Bigelow and Tim Swinehart

Engaging environmental teaching activities from *Rethinking Schools* magazine alongside classroom-friendly readings on climate change, energy, water, food, pollution, and the people who are working to make things better.

Paperback • 433 pages • ISBN: 978-0-942961-57-7 **Print $24.95***

* Plus shipping and handling
Use discount code RSBK19 for a 10% discount on your next order.

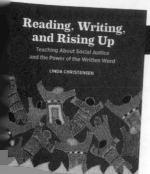

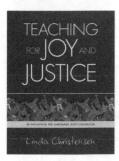

Resources from RETHINKING SCHOOLS

Reading, Writing, and Rising Up SECOND EDITION
Teaching About Social Justice and the Power of the Written Word
By Linda Christensen

Essays, lesson plans, and a remarkable collection of student writing, with an unwavering focus on language arts teaching for justice.

Paperback • 196 pages • ISBN: 978-0-942961-69-0 **Print $24.95***

Rhythm and Resistance
Teaching Poetry for Social Justice
Edited by Linda Christensen and Dyan Watson

Rhythm and Resistance offers practical lessons about how to teach poetry to build community, understand literature and history, talk back to injustice, and construct stronger literacy skills across content areas—from elementary school to graduate school. *Rhythm and Resistance* reclaims poetry as a necessary part of a larger vision of what it means to teach for justice.

Paperback • 272 pages • ISBN: 978-0-942961-61-4 **Print $24.95***

Teaching for Joy and Justice
Re-imagining the Language Arts Classroom
By Linda Christensen

Demonstrates how to draw on students' lives and the world to teach poetry, essays, narratives, and critical literacy skills. Part autobiography, part curriculum guide, part critique of today's numbing standardized mandates, this book sings with hope—born of Christensen's more than 30 years as a classroom teacher, language arts specialist, and teacher educator.

Paperback • 287 pages • ISBN: 978-0-942961-43-0
Print $19.95* PDF $14.95

Teaching a People's History of Abolition and the Civil War
Edited by Adam Sanchez

A collection of 10 classroom-tested lessons on one of the most transformative periods in U.S. history. They encourage students to take a critical look at the popular narrative that centers Abraham Lincoln as the Great Emancipator and ignores the resistance of abolitionists and enslaved people. Students can understand how ordinary citizens — with ideas that seem radical and idealistic — can challenge unjust laws, take action together, and fundamentally change society.

2019 • Paperback • 181 pages • ISBN: 978-0-942961-05-8 **Print $19.95***

ORDER ONLINE: www.rethinkingschools.org
CALL TOLL-FREE: 800-669-4192

Resources from RETHINKING SCHOOLS

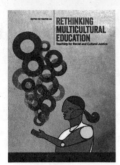

Rethinking Multicultural Education
Teaching for Racial and Cultural Justice
Edited by Wayne Au

This new and expanded second edition demonstrates a powerful vision of anti-racist social justice education. Practical, rich in story, and analytically sharp, *Rethinking Multicultural Education* reclaims multicultural education as part of a larger struggle for justice and against racism, colonization, and cultural oppression—in both schools and society.

Paperback • 418 pages • ISBN: 978-0-942961-53-9 **Print $24.95***

Rethinking Mathematics
Teaching Social Justice by the Numbers
Edited by Eric "Rico" Gutstein and Bob Peterson

This expanded and updated edition shows how to weave social justice issues throughout the mathematics curriculum, and how to integrate mathematics into other curricular areas.

Paperback • 300 pages • ISBN: 978-0-942961-55-3 **Print $24.95***

Rethinking Elementary Education
Edited by Linda Christensen, Mark Hansen, Bob Peterson, Elizabeth Schlessman, and Dyan Watson

Practical insights on how to integrate the teaching of social justice content, seek wisdom from students and their families, and navigate stifling tests and mandates. This book contains some of the finest writing about elementary school life and learning.

Paperback • 320 pages • ISBN: 978-0-942961-52-2 **Print $24.95***

Rethinking Bilingual Education
Welcoming Home Languages in Our Classrooms
Edited by Elizabeth Barbian, Grace Cornell Gonzales, and Pilar Mejía

This collection shares how teachers bring students' home languages into their classrooms—from powerful bilingual social justice curriculum to strategies for honoring students' languages in schools that do not have bilingual programs. Bilingual educators and advocates share how they work to keep equity at the center, build solidarity between diverse communities, and about the inspiring work to defend and expand bilingual programs.

2017 • Paperback • 343 pages • ISBN: 978-1-937730-73-4 **Print $24.95***

* Plus shipping and handling
Use discount code RSBK19 for a 10% discount on your next order.